POPULAR THEATRE

Bertolt Brecht turned to cabaret; Ariane Mnouchkine went to the circus; Joan Littlewood wanted to open a palace of fun. These were a few of the directors who turned to popular theatre forms in the last century, and this sourcebook accounts for their attraction.

Popular theatre forms introduced in this sourcebook include cabaret, circus, puppetry, vaudeville, Indian jatra, political satire, and physical comedy. These entertainments are highly visual, itinerant, and readily understood by audiences. *Popular Theatre: A Sourcebook* follows them around the world, from the bunraku puppetry of Japan to the masked *topeng* theatre of Bali to South African political satire, the San Francisco Mime Troupe's comic melodramas, and a 'Fun Palace' proposed for London.

The book features essays from the archives of *The Drama Review* and other research. Contributions by Roland Barthes, Hovey Burgess, Marvin Carlson, John Emigh, Dario Fo, Ron Jenkins, Joan Littlewood, Brooks McNamara, Richard Schechner, and others, offer some of the most important, informative, and lively writing available on popular theatre. Introducing both western and non-western popular theatre practices, the sourcebook provides access to theatrical forms which have delighted audiences and attracted stage artists around the world.

Joel Schechter is Professor of Theatre Arts at San Francisco State University. He is the author of several books on political satirists and circus clowns, including *Durov's Pig: Clowns, Politics and Theatre* (1985), *Satiric Impersonations* (1994), and *The Pickle Clowns* (2001).

WORLDS OF PERFORMANCE

What is a 'performance'? Where does it take place? Who are the participants? What is being enacted? Does it make a difference if the performance is embodied by live performers or represented on film, video, or digital media? How does the performance interact with individuals, societies, and cultures? Not so long ago, many of these questions were settled. But today, orthodox answers are misleading, limiting, and unsatisfactory.

'Performance' as a practice and as a theoretical category has expanded exponentially. It now comprises a panoply of genres, styles, events, and actions ranging from play, sports and popular entertainments, to theatre, dance and music, secular and religious rituals, the performances of everyday life, intercultural experiments, and more. And beyond performance proper is the even more dynamically unsettled category of the performative.

For nearly fifty years, *The Drama Review (TDR)*, the journal of performance studies, has been at the cutting edge of exploring performance. In *TDR*, artists and scholars introduce and debate new ideas; historical documents are published; new performance theories are expounded. The Worlds of Performance Series is designed to mine the extraordinary resources and diversity of *TDR*'s decades of excellence.

Each World of Performance book is a complete anthology, arranged around a specific theme or topic. Each volume contains hard-to-get seminal essays, artists' notes, interviews, creative texts, and photographs. New materials and careful introductions insure that each book is up to date. Every Worlds of Performance editor is a leader in the field of performance studies. Each World of Performance book is an excellent basic resource for scholars, a textbook for students, and an exciting eye-opener for the general reader.

Richard Schechner
Editor, *TDR*
Series Editor

OTHER TITLES IN THE SERIES

Acting (Re)Considered 2nd Edition edited by Phillip B. Zarrilli
Happenings and Other Acts edited by Mariellen R. Sandford
A Sourcebook of Feminist Theatre and Performance: On and Beyond the Stage
  edited by Carol Martin
The Grotowski Sourcebook edited by Richard Schechner and Lisa Wolford
A Sourcebook of African-American Performance: Plays, People, Movements edited by
  Annemarie Bean
Brecht Sourcebook edited by Carol Martin and Henry Bial
Re: Direction. A Theoretical and Practical Guide by Rebecca Schneider and Gabrielle Cody

POPULAR THEATRE

A SOURCEBOOK

Edited by Joel Schechter

Routledge
Taylor & Francis Group

LONDON AND NEW YORK

First published 2003 by Routledge
11 New Fetter Lane, London EC4P 4EE

Simultaneously published in the USA and Canada
by Routledge
29 West 35th Street, New York, NY 10001

Routledge is an imprint of the Taylor & Francis Group

Selection and editorial matter © 2003 Joel Schechter

Typeset in Times New Roman by Bookcraft Ltd, Stroud, Gloucestershire
Printed and bound in Great Britain by TJ International Ltd, Padstow, Cornwall

British Library Cataloguing in Publication Data
A catalogue record for this book is available from the British Library

Library of Congress Cataloging in Publication Data

Popular theatre : a sourcebook / edited by Joel Schechter.
      p. cm. – (Worlds of performance)
   Includes bibliographical references and index.
   1. Theater. 2. Theater and society. I. Schechter, Joel, 1947– II. Series.

   PN2020 .P67 2002
   792–dc21   2002026941

ISBN 0–415–25830–8 (pbk)
ISBN 0–415–25829–4 (hbk)

CONTENTS

Part III Masks: *commedia dell'arte* and *topeng*

Part IV Circus, clowns and jesters

Part V Cabaret, vaudeville and the Fun Palace

Part VI   Political theatre as popular entertainment

ILLUSTRATIONS

ACKNOWLEDGMENTS

This volume could not have been completed without the encouragement and support of Worlds of Performance Series Editor Richard Schechner, and the Editors at Routledge, Talia Rodgers and Rosie Waters. Most of the essays previously appeared in *The Drama Review*, and I am grateful to *TDR* contributors who have permitted their writing to be reprinted here. Advice from colleagues and friends has helped me develop the introductory essays in this volume; and I want to thank John Bell, Eric Bentley, Denis Calandra, Dan Chumley, Roy Conboy, R.G. Davis, Larry Eilenberg, Joan Holden, Geoff Hoyle, Ron Jenkins, Stanley Kauffmann, Mohammad Kowsar, Rocco Landesman, Bill Peters, Jeff Raz, Nahma Sandrow, Diana Scott, and Laurence Senelick for their discussions about popular theatre which influenced my own views. I also am grateful to the students in my course on popular theatre at San Francisco State University; their research and performances in the field have shown me that popular theatre has a promising future as well as a reconstructable past. Last but not least, the creators of popular theatre, many of whom go unnamed in this book if not in theatre history, deserve special acknowledgement. Popular theatre has a largely unwritten history, and the names of its artists have often been forgotten; not all of them could fit into this volume's pages. But I hope that this collection will allow some of the popular entertainers and their history to reach a new audience.

"Wordless Speech," by Dario Fo originally appeared in *The Tricks of the Trade,* by Dario Fo, translated by Joe Farrell (Routledge, London, 1991), pp. 56–9, and is reprinted by permission.

"Ridiculing Racism in South Africa," by Ron Jenkins first appeared in *Subversive Laughter* by Ron Jenkins (Free Press, New York, 1994), pp. 86–92, and is reprinted by permission of the author.

"Part Circus, Part Sideshow, Part Burlesque. Thoroughly Grotesque" by Hovey Burgess, first appeared in the journal *Spectacle* (Spring 1999), pp. 31–3, edited by Ernest Albrecht, and is reprinted by permission of the editor and the author.

"Legislative Theatre," by Augusto Boal originally appeared in the book *Legislative Theatre* by Augusto Boal (Routledge, London, 1998), pp. 19–20 and is reprinted with permission.

The following articles, cited in the order in which they appear in this book, were previously published in *TDR* and are reprinted by permission of *TDR*/MIT Press and/or the authors.

"The Scenography of Popular Entertainment" by Brooks McNamara 18, no 1 (T61, 1974), 16–24

"The Golden Age of the Boulevard" by Marvin Carlson 18, no 1 (T61, 1974), 25–33

"Bread and Puppets" by Peter Schumann 12, no 2 (T38, 1968), 35

"The Radicality of Puppet Theatre" by Peter Schumann 35, no 4 (T112, 1991), 75–83

"On Bunraku" by Roland Barthes, translated by Sandy MacDonald 15, no 3 (T15, 1971), 76–9

"Wayang and Ludruk: Polarities in Java" by Barbara Hatley 15, no 3 (T15 , 1971), 88–101

"Julie Taymor: From Jacques Lecoq to *The Lion King*" by Richard Schechner 43, no 3 (T163,1999), 36–55

"Commedia and the Actor" by Carlo Mazzone-Clementi and Jane Hill 18, no 1 (T061, 1974), 59–64

"The Dell'Arte Players of Blue Lake, California" by Misha Berson 27, no 2 (T98,1983) 61–72

"Théâtre du Soleil: *The Golden Age, First Draft*" by Christopher Kirkland 19, no 2 (T66, 1975), 53–60

"Playing with the Past: Visitation and Illusion in the Mask Theatre of Bali" by John Emigh 23, no 2 (T–82, 1979), 11–36

"Circus and the Actor" by Hovey Burgess 16, no 1 (T53, 1972), 39–46

"Pitu's Doubt: Entrée Clown Self-Fashioning in the Circus Tradition" by Kenneth Little 30, no 4 (T112, 1986), 51–64

"Hajari Bhand of Rajasthan: A Joker in the Deck" by John Emigh 30, no 1(T109, 1986), 101–30

"Clown Politics: Report on the International Clown–Theatre Congress" by Fred Siegel 33, no 2 (T134, 1992), 182–6

"The Origins of the Cabaret Artistique" by John Houchin 28, no 1 (T101, 1984), 5–14

"A Visit to the Cabaret Dada" by "Alexis" 18, no 2 (T62, 1974), 26–8

"Karl Valentin and Bertolt Brecht" by Denis Calandra 18, no 1 (T61, 1974), 86–98

"From Vilna to Vaudeville: Minikes and *Among the Indians*" by Mark Slobin 24, no 3 (T87, 1980), 17–26

"A Laboratory of Fun" by Joan Littlewood 12, no 3 (T39, 1968), 130–4

"The AgitProp and Circus Plays of Vladimir Mayakovsky" by Frantisek Deák 17, no 1 (T57, 1973), 47–52

"El Teatro Campesino: Interviews with Luis Valdez" by Beth Bagby 11, no 4 (T36 , 1967), 71–9

"Dario Fo Explains" by Luigi Ballerini and Giuseppe Riso 22, no 1 (T77, 1978), 33–48

"Theatre as a Weapon" by A.J. Gunawardana 15, no 3 (T15, 1970), 225–37

"Political Theatre as Popular Entertainment: The San Francisco Mime Troupe" by Theodore Shank 18, no 1 (T–61, 1974), 110–17.

The editor and publishers have made every effort to contact copyright holders. Any omissions brought to our attention will be rectified in future editions.

CONTRIBUTORS

Luigi Ballerini teaches Italian literature at UCLA. He has published several volumes of poetry including *The Cadence of a Neighboring Tribe, Shakespearean Rags*, and *Uno monta la luna*. He has translated Gertrude Stein, William Carlos Williams, Amiri Baraka, and other American poets and writers into Italian.

Roland Barthes (deceased 1980) was the author of *Against the Grain, Barthes on Barthes, Camera Lucida, Empire of Signs, Mythologies, Racine, Writing Degree Zero*, and other volumes. He was also an editor of the journal *Théâtre Populaire*.

Misha Berson has been the theatre critic of the *Seattle Times* since 1991. She is also a frequent contributor to *American Theatre, Stagebill* and other publications, and the author of *The San Francisco Stage* and *Between Worlds: Contemporary Asian American Plays*.

Augusto Boal is a Brazilian director, creator of Theatre of the Oppressed around the world, former Rio city council member, and author of books including *Games for Actors and Non-Actors, The Rainbow of Desire, Theatre of the Oppressed*.

Hovey Burgess is the author of *Circus Techniques*, and has taught circus arts at Sarah Lawrence, the Julliard School, the Dell'Arte School, American Conservatory Theatre, the Ultimate Clown School, the Ringling Brothers Clown College, and other centers of learning. In 1999 he was inducted into the New York People's Hall of Fame for mentoring a new generation of circus artists. He is an adjunct teacher at New York University's Tisch School of the Arts, dramaturge for Circus Flora, and a contributing editor of *Spectacle*.

Denis Calandra is Professor of Theatre at the University of South Florida in Tampa. His publications include *New German Dramatists* and *Fassbinder: Plays*. His Fassbinder translations are regularly produced in all major English-language venues. He is currently translating Berlin playwright David Gieselmann's new play, *Eine Amerikanische Hand*, and writing a play about family, popular culture and politics among Tampa's Cuban cigar workers in the early 1930s.

Marvin Carlson, Sidney E. Cohn Professor of Theatre and Comparative Literature at the Graduate Center of the City University of New York, is the founding editor of *Western European Stages* and has published widely in the areas of theatre history, theatre theory and dramatic literature. His most recent book, on theatre and memory, is *The Haunted Stage*.

Frantisek Deák is Dean of Arts and Humanities and a Professor of Theatre at the University of California at San Diego. He has written *Symbolist Theatre* and served as a contributing editor of *The Drama Review*.

John Emigh is a professor in the Theatre, Speech and Dance and English Departments at Brown University, and is author of *Masked Performance: The Play of Self and Other in Ritual and Theatre*. He has directed more than sixty plays and his own performances have been documented in the *Drama Review* and the *Asian Theatre Journal*. He was founding chairperson of the Association for Asian Performance.

Ulrike Emigh has directed *Pamphilus*, an early medieval secular play, has made several trips to Asia with her husband, John Emigh, and is a professional translator of German.

Dario Fo, Italian satirist, actor, director, and Nobel Laureate in Literature, is author of many plays, including *Accidental Death of an Anarchist, We Can't Pay, We Won't Pay!*, and *Archangels Don't Play Pinball*. He is also the author of *The Tricks of the Trade* (translated into English by Joe Farrell), from which his essay here is excerpted.

A. J. Gunawardana, until his death in 1998, was a journalist and screenplay writer in England. The interview with director Utpal Dutt excerpted here was first published in *TDR* in 1970.

Barbara Hatley heads the School of Asian Languages at the University of Tasmania. She has published widely on Indonesian theatre and literature.

Jane Hill is Executive Director of Opera Omaha. With Carlo Mazzone-Clementi, she co-founded the Dell'Arte Players Company and the Dell'Arte School of Physical Theatre. She previously served on the faculties of the American Conservatory Theatre, the University of California at Berkeley and Humboldt State University.

John Houchin is Associate Professor of Theatre at Boston College, where he teaches theatre history, American theatre, experimental theatre and acting. He is the author of a forthcoming book on theatre censorship in the United States.

Ron Jenkins is Chair of Theatre at Wesleyan University, and author of the books *Acrobats of the Soul, Subversive Laughter*, and *Artful Laughter: Dario Fo and Franca Rame*. He has served as the onstage translator for Dario Fo and Franca Rame during their American tours, has also translated the plays of Joshua Sobol, and frequently writes about theatre for the *New York Times*.

Kenneth Little is an Associate Professor of Anthropology at York University. He has an abiding interest in the contemporary world as exhibition and in late-capitalist culture as spectacle consumption. His research is on public spectacles like the circus, on tourism, and most recently, on specters of the city.

Joan Littlewood (deceased 2002) served for many years as artistic director of the Theatre Workshop in East London, where she produced the premieres of *The Hostage, Oh, What a Lovely War!, Mrs. Wilson's Diary*, and *A Taste of Honey!*, among other plays. She has written an autobiography, *Joan's Book*, and a biography of Baron Philippe de Rothschild.

Brooks McNamara served as a Professor in the Department of Performance Studies at New York University's School of the Arts for many years. His books include *Step Right Up!, The American Playhouse in the Eighteenth Century, American Popular Entertainments*, and (with Jerry Rojo and Richard Schechner) *Theatres, Spaces and Environments*.

Carlo Mazzone-Clementi (1921–2000) was a founder of the Dell'Arte School and Dell'Arte Players in Blue Lake, California. His teaching of commedia tradition and mime influenced actors around the world. He and his former wife, Jane Hill, often collaborated in writing about commedia.

Richard Schechner is the Editor of *TDR, A Journal of Performance Studies*, and University Professor and Professor of Performance Studies, Tisch School of the Arts, New York University. He is also the founder of the Performance Group, and artistic director of East Coast Artists. Schechner's books include *Environmental Theatre, Between Theatre and Anthropology, The Grotowski Sourcebook* (co-edited with Lisa Wolford), and *The Future of Ritual*.

Joel Schechter is Professor of Theatre Arts at San Francisco State University, where he teaches courses in popular theatre and theatre history. He is the author of *Durov's Pig: Clowns, Politics and Theatre, Satiric Impersonations: From Aristophanes to the Guerrilla Girls*, and *The Pickle Clowns: New American Circus Comedy*. For over a decade he was Editor of the journal *Theater* at Yale, and he has served as West Coast correspondent for *Spectacle*, the circus quarterly.

Peter Schumann founded Bread and Puppet Theatre in 1963. He has directed the company throughout its residency in New York City, and Glover, Vermont, where it is currently based, and he has toured with Bread and Puppet around the world.

Theodore Shank is the founding editor of *TheatreForum*, an international journal of innovative performance. He is also a prize-winning playwright and director. His latest book is *Beyond the Boundaries: American Alternative Theatre*. He is on the Theatre faculty of the University of California, San Diego.

Fred Siegel teaches in the English and Philosophy Department at Drexel University in Philadelphia. He is a magician, improv performer, former sideshow talker, and currently artistic director of El Teatro Narcistico, Philadelphia's autobiographical vaudeville troupe.

Mark Slobin is Professor of Music at Wesleyan University and the author or editor of a dozen books on the musics of Central Asian and East European Jews, two of which have received the ASCAP-Deems Taylor Award: *Tenement Songs: The Popular Music of the Jewish Immigrants* (1982) and *Fiddler on the Move: Exploring the Klezmer World* (2001). He has been the president of both the Society for Ethnomusicology and the Society for Asian Music.

Publisher's Note: Contributors' details on Bagby, Kirkland and Risso were unavailable at the time of going to press. The identitiy of "Alexis" is unknown.

Part I

WHAT IS POPULAR THEATRE?

1

BACK TO THE POPULAR SOURCE
Introduction to Part I

Joel Schechter

"Every attempt to revitalize the theatre has gone back to the popular source."

Peter Brook, *The Empty Space*

Popular theatre rarely ends up in print. Circus clowns in Paris, shadow puppeteers in Java, *commedia dell'arte* troupes in Venice, Yiddish vaudevillians in New York have not been reviewed regularly by the press; and few of them published program books, scenarios or plays. The artists kept their work alive by performing it, and passed scenarios to future generations through oral transmission or apprenticeship. Their art lives in bodies and voices, in their memories and stage acts, and those of people who know them; their repertoire reposes in people, and in that sense among others their theatre is popular.

The term "popular theatre" as we know it in English comes from the French "théâtre populaire." References to people's and popular theatre in France date back to Jean-Jacques Rousseau (who in 1758 wanted to see People's Festivals feature dances instead of stage plays) and Louis-Sébastien Mercier, disciple of Rousseau and Diderot. By 1778 Mercier had called for a people's theatre which would "mould the morals and manners of the citizens," and his proposal influenced later ventures to make theatre affordable and educational to the masses.[1] The concept of people's theatre was further advanced by Rolland Romain's 1903 publication of *Théâtre du peuple*. Romain called for recreation, energy and intelligence in people's theatre; he cautioned against excessive preaching and empty amusement. Some of his theory was realized in practice by Firmin Gemier's Théâtre National Ambulant (1910–12) and Jean Vilar's direction of the Théâtre National Populaire at Chaillot in the 1950s, where plays were made available to the working class in a subsidized cultural center. Brecht may have had the creation of this new kind of theatre in mind when he wrote that "besides *being popular* there is such as thing as *becoming popular*."[2] Today the term "popular theatre" is still associated with democratic, proletarian, and politically progressive theatre.

But other popular theatres existed before the publication of treatises or artistic manifestoes about them. John McCormick notes in his study of French popular theatre that, while Romain and others were calling for the "creation of a state-directed (or at least state-subsidized) people's theatre," there already existed self-supporting popular theatres within late eighteenth and most of nineteenth-century France, in the circus and on stages presenting vaudeville, melodrama, fairy tales and pantomime.[3] Victor Fournel in his 1863 volume, *Les Spectacles Populaires et les Artistes des Rues*, provides descriptions of popular Parisian street performances, "spectacles populaires," including the outdoor *parades* (comic sketches and come-ins) created by the famous team of Bobèche and Galimafré on the Boulevard du Temple. This street filled with popular entertainments was also known as the Boulevard of Crime, due to the many murders and thefts its plays depicted; its teeming nineteenth-century life was magnificently recreated in the film *Children of Paradise*. (The Boulevard's exemplary popular theatre is discussed later in an essay by Marvin Carlson.)

Popular theatre also thrived outside Paris, centuries earlier, minus the French terminology. The theatre which this volume explores began with the performance of ancient Greek mimes and their non-western counterparts. For several thousand years, popular forms such as mime, pantomime, shadow puppetry, and clowning have been available to diverse populations including urban lower classes and villagers across Europe and Asia. The names of these popular forms vary from one continent to another. They may be called folk art or traditional entertainments, rather than popular theatre; and India's jatra should not be equated with France's melodrama, although they share characteristics. In general, popular theatre performances were and still are publicly supported, highly visual and physical, portable, orally transmitted, readily understood, not flattering to wealth or tyranny; and for these reasons, as well as for low or no admission cost, they have been widely appreciated. While most popular theatre

> draws from the tradition of legitimate theatre to one extent or another, [as Brooks McNamara has observed, the works] possess few of the artistic and intellectual pretensions common to the regular stage. Subtlety and conventional good taste are usually secondary to action, fantasy, and physicality. The script of a popular theatre piece is often little more than a scenario or framework for improvisation, comic business, and spectacular effects.[4]

It would be misleading to define popular theatre as text-free or wholly non-literary performance. Even the earliest western popular theatre, mime in ancient Athens, presented spoken words and dramatic characters to the public. Historian Arnold Hauser states that Greek mimes were "popular" performers in the ancient period because they "received no subvention from the state, in consequence did not have to take instruction from above, and so worked out [their] artistic principles simply and solely from [their] own immediate experience with audiences."[5] Mimes performing outdoors on the street or in city squares did not enter state-sponsored contests like the Greek tragedians at the Festival of Dionysus.

Popular theatre performers who depend on the audience for support also usually speak for the audience by voicing its social concerns. Greek mimes such as Herodas (third century BC) portrayed everyday domestic scenes featuring people much like the audience, not kings or mythical heroes seen in the festival tragedies. Similarly, later popular stage artists addressed the lives of their audience in performances paid for by the general public, and therefore not subject to the court's or government rulers' pleasure. Popular theatre along these lines can be found in the itinerant minstrelsy of the Middle Ages; in carnival clowning, *commedia dell'arte*, farce and stage jigs of the Renaissance period; vaudeville, circus, pantomime, Punch and Judy, and melodrama from the eighteenth century to the twentieth, to mention but a few of its western incarnations. In non-western countries, popular theatre has survived to this day in the jatra of India, *topeng* and *wayang kulit* of Indonesia, and kabuki and bunraku of Japan, although some of these forms were far more popular in past centuries, and now survive through state subsidy.

Popular theatre still flourishes in performances which sustain or revitalize its traditions. I have been fortunate enough to see Italian *commedia dell'arte* and medieval minstrelsy alive in the stage satire of Dario Fo and Franca Rame; immensely comic puppetry by British Professor John Styles (who was hidden inside his Punch and Judy

Fig. 1.1 Clown at fair, from Mayhew's *London Labour and the London Poor*, 1861.

booth at the time); Balinese clowning with new, western references incorporated into the act by I Nyoman Catra; circus clowning by masters such as Bill Irwin, Geoff Hoyle, and Larry Pisoni; and reinventions of nineteeth-century melodrama, minstrelsy and farce by the San Francisco Mime Troupe. The popular traditions upon which these entertainments draw have specific sites of origin; but their artists have moved some distance away, geographically and artistically, and have attracted new audiences around the world through international tours and festivals.

It has been argued that European playwrights of the sixteenth and seventeenth century "lost touch with the popular masses in order to create theatre that would be pleasing to a small, aristocratic elite that supported them financially ... [although] small traveling troupes continued to play to the masses at country fairs and public celebrations."[6] It is tempting to call the other tradition of theatre, the one enjoyed by the elite, "unpopular theatre;" but in fact many plays were created in the Renaissance period and later mixed popular and so-called higher forms of theatre, allowing clowns and kings, farcical and noble characters, to appear together on stage. Popular theatre and its stage characters are not always neatly separated from the rest of culture. Shakespeare's Prince Hal lives in Falstaff's world of taverns and earthy jests for a time. The clowns (*punakawan*) Semar, Bagong, and Gareng follow a knight, Lord Arjuna, onto the puppet stages of Indonesia. Popular theatre's appearance in hybrids, and its wide range of forms are consonant with the genre's tendency to transgress limitations and boundaries (a tendency which plump Jack Falstaff shares).

Dario Fo offers another perspective on the transgressive tendencies of popular theatre in his comments on ancient Greek mime: "Mime in ancient times was considered an inferior, dubious, and scurrilous genre, and was censured, as has been everything which authorities have been unable to control and manipulate for their own ends."[7] Persecution from authorities might be expected for theatre which departs from "legitimate" forms, and goes unsponsored or dismissed by government and academia. In 1594, when the Lord Mayor of London objected to new theatre, he said plays were attracting "base & refuse sort of people…. Vagrant persons & Maisterles men that hang about the Citie…."[8] He was not objecting to theatre at court. At times, popular theatre does not provoke such objections from authorities; they may simply dismiss it as frivolous.

But that accusation could be regarded as praise, too. Brecht observed in his *Short Organum for the Theatre*: "The theatre must in fact remain entirely superfluous, though this means that it is the superfluous for which we live. Nothing needs less justification than pleasure."[9] John McCormick unwittingly reiterates Brecht's premise when he notes that nineteenth-century French popular theatre had enough public support that it "did not need to justify its existence," and "for most of these [French popular] theatres literature and literary criticism were irrelevant."[10]

Bread and Puppet Theatre founder Peter Schumann regards the "illegitimate" standing of his art as its saving grace:

> Puppet theater in the Western world has been illegitimate more often than not and is there-fore referred to as: only puppet theater. The puppet theater's traditional exemption from seriousness and its quasi-asocial status acted also as its saving grace, as a negative privilege which allowed the art to grow.[11]

The same might be said of other popular forms: without having to conform to externally-imposed standards or depend on institutional approval, artists can say what they please, and may please the public in ways that more controlled, formulaic art cannot.

In the past, popular theatre training took place outside university centers, and was removed from academic standards, as the artistry was passed from father to daughter, son, or colleague, or from master to apprentice. Successors were not necessarily taught a wide range of roles, either. One bunraku puppeteer would manipulate only the arms of puppets for many years. A commedia actor might learn only Arlecchino's role. Those trained were generally guaranteed a character part or a puppet stage space upon comple-tion of apprenticeship. They learned through imitation and study of popular traditions, initially performing much like their master teachers did, until they were on their own. Originality has not been an overriding concern in popular theatre training, although popular forms often allow for improvisation and topical references.

Eventually, indigenous popular forms may be copied by outsiders, who remove the work from its original context or creator's circuit, and sell it for profit in adulterated form. This happened when melodrama and farce moved from stage venues to Hollywood film studios and television; popular characters and plot structures ended up serving other forces besides the artists: namely corporate sponsors, stockholders, and network execu-tives. It might be said that this is the outcome of giving the public what it wants, which popular theatre usually does; but since the advent of corporate-controlled mass media entertainment, it can also be said, to rephrase Brecht, that besides being popular, there is such a thing as being profitable.

Carlo Mazzone-Clementi and Jane Hill suggest in their essay, "Commedia and the Actor," that theatre's popularity should not be measured by box office profits or atten-dance records, but rather

> in terms of what it depicts and to whom it appeals … . There is only one audience to please at each [commedia] performance. When one plays Verona, one does not worry about the

reactions of the Romans. The piece is shaped and colored by the local audience, by the moods and responses … . Each performance 'on the road' was custom-tailored to a specific audience. Mass appeal was unimportant. In fact, had television existed in the Renaissance, commedia might have died an early death.[12]

Half a century ago, Eric Bentley suggested that popular theatre was alive and well, and living on film and television. He wrote: "while high theater has a harder time than any other high art, the popular theater, dedicated to entertainment, and today functioning on the screen and over the air, is perpetually the most flourishing of the arts."[13] That situation has not changed, if we agree that "popular theatre" can exist on screen and over the air, on camera as well as in live performance, and that electronic media can take over popular stage forms without substantially changing the experience. Mazzone-Clementi and Hill's view of commedia suggests that the experience is not transferable. Lacking live performance adjustments in front of an audience, an electronically recorded act is likely to lose some of its suspense, immediacy, and interaction between actors and spectators. For popular theatre the loss is considerable; to achieve its full, unscripted promise, complete with improvisations and direct addresses to spectators, this theatre requires the presence of live bodies onstage and offstage. Even popular puppetry involves a form of "body-fetish," Roland Barthes notes in his discussion of bunraku puppetry.[14]

Judging from the diversity of popular theatre forms and their audiences, there is no critical mass, no minimum number of bodies required to make theatre popular; but it cannot exist without a supportive audience. Audience size might range from 20,000 spectators surrounding a jatra performance in Calcutta, to a few hundred groundlings standing (and others seated) in an Elizabethan theatre, to a few New Yorkers eating hot dogs in front of a Coney Island puppet booth. As Robert Weimann writes in his study of Shakespeare and popular theatre:

> The relationship between actor and audience is … not only a constituent element of dramaturgy, but of dramatic meaning as well. While Ibsen, Chekhov, and the theatre of dramatic illusion can largely, or to a certain extent, be understood by a reading of the text, the purely literary interpretation remains quite unsatisfactory in dealing with the older popular theater.[15]

In new popular theatre, too, artists often develop a following, a tour circuit or schedule, and their return is eagerly awaited by supportive communities; touring, common to North American vaudevillians, England's Punch and Judy professors, and India's jatra players in the past, continues to keep some popular theatre ensembles alive.

The "popular" component of people present as an audience remains inseparable from the genre's history and reception; the genre cannot be defined without defining their roles, too. As David Mayer observes in his pioneering essay "Towards a Definition of Popular Theatre:"

> Popular, in the widest sense, is something 'of the people,' for our purposes in drama that is principally concerned with the widest reach of audience available at a given moment or place … . Often it happens that for these groupings the adjective 'lower' is significantly appropriate: lower per capita income, lower level of education and literacy, lower interest in or knowledge of aesthetic criteria.[16]

Mayer suggests there are class-based differences between those who attend "high theater" and those who attend "popular theater." For him the latter group often consists of "farmers, artisans, factory workers, shopkeepers, laborers, the rural and urban poor and middle classes." That leaves out the upper class, the factory owners, the rural and urban rich; but the history of popular theatre includes famous episodes where carriages and motor cars drove the wealthy to see actors in a working-class district: Jean-Gaspard Deburau's pantomime performances as Pierrot at the Théâtre des Funambules attracted the carriage trade in nineteenth-century Paris, and Brendan Behan's farce, *The Hostage,* at Joan Littlewood's Theatre Workshop, lured some limousines to the East End of London mid-twentieth century. Wealthy spectators are not immune to the attractions of great comic actors, pantomime artists, and clowns, even if the performance lacks sympathy for the leisure class.

Not all popular theatre is anti-capitalistic or subversive of the status quo. In Asia, as several essays in this volume explain, popular forms and the myths and religions within them uphold old orders and hierarchy. Peter Brook once proposed that "by nature the popular theatre is anti-authoritarian, anti-traditional, anti-pomp, anti-pretence;"[17] but exceptions abound. Japanese bunraku puppetry began as a popular art wholly supported by its middle-class merchant audiences three centuries ago; it now depends on the state for preservation of its revered tradition, and some bunraku artists are known as "living treasures" (a term with which the government honors master artists, including puppeteers and doll-carvers). Subversive tendencies, if there are any, may decrease under state-sponsored conditions.

Some popular theatre artists are articulate advocates of social change and class-consciousness. Walter Benjamin saw popular art representing the struggle of those for whom it is created, when he wrote in 1931:

> in the long run every class and every social stratum will open the door to the forms of their life and language only to the person who is active on their behalf … . Every form of art that systematically sets out to dispense with popularity will rightly find itself consigned to the luxury section of the market.[18]

Benjamin's description of engaged, socially committed artistic work is amplified in Brecht's essay on "The Popular and the Realistic," written in 1938. Brecht defines "popular" as that which is "intelligible to the broad masses, taking over their forms of expression and enriching them/ adopting and consolidating their standpoint/ representing the most progressive section of the people in such a way that it can take over the leadership."[19] Neither Brecht nor Benjamin suggests that popular theatre is created by the masses, or only by the working class, but rather *for* that social stratum among others. This distinction is reiterated by Jean Variot in *Théâtre de tradition populaire.* Variot asks, "Who were the authors of popular plays?" and answers that the plays did not come from the spontaneous imagination of peasants, manual laborers *per se*, rather from practiced artists affiliated with traveling theatre companies.[20] The plays were created by and for the response of audiences who saw them performed in villages, at fairgrounds, and on the outskirts of great cities.

Among the popular theatre artists who represent, in Brecht's phrase, "the most progressive section of the people," one could easily include Dario Fo and Franca Rame, Utpal Dutt, Augusto Boal and the San Francisco Mime Troupe. Other popular theatre creators are less politically active and less didactic. The concept of popular theatre as subversive, anti-authoritarian, or anti-traditional is not necessarily at odds with that of theatre as diverting, relaxing entertainment; a performance may reassure its audience by calling for social change the audience also wants to see. In 1965, French critic Emile Copfermann published *Le théâtre populaire. Pourquoi?* which questioned the political leanings of popular theatre ensembles receiving state subsidies; he suggested that dependence on subvention brought to large companies like Jean Vilar's Théâtre National Populaire "an element of social adaptation, of acquiescence to the values of a repressive society."[21] Without question, some popular theatre presentations are less disturbing and more reassuring than others. Still, there is a segment of past and current popular theatre which is entertaining and fervently dedicated to political change, and examples are offered in the last section of this volume.

Creators of popular theatre rarely depend on critics or favorable press to survive, especially if they have a tour circuit where they are known ahead of their arrival. But the prospects of accurate written documentation have improved for popular theatre in recent decades. Performances at fairgrounds, in one-ring circus tents, and on boulevards are covered in print with greater frequency since the advent of performance studies, which has increased the chances of a scholarly visit to a clown, a bunraku master or a fire-eater. (I have made a few of those visits myself.) Essays and interviews on popular theatre around the world have been published in *The Drama Review*, the leading journal of performance studies; and *TDR* articles collected here, along with a few essays from other sources, offer a unique introduction to popular theatre's history and practices in Asia, Africa, Latin America, Europe and North America. (There were, of course, earlier, landmark studies of popular theatre; unfortunately many of them are now out of print, including books by Allardyce Nicoll, Tristan Rémy, George Speaight, David Mayer, J. R. Goodlad, Jean Duvignaud, Laurence Senelick, Brooks McNamara and Don Wilmeth, among others.)

A number of books on popular theatre have focused either on western popular theatre or non-western forms as if they had nothing in common. At the very least, they have shared the pages of *TDR*. But more than that, forms of puppetry, physical comedy, melodrama, jatra, bunraku, and political satire discussed here have become internationally popular and renowned through tours made by the artists, through studies by scholars, and through the practical interest that innovative stage directors have taken in them. Asian popular forms have attracted western stage directors and their audiences in recent decades; for example, productions by Peter Brook, Ariane Mnouchkine, Lee Breuer, and Julie Taymor draw on shadow puppetry, bunraku, and Indian epics.

A revitalization of popular forms by avant-garde directors began early in the twentieth century. "It is always the popular theatre that saves the day," Peter Brook writes in *The Empty Space*, and he adds that "every attempt to revitalize the theatre has gone back to the popular source. Meyerhold … [turned] to the circus and the music hall … . Brecht was rooted in the cabaret; Joan Littlewood longs for a funfair."[22] (Brook himself brought a circus trapeze, clowning and acrobatics into *A Midsummer Night's Dream*, and knowledge of Asian theatre traditions to his adaptation of *The Mahabharata*.)

Popular theatre does not survive only in avant-garde reinterpretations. While a number of historically important popular forms such as pantomime and melodrama are not staged now as often as they were in the nineteenth century, others, such as *wayang kulit* and jatra, continue in their countries of origin. The popularity of such forms is greater in regions where television and film are not pervasive. But even in the western countries where one might expect mass media and electronic recording to have overwhelmed the low-tech, itinerant competition, there has been a renewal of interest in live puppetry, circus clowning, cabaret and vaudeville. Perhaps this is due to a weariness or mistrust of prerecorded life. In any event, tours by Cirque du Soleil, Cirque Eloize, the Bindlestiff Family Cirkus, performances in London's Circus Space and at New York's Coney Island USA, puppet festivals such as New York's Henson-sponsored showcase and HERE's Lower Manhattan Puppet Parlour are signs of new and increasing English language interest in popular theatre. The acclaim for Julie Taymor's stage work, notably *The Lion King* and *The Green Bird* on Broadway and in other commercial venues, suggests that her productions adapting Asian puppetry and Italian commedia have broad appeal.

Popular theatre forms lend themselves to adaptation, reinterpretation and changes of content because they originate in unwritten and improvised performance traditions. A mischievous servant like Arlecchino may be, and has been, disobedient for very different reasons over the centuries; but the character's mischief continues to amuse, and to survive his master's orders onstage as the times and comic plots change. The San Francisco Mime Troupe, discussed by Theodore Shank later, once announced:

> 'Adaptation' may be a misleading term for the relation of our commedia shows to their originals … we exploit this work to suit our own; using what we can and discarding the rest … . Our interest in this sixteenth-century form is not antiquarian; we use it because it is popular, free, engaging, and adaptable.[23]

The same could be said of Théâtre du Soleil and Dell'Arte Players' adaptations of commedia characters discussed in this volume.

Commedia and other popular forms have proven surprisingly malleable; that is one reason for their endurance. John Emigh in his study of India's wandering comedian (*bahurupiya*) Hajari Bhand finds that, while itinerant minstrels were subsidized for centuries as court jesters, in the past century, "with the dwindling of royal patronage after [India's] Independence, Hajari Bhand has had to rely more on village audiences and especially the merchant castes for support."[24] Bhand developed a circuit of 460 villages, and "kept expanding his repertory, picking up ideas from other wandering mimics and inventing new roles based on people he observed in the courts, towns, and villages." Here a wonderful non-western popular artist's life confirms Brecht's view that "there is such a thing as *becoming popular*." Another example is offered in Barbara Hatley's account of the Javanese Ludruk, a relatively new popular theatre form featuring clowns and transvestite singers; it represents, in Hatley's words, "a great innovation in Javanese theatre, to present stories which are not part of a well-known mythical tradition but have been newly created … ."[25]

With their tendency to become popular now and again, to be revived and altered, many of the theatre forms described in this volume have a promising future; for the same reason, some of the essays describing performances are already out of date. The essays stand as documents and sources of information about theatre that has been popular, and may be popular once more. Meyerhold, praising the popular theatre of strolling players and fairground entertainment in 1912, wrote that

> the fairground booth is eternal. Its heroes do not die; they simply change their aspects and assume new forms … . Their audience came not so much to listen to dialogue as to watch the wealth of movement, club blows, dizzy leaps, and all the whole range of tricks native to the theatre.[26]

The pages that follow constitute a record of such theatre's creativity; but it is an incomplete record, which continues to change and expand in the twenty-first century, thanks to directors like Mnouchkine, Taymor, Fo, Brook, Schumann, and the uncounted performers who give popular theatre new stage life.

NOTES

1 Jean Louis Mercier quoted by Romain Rolland in "The People's Theater," *The Theory of the Modern Stage*, edited by Eric Bentley. New York: Penguin Books, 1980, p. 461.

2 Bertolt Brecht, "The Popular and the Realistic" in *Brecht on Theatre*, edited by John Willett. New York: Hill and Wang, 1964, p. 108.

3 John McCormick, *Popular Theatres of Nineteenth-Century France*. Cambridge: Cambridge University Press, 1993, p. 5.

4 Brooks McNamara, "The Scenography of Popular Entertainments," reprinted in this volume.

5 Arnold Hauser, *The Social History of Art,* Vol. I. Baltimore: Penguin, 1951, p. 86.
It should also be noted, as Raymond Williams observed in *Keywords*, that the word "popular" is derived from the Latin *popularis*, "belonging to the people." Although French nineteenth-century references to popular theatre most fully anticipate the developments discussed in this volume, there were antecedents, linguistically and artistically, in ancient Rome and Greece.

6 Eugene van Erven, *Radical People's Theatre*. Bloomington: University of Indiana, 1988, p. 6.

7 Dario Fo, *The Tricks of the Trade*, trans. by Joe Farrell. New York: Routledge/Theatre Arts, 1991, p. 143.

8 A. M. Nagler, *A Source Book in Theatrical History*. New York: Dover, 1952, p. 115.

9 Bertolt Brecht, "Short Organum for the Theatre," in *Brecht on Theatre*, edited by John Willett. New York: Hill & Wang, 1964, p. 181.

10 John McCormick, op. cit., p. 227.

11 Peter Schumann, "The Old Art of Puppetry in the New World Order," Bread and Puppet Theatre, Glover. Vermont, 1999, p. 7. This statement differs slightly from the one made in "The Radicality of Puppet Theater."

12 Carlo Mazzone-Clementi and Jane Hill, "Commedia and the Actor," reprinted in this volume.

13 Eric Bentley, *The Playwright as Thinker*. New York: Harcourt, Brace & World, 1967, p. 233.

14 Roland Barthes, " On Bunraku," reprinted in this volume. Richard Howard's translation of this essay in Barthes' book, *The Empire of Signs*, does not include it in entirety, as Sandy MacDonald's translation did in *The Drama Review*.

15 Robert Weimann, *Shakespeare and the Popular Tradition in the Theater*. Baltimore: Johns Hopkins, 1978, p. 7.

16 David Mayer, "Towards a Definition of Popular Theatre," in *Western Popular Theatre*, edited by David Mayer and Kenneth Richards. London: Methuen, 1977, p. 263. This essay was originally a speech delivered by Mayer at a conference on popular theatre; the volume in which it appears includes many other useful and original perspectives on western popular theatre.

17 Peter Brook, *The Empty Space*. New York: Atheneum, 1968, p. 68.

18 Walter Benjamin, *Selected Writings*, Vol. II. Cambridge: Harvard Belnap, 1996, p. 504.

19 Bertolt Brecht, op. cit., p. 108.

20 Jean Variot, *Théâtre de Tradition Populaire*. Marseille: Robert Laffont, 1942, pp. 16–17.

21 Emile Copfermann translated by Eugene van Erven in *People's Radical Theatre*, op. cit., p. 13.

22 Peter Brook, op. cit., p. 68.

23 Quoted by Theodore Shank in "Political Theatre as Popular Entertainment: The San Francisco Mime Troupe," reprinted in this volume.

24 John Emigh, "Hajari Bhand of Rajasthan: A Joker in the Deck," reprinted in this volume.

25 Barbara Hatley, "Wayang and Ludruk: Polarities in Java," reprinted in this volume.

26 Vsevolod Meyerhold, "The Fairground Booth" in *Meyerhold on Theatre*, edited by Edward Braun. New York: Hill and Wang, 1969, p. 135.

2

THE SCENOGRAPHY OF POPULAR ENTERTAINMENT

Brooks McNamara

There have been few attempts to examine seriously the architecture and design of traditional popular entertainments. For the most part, popular forms have not been thought to involve a high level of design or systematic organization of performance space. Yet, over the years, there has emerged a distinctive scenography of popular entertainment. It has borrowed from conventional theatre, festivals, and folk performance. Essentially, however, it constitutes a highly independent scenographic strain. While interest in that strain continues to grow, the scenography itself is rapidly disappearing. Increasingly, traditional popular forms are influenced by the scenography of the newest popular entertainments, television and film. The scenographic base of these new forms is quite different from that of traditional amusements: film and television are naturalist in their orientation. They are concerned more with presenting a seemingly coherent reality than with creation of spectacle and fantasy for their own sake – and the naive art of traditional popular forms is gradually giving way to the orderly and precise scenography of mass culture.

Traditional popular scenography may be divided into seven broad categories based on the ways in which space and design are employed by the showman:

1. booths and other arrangements of space by itinerant street performers;
2. improvised theatres;
3. the scenography of variety entertainments;
4. the scenography of popular theatre;
5. performance spaces devoted to spectacle or special effects;
6. processional forms;
7. entertainment environments such as the traveling carnival and the amusement park, where the spectator himself organizes the event.

Although nothing may be said to be universally true about these approaches to scenography, it is clear that they often involve a naive and casual view of design, a strong emphasis on trick-work, fantasy and spectacle, and a lack of interest in such conventional scenic values as verisimilitude, consistency, and so-called good taste. Popular design seems to be strongly traditional and non-academic, far more concerned with craft than art and far more involved with objects than with ideas. At its best, however, it produces vital and imaginative solutions to basic problems of performance space and design.

THE STREET BOOTH AND THE MOBILE ENTERTAINER

Many traditional street entertainers have worked without any sort of formal stage, performing on the ground or on a bench or barrel head. These performers tended to use space pragmatically, not altering it in any significant way for theatrical purposes. Like many folk performers who played in the streets, their costumes and properties served as a kind of basic scenery, announcing them immediately as entertainers. Mountebanks, or performing quacks, were especially well known for their eccentric costumes and properties, often dressing as sorcerers, Turks or Indians, and seemingly burning money or slashing their bodies with swords or knives to attract a crowd. Such performers became, in effect, self-contained mobile theatres, with their properties and costumes fulfilling the function that scenery and lights have in more complex productions.

Where a temporary stage was possible, a simple platform was erected by the showmen. Frequently, this was no more than a few planks arranged on top of trestles or barrels, but often it gave way to a more elaborate booth stage – a form used by British Pierrot troupes and American medicine show companies as late as the mid-twentieth century. A typical booth stage consisted of a platform raised to approximately head height, with a room formed out of curtains suspended from a framework of poles covering the rear half of the stage. The players used the open front portion of the platform for their performance and the rear room for storage and living quarters. Entrances and exits were made through one of the openings in the curtain that separated the stage from the booth behind. In some later versions, the stage was fully enclosed with an ornamented proscenium arch, elaborately painted backdrop, and side wings. In some cases even rudimentary stage boxes were attached to either side. The basic two-part booth stage, however, remained the staple of the itinerant street performer.

The booth stage entertainer was elevated and distanced from his audience. Unlike the street performer who worked against the background of the town and its activities, his territory was clearly distinguished from that of his spectators, becoming "theatricalized" space, over which he exercised complete design control. Unlike designers for conventional theatres since the Renaissance, the booth showman was not overly concerned with a need to create verisimilitude in the space that he controlled. Like the simple sketches and variety entertainments performed on them, booth stages reflected casual attitudes toward nice distinctions about time and place. Most booths, in fact, seem to have been used as generalized locations for performance, with changes of scene indicated by the shifting of a few simple emblematic properties. When complex design was introduced by the booth showman, it was used to highlight the booth as theatricalized space through bright colour, blatant design, and gratuitous ornament, all of which were to become typical of later popular scenography.

IMPROVISED THEATRES

The booth stage provided the showman with design opportunities that were beyond the means of the mobile street entertainer, but it gave him little more control over his audience and the conditions of his performance. In order to establish more control, he needed some sort of cheap, easily adaptable space that could contain both actors and spectators. The result was a whole range of crude, improvised theatres in which the traditions of the booth stage were continued and developed.

A high level of poverty and a low level of design were typical of the traditional English-fairground theatre, variations of which survive today at traveling carnivals. A theatre of this sort was, and still is, little more than a simple platform or booth stage set down inside a flimsy wooden "fit-up" or tent. Because it was the exterior of the theatre that attracted crowds, it was there that the showman spent his money and his creative energy. Many showmen used an extravagantly decorated platform called a balcony or parade near the entrance – the "bally" platform of the modern carnival booth – on which performers gave a sample of the show to be seen inside. Behind them rose a high false wall of banners, boldly painted with scenes from the showman's play. This "front," still in use at modern side-shows, gave the showman's theatre an apparent size and magnificence belied by the interior of the booth. Inside, audiences stood on the bare ground or sat on rough plank benches while on a platform at one end – fitted out with a pair of paper wings and a tattered roll drop and often made from the wagons that hauled the show – the performers presented "a melodrama (with three murders and a ghost), a pantomime, a comic song, an overture, and some incidental music, all done in five-and-twenty minutes."

A slightly more sophisticated example of an improvised theatre was the "penny gaff." Located in former stables, shops, or sheds, this form catered to working-class audiences in nineteenth-century England. Henry Mayhew visited a typical penny gaff and set down a description of its curious mixture of poverty and strident design in *London Labour and the London Poor* (1851). Mayhew wrote:

> The front of a large shop had been entirely removed and the entrance was decorated with paintings of the 'comic singers' in their most 'humorous' attitudes. On a table against the wall was perched the band, playing what the costers call 'dancing tunes' with great effect.

Inside, the former shop had been turned into a lobby of sorts. Behind it lay the stage and auditorium.

> To form the theatre, the first floor had been removed; the whitewashed beams, however, still stretched from wall to wall. The lower room had evidently been the warehouse, while the upper apartment had been the sitting-room, for the paper was still on the walls. A gallery, with a canvas front, had been hurriedly built up, and it was so fragile that the boards bent under the weight of those above. The bricks in the warehouse were smeared over with red paint and had a few black curtains daubed upon them. The coster-youths require no great scenic embellishment, and indeed the stage – which was about eight feet square – could admit of none.

VARIETY ENTERTAINMENT

The offhand approach to the function of scenery seen at the penny gaff and the fairground theatre was in part the result of poverty and in part based on a shrewd analysis of when design was really necessary and – when it was – of what elements were best received by an unsophisticated audience. Even when poverty was not such an important factor in the showman's handling of design, the same casual and pragmatic approach often continued to guide his view of the function of design in performance. Vaudeville, music hall, minstrel shows, and burlesque often played in conventionally equipped legitimate theatres. Yet, their approach to design was frequently quite different from that of other theatrical forms that played the same houses.

The scenography of such forms was based on the principle of variety structure in which there is no transfer of information from one act to another. The shape of an entire vaudeville bill, for example, was not the result of plot or theme – it had none – but of the way in which the various acts or "compartments" were combined by the showman in charge. The scenography of variety entertainments has always reflected this basic structural idea. Ordinarily there is no strong attempt to create an integrated scenography that somehow encompasses all of the acts on the bill. Instead, each act independently determines its own scenic requirements, which have no particular relationship to those of other acts but which must somehow be accommodated within the total framework of the performance.

A common device in such forms as vaudeville and burlesque, for example, was to use a conventional proscenium stage decorated for each act with stock house scenery more or less appropriate to the premise of each act. Alternatively, neutral curtains were used to create a generalized background for the entire performance, or stock scenery was combined with the special properties and scenery carried by each act on the bill, often producing curious scenic hybrids. The urge toward consistency and verisimilitude was notably weak; for the most part, backgrounds were not designed to establish the act of a compartment except in an emblematic way.

Some variety forms avoid the problem of settings altogether by building a neutral performance space, and allowing the individual entertainer to alter the space through his properties and costumes somewhat in the manner of the street performer. Early London music halls such as The Oxford, Evan's, and The Canterbury, for example, used a simple projecting platform stage against a permanent architectural facade containing one or more doors. In many variations, the idea appeared at countless lesser concert saloons and tavern theatres that had little interest in providing more than the simplest background for their entertainers. Perhaps the most familiar example of a neutral performing space, however, is the circus arena, which makes no attempt to create an environment for the

Fig. 2.1 Harry Hill's Concert Saloon. Detail from *The National Police Gazette,* 1879. A variation of the platform stage used at many variety theatres, in this case combined with a simple proscenium. (*TDR* 18: 2.)

performers separate from that of the audience. Furthermore, the events that take place in the circus arena exist in the present time and place in which they are being presented. The arena is constantly transformed by lights, costumes, and scenic displays. But it always remains a practical working space, filled with purely functional equipment, such as lights, rigging, and cages, the function of which is neither concealed nor integrated into some overall design scheme. Equipment is there simply because it needs to be, while the scenic elements that appear from time to time are frankly gratuitous, existing purely and simply for the sake of spectacle.

POPULAR THEATRE

In forms of popular theatre such as cheap melodrama, Tom Shows, and knockabout farce there was – unlike the variety forms – the same sort of cause-and-effect structure typical of most legitimate plays, as well as an acknowledgement that the locations were all somehow bound together within the same work. Showmen involved with such productions also borrowed from the scenic conventions of legitimate theatre. Typically, however, they made only perfunctory attempts to create scenery appropriate to the events taking place, since their audiences were less concerned that a stage be set convincingly than that there be occasional bits of impressive trickwork or special effects.

Well into the twentieth century, repertory companies playing rural areas with a stock of popular melodramas often carried only four battered utility settings, little different in their function from the Serlian scenes of the Renaissance. Known to showmen as "front room," "back room," "timber," and "town," they represented theatrical generalizations about locale. The "town" set was a backdrop painted with a conventional street scene, the "timber" a forest drop, and the "back room" a simple chamber often used for kitchen scenes. Sometimes the "front room" was in fact two different settings, an ordinary parlor and a "center door fancy" set, understood by audiences to stand for a rich man's drawing room in any place and period. Some traveling companies merely trusted to luck and used the house scenery in the small town theatres in which they played, carrying only the special settings necessary for a "sensation" scene or two.

Many showmen chose plays that provided opportunities for trickwork, fantasy and spectacle. It was on these aspects of their productions that they lavished money and attention since it was the sensational and the spectacular that invariably brought crowds into the theatre. *The Black Crook,* which consisted primarily of bits of spectacle and pageantry, cost more than $55,000 to produce, a fabulous sum in 1866, but it returned more than $660,000 to its backers in a single year. This was partly a result of elaborate scenes containing "hosts of fairies, sprites, water nymphs, amphibia, gnomes, ... calcium lights, brilliant fires, and a slow curtain." So popular was trickwork and spectacle with nineteenth-century audiences, in fact, that hundreds of plays were written solely as vehicles for magic, special effects, or elaborately trapped settings. Many of the traditional English Christmas pantomimes, for example, were little more than frameworks for elaborate transformation scenes, and a late nineteenth-century company of trickwork specialists, the Hanlon-Lees, fascinated audiences with such nightmarish productions as *The Voyage to Switzerland* in which elaborately trapped walls concealed disappearing demons and a character's boots walked across a room, up a wall, and into the ceiling.

Fig. 2.2 A scene from *The Black Crook* as depicted on a cover of sheet music from the production. (*TDR* 18: 2.)

SPECTACLE THEATRES

The interest of nineteenth-century audiences in spectacle led to the creation by prosperous showmen of a number of specialized theatres for the production of elaborate equestrian pageants and "aquadramas." Many of these theatres were, in effect, hybrids of an elaborately equipped proscenium stage and a circus arena. Astley's amphitheatre in London, for example, at one time contained a 44-foot arena backed by a stage filled with huge platforms.

> The horsemen gallop and skirmish over them [wrote a contemporary commentator] and they will admit a carriage equal in size and weight to a mail coach, to be driven across them. They are, notwithstanding, so constructed as to be placed, and removed, in a short space of time, by manual labour and mechanism. When exhibited they are masked with scenery, representing battlements, heights, bridges, mountains, etc.

On the stage at Astley's and the other hippodrome theatres, there appeared a bizarre assortment of pageants, spectacles, and conventional plays turned into panoramas of horseflesh, among them equestrian versions of *Richard III* and *Macbeth*. At Sadler's Wells, another brand of spectacle performance, the aquadrama, provided recreations of famous naval battles or combinations of pantomime and melodrama. Such performances depended heavily on effects achieved with pressure hoses, fireworks, and transparencies. Many simulated floating sea monsters, sea-shell chariots, and scale-model warships, often manned by crews of children to maintain proper perspective.

In another variation of spectacle theatre, the diorama, the audience usually sat on a platform that revolved every few minutes to disclose one of two proscenium stages – at Daguerre's Diorama, 71 feet wide and 45 feet high – containing paintings lit from above by natural light that was varied in color, intensity, and direction in order to create an impression of constant change. The actor in the hippodrome, aquatic theatre, and diorama, when he existed at all, became a mass-performer, as mechanical as the elaborate special effects that were the central reason for the existence of these theatres. The

Fig. 2.3 **The stage and arena of the fourth Astley's Amphitheatre, c.1856, with an equestrian version of** *Richard III* **in progress. (***TDR* **18: 2.)**

chief actor became the effects themselves, organized into a kind of controlled fantasy based on carefully planned distortions of reality by the scene designer, the technician, and the machinist.

PROCESSIONAL FORMS

Processional forms brought into the streets many of the same qualities developed in the spectacle theatre. The procession has been involved with various kinds of festival performance since antiquity, perhaps reaching its highest point in the entries and street spectacles of the late Middle Ages and Renaissance given by municipalities in honor of royal

Fig. 2.4 **Artist's conception of a circus parade leaving the lot of Barnum's Great Traveling World's Fair. (***TDR* **18: 2.)**

weddings, military victories, coronations, or visiting royalty. The street parade was adopted by showmen as an adjunct to their regular performances. Street parades were once a feature of many nineteenth-century traveling repertory companies, medicine shows, Wild West shows and circuses. Because they competed with the streets themselves for attention, most processional forms tended to be made up of elements that were oversized, decorated with extreme boldness, and thematically very simple. The tableau wagons used in American circus parades, for example, were often of great size and complexity, heavily carved with exotic or allegorical scenes based on fairy tales, patriotic themes, or traditional stories, and designed frankly for instant recognition by the spectator who might view it for no more than a few seconds before it passed by.

Processional forms gave the spectator considerable latitude to deal with the event in his own way because it was lacking dialog and was in motion through space rather than being fixed on a stage or in a circus arena. Instead of requiring the spectator's close attention, processional forms allowed him to watch some parts and not others. Because they are bold and direct and simply organized, it makes little difference whether the spectator involves himself in every minute of it. In any case, he is still connected to the total event, which is as much a festival alteration of space as it is a performance.

ENTERTAINMENT ENVIRONMENTS

In the entertainment environment, it is the events that are fixed, and not the spectator, who is often completely mobile and presented with a large number of choices around which he organizes his own "event." Entertainment environments are of two types: those that redefine an already existing area for a short time and those that make up what might be called a self-contained or autonomous environment. The first type is an ancient one, stretching back as far as the trading fairs and religious pageants of the Middle Ages. In it, a street or a square is transformed for the duration of a fair or festival into an entertainment area filled with merchants' stalls and the booths of showmen.

The Italian street fairs of New York's Little Italy are striking examples of the way in which existing space may be redefined through complex fantasy architecture into an entertainment environment. The main entrance to the St. Anthony festival, which stretches for half a dozen blocks down Sullivan Street, is flanked by the Saint's church and a small traveling carnival set up in a parking lot. Over Sullivan Street stretch dozens of huge lighted arches, creating at night a corridor of light, the sides of which are packed with food and novelty stalls and game booths that virtually block out the shops and apartment buildings. The environment is, in effect, overlaid on the life of the neighborhood, creating a temporary, special area with its own character superimposed on the usual function of the street.

Self-contained or autonomous environments use spaces solely devoted to entertainment. The simplest self-contained environments are based on a single kind of experience for the spectator. The carnival "glass house" or "hall of mirrors," for example, is simply a maze of mirrored rooms through which the visitor wanders until he has groped his way to the exit. The fun house takes patrons through black rooms with shifting floors and other mock-terrifying experiences. A somewhat more extensive and varied set of experiences was provided by Barnum's and the countless other "dime" museums and waxworks popular during the nineteenth century, forms that survive in London's Mme Tussaud's and the Musée Grévin in Paris. A Philadelphia "museum" of the late nineteenth century contained a first floor fitted out as a penny arcade, with fun house distorting mirrors, "Trial-

Fig. 2.5 William Hogarth's "Southwark Fair," (1733) an eighteenth-century "entertainment environment" with open-air street performers, including a peep-show operator, a slack-wire walker, and a musician who exhibits puppets and a trained dog.

Test Machines of all descriptions" (including "Lung Tester, Health Lift and Registering Striking Machine"), as well as "Cosmic and Dioramic Views." On the second floor, patrons saw a menagerie, and on the floor above was the so-called Curio Hall. There, on platforms around the room, were live freaks, among them the "Minnesota Wooly Baby"; "General Rhinebeck, the Military Midget"; and "Joe Berliner, the Human Fire Alarm." The featured attraction, who may have performed in another room for an additional admission charge, was Layman, the "Man of a Hundred Faces." On the hour, the crowd that collected in the Curio Hall was permitted to descend to a theatre where they viewed a 45-minute version of a standard play with much doubling and tripling of roles.

Such forms as the traveling carnival and the amusement park represent still more complex environments. The carnival becomes, in effect, a kind of temporary city with a specialized purpose and a distinctive brand of architecture. Traditional carnivals generally contain rides, booths, and "joints." The joints represent an evolution out of the traditional market traders' stalls and the booths are variations of the old fairground showman's theatre. Each structure reflects its owner's personal prejudices about design and there is virtually no consistency in terms of their scale or decoration. A booth that is well designed from the showman's point of view is said to have "flash." Flash is a hazy word, used in many different ways, but basically it is anything that attracts the eye. It comes from startling design, bright paint, use of chrome or steel, or from a strident front. Light and music may in themselves be flash and are basic elements in the scenography of the entertainment environment.

The effect of an entertainment environment on the spectator is a kind of disorientation, and the showmen attempt to use that disorientation to draw the spectators through the environment from attraction to attraction. In most cases, organization of the elements in the environment is far more carefully calculated than it would appear to be. A typical carnival midway, for example, is laid out in a horseshoe shape. Down the sides of the lot are the joints devoted to games, food, and merchandise. At the rear are booths devoted to the freak, thrill, and girl shows, animal attractions, and fun houses. A spine down the center of the lot contains open joints and rides that can be approached by the crowd from two sides. The largest and most spectacular rides, located toward the back, draw spectators automatically down one leg of the horseshoe toward the rear of the lot. Showmen speak of "balancing" a lot – that is, of creating combinations of booths, rides and joints that will draw customers to all in a regular and systematic way.

The amusement park is, in effect, a more permanent version of the carnival, but with precisely the same objectives. Unlike the meticulously consistent environments created by the Disney organization, with their concern for illusionism, tidiness and what passes for good taste, the traditional amusement park offers a chaotic, jarring and somewhat sinister environment, created with unrestrained indulgence in fantasy architecture and "flash." Coney Island, wrote e. e. cummings in the 1920s, is made up of

> a trillion smells; the tinkle and snap of shooting galleries; the magically sonorous exhortations of barkers and ballyhoomen; the thousands upon thousands of faces paralyzed by enchantment to mere eyeful disks, which strugglingly surge through dizzy gates of illusion; the metamorphosis of atmosphere into a stupendous pattern of electric colors, punctuated by a continuous whisking of leaning and cleaving ship-like shapes; the yearn and skid of toy cars crammed with screeching reality, wildly spiraling earthward or gliding out of ferocious depth into sumptuous height or whirling eccentrically in a brilliant flatness … . Coney has a distinct drop on both theatre and circus. Whereas at the theatre we are merely deceived, at Coney we deceive ourselves. Whereas at the circus we are merely spectators of the impossible, at Coney we ourselves perform impossible feats … the essence of Coney Island's 'circus theatre' consists of *homogeneity*. THE AUDIENCE IS THE PERFORMANCE, and vice versa.

3

THE GOLDEN AGE OF THE BOULEVARD

Marvin Carlson

To the theatre historian, the year 1830 means Hugo and the premiere of *Hernani*. For the great majority of the theatre public of the period, however, Hugo was a name scarcely known and the battle of *Hernani* was a minor passing scandal. Neither the new romantic experiments nor the declining neoclassic tradition they were attempting to replace represented theatre to this public. For them, theatre was the rope-dancing of Mme Saqui, the pantomimes of Déburau, Kiony the elephant performing in plays written especially for him, the view of Timbuktu at the Cosmorama, the spectacular melodramas of Bouchardy, or the full-scale Napoleonic battle recreated at the Cirque Olympique.

This astonishingly varied popular theatre was the direct descendant of the fair theatres, which had challenged the entertainment monopoly of the state-supported theatres, with varying degrees of success, for two hundred years. Then, primarily because of the rapidly changing political situation, the great fairs had disappeared. The Foire Saint-Germain, destroyed by fire in 1762, was never rebuilt. The famous *parades*, the most popular theatrical entertainment at the fairs, were steadily discouraged by the police, and the last was closed in 1777. The last two major fairs, Saint-Laurent and Saint-Ovide, closed in 1786, and their few remaining minor successors did not survive the storms of the Revolution.

One might expect that these changes would mean the end of the entertainments sheltered by the fairs. But entertainments that had survived for so long under all the legal harassments that the authorities, spurred on by the Comédie-Française and Opéra, could devise, refused to disappear so easily. With their homes outside the city walls disappearing, they moved boldly into Paris itself, and, more accessible to their audiences, became more popular than ever. The leader in this movement was Jean-Baptiste Nicolet, who, in 1759, established a permanent theatre in the north of Paris on the Boulevard du Temple. Although his permit allowed him to present only rope-dancing, the Comédie, knowing from experience how easily such permits were gradually expanded, protested the establishment of any permanent popular entertainment within the city. But the Minister replied that the people needed their spectacles and that the times of Louis XIV were past. The fears of the Comédie were not in vain. Other directors followed Nicolet, and, although rigid restrictions were placed on each, the Comédie and Opéra complained

Fig. 3.1 Acrobats on the Boulevard, Paris. (*TDR* 18: 2.)

regularly, and not always successfully, about the erosion of these restrictions. Nicolet
added trained animals to his acrobats, then marionettes and *parades*, then full-scale plays
and harlequinades.

Although Nicolet's was the first permanent theatre on the Boulevard, the area had
already developed as a popular entertainment center. The Boulevard du Temple had been
constructed under Louis XIV. For almost a century, it remained little more than a pleasant,
tree-lined drive for Parisians out for Sundays and holidays. During the early 1750s, cabarets, cafés, and a few marionette booths began to appear, and a diary of 1753 reports that
the area had "almost the atmosphere of a fair." Mountebanks, jugglers, acrobats, trained
animals, and every sort of street spectacle soon appeared on the Boulevard, aimed at tourists and at every level of Parisian society. Rough booths erected for marionettes gave way
to more ambitious structures, one of which housed an ephemeral "marine spectacle," then
a display of "architecture and mechanical devices" by Antoine Fouré, a student of the
famous designer Servandoni, and finally Nicolet's new Théâtre de la Gaîté.[1]

The arrival of the Gaîté spurred an even more rapid development of this new entertainment center, and for the next century the Boulevard du Temple became synonymous with
popular non-Establishment theatre, despite the opposition of the Comédie and Opéra and
every sort of legal restriction on performance conditions – repertoire, size of casts, number
of musicians, and whether dialog or song could be added to pantomime. When all legal
restrictions were removed in 1791, Paris already had thirty-five theatres, most of them on,
or near, the Boulevard, and in the years that followed, the number rose to nearly one
hundred. Around them gathered many other forms of popular entertainment. The fairs had
disappeared, but the Boulevard itself now became a perpetual fair – lined with theatres,
cafés, and music halls, its wide streets crowded at all hours with strollers and with a rich
variety of spectacles for their amusement. There were tumblers, giants and dwarfs; wild
men and wild animals; marionettes, monsters and magicians; Osage Indians, trained dogs,

bears, and fleas; men who swallowed serpents, stones and cutlery; children who drank boiling oil and walked on bars of red-hot iron; wandering musicians, fortune-tellers, astrologers, and wandering "physicists" who, for a sou, offered a look through a microscope at a flea made as large as a fist, and, for two sous, treated their patrons to a shock from a revolving electrical apparatus. Behind this constantly varied scene, music poured from the pleasure gardens and the cafés. Many of the established theatres added to the display by employing barkers or presenting lively vaudeville entertainments, the popular *parades*, before their doors to draw prospective patrons inside.

Despite the storms of the Revolution, it was a period of amazing richness in popular entertainment. The competition, encouraged by the removal of all privileges, forced every entrepreneur to search continuously for new attractions simply to survive. After 1791, having nothing to fear from either the Comédie or the Opéra, Nicolet varied his acrobatics, farces, and pantomimes with Corneille, Molière, and mythological ballets. The genres began to mix. When Nicolet's major rival, Audinot, invented the *pantomime dialoguée*, adding verses and music to previously mute pantomimes, Nicolet responded by adding musical themes, which he called *Leitmotifs*, to his short plays. From these experiments the first melodramas developed.

Throughout the Revolution, the theatres suffered under an arbitrary and constantly shifting policy of censorship, but there was never an attempt to limit their numbers or define their modes of production in the manner of the *ancien régime*. It was Napoleon who restored this tradition in 1807, reducing the number of Parisian theatres from the thirty-three that had survived the Revolution to eight, each with a clearly defined repertoire. He set up four major national theatres: the Théâtres de l'Empereur and de l'Impératrice (later the Comédie-Française and the Odéon), the Opéra, and the Opéra-Comique, and four minor boulevard theatres, the Gaîté and the Ambigu-Comique (the oldest Boulevard theatres, founded by Nicolet and Audinot), the Variétés, and the Vaudeville. The Empereur had exclusive rights to the pre-Revolutionary Comédie repertoire and part of the repertoire of the old Comédie Italienne. The Impératrice possessed the rest of this repertoire, plus whatever new plays it would henceforth premiere. The Opéra and Opéra-Comique, of course, controlled their respective genres.

The Gaîté and Ambigu were required to share the new melodrama, now a fully developed form embellished not only with song but with other spectacular trappings – ballet, lavish and often exotic settings and costumes, even performing animals. The genre assigned to the Vaudeville was the light comedy or parody ornamented with songs from which it took its name. Its subjects were decorous and frequently literary; no other minor theatre made so strong an effort to attract refined audiences. The Variétés, on the contrary, held most closely to the broad and extravagant spirit of the old fair theatres – gross buffoonery, snatches of song, acrobats, crude puns, and irreverent satire were staples here. Members of polite society affected never to attend the Variétés, but after 1807 the theatre was provided with a large number of grilled boxes, and the popularity of these proved that the theatre had a strong appeal to persons who wished to see without being seen. The Variétés was also very popular with foreigners, who could enjoy its gross physical humor and its emphasis on spectacle and action without troubling over the dialog.

Since Napoleon made no attempt to regulate spectacles that he did not consider theatrical, the decree of 1807 had little effect on Paris' other popular entertainments. In most of the city's large squares, and especially near the Pont Neuf, the mountebanks, musicians, and acrobats continued to display their skills to a delighted public, as they had in most of these same locations since the days of Henri IV. A vast market of mountebank doctors was on the Place des Victoires, their booths festooned with many-colored flags, the air ringing with songs and spiels and with the sounds of cymbals, clarinets and hunting horns. The public pleasure gardens, an invention of the Revolutionary years, featured other entertainments. Concerts were an inevitable feature, and acrobats, fireworks, trained animals and balloon ascensions were common. New attractions appeared yearly, however, such as the popular "Russian mountains," the ancestor of the modern roller-coaster, or a mechanical giant representing Gargantua that regularly consumed a titanic meal at Tivoli.

The Napoleonic decree had little effect on the carnival atmosphere of the Boulevard du Temple. Few theatres closed, most simply retreating from regular dramatic offerings to exhibitions of the sort from which they had developed – acrobatics, magicians, clowns, concerts, and marionettes. A traveler, strolling down the Boulevard from the Porte-Saint-Martin at this time, would pass not only a constantly changing array of street entertainments, but an almost unbroken line of more permanent pleasure resorts on both sides of the avenue. First, on the left, came a pair of popular cafés and, on the right, the rotunda and public garden of Paphos, a resort of somewhat dubious reputation. Except for Sundays and holidays, a journal of the time reports, the Paphos was "the haunt of criminals and vagrants, of depraved working girls and of women as ugly as they are importunate."[2] Next, on the left, came a series of theatres alternating with cafés: the Délassements, closed by Napoleon but now sheltering Dujon and his trained birds, the closed Théâtre des Jeunes Troubadours, Hurpin's Ombres Chinoises, and the Théâtre des Patagoniens, now the home of the popular acrobat Malaga. Next came the two official Boulevard theatres, the Ambigu and Gaîté, separated by a café, then the wax museum of Curtius, one of the great attractions of pre-Revolutionary Paris.

After the popular Café-concert Apollo (the former Théâtre Sans-Prétention) came the Théâtre des Pygmées, which featured magical transformations and miniature scenes enlarged by an ingenious system of mirrors. The Pygmées was best known, however, not for any of these marvels, but for the *parades* performed outside its doors by Bobèche and Galimafré, the last great practitioners of this genre which, at this time, was one of Paris' favorite attractions. In the traditional manner of clown pairs, the two set each other off perfectly both in style and physique, and though their *parades* might contain easily recognizable French types of commedia figures, most of their routines were based on their own contrast. Bobèche was elegant and handsome, dressed invariably in a red vest, yellow breeches, blue stockings, a black cravat, a red wig and a three-cornered hat. His style and sharp wit made him the ideal of the *beau monde*. Galimafré, on the other hand, was adored by the populace. His dress was that of a Norman peasant with hunting cap and rough wig, not always tidy or particularly well brushed. His large face was fixed almost continuously in a foolish smile and his wit was no match for his partner's. Still, his broadsword approach could occasionally defeat Bobèche's rapier; but, win or lose, his follies were the delight of his public. Many of their *parades* were preserved by this public in diaries and journals, and their humor is often surprisingly undated:

> "Here is a letter from a friend of yours. I'll read it to you, since I imagine you've forgotten how. Listen. (*reads*) My dear friend, I must inform you that since your departure your sister has committed several indiscretions; in fact she has had twelve lovers in six months."
>
> "The miserable creature! I must go at once to kill her and preserve the family honor!"
>
> "Wait. (*reads*) She has earned some ten thousand francs by this light conduct and half of it is yours."
>
> "Well, after all, she's a good girl with certain qualities … "

"Wait a bit, my friend. (*reads*) Unhappily, thieves broke into her house while she was out and carried off the whole sum."

"The rogue! The rascal! Master, don't hold me back any longer. I must go punish her!"

"One moment more. (*reads*) Happily, the thieves were arrested the next day and the entire sum was found on them."

"In fact, the poor girl has perhaps been the victim of gossip ... "

"(*reads*) The ten thousand francs, however, have been confiscated by the police and no one knows when they will be released."

"Sir, I see that I must wait a bit before making a judgment."[3]

Beyond the Pygmées, the appeal of the Boulevard lessened, but strollers who continued were offered the attractions of several café-théâtres and cabarets, Thévenélin's automats (a group of mechanical figures that were reported to move in a surprisingly realistic manner), and two more wax museums. On the other side of the Boulevard, the whole area beyond the garden of Paphos was taken up by the far more popular and respectable cafés, and Jardin Turc, with its kiosks of colored glass, a Chinese bridge, verdant walks, sheltered nooks, and hanging lanterns. The garden was not lacking theatrical fare. "Vaudevilles and harlequinades are offered all over the garden," a contemporary journal reported. "The refreshments are not particularly good, but the musicians and actors must be paid for somehow."[4] From four in the afternoon, just after dinner, until eleven in the evening, this was one of the most frequented gathering places in Paris.

Two of the great spectacle theatres of the capital managed, like the humbler cafés and mountebanks, to escape Napoleonic legislation – the Cirque Olympique and the Porte-Saint-Martin. The Cirque Olympique had been founded in 1782 by Philip Astley, an Englishman and a former Sergeant Major of Dragoons, who created the first modern circus by adding acrobats, rope-dancers and brief pantomimes and spoken scenes to his popular equestrian spectacles. The war with England and the coming of the Terror forced Astley to leave his profitable venture and sell out to Antonio Franconi, founder of a famous circus family. Franconi's sons, Laurent and Henri, succeeded their father in 1805, and resisted the decree of 1807 by arguing, successfully, that their venture was a circus, not a theatre, and therefore exempt from the general closing.

Laurent's wife was an outstanding rider, Henri's a pantomimist of grace and skill; but the real stars of the theatre were the stag Coco and the elephant Baba. Coco was tame enough to wander freely among the audience, presenting flowers to ladies and eating from their hands, but he was also a featured performer in a whole series of elaborate dramas such as Hapdé's *Acteon changé en cerf* (1811) and Henri Franconi's *Le pont infernal* (1812). The central scene in each was invariably a hunt with the stag pursued by men and dogs through the roughest mountain wilderness the carpenters and machinists of the Cirque could design, saving himself at last by a spectacular leap across a gaping chasm. Baba, scarcely larger than a bull, had less thespian skill, but could uncork champagne bottles, remove a handkerchief from his trainer's pocket and dance the gavotte. His successor, Kiouny, proved far more versatile and, like Coco, inspired a number of plays. The greatest of these, *L'Eléphant du Roi de Siam*, called on the talents not only of Kiouny and accompanying human actors, but on Sergent, a composer, Bertotto, a ballet designer, and some of the major scene designers of the period – Leroux, Dumay, and Philastre. With such attractions, the Franconis soon established a reputation throughout Europe.

The Porte-Saint-Martin was the only theatre closed by the 1807 decree that raised a serious protest. Its position was a strong one; it had a large, well-equipped house and it was popular and financially stable. In melodrama and in the spectacular fairy play that had developed along with it, the Porte-Saint-Martin rivaled the Ambigu and Gaîté, which had been established longer; its ballets were considered superior even to those of the Opéra; its mime, Mazurier, was judged by Talma himself as one of the three "true actors" then living. As the monkey Jocko, he created a vogue for simian pantomimes that swept Europe. For two years, the theatre's directors submitted petition after petition until at last they were allowed to reopen as the Jeux Gymniques. To protect the establishment theatres, the new house was restricted to "acrobatics, historic tableaux, military displays, and prologs," with any dramatic works to be presented by no more than two actors.[5] It was the same sort of restrictive legislation common for minor theatres before the Revolution, and the Jeux Gymniques followed the pattern of most of those, gradually departing farther and farther from its legal bonds until a protest from the Opéra caused it to be closed again in 1811.

Napoleon's restrictions on the number of Parisian theatres were repealed in 1815, but the restored monarchy retained the practice of granting new privileges only with severe limitations on the genre or the method of production. When the Funambules opened in 1816 it was restricted to "acrobatic displays," so that when the theatre began to present pantomimes, each actor was still required to make his entrance on a tightrope, which was stretched permanently across the stage. The *Almanach des Spectacles* of 1822 reported that "The leading man is forbidden to take part in the action and to concern himself with affairs of the heart without having first performed a few leaps and done some cart-wheels."[6] Even Frédérick Lemaître, greatest of the Boulevard actors, performing at the Funambules early in his career, entered walking on his hands and going into a forward somersault, though his part was a "Count Adolph" of illustrious lineage. Perhaps the most ingenious director in circumventing such restrictions was Pierre Alaux of the Panorama-Dramatique, who was given permission in 1819 to present dramas, comedies, and vaudevilles on the condition that he never have on stage more than two speaking actors. By hiring a quick-change artist, who could appear as a new character every few minutes, and employing life-size marionettes whose lines were spoken from the wings, Alaux managed to create the impression of working with a full company.

Despite these ingenious adaptations, the major attraction at the Panorama-Dramatique was the scenery, as it was in many Parisian theatres. The love of visual spectacle, brought to the Opéra and the fairs by Servandoni early in the eighteenth century and fed by a growing interest in the exotic, the supernatural, and the sublime, reached its high point in the French theatre of the Empire. Melodrama houses such as the Ambigu and Gaîté were scarcely less lavish in such display than the Cirque Olympique or the Porte-Saint-Martin. Even more significantly, Paris experienced a vogue for theatres of pure scenic spectacle, without a single actor – human or animal. The first panoramas were exhibited to Londoners by the painter Robert Barker in 1787 and to Parisians by the American inventor Robert Fulton in 1799. During the next several years, the painter Prévost created a series of panoramas along the Boulevards and in 1804, Daguerre, the pioneer in photography, opened his Théâtre Pittoresque, which offered, instead of plays, scenes of sunrises, seas, gardens, streets, and famous buildings. More than twenty similar establishments opened between 1815 and 1820. There were panoramas of London, Jerusalem, Rome, Athens, Constantinople, and Timbuktu; panoramas of famous historical events, and a whole series of variations – a Néorama and Géorama, a Europarama, even a Cosmorama. The most ambitious and successful of these establishments was the Diorama, opened by Daguerre and Bouton in 1822. Here 350 spectators could be seated on a circular platform and turned 360 degrees to view a huge painting 42 feet high which completely surrounded them and could be illuminated from both front and back to create a variety of atmospheric effects.

Many of the minor houses closed by Napoleon were reorganized and revived under the more relaxed conditions of the Restoration. The Associés survived during the Empire as a café-theatre, the Apollon, offering its guests pantomimes, harlequinades, and eventually even operas with the 16-sou cup of coffee or chocolate. Soon after the Restoration a new theatre patent was sought for the house by a well-known rope-dancer of the time, Mme Saqui, whose father was an acrobat in the fairs and at one time a performer for Nicolet. During the Revolution, Mme Saqui trained herself in rope-dancing in the provinces with such success that, on her return to Paris, Napoleon called her "his passion" and bestowed on her the title of "first dancer of France." Not a festival was given at Saint-Cloud or an imperial victory celebrated without her participation, and her performances at imperial celebrations outside of France gave her a European reputation as great as Talma's. Mme Saqui's new Théâtre Acrobate was restricted to rope-dancing, though she could introduce other non-theatrical fair entertainment for variety, such as Jacques de Falaise, "the polyphage," who would swallow any object submitted to him by a member of the audience.

Her bright prospects were dimmed considerably by the appearance of a major competitor only a few months later. As a result of a quarrel with the noted acrobat, a coach driver named Bertrand decided to gain revenge by opening a rival theatre next to hers. With capital provided by a friend, an umbrella merchant who was devoted to Boulevard entertainment, Bertrand gained not a patent, but a *tolérance*, which could be withdrawn at any moment without notice or explanation. On this shaky basis he opened the Funambules, a house restricted, at least in theory, to acrobatic displays. Bertrand prospered despite his unstable legal position. In 1817, he discovered a talented family of acrobats and rope-dancers, the Déburaus, performing in the Cour Saint-Maur and engaged them for the Funambules. One of the sons, Jean-Gaspard, appeared without much success in brigand roles until, by chance, he was given the opportunity to substitute for the theatre's Pierrot in 1819. His success was immediate and enormous and, until his death in 1846, his Pierrot was one of the great attractions of the Parisian stage. Earlier Pierrots had been secondary characters, cynical, unfaithful servants who were generally little more than the butt of the more fanciful Harlequin's jokes. Now Harlequin and Columbine, the Captain and the traditional young lovers of the pantomime were all pushed into the background by Déburau's fascinating Pierrot – graceful, svelte, naive and open as a child yet able to assume all the elegance and splendor of the most refined aristocrat. Déburau's Pierrot took on a different character in almost every play, but a warmth and rich observation of humanity united them all.

After 1820, the authorities rarely attempted to check the steady erosion of the regulations imposed on almost every minor theatre. The state-supported theatres no longer found it worthwhile to complain except in cases of outright theft of their repertoire. Complaints of infractions now came to authorities mainly from disgruntled minor rivals, and were generally ignored. The legislation that restricted each theatre to a distinctive genre had been repealed and most minor houses now mixed melodramas with comedies, vaudevilles, and pantomimes – perhaps all on the same evening, since two, three, or even four plays were offered nightly. As programs changed at least once a week, this was a period of enormous productivity. The vogue for melodrama was still great, and brigands, plots, and violence were so favored on Boulevard stages that during the 1820s it became popularly known as the Boulevard du Crime. The *Almanach des Spectacles* of 1823 demonstrated the appropriateness of this title. By counting up the crimes on Boulevard stages for the previous two decades, the *Almanach* claimed, it found "Tautin has been stabbed 16,302 times, Marty has been poisoned in various ways 11,000 times, Fresnoy has been murdered 27,000 times, Mlle Adèle Dupuis has been the innocent victim of 75,000 seductions, abductions, or drownings, 6,500 capital charges have tested Mlle Levesque's virtue, and Mlle Oliver, whose career is scarcely launched, has already tasted the cup of crime and vengeance 16,000 times."[7] The period from 1815 to 1830 produced 280 new melodramas to add to the hundreds of revivals, but even though these violent entertainments gave the Boulevard much of its distinctive tone, they were only a small part of the minor theatres' total production. The same period produced 369 new come- dies, 200 new comic operas, 1,300 new vaudevilles, and innumerable lesser dramatic works.

Because of their diversity, a large number of theatres were able to coexist on the Boulevard without serious problems of competition. As their fortunes improved, so did their physical surroundings. Gas lighting was installed along the Boulevard, the rough paving was smoothed, wooden barriers were erected to control each theatre's queues, marquees were built to give protection from the weather, the theatres themselves were steadily remodeled and improved, and the humble structures previously mixed in among them were replaced by elegant town houses and cafés. The proprietors of these new establishments began to make common cause with the directors of the Boulevard thea- tres to drive out the street vendors and entertainers, pleading that they created a continual disturbance and were an affront to their respectable neighbors. By 1830, they were able to rid the Boulevard of every mountebank, marionette, and *parade*, and, naturally, of much of its color. Now, only in the theatre of Mme Saqui could audiences find displays like those of the former fairs. Some street entertainments, most notably the *parade*, disappeared after 1830, but others, seemingly indestructible, simply returned to their traditional haunts around the Pont Neuf or into the area of the present Place du Châtelet.

With the departure of such performances, the quarter was as peaceful as any in Paris during the day, but the crowds that 'began to gather about five, when the box offices opened, proved that the Boulevard had lost none of its popularity. Major houses like the Comédie now opened at 7, but the Boulevard theatres, with their long programs, often began at 5.15 or 5.30 p.m. Even so, a police decree of 1834 requiring all theatres to close at 11 p.m. met with considerable protest.

The greatest theatrical artists of France were to be found at these minor houses. At their head was the brilliant Frédérick Lemaître, greatest of the French romantic actors. Close to him in popularity and frequently performing with him were Marie Dorval and Pierre Bocage. Déburau still reigned at the Funambules, supported by Laurent, a clown from England. A whole galaxy of lesser stars filled the minor theatres – Virginie Déjazet, Mlle George, Mélingue, Lockroy, Ligier, and Laferrière, to name only a few – so that a number of houses could offer performers as capable as, and in some cases superior to, those at the Comédie itself.

The symbolic importance of the Comédie was still great, however, and Hugo and Dumas were clearly correct in their judgment that romantic drama must capture this citadel before it would be taken seriously by French men of letters. Their opponents obviously agreed, as the famous battle over *Hernani* and the less famous struggles within the Comédie over the presentation of other works by Hugo, Dumas, and Vigny clearly demonstrated. Once this battle was won, the romantics were quick to leave the hostile ground of the Comédie for the more congenial Boulevard theatres.

Everyone, save a few embittered classicists, attended the Porte-Saint-Martin, and its program was as varied as its public. Visual spectacle was its specialty, not only in the romantic works but in melodramas, historical pageants, and fairy plays – all popular forms presented at the theatre. Only the Cirque Olympique could rival the Porte-Saint-Martin in such spectacle, and, unwilling to miss any opportunity to win audiences, the latter house challenged the Cirque even in the presentation of animal acts. Behind a heavy wire screen that protected the audience, the admired trainer Martin starred in plays that required him to fight lions, tigers, and hyenas with his bare hands. The Parisian stage had departed so far from Napoleonic ideals that neither Harel nor his audiences saw any incongruity in alternating lion taming and premieres by Victor Hugo on the same stage.

The particular specialty of the Cirque during this period was vast historical pageants, for which the theatre employed a permanent company of more than 100 actors, 30 horses, and a large staff of designers and technicians. Entire battles were recreated at the Cirque on a huge stage connected by ramps to a circus-style arena in the midst of the audience. Here, too, the fairy play reached its apogee in such works as *Zazezizozu* (1834) and *Les Pilules du Diable* (1839) with underwater scenes, erupting volcanoes, dancing bears, monsters, enchanted forests, castles, and grottos. Advances in technology were quickly utilized too. *Pilules* featured the first train on a Parisian stage, which not only rolled onto the stage but exploded.

The Revolution of 1830 destroyed the last vestiges of imperial theatrical restrictions. Anxious to demonstrate his love of liberty, Louis-Philippe removed any restrictions on the opening of new theatres, allowed theatres access to the repertoires of all the others, and abolished censorship, giving Parisian playhouses a freedom that they had not enjoyed since the first enthusiastic legislation of the Revolution. The results were as catastrophic in 1830 as they had been in 1791, and within months the government was besieged with complaints from the church and from moralists about profane or obscene performances, and from all sorts of prominent citizens who found themselves being publicly represented and mocked in the Boulevard theatres. Within three months, the government felt obliged to forbid the theatres

> instigating any action considered a crime or misdemeanor, attacks against the king and royal dignity, offenses toward the Chambers, foreign sovereigns, and the legally recognized religion, seditious expressions, outrages to public or religious morality, the representation of any person living or alive within the past 25 years, whether named or presented in such a way that he can be recognized,

and further, to require all plays to be submitted to a censor fifteen days before production so that these regulations could be enforced.[8]

The arrival of Rachel at the Comédie in 1838 restored a measure of the popularity to the national theatre that it had last enjoyed in the days of Talma, but the minor houses offered too varied and attractive a competition to be much affected. For a century and a half, the major dramatic artists and authors of France had been found exclusively at the national theatres, but these post-Revolutionary years had broken that pattern. Lemaître, generally considered the greatest French actor of the period, never appeared at the Comédie at all. Hugo and Dumas felt the necessity of proving themselves by productions at the Comédie, but found that their plays were in fact better interpreted elsewhere. Augier and Dumas *fils*, the leading dramatists of the next generation, established their reputations entirely outside the national theatres, at the Gymnase and Vaudeville. For such major artists of the late nineteenth century as Bernhardt, Coquelin, and Réjane, the

Comédie was only one of many theatres where they might display their talents, and not even their favored one.

The status and respectability gained by the Boulevard theatres during the nineteenth century was achieved, not surprisingly, with some loss in color and variety. The popular roots from which they sprang – the *parades*, pantomimes, and acrobats of the fairs – were gradually expelled, first from the theatres themselves, then even from their environs. Gradually, the memory of these entertainments faded until, by the late nineteenth century, Boulevard entertainment came to mean a highly polished but insubstantial and largely predictable fare designed for a rather monochromatic bourgeois audience. The old Boulevard du Temple itself was destroyed in Haussmann's rebuilding of Paris, but the theatres, relocated elsewhere in Paris, had already become an important part of the Establishment against which they were originally pitted. Gone forever was the heady mixture of the early nineteenth-century Boulevard, where acrobatics, major literary premieres, romantic ballets, trained dogs and horses, and spectacular melodramas and fairy plays competed for audiences within a few hundred yards of each other. The constant borrowing, or stealing, of ideas and techniques among artists had created a theatrical period of unusual richness and diversity.

NOTES

1 Campardon, *Spectacles*, 1, 332.
2 *Tribunal volatile*, 28, 29, quoted in Henri Beaulieu, *Les Théâtres du boulevard du Crime* (Paris, 1904), p. 175.
3 Théodore Faucher, *Histoire du boulevard du Temple* (Paris, 1863), pp. 43–4.
4 *Tribunal Volatile*, 32–4, quoted in Beaulieu, op. cit., p. 173.
5 Albert, *Les Théâtres des boulevards* (Paris, 1902), p. 230.
6 *Almanach des spectacles*, 1822, quoted in Gustav Cain's *Théâtres de Paris* (Paris, 1906) p. 110.
7 Quoted in Beaulieu, op. cit., pp. 5–6.
8 Albert, op. cit., pp. 335–9.

Part II

PUPPETS FROM BREAD AND PUPPET THEATRE TO BUNRAKU AND BROADWAY

4

INTRODUCTION TO PART II

Joel Schechter

Some of the world's most popular theatre is performed on small stages without actors, as puppets play all the roles. Gordon Craig, the visionary director and designer, proposed universal replacement of live stage-performers with marionettes in 1907;[1] but long before that, puppetry was threatening the livelihood of actors. It is a measure of the art's popularity, and the insecurity of human performers, that hand puppets arrived in Paris in the seventeenth century, and by the eighteenth century, French stage actors were complaining about the competition.[2]

Actor antipathy to puppetry in Paris and other European cities was driven by economics, not aesthetics. A cast of puppets costs almost nothing to maintain, and if earnings are low in one location, a director can pack his or her troupe into a trunk and move to another street or town, as many itinerant puppeteers did. Punch and Judy shows could be seen on different London streets by 1713, and antic characters appeared even earlier on puppet stages in Italy and France. A German account of 1744 reports the appearance of Pickle Herring – a farcical puppet character, like France and Italy's Polichinelle and England's Punch, based on a stage clown – in "the kind of puppet show where the hand is put inside the puppet."[3] These puppets spread across Europe, and the comic characters were so popular by Gordon Craig's time that he lamented "all puppets are now but low comedians."

(At the time he wrote these words, Craig could have seen or at least known the avant-garde puppetry of Alfred Jarry. Paris welcomed Jarry's puppet-theatre staging of *Ubu Roi,* which ran for sixty-four performances in 1898; whereas the actor-performed production of *Ubu* set off a riot two years earlier, the puppets, designed by Pierre Bonnard, won audience favor, and may have better served Jarry's comic vision of political upheaval.)

Comedy is a mainstay of popular puppetry, but the genre is not entirely low or comic. Craig in his 1907 essay described Asian puppets as "the symbols of all things on earth and in Nirvana."[4] They "are the descendants of a great and noble family of Images, images which were indeed made 'in the likeness of God,'" Craig observed, and such images of divinities and epic heroes can still be seen in the puppetry of masters in Java, China, India, Vietnam, Burma, Thailand, Japan.

Age-old traditions of shadow and rod puppetry in some of these nations still present versions of the *Mahabharata* and *Ramayana*, religious epics which in puppet-forms "cut across time and space for a meeting of popular, traditional, folk, high and elite culture."[5] Within these puppet epics, low comedy can be found; topical, irreverent and local commentary from clowns and servants gives the Asian forms the puppet equivalent of the punch in western culture's Punch and Judy: which is to say, their popular appeal comes from farcical interludes, disruptive asides, slapstick and comic resistance to religious order, law, and social hierarchy. Barbara Hatley notes of Javanese shadow puppetry (*wayang kulit*), in the essay reprinted here, that "through joking the clowns demystify the sacred Wayang symbols and reduce tensions and anxieties produced by Wayang's social and religious prescriptions. The clowns' satirical commentary on contemporary political and social evils probably has a similar cathartic effect."[6] (The fact that some of the puppets are clowns, and share satirical tendencies found in circus clowning, attests to an intersection of popular theatre forms which is not uncommon.)

As noted in the introductory pages of this volume, Asian puppetry such as bunraku was once far more popular, and more fully supported by the paying public, than it is today. The large bunraku dolls, each manipulated by three highly trained operators clothed in black, still appear onstage in Japan. Donald Keene observed that while

> Bunraku attracted large audiences in the eighteenth century because the theatre staged plays of immediate appeal, the problem in appreciation of Bunraku today is that the plays belong to a Japan which either no longer exists or is buried so deeply as to be undiscoverable ... many young Japanese declare that they can understand neither the old-fashioned poetic language of the plays nor their outmoded philosophy.[7]

Unlike some western traditions of puppetry, bunraku resists the illusion that its dolls speak. Trained chanters are seated near the puppet stage, not hidden from spectators; the vocalizing of a prepared text is visibly separate from the bodies of the bunraku dolls. Roland Barthes suggests in the essay reprinted here that this separation of elements is Brechtian. "As Brecht saw," writes Barthes, "here reigns the *quotation* – the pinch of a script, the fragment of code – because none of the promotives of the action can take on himself responsibility for something he never writes alone."[8] In other puppetry, we experience what Barthes terms "not so much the illusion of reality as the illusion of totality." Although western puppet handlers for Punch and Judy are artists whose voices we hear, their human bodies are concealed inside a booth, or behind a curtain, to foster an illusion that bodies made of inanimate objects have a unity of movement and voice.

This illusion of totality imbues western puppetry with some of its humor and fascination; it gives the performance a sense of incongruity, bordering on absurdity, as constructions of leather, cloth, wood, and string appear to speak. By contrast, as Barthes notes, "it is not the simulation of the body which Bunraku seeks, it is – if this can be said – the body's tangible abstraction." At the same time, human bodies are essential to bunraku, and their presence reminds us why popular theatre, even in puppetry, is so dependent on the body. As Donald Keene notes, the bunraku puppet operator "is bound by traditions no less than [the chanters of text and musicians], but these traditions are completely unrecorded, and are remembered more by the body than by the mind ... . The operator['s] memory is physical rather than verbal ... ."[9] Physical memory of this order is required of other theatre performers; but in puppetry the human bodies capable of complex muscle memory are usually hidden.

Bunraku puppetry, like other Japanese theatre arts, has traditionally been the province of men; they chant the lines and operate the dolls. Women perform roles in other non-western puppet shows, particularly those created by families of artists. For India's Karnataka shadow puppeteers, "the wife of the puppeteer plays the harmonium, sings, and speaks for the female puppets."[10] Traditional western puppetry is not exempt from charges that it favors men, too. Punch and Judy Professor Caz Frost recalls that feminists once derided her for portraying Punch's violent assault on Judy. Frost responds that to show "male/female stereotypes … [in a style] so grossly exaggerated and comic is not to condone them."[11]

Puppet traditions in Europe, the United States and non-western regions have quite distinct histories, but in recent times these traditions are more likely to be mixed, and derive inspiration and techniques from one another. Asian puppetry has been adapted by wWestern stage directors Ariane Mnouchkine, Lee Breuer, and Julie Taymor, for example. There is some irony that inexpensive popular puppetry traditions from Asia and from Peter Schumann's Bread and Puppet theatre reappeared, in altered form, in the multimillion dollar Broadway production of *The Lion King*, and returned great profits to its producer, the Disney Corporation. In Julie Taymor's defense, it should be noted (as is clear from Richard Schechner's interview with her, reprinted here) that her success on Broadway with *The Lion King* came only after many years of non-commercial, non-profit experimentation and immersion in popular traditions.

Today, English language audiences are more likely to see puppets in a commercial stage production of *The Lion King* or *Shockheaded Peter* than on a stage set up on the street, or at a fairground or village square. (The recent film, *Being John Malkovich*, humorously portrays a New York City street puppeteer assaulted by a citizen who regards the marionette enactment of a medieval love story as pornography; the streets of New York are not safe for serious puppetry, at least not in Hollywood's vision of New

Fig. 4.1 *Punch and Judy* **on a London street, drawing by George Cruikshank, 1837.**

York.) In earlier periods, itinerant life was common among puppeteers in western and non-western regions. In southern India, for example, the Ganesh Yakshagana Gombeyata Mandali puppet theatre group used to perform 150 shows a year, travelling from one village to another, to weddings and birth ceremonies, to support itself and impart blessings as well as entertainment through its art.[12] This practice of travelling has an interesting western counterpart documented by Henry Mayhew in his 1850 interview with a London Punchman. In neither region is the itinerant life one most artists can sustain today. Even 150 years ago, Mayhew's anonymous Punch and Judy operator said, "business gets slacker and slacker every season … . People isn't getting tired of our [street] performances, but stingier – that's it."[13] Today if puppeteers travel, it is most likely from one festival to another, with advance bookings, or from one television studio workshop (such as that founded by the late Jim Henson) to another.

Besides the muppeteers and Sesame Street puppets on television, which are seen by millions of children and their parents, there exists within North America, Europe and Asia a large group of puppeteers who draw on diverse cultures and popular traditions. In the United States, artists Theodora Skipitares, Bob Hartman, Bruce Schwartz, Paul Zaloom, Wise Fool Puppet Intervention, In the Heart of the Beast Puppet and Mask Theatre, and Great Small Works are a few of the creators who have developed highly original shows, and, like their European and Asian counterparts, present innovative and topical theatre on small stages. These indigenous puppeteers and their ensembles in the United States owe a huge debt to Peter Schumann and his pioneering Bread and Puppet Theatre. Schumann offered guidance and apprenticeships around the world to hundreds of aspiring artists. His statements on puppetry (reprinted here from *TDR*) pay homage to it as

> an anarchic art, subversive and untamable by nature, an art which is easier researched in police records than in theater chronicles, an art which by fate and spirit does not aspire to represent governments or civilizations, but prefers its own secret and demeaning stature in society, representing, more or less, the demons of that society and definitely not its institutions.[14]

Bread and Puppet Theatre presented widely seen street theatre during the 1960s, the period of America's war in Vietnam, when the ensemble's huge sculpted masks of mourners and floating cloth birds of peace led protest parades. In the interview included here, Julie Taymor says, "Bread and Puppet was one of the first things [in American popular arts] that really grabbed me during the Vietnam War. It was *that* power of parade." For years Bread and Puppet's annual festival, "Our Domestic Resurrection Circus" in Glover, Vermont, demonstrated the tremendous power of popular theatre, as it charged no admission, hardly advertised, and attracted thousands of people from around the world to eat Peter Schumann's homemade sourdough bread and watch his legendary puppets perform. Schumann's puppets deliver the radicality he seeks in art which is "conceptual sculpture, cheap, true to its popular origins, uninvited by the powers-that-be … ," and welcome by just about everyone else.

NOTES

1 Gordon Craig, "The Actor and the Ubermarionette" in *On the Art of the Theatre* London: Mercury Books, 1962, pp.54–94.
2 Max von Boehn, *Puppets and Automata* New York: Dover, 1972, p. 60.
3 Max von Boehn, op. cit., p. 66.
4 Craig, op. cit., p. 92.

5   *A World View of Puppets*. San Francisco: San Francisco Airport Museums, 1999, p. 3. [No author named].

6   Barbara Hatley, "Wayang and Ludruk: Polarities in Java," reprinted in this volume.

7   Donald Keene, *Bunraku: The Art of the Japanese Puppet Theatre*. Tokyo: Kodansha International Ltd., p. 35.

8   Roland Barthes, "On Bunraku," reprinted in this volume.

9   Keene, op. cit., p. 49.

10 Unsigned statement in *Asian Puppets, Wall of the World*. Los Angeles, UCLA Museum of Cultural History, University of California, Los Angeles, 1979, p. 41.

11 Caz Frost, "Judy Punches Back," in *Mr. Punch's Progress*. Norfolk: Monkeypuzzle, 1987, p. 10.

12 Theodora Skipitares, "Once Were Warriors: The Struggle to Preserve Tradition in Southern Indian, in a Changing World," in *Puppetry International*, Spring 2000, Atlanta, UNIMA–USA, p. 15.

13 Henry Mayhew, *London Labour and the London Poor*, Vol. III. New York: Dover, 1968, p. 46.

14 Peter Schumann, "The Radicality of Puppet Theatre," reprinted in this volume.

5

BREAD AND PUPPETS

Peter Schumann

We sometimes give you a piece of bread along with the puppet show because our bread and theatre belong together. For a long time the theatre arts have been separated from the stomach. Theatre was entertainment. Entertainment was meant for the skin. Bread was meant for the stomach. The old rites of baking, and eating, and offering bread were forgotten. The bread decayed and became mush. We would like you to take your shoes off when you come to our puppet show or we would like to bless you with the fiddle bow. The bread shall remind you of the sacrament of eating. We want you to understand that theatre is not yet an established form, not the place of commerce that you think it is, where you pay and get something. Theatre is different. It is more like bread, more like a necessity. Theatre is a form of religion. It is fun. It preaches sermons and it builds up a self-sufficient ritual where the actors try to raise their lives to the purity and ecstasy of the actions in which they participate. Puppet theatre is the theatre of all means. Puppets and masks should be played in the street. They are louder than the traffic. They don't teach problems, but they scream and dance and hit each other on the head and display life in its clearest terms. Puppet theatre is an extension of sculpture. Imagine a cathedral, not as a decorated religious place, but as a theatre with Christ and the saints and gargoyles being set into motion by puppeteers, talking to the worshippers, participating in the ritual of music and words. Puppet theatre is of action rather than of dialogue. The action is reduced to the simplest dance-like and specialized gestures. Our ten-foot rod-puppets were invented as dancers, each puppet with a different construction for its movement. A puppet may be a hand only, or it may be a complicated body of many heads, hands, rods, and fabric. Our puppeteers double as musicians, dancers, actors, and technicians.

6

THE RADICALITY OF THE PUPPET THEATRE

Peter Schumann

I wrote this essay at the request of Irina Uvarova and Viktor Novatsky for a brand-newborn Russian puppetry magazine, during Bread & Puppet Theatre's first tour to Siberia, in May 1990, between rehearsals in Tomsk, Novii Vasyugan, and Abakan, while being overwhelmed by totally new impressions. Naturally, my observations and conclusions are from a distinctly western perspective. But even though puppet theatre in Communist countries has, until now, been an official branch of the government-sponsored culture, the malaise of puppet theatre, as well as its background and future possibilities, are essentially the same in both worlds. Where the polemics don't apply, they may serve as a warning for what could be in store as an inevitable by-product of culture liberation.

Thinking is an activity which takes bulky, disorganized storage in the brain, and attempts to put the pieces into a harmonious relationship. The result pleases the brain and makes the thinker happy. But to inspire such a process there needs to be a desire to communicate the happy conclusion to the world-at-large where its validity is tested. In the case of any revelations that can be made about the true nature of puppet theatre, I am not sure that I feel the communicative urge, that I don't prefer the confused and obscure circumstances which typify the situation of puppet theatre.

Puppet theatre, the employment and dance of dolls, effigies, and puppets, is not only historically obscure and unable to shake off its ties to shamanistic healing and other inherently strange and hard-to-prove social services. It is also, by definition of its most persuasive characteristics, an anarchic art, subversive and untameable by nature, an art which is easier researched in police records than in theatre chronicles, an art which by fate and spirit does not aspire to represent governments or civilizations, but prefers its own secret and demeaning stature in society, representing, more or less, the demons of that society and definitely not its institutions.

The puppeteers' traditional exemption from seriousness – e.g. from the seriousness of being analytically disciplined and categorized by the cultural philosophy of the day – and their asocial status acted also as their saving grace, as a negative privilege that allowed their art to grow. The habitual lament of modern puppeteers about their low and ridiculous status is unfortunately disrespectful of their own art, or proves an impotent attempt

SERIOUSNESS

Fig. 6.1 All drawings (Figs. 6.1–5) by Peter Schumann. (*TDR* 1990 issue.)

to market their works as so-called serious art. (The physiognomy of modern puppetry is often a sad example of this impotent seriousness, especially where animals are portrayed with the jolly stupidity of chewing-gum advertisements, adding the creatures' fateful features to the already existing set of human stereotypes, defunct physiognomies, really meant to be cute but desperately sarcastic at heart.)

In the meantime, the modern German puppet-interpreters have come up with a grand solution to the social-status problem of puppetry, rebaptizing it "Figurentheater," so that nobody will find them guilty of complicity with Kasper, Punch, or Petroushka. Luckily, the art of puppetry is much too old to be seriously affected by such silly ploys, and luckily there are plenty of live examples to prove it.

And yet, despite the general tendency of our cultural effects to be subservient to the power of the market, to money-making and to the associated steeping of our souls into as much nonsense as possible, despite the fact that puppet theatre exists mostly in the feeble manner of an art obedient to the demands of the entertainment business, puppet theatre also exists as a radically new and daring art form: new, not in the sense of unheard-of newness, but in the sense of an uncovered truth that was there all along but was so common it couldn't be seen for what it was. Radical in the sense of not only turning away from established concepts, it also succeeded in a widening of the heart that allowed for greater inclusion of more modern and ancient art into the ancient art of puppetry.

The radicalism of the puppet theatre includes a redefinition of language as not merely a tool of convenient communication. Puppet language is more than an instrument of fine-tuned information. It is an experiment which strips words and sentences of their secondary

Fig. 6.2

fashionable contexts and condenses quantities of habitual gossip into singular terms. The puppets need silence, and their silences are an outspoken part of their language.

In puppet language, words sing and stutter in the mouths of singers and stutterers who are especially equipped for this task, whose vocabulary is not academically learned or extracted from everyday uses of language, but shows an ongoing struggle to come to terms with the naming of things by their right names in a slow, haphazard way. In the puppet theatre, words are attached to faces which don't move externally but are all the more obviously able to produce meaning.

Language in the dramatic arts is the reflector of human thought and trivia through the actors' imitative efforts. Acting is an art that the actor knows about from the growing-up practices of children, who mimic adults as a means of entering their world just as they mimic animals to cast off their fear of the wild. Unfortunately, the actor lacks the child's sincerity at this game and has to replace the child's urgent need with an education of trickery, with facial and vocal gymnastics aimed at a most naturalistic pretending of something irreal and intangible: the ghost of a reality is not there but insists on our acceptance of its existence. His whole education is geared towards the intensification of this fakery that is supposed to transport the viewer over the gap of the missing reality. It isn't this gap between made-up and real reality, though, which is so bothersome. The weightiness of the unasked-for and affected sincerity in the aping of kitchen and bedroom intimacy, and the intimacy of pain – that is what is so demeaning. Real pain in life is a serious relative of death, a terrorizer, usually a visitor of great consequence. The detailed, imitated pain in movies makes a mockery of the vital resources which enable our nature to fight pain or even submit to pain gracefully.

Sincere intimacy, if anything, seems to be the addictive spice with which the movie industry – the most visible exponent of the art of acting – has modern humankind hooked. Subject matter and visual adornment are secondary to this technique: the peep-show secrecy blown up into the dimension of public frenzy, but a frenzy without teeth because of the regularity with which it occurs. Eventually, real intimacy has to bear the weight of the imitated intimacy.

Because of its domineering status in the consciousness of the general public, acting performs an unquestioned political role in the manipulation of public self-consciousness. The self-conscious viewer's second-nature sincerity feeds entirely on the viewer's educated identification with nothing much, with replay of his own littleness. And even if one would consider this an endearing trait which is generally justified considering our decrepit circumstances, it is defeatist by nature, not modest. On the whole, it amounts to weeping and whining in the face of the harsh world.

I find acting sad, a sad art, especially in the movies: the jollier they try to be, the sadder they are. (The glib, self-satisfied expressions on so many faces of First World beneficiaries are a direct result of the movies. The faces seem to belong to actors who use their features to perform the standard role of the Good Life for the benefit of everybody else.)

Remember, not long ago, B. Brecht took a look at the Chinese theatre (and, also, I suppose, at puppet theatre) and realized that the actor's service to the dramatic arts could be salvaged from this psychological dilemma if the actor was allowed to enjoy his art as an art of faking, and with that be liberated from the self-possessed art of acting, and instead be allowed to concentrate on the text. And Brecht went to Hollywood and half-heartedly fought with Hollywood about this issue. But Hollywood understood very well the human weakness for perfect recreation, the abandoning of ourselves and our unrewarding lives, the need for a pillow for our brains which translates into the sentimental excuse for any brutality whatsoever, and has since served us countless sentimental brutalities, successfully avoiding Brecht's message.

If the movies were not so big and acting so glorious, I would say: let it go as it goes, they will eventually act themselves to death anyway. But here it is, the perfectly adequate symbol of our culture, exposed in what it presents to us with oppressive regularity: a pretty face in distress, on the surface nothing more than a pitiful story, but in reality a corporate giant, a political powertool, very able to hurt, very willing to be used in any direction, very able as we all know now, to serve up presidents, dwarfs, and demagogs at random.

Compared to the high-falutin aspirations of actors, the puppeteers' handling of themselves and of the objects and effigies entrusted into their hands seems quite formal and modest. The considerable talents for the puppeteers' bag-of-tricks showmanship all originate in their preoccupation with things. The puppeteers harvest piles of human-like and yet other-worldly qualities from their observation of objects, especially from their practice of moving these objects. The souls of things don't reveal themselves easily. What speaks out of a doll's eyes is often beyond control. The manipulation of puppets is over and above the willful targeting which aims for certain results from an audience. The puppeteers' only hope of mastering their puppets is to enter their puppets' delicate and seemingly inexhaustible lives. Puppets are not made to order or script. What's in them is hidden in their faces and becomes clear only through their functioning. They are born from the raw clay. Their creation has to be as far removed as possible from the purposeful definitions of dramatic characters or story. Only through this disconnected distance are they able to enter actively into the story as independent agents, not as providers of purposes.

Fig. 6.3

The radicalism of the puppet theatre is further evident in its employment of music as music, as sound production in its own right, operating in its own sphere, parallel to and not governed by the visual theatre. The listening which the puppet theatre teaches is diametrically opposed to the modern notion of music as a service tool for the consumer and his vacationing and working habits, a wishy-washy something between Muzak and white noise, meant to stimulate the desired moods in an exhausted brain. It is exactly this service attitude, culminating in the unquestioned duplicity of effect of vision and sound, or rather, the misuse of sound for the purposes of vision, which keeps music from acting as music for the benefit of the larger scheme of collaborative production.

(Modern puppet theatre suffers from the tape recorder just as much as it suffers from foam rubber. As in so many other examples of twentieth-century inventiveness, the genius of engineering also seeds the virus of decay. The all-purpose, multi-talented cassette player, loaded to the brim with wonderfulness, inhibits modern puppetry like nothing else. The little machine is an international omnipresence in the puppet world. It stinks. It takes the guts out of the trade.)

Music hurts as the animal kingdom hurts. From what? From the dispirited understanding of its sense, from the exploitation of its innards by a race of spoilers and manipulators, from not being allowed the circumstances it needs for its own growth and life.

The tolerance and indiscriminate loving-power of music are proverbial. But the political use of the healing and soothing traits of music makes it hard for musicians to create actively helpful sounds or to extract already existing sounds from the world of sound without losing them to an exploitative culture. Air which is burdened with tons of carelessly discarded sounds has trouble carrying selective sounds and needed sounds. If

Fig. 6.4

music is the relationship of some and all sounds to each other and the psychic effects of these, but also if music is one of the rare, wholesome utterances of self, where the self is not only bone and brain but an attuned part of a large body of selves, like ourselves and more than ourselves, then the concert stage with its thoroughly specialized clientele is too small a forum for the messages of music.

I think of puppet theatre as a possible context for music, a place where music can be useful without being corrupted.

Finally, the radicalism of puppet theatre derives from the definition of puppet theatre as applied and socially embedded sculpture. Puppet theatre is committed to common sense as a guiding principle in the making of sculpture. The sculptural effigies which try to give meaning to our public places have long ceased to represent public heartbeat and yearning. They also don't frighten us any more, other than intellectually, as symbols of status quo cultural politics. The meaning of sculpture has long been connected to its expense, and with that, to its sponsorship. The shift of sponsorship from princes and churches to governments and cigarette-makers is as sad as the drudgery of history, a shift from one oppressive authority to another. The liberating momentum of sculpture in puppet theatre lies in the fact that it provides a better *raison d'être* for sculpture than that of sculpture's retirement into statues, be they in private chambers or public places. In the puppet theatre sculpture serves a quasi-narrative purpose, if narration is understood as the revelation of an inner world and if we allow the possibility that the narration hinges on and is inspired by the sculpture.

Puppetry is conceptual sculpture, cheap, true to its popular origins, uninvited by the powers-that-be, its feet in the mud, economically on the fringe of existence, technically

CONCEPTUAL ART

Fig. 6.5

a collage art combining paper, rags, and scraps of wood into kinetic two- and three-dimensional bodies. The conceptual element, the sheer concentration on concept at the expense of communicative pleasantness, the sacrificing of the decorative or handsome appearance of an inner theme in an outside form or art object for a greater adherence to this inner theme, are practiced with a certain restraint in puppet theatre.

Unlike most modern conceptual art, puppet theatre realizes its conceptualizations in an atmosphere of what is possible or of what can be understood and taken from it, and not as an exercise which demonstrates an extreme example of concept. This excessive exhibition of process and avoidance of the art object confine most modern conceptual art to a tiny clique of makers, interpreters, and investors.

Basically, I think of conceptual art or of the pre-eminence of concept in art as the result of a lot of art-making, as in old artists' art, in the sense of a much higher concentration on essentials like gesture and meaning of gesture, or the daring of bare-bones composition in lieu of the show and its opulence. The priest in the Russian Orthodox church service is so sure of his performance of accurate motions, which are given to him and which are totally inaccessible to his private interpretations, that, indeed, he can afford to gossip between his sacramental duties. The shaman, whose handling of objects is an accumulation of pointed, purposeful gestures which derive from attempts at divine communication, can turn his back to the audience.

The puppeteer whose performance starts somewhere else, namely with a passion for the correct or right raw materials, judged by their former uses, availability, origin, cost, weight, beauty, can perform confidently with the help of these raw materials. None of these qualities is immediately obvious to an audience. The process of their selection, their actual importance as participatory forces in the final product, are nothing more than a subtle presence, and yet he owes his show to these invisible ingredients.

To wrap it up: the modernist puppeteer struggles with the same basic questions which bother or don't bother and provoke or don't provoke all modernist artists. All art producers, even puppeteers, are children of Modernism.

What has Modernism achieved? It has destroyed taboos of perception. It has released powers of hand and brain of which hand and brain were not aware before. The tragedy of Modernism is its political and social failure, its inability to apply more than the formal discoveries to the historical situation. The liberation process of Modernism has been confined to art and art-related production. The lofty ideals of Modernism did not penetrate the social sphere of habit or of the oppressive exercises of organizational authority. Maybe the question is: how far did Modernism mean to go? Did it ever direct its dreams beyond the Russian Revolution which it failed to survive? Kandinsky and Schoenberg believed in some higher, quasi-religious aspirations of Modernism, but Nazi Germany and modern capitalism dwindled these hopes into the specialization of sheer esoteric practices which we now think of when we say "Modern Art."

The homeless look into the elegantly empty, super-expensive gallery spaces of Soho and defy progress in art.

Does the idea of doing with art more than art still exist? Are the arts interested in more than themselves? Can puppet theatre be more than puppet theatre by giving purpose and aggressivity back to the arts and make the gods' voices yell as loud as they should yell?

7

ON BUNRAKU

Roland Barthes

Translated by Sandy MacDonald

THE THREE SCRIPTS

Bunraku puppets are up to 3 feet tall. They are little men or women with mobile limbs, hands, and mouths; each puppet is moved by three visible men, who surround it, support it, accompany it. The master puppeteer controls the puppet's upper body and right arm; his face is uncovered, smooth, light, impassive, cold as "a white onion which has just been washed" (Basho). His two assistants are dressed in black; cloths cover their faces. One, gloved but with his thumb left uncovered, holds a large, stringed, scissor-like extension, with which he moves the puppet's left arm and hand; the other, crouching, supports the puppet's body and steadies its course. These men move along a shallow trench, which leaves their bodies visible. The scenery is behind them, as in the theatre. On a platform to one side are the musicians and narrators; their role is to express the text (the way one squeezes a fruit). This text is half-spoken, half-chanted; punctuated by the samisen players' loud plectrum beats, it is both restrained and flung, with violence and artifice. Sweating and still, the narrators are seated behind little lecterns on which is placed the large script they vocalize. One can perceive the vertical characters from afar when the narrators turn the pages of their librettos. Triangles of stiff cloth, attached to their shoulders like kites, frame their faces, which are prey to all the throes of their voices.

Bunraku thus uses three separate scripts and presents them simultaneously in three places in the spectacle: the puppet, the manipulator, the vociferator, the effected gesture, the effective gesture, the vocal gesture. Bunraku has a *limited* idea of the voice; it doesn't suppress it but assigns it a very definite, essentially vulgar function. In the voice of the narrator there converge: exaggerated declamation, the tremolo, the shrill feminine tone, broken pitches, weeping, paroxysms of anger, moaning, supplication, astonishment, indecent pathos – every emotional recipe, openly elaborated at the level of this internal, visceral body, whose larynx is the mediatory muscle. Also, this outbreak is given solely under the very code of outbreak: the voice moves only through some discontinuous signs of outburst. Thrust from an immobile body triangulated by its clothing, bound to the book which, from its lectern, guides it, and sharply hammered by the samisen player's slightly out of phase (and therefore impertinent) beats, the vocal substance remains written, discontinuous, coded, subjected to a certain irony (excluding from the word any caustic sense). Also, what the voice exteriorizes, finally, is not what it conveys ("feelings"), but itself, its own prostitution. The signifier, cunningly, only turns itself inside out like a glove.

Without being eliminated (which would be a way of censoring it, that is, designating its importance), the voice is thus put to one side (scenically, the narrators occupy a lateral platform). Bunraku gives the voice a balance, or better, a check: gesture. Gesture is double: emotive gesture at the puppet's level (people cry at the suicide of the puppet-lover), transitive act at the manipulators' level. In western theatre, the actor pretends to act but his acts are never anything but gestures; onstage, there is only theatre, and ashamed theatre at that. Bunraku, though (by definition), separates act from gesture: it shows the gesture, allows the act to be seen, exposes art and work simultaneously and reserves for each its own script. The voice (and there is then no risk in letting it attain the excessive regions of its gamut) – the voice is plated with a vast volume of silence, on which, with all the greater subtlety, other tracts, other scripts are inscribed. And here, an unparalleled effect is produced: distant from the voice and nearly without pantomime, these silent scripts – one transitive, the other gestural – produce an exaltation as unique, perhaps, as the intellectual hyperesthesia attributed to certain drugs. Speech is not puri-fied (Bunraku in no way strives for asceticism) but – if this can be said – is amassed next to the action; the sticky substances of western theatre are dissolved. Emotion no longer inundates, no longer submerges, it becomes reading material; stereotypes disappear, without, however, the spectacle resorting to originality, or "felicity." All of this achieves, of course, the *Verfremdungseffekt* advocated by Brecht. This distance, was reputed in the west to be impossible, pointless, or ridiculous and readily abandoned, although Brecht very specifically placed it at the center of revolutionary dramaturgy (and the following undoubtably explains why) – Bunraku shows how this distance can work: through the discontinuity of the codes, through this censorship imposed on the performance's different tracts, so that the copy elaborated onstage is not destroyed, but as if broken, stri-ated, saved from the metonymic contagion of voice and gesture, soul and body, which mires the western actor.

A total though divided spectacle, Bunraku of course excludes improvisation; to return to spontaneity would be to return to the stereotypes which constitute western "profundity." As Brecht saw, here reigns the *quotation* – the pinch of script, the fragment of code – because none of the promotives of the action can take on himself responsibility for some-thing he never writes alone. As in the modern text the braiding of codes, references, detached statements, and anthological gestures multiplies the written line, not by virtue of some metaphysical appeal, but through a combinative activity which unfolds in the thea-tre's entire space. What is begun by one person is continued by another, without pause.

ANIMATE/INANIMATE

In dealing with a fundamental antimony, the *animate/inanimate*, Bunraku muddies it, makes it fade, without benefiting either of its terms. In the west, the puppet (Punch, for example) is expected to offer the actor the mirror of his contrary; it animates the inani-mate, but the better to show its degradation, the indignity of its inertia. A caricature of "life," the puppet thereby affirms life's *moral* limits and presumes to confine beauty, truth, and emotion in the living body of the actor, who, however, makes of this body a lie. Bunraku, though, does not put its own stamp on the actor; it gets rid of him for us. How? Through a certain conception of the human body, which inanimate matter rules in Bunraku with infinitely more rigor and trembling than the animate body (endowed with a "soul"). The western (naturalistic) actor is never beautiful; his body would be of a physi-ological, not plastic, essence. He is a collection of organs, a musculature of passions, whose every spring (voice, facial expressions, gestures) is subjected to a sort of gymnastic exercise. But by an absolutely bourgeois reversal, although the actor's body is constructed according to a division of passional elements, it borrows from physiology the alibi of an organic unity, that of "life"; it is the actor who is a puppet here.

The basis of western theatre is, in fact, not so much the illusion of reality as the illusion of totality: periodically, from the Greek *choreia* to the bourgeois opera, lyrical art has been conceived as the simultaneity of several expressions (acted, sung, mimed) with a single, indivisible origin. This origin is the body, and the totality claimed is modelled on organic unity. The western spectacle is anthropomorphic; in it, gesture and speech (not to mention song) form but one fabric, conglomerated and lubricated like a single muscle which puts expression into play but never divides it. The unity of movement and voice produces *he who acts*; in other words, it is this unity which constitutes the "person" of the personage; that is, the actor. Actually, under his "living" and "natural" exterior, the western actor preserves the division of his body and, consequently, food for our phantasms: now the voice, then the look, now again the figure are eroticized, like so many pieces of the body, like so many fetishes. The western puppet, too (it's quite apparent in Punch), is a phantasmic subproduct: as a reduction, a grating reflection whose place in the human order is constantly recalled by a caricatured simulation, it lives not as a total body, totally trembling, but as a rigid part of the actor from whom it is derived; as an automaton, it is still a piece of movement, a jerk, a shove, the essence of discontinuity, a decomposed projection of the body's gestures; finally, as a puppet – reminiscent of a scrap of rag, of a genital dressing – it is quite the phallic "little thing" (*"das Kleine"*), fallen from the body to become a fetish.

It is very possible that the Japanese puppet retains something of this phantasmic origin, but the art of Bunraku imprints on it a different meaning. Bunraku does not aim to

Fig. 7.1 Bunraku puppet in *Chusingura*. (Photo courtesy of Yomiuri Shimbun Osaka.)

"animate" an inanimate object so as to bring a piece of the body, a shred of man, to life, all the while keeping for it its vocation as a "part." It is not the simulation of the body which Bunraku seeks; it is – if this can be said – the body's tangible abstraction. Everything we attribute to the total body and which is refused western actors under the name of "living" organic unit, the little man in Bunraku collects and states, without any lies. Fragility, discretion, sumptuousness, unparalleled nuance, the abandonment of all vulgarity, the melodic phrasing of gestures – in short, the very qualities ancient theology accorded to heavenly bodies, to wit, impassivity, clarity, agility, subtlety – this is what Bunraku accomplishes, this is how it converts the body-fetish into a body worthy of love, this is how it rejects the animate/inanimate antinomy and banishes the concept hidden behind all animation, which is, quite simply, the "soul."

INSIDE/OUTSIDE

The function of the western theatre of the last few centuries has been essentially to show what is said to be secret ("feelings," "situations," "conflicts"), while hiding the very artifice of the show (stage effects, painting, powder, light sources). The Italian-style stage is the space of this lie; everything takes place in an interior which is surreptitiously opened, surprised, spied upon, savored by a spectator hidden in the shadow. This space is theological, a space of Guilt: on one side, under lights which he pretends to ignore, the actor (gesture and speech); on the other, in the darkness, the audience (conscience).

Bunraku does not directly subvert the relation of the seats to the stage. It changes most profoundly the motive link going from character to actor, which westerners always conceive of as the expressive path of an interiority. In Bunraku the agents of the spectacle are both visible and impassive. The men in black busy themselves about the puppet, but without any affectation of competence or discretion, or any advertising demagogy; quiet, rapid, elegant, their acts are eminently transitive, operative, colored by that mixture of force and subtlety which marks the Japanese gestuary and is like the aesthetic envelope of efficacity. The leader's head is uncovered; smooth, naked, without powder – this confers on him a civil (non-theatrical) cachet – his face is offered for the spectators' perusal. But what is carefully, preciously given to read is that there is nothing to read; one finds here this exemption of meaning which we in the west scarcely understand, since, for us, to attack meaning means to hide or invert it, but never to keep it away. Bunraku exposes the sources of theatre in their emptiness. What is expelled from the stage is hysteria – that is, theatre itself – and what replaces it is the action necessary to the production of the spectacle. Work substitutes for interiority.

It is thus vain to wonder whether the spectator can forget the presence of the manipulators. Bunraku practices neither the occultation nor emphatic manifestation of its springs; it rids the actor's animation of all sacral staleness and abolishes the metaphysical connection the west cannot keep from making between the soul and the body, cause and effect, motor and machine, agent and actor, destiny and man, God and creature. If the manipulator is not hidden, why – how? – do you want to make him a god? In Bunraku, the puppet is not controlled by strings. No more strings, therefore no more metaphors, no more destiny. The puppet no longer apes the creature, man is no longer a puppet in the hands of divinity, the *inside* no longer rules the *outside*.

8

WAYANG AND LUDRUK
Polarities in Java

Barbara Hatley

In contemporary western society, theatre has become primarily a source of entertainment and sometimes of social criticism; its older function of articulating and instilling prevailing values is now performed by the mass media and specialized educational and propaganda institutions. In Indonesia, however, and elsewhere in Asia where mass media and educational facilities are less developed and private reading is not a widely established habit, popular drama still transmits sociopolitical ideals between the court (or city) and the countryside, and reinforces religious tradition. While some of its communicative role is now shared with movies and other new media, live theatre is still a vital and popular teacher.

In Java the Wayang Kulit, or shadow-puppet theatre, epitomizes the traditional Javanese world view; it has functioned as an art form, a religious rite, and a medium of instruction for more than a thousand years. Yet during the past century, Indonesian society has been changing rapidly, forcing adjustments in the Javanese value system. Several new types of popular drama have grown up which often present stories of contemporary life rather than the legendary tales of the Wayang tradition and perhaps better reflect contemporary values. A comparison of Wayang Kulit with new dramatic forms should show the theatre's response to these changes in Javanese society and its values.

THE SHADOW PLAY

In the all-night ritual/performance of the shadow play, the *dalang,* or puppeteer, seated on the floor with an oil-lamp above his head casts the shadows of the intricately carved, flat, leather puppets on the screen before him. Through narration and song, he weaves his puppets' actions and dialogue with the moral lesson of the story. He knows by heart the hundreds of Wayang stories, or *lakons*, which, though based on the Indian epics, the *Mahabharata* and the *Ramayana*, have been adapted to fit the Javanese setting: the Indian kings and gods are regarded as the ancestors of the Javanese, and a group of characters not present in the original have been added – the only ones with Javanese rather than Indian names. These are the *punakawan*, or clown-attendants, who are simultaneously the servants, advisors, and protectors of the epics' heroes. And while the plots

Fig. 8.1 Javanese *dalang* (shadow theatre puppeteer, upper left) and *gamelan* (orchestra, right). (Photo by Barbara Hatley.)

and characters of the legendary/historical dramas are fixed, the *dalang*, by choosing a *lakon* he sees as analogous to contemporary events and adding satirical remarks through the clowns, is free to comment on local political and social conditions.

The social philosophy and stories of the Indian epics fused with the Javanese magico-religious tradition and were elaborated in the Javanese courts to form Wayang.[1] From these origins the shadow-puppet performance became both a medium conveying the social ethos and a mystical ritual sanctifying the social structure which embodies this ethos. The central ethos of the Wayang is that of a rigidly stratified society in which each social rank shares in the downward-flowing power of the king and in which each person acts in accordance with his social position. In watching the shadow play, the king and his court (or in contemporary performances, government officials) find justification for their position as rulers. They see their *ksatrya* ("noble") counterparts praised extravagantly and compared to gods in strength and wisdom. They witness the Wayang kings making wise pronouncements which their subjects follow obediently. And they are reminded that the *ksatrya* holds honor and duty to his king above family loyalty or personal sentiment. Meanwhile the peasants (or "little people") are instilled with belief in the moral and social superiority of their political overlords; they see that "little people" should act as the king's loyal supporters, on the model of the *punakawan*. These clown-servants, particularly Semar, are interpreted as "a master-symbol of the peasantry."[2]

In addition to its sociopolitical message, Wayang provides a set of moral qualities, embodied in the characteristics of particular Wayang figures, as standards of social behavior. From childhood, a Javanese is acquainted with the physical, psychological, and ethical traits of the Wayang heroes and is free to follow whichever example best fits his own personality. In theory, there is no hierarchy among the main characters and their virtues.[3] Yet through the puppets' behavior and iconography, certain characteristics emerge as the most valued: refinement, patience, self-control, and devotion to duty. Thus, the most admired characters have elongated, narrow eyes, long noses – indicating refinement – and bowed heads – showing patience and imperturbability. These qualities are consonant with the Javanese aristocratic ideal of emotional quiescence within – reflected in exquisitely *alus* ("refined") outward behavior – and strict adherence to formal etiquette. Crude, violent characters with excitable dispositions have round, bulging eyes, bulbous noses, heavy builds, and upturned faces, though in some revered heroes, notably Bima and his son Gatutkatja, round eyes and upturned faces are not unfavourable characteristics but indicate bravery as well as directness. Thus, while each member of society has a place in the moral universe of Wayang, the equating of moral virtue and social and political prominence helps sanctify social differences.

A Wayang performance is also a religious ritual: while the shadow play is a form of entertainment and today may be performed as a strictly commercial venture, most Wayangs are presented in conjunction with life-cycle rituals. An integral extension of the *slametan*, or communal feast, which celebrates birthdays, weddings, and circumcisions, the Wayang performance binds all present in a shared security and communion. Besides being an artistic performer, the *dalang* is also officiant at the Wayang communal ritual; he recites prayers and presents offerings in conjunction with the performance and draws his audience into the experience by commenting on people present and local issues. Indeed,

Fig. 8.2 Head of Kresna, Javanese shadow puppet. (Courtesy of the British Museum, Raffles Collection.)

the Wayang is as much a social gathering as a performance. As the well-known stories do not require the audience's full concentration and the performance is held in the open air, people are free to move about and chat with one another. Children occasionally doze off, young lovers retreat to the shadows, others wander off for coffee – only to be lured back when the music and action pick up again. The very experience of spending the entire night together creates a feeling of intimacy. For the duration of the shadow play performance, young and old, high and low, rich and poor, audience and performers are one.

Yet social distance is still maintained – the best seats are always occupied by the leaders of the community, who usually provide the performance. The politically and socially powerful have always supported the shadow-puppet theatre, for they have an interest in communicating Wayang's picture of a stable society and can use the drama to convey particular educative and propagandistic messages.

Javanese culture demands suppression of all disruptive, antisocial desire and interpersonal hostility in order to preserve outward calm and social harmony. This social ideal is depicted in the Wayang stories and acted out in the harmonious communal experience of the Wayang audience. In reality, of course, society is not united, and conflicts symbolically absolved may not be ended. But on the Wayang stage, conflicts and desires can be objectified, and the audience can, by identification with the characters, work out solutions to their personal problems. Perhaps the Wayang audience gains gratification through the heroes' success in slaughtering demons, who symbolize the baser passions. And they may take vicarious pleasure in the battle scenes, since open conflict is proscribed in everyday life. The struggle of the Pandawas and the Kurawas (the two feuding factions of the *Mahabharata*) may embody the whole movement of the cosmos, where good and evil, light and darkness, youth and age, though ever opposed, are yet complementary and, in some ultimate sense, all one.

Fig. 8.3 Javanese shadow puppet clown-attendants Sarwita, Togog, Semar (center), Petrok (center back) and Bagong (far right). (Courtesy of British Museum, Raffles Collection.)

While the values of the mythical Wayang stories might apply in an idealized Javanese society, they are sometimes difficult to maintain in real life. In this situation the *punakawan* play a vital role, through their criticism and clowning making Wayang symbols more understandable and acceptable to the "little people." They often poke fun at the high-minded ideals of their aristocratic masters and, through their earthy humor and *kasar* ("coarse" or "rough") ways, seem to criticize the dominant values of the drama. Semar, one of the best loved of the Wayang figures, is really a powerful god, yet his appearance is grotesque, his manner entirely lacking in refinement. Perhaps Semar and his sons represent the realistic view of life as opposed to the idealistic, to remind the noble heroes (and the audience) of their humble animal origins – to express "the more earthy sense of life of the villagers" (Geertz, p. 277).

Being the only completely Javanese figures, the *punakawan* domesticate and "Javanize" Wayang. Through joking, the clowns demystify the scared Wayang symbols and reduce tensions and anxieties produced by Wayang's social and religious prescriptions. The clowns' satirical commentary on contemporary political and social evils probably has a similar cathartic effect. The clowns represent not so much a rebellion against the prevailing values of Wayang – and society – as a mode of adjusting to them, a humanizing counterpoint.

WAYANG IN A CHANGING SOCIETY

The Wayang ethos survived the impact of colonialism. The highly stratified feudal society symbiotically related to Wayang was preserved rather well by the Dutch policy of using Javanese aristocrats in influential positions in the colonial civil service and of "protecting" Indonesian society from the disruptive effects of modernization. But the introduction of a money economy, urbanization, and western education began to make inroads into the old social order, especially during the last century. While the 1945–9 revolution which brought independence did not cut off Indonesia from her past or produce an instant "classless" society, it did alter the hierarchical patterns of prestige by which Javanese society had been ordered. And the modern ideologies of nationalism and democracy have stimulated changes in the value system, even if social reality lags behind.

Developments in the theatre reflect these changes. New dramatic forms and westernized entertainment have gained popularity, but Wayang has not lost its following. Although commercial urbanism and nationalism are undermining its social and religious base, Wayang still has a definite, if slightly different, place in Indonesian life. Among older people and in rural areas (where the majority of Javanese still live), new values have had less impact and Wayang is as popular as ever, but, for financial reasons, village performances are less frequent now. The contemporary elite, including Indonesian presidents, support most performances; neotraditionalists as well as nationalists, they recognize the appropriateness of presenting shadow plays in the still partially traditional society. And life-cycle rituals still require celebrations; indeed, the birthdays of modern organizations, government offices, and buildings are now marked by Wayang performances.

However, a growing body of Indonesians, influenced by ideals of social equality and personal achievement, sees the stratified, court-centered society pictured in the Wayang as *kuna*, or old-fashioned. Their image of the dynamic modern man hardly fits the refined quiescence and acceptance of the traditionally revered Wayang heroes. The westernized urbanite of present-day Indonesia is more interested in light evening entertainment than in the all-night aesthetic ritual of Wayang. In response, some changes are occuring in the shadow play which make it more appealing to contemporary audiences. Among the Wayang characters, unhesitating bravery and uncritical loyalty are replacing gentleness and contemplation as values for the "new Indonesian man." Young *dalangs* are attempting to make Wayang more relevant to the present through increasing the use of Indonesian language, expanding the joking sequences with contemporary references, and shortening the length of the performance. But apart from such minor changes, the possibilities for innovation in Wayang are limited: the stories, characters, and underlying philosophy are fixed. (For example, when the Indonesian government in the 1950s attempted to use Wayang as a medium of explicit nationalist propaganda in creating two new forms, Wayang Suluh, which depicted present-day leaders through naturalistic puppets and Wayang Pantjasila, in which the five main heroes of the *Mahabharata* became symbols for the five principles of the Indonesian state, neither form became popular.) Shadow theatre seems to be too deeply rooted in traditional morality and religion to survive major changes in its symbols or ethos. And without such changes, Wayang, in a society concerned with the exigencies of achieving "progress" and prosperity, is likely to lose its educative role, becoming simply entertainment.

LUDRUK – A NEW DRAMATIC FORM

In keeping with recent changes in Indonesian society, modern popular theatre forms have appeared. As it is not closely connected with the traditional social order and religion, this new theatre should reflect social change more accurately and can be used as a vehicle of new ideas. Such new forms include the Ketoprak of Central Java, the Legong of Jakarta, the Balinese Ardja, and the Ludruk of East Java. (Ketroprak and Ardja, performed as popular entertainment particularly in rural areas, are associated with the *alus* tradition of the court and present mythical stories like those of the Wayang. Legong stories, set in the world of Malay seafarers, use Jakarta dialect and express the rough commercial ethos of coastal traders.)

Ludruk, which concentrates on contemporary themes and is performed commercially by troupes based in cities, perhaps provides the best modern contrast to traditional Javanese theatre. Ludruk, being East Javanese, is considered *kasar*, compared to the *alus* drama, like Wayang, associated with the court culture of Central Java. Ludruk performers and audiences are usually lower-class city-dwellers, who are personally affected by urbanization, secularization, and the accompanying value changes – all of which also influence their drama. Both actors and audience regard Ludruk, which depicts scenes from everyday life and encourages them to be "modern," as an art form, "of the people." And it has been frequently used to influence popular thinking. During the colonial period and the revolution, Ludruk became a vehicle of anti-Dutch propaganda and nationalist ideas and since independence has been used by various political groups to promote their viewpoints. In the early 1960s, when the Indonesian Communist Party had a strong influence among the urban lower class, Ludruk participants looked on themselves as belonging to a distinct social group of "proletarians" (hence the title of James Peacock's study of Ludruk during this period: *Rites of Modernization: Symbolic and Social Aspects of Indonesian Proletarian Drama*, Chicago: University of Chicago Press, 1968). Since the crushing of the Communist Party in 1965–6, however, the terminology and specific ethos of the proletariat has disappeared from Ludruk. (When Peacock wrote, some of the Ludruk troupes had ties with the Communist Party, while others were associated with the army. Now all troupes must have an official government sponsor and many are associated with the military.)

Ludruk originated as a simple entertainment routine featuring a clown and a transvestite singer. Later it developed into a full dramatic form, but the clown and the transvestite – particularly the clown, the traditional symbol of the "little man" in Javanese drama – remain the dominant figures. Each Ludruk performance is a collection of "prefabricated" parts: the opening *ngremo* (a traditional East Javanese dance); a prologue consisting of songs and comic skits performed by clowns; a melodrama, in which the female parts are played by transvestites. Songs and dances by female impersonators are inserted between the acts.

There are several kinds of Ludruk stories: histories and legends about heroes of the nationalist struggle; *dongeng* ("folk tales"); and contemporary melodramas. The melodramas are the most typical of Ludruk form and are more "hand-crafted" than Ludruk adaptations of old myths and historical tales. For example, one Malang troupe has a four-man team to create new plots, which are then discussed by the group; the actors are given outlines of their parts and improvise the dialogue.

This is a great innovation in Javanese theatre, to present stories which are not part of a well-known mythical tradition but have been newly created by a particular person or group of people; when played in village communities, Ludruk still had the ritualized quality of traditional drama, but when it moved to the city, where there was no longer a sense of the stage as a magical domain, performers probably felt free to change the prescribed, traditional forms. Since Ludruk stories may be created or varied to suit the times and the audience, it is chiefly through these contemporary melodramas, and the accompanying comic routines and songs, that Ludruk troupes succeed in conveying new ideas.

The melodramas contain a number of common themes, all concerning adjustment to modern life. Ludruk audiences often consist of new arrivals from the country or townspeople experiencing changes in their lives because of growing urbanization, so Ludruk stories frequently involve movement from the village to the city. The city is portrayed as a *madju* ("progressive") place, where people wear western dress, use modern mechanical devices, speak Indonesian rather than the regional language, Javanese, and act more forthrightly than their village counterparts. A typical scene is one in which a newcomer to the city appears at a job interview or in a government office wearing traditional clothes, speaking Javanese, and following village etiquette. He finds he must discard all these things in order to adjust to the new setting. So in Ludruk, the city becomes a source of new values and patterns of behavior.

But life in the city can also be disturbing. Cities produce more crime and exploitation, and in many melodramas young hoodlums rob, shoot, or kidnap people. Frequently an older, more *kuna* character is outwitted by young, antitraditional reprobates. The old man is vulnerable to exploitation because he is thrown off balance by their neglect of traditional norms. Following village ways, he feels obliged to comply with their demands in order to preserve harmony. The conflict of old and new ways, of the village and the city, also becomes one of generations.

Generational differences and urbanization have had profound effects on the nature of marriage. Most Ludruk plots focus on marriage, often depicting the conflicts involved in an arranged match. Though young city-dwellers have increased opportunities for meeting members of the opposite sex and choosing their own mates, they usually must marry someone of their parents' choice. Ludruk teaches that marriages arranged according to class considerations and family connections can often lead to unhappiness and that marriage based on romantic love is the modern ideal. And indeed, marriage across class lines forms the most important channel of mobility for low-status Ludruk characters; a common Ludruk figure is the village girl who is forced to leave her home and become a servant in the city but eventually marries into the elite. Such matches – unthinkable in traditional Javanese society – are possible now, especially in the city.

Urbanization often causes strain in the relationships of people married before they come to the city. A villager, going to work in the city, may have to leave his wife and children for long periods or, if he does bring his family, finds that his low-status, poorly paid job will not support them. His wife assumes a dual role as breadwinner and home-maker and comes to dominate the family unit, while he is left with a rather redundant role. So the stock Ludruk figures of the hen-pecked husband and the domineering wife have a factual basis in Javanese social life.

LUDRUK AS TRANSITIONAL DRAMA

Ludruk stories are closely related to contemporary social reality and so portray a very different world from that of traditional drama. But Ludruk does much more than reflect trends in Javanese society: it makes the changes people are experiencing comprehensible and helps them to adjust to the tensions. Ludruk's symbols – Indonesian language, western dress, and modern material goods – and action encourage the acceptance of new social values. As the new drama brings out the importance of *madju* qualities such as rationality and frankness, the old Wayang virtues of self-control and refinement of manner lose some of their vitality as models for action. In the Wayang drama there is a sense of underlying stasis, as characters act out the roles determined for them by their personality traits and social status. In Ludruk, however, some characters do overcome the bounds of social class and become prosperous and "modern".

James Peacock, in *Rites of Modernization*, concluded that Ludruk stories encourage people to favor goal-oriented behavior and to strive for social advancement. But Ludruk seems to promote social change and modernity only up to a certain point. It is easy to see how it helps people to feel at home in their new environment; less clear is the fact that it really teaches them that, by following new norms, they too may gain access to the desired new material goods and social prestige. Current Ludruk performances do not consis-tently stress the theme of social advancement; not every story involves a lower-class character who makes good – a number of plots depict the "little man" who tries to get ahead but fails because he uses underhand methods. Not all progressive behavior is regarded favourably; a very "modern" girl, for example, may be portrayed as bold and coarse. Most importantly, the lowly characters who do improve their social position, the models for social advancement, rise not through an acquired ability, but through an innate characteristic, sexual attractiveness. Marriage, rather than education or hard work, is the ladder to elite status.

Since not every lower-class person has the opportunity of meeting and attracting someone from the elite, such stories may more often provide wish-fulfilling day dreams than blueprints for action. And even when this ideal of rising socially through marriage is successfully attained, there is little social change or modernity reflected, for the goal is elite status *per se*, which is acquired through an innate characteristic, not achievement. Ludruk promotes the idea of a new society based on such "modern" values as education and career achievement, but these ideals are still depicted as traits of the socially privileged and pros-perous, rather than as a means used by "little people" to become "better off".

CLOWNS, TRANSVESTITES, AND THE NEW ORDER

The clown, symbol of the "little man," also relates to the issue of progress and modernity, but in a very different way. By making light of the problems brought about by change and exposing the hypocrisies of old and new alike, the clown acts as both social critic and popular psychologist. In Ludruk the first clown appears immediately after the opening dance and sings of the need for national unity, the importance of the coming general elections, and the good intentions of the army government. He skips quickly through this song and then usually begins a monologue about his own poverty and misfortunes, and the general problems of the times, commenting on declining moral standards among modern youth, and the like. His own sufferings – he has no money or job and only beans to eat – are pictured as quite harrowing and are probably uncomfortably close to the audience's experiences. Yet the audience invariably laughs. (Suffering has always been handled in an indirect, ritualized way in Javanese culture. A common Javanese habit is to break into giggles or open laughter when relating the story of some gruesome or pitiful personal experience, or tragedy of a close friend or relative. This anxious laughter seems to be a socially accepted way of coping with feelings too strong to be expressed more openly – a way of adjusting to harsh reality rather than fighting it. Ludruk clowns may perform a similar function, helping people to adjust to their day-to-day problems through empathy and laughter.)

After this monologue a second clown joins the first, and there is banter and horseplay. The theme of change and how to handle it appears frequently in these sequences. Much humor derives from the *kuna* figures' errors in confronting new ways, such as a villager's mistaking a telephone for a coffee-maker. Another clown is ridiculed by his friend when he tells of his plans to join a modern band and travel around the world, though, as it turns out, he has no modern clothes, speaks no foreign languages, and doesn't know where the various countries of the world are located. Then there is the successful clown who rejects his old friends and boasts that he can no longer speak Javanese, only *madju* Indonesian, yet slips unconsciously into Javanese and shows that he is really still a naive hick.

Some Ludruk actors, as members of military/government-supported entertainment troupes, are also civil servants. At one performance in which their performing skill was being judged by a panel of army officers to see whether they deserved promotion, several actors staged a very "modern" mock singing contest involving many "novel" elements. A judge, who wrote things down officiously with an outsize pencil, awarded such prizes as a cigarette butt, a dirty rag, and a rusty chain. Even after it was explained that these were lofty symbols of nation-building – the chain, for example, represented the unity of the scattered islands of Indonesia – the clown-performers remained nonplussed. It is possible that the actors were being satirical about the futility of the exercise in which they were engaged, and the uselessness of the anticipated rewards. But this seems unlikely, given that their livelihood depended on favorably impressing the judges testing them for promotion. A further insinuation is contained here – that in the wilder society, the symbols of "progress" proffered by the New Order government might prove as insubstantial as these competition prizes. Clowns have traditionally had license to make satirical gibes about contemporary politics, so perhaps these clowns were acting out their age-old role, daring to mock the present political powers. More likely, though, they were trying to show in an amusing way, that the benefits of being up to date are not always obvious. The general impression gained from all these jokes is that it is not easy for "little people" to keep up with *madju* ways; sometimes they appear foolish by trying too hard, and "modernity" may not be completely desirable anyway.

Clowns also appear as servants in the Ludruk melodramas, and their relationship to their masters is similar to that of the Wayang clowns. They tease their masters and sometimes play embarrassing tricks; for example, a servant parodies the way his master offers coffee to guests, telling them to "Slurp it up!" (Peacock, p. 155). Yet Ludruk clown-servants are loyal and accept their role without complaint.

That clowns as "little people" are never in the forefront of "progressive" trends or social advancement is emphasized by their dress: the traditional sarong or urban lower-class clothes. The clown is hardly a rebel against traditional social values or spokesman for new ways – more the opposite. His criticisms are light-hearted; they do not undermine new values and ways but allow people to laugh away the tensions arising from these changes.

Thus the general role of the clown in Ludruk does not seem very different from that of the Wayang clowns. While the social ideal might be changing from an emphasis on refinement, politeness, and outward calm to a more dynamic ethic, the clown's relationship to prescribed social ideas is the same – he provides a counterpoint, bringing them down to earth and softening their impact.

The transvestite, however, is an outspoken proponent of new ways and ideas. Playing the female role in the melodramas, he is able to depict modern behavior patterns more realistically and openly than a woman could. The traditional woman, particularly as represented in drama, is submissive and retiring, yet in modern Javanese society women are supposed to have equal rights, and relations between the sexes are expected to be open and free. Traditional conventions are still strong enough to make it improper for a woman, either in real life or onstage, to act as freely with men as the female impersonators do, initiating contact with them and arguing publicly. The transvestites, dressed in feminine and flattering traditional dress, are both beautiful and sexy, and it is fascinating to watch their artistry in portraying a woman's voice and movements. Their presence increases Ludruk's popular appeal, but it is difficult to know how the illicit sexual appeal of the female impersonators affects their role as spokesmen for government propaganda in the songs they sing between the acts of the melodrama – the audience may become too involved in watching the singer to listen carefully to his message. And it is equally difficult to know the effect on this "modern" message of its association with a figure dressed in traditional clothes, symbolizing the traditional idea of beauty and status.

Some of the transvestites' songs are popular love songs or traditional tunes, but often the singers exhort people to work together to build their nation and make a success of the five-year development plan, or praise the *Pantjasila* and the New Order government as defenders of the nation. The content varies little among different troupes or performers as the Ludruk actors apparently are provided with standard instructions from the government concerning the propaganda messages they are to convey. The clowns also include these themes in their opening song but quickly move on to other subjects, whereas the transvestites appear intermittently throughout the evening with the same message. The reason propaganda is incorporated into the performance through the transvestite singers is not clear, but it may be that the clowns' traditional role as social and political critics makes them unsuitable spokesmen for the government line and this role devolves on the other singers, the transvestites. But at least one conclusion is obvious – the ideals and goals which the Ludruk passes on to the "little people" are set by their social and political superiors, and the "voice of progress" in the dramas is not the "little man's" symbol, the clown, but a more remote, mysterious figure, the transvestite.

LUDRUK AND WAYANG

Ludruk and traditional Javanese drama appear to be worlds apart, but for all their differences, both have the same fundamental view of society: society is divided into two distinct classes, and it is the upper class which embodies all that is good and desirable in life, whether that ideal be traditional grace and refinement of behavior or progressive modernity. As the composition of the elite in the wider society has altered, so, in Ludruk, have dramatic representations of the social idea – the heroes are no longer nobles and princes, but doctors, government officials, and, especially, policemen and soldiers. Ludruk shows an important change of ethos – individual mobility from the lower to the upper class is now possible – but it has not obliterated the distinction between the two groups, or undermined belief in the superiority of elite life. Characters of low status make no attempt to assert, individually or collectively, an alternative viewpoint. Instead, they strive for acceptance into the elite.

All this affects the social role of drama itself. A vital function of Wayang, the dissemination of the world view of court and city to the rural masses, may disappear as the content of that world view changes. Ludruk, having grown up in villages and lower-class urban neighborhoods, prides itself on being the art form "of the people" and does indeed speak to and for the urban masses, yet it continues to play the ancient role of drama in Javanese society, communicating to the "little people" the values and standards set by the elite. As traditional drama promoted acceptance of social roles and helped people overcome conflicts and tensions through laughter, so Ludruk assists in the adjustment to social change, turning the accompanying frictions into sources of amusement rather than resentment.

NOTES

1 See Claire Holt, *Art in Indonesia: Continuities and Change*, Ithaca, N.Y.: Cornell University Press, 1967.

2 Clifford Geertz, *The Religion of Java*. Glencoe, Ill: the Free Press, 1960, p. 277.

3 See Bendict, R., O. G. Anderson, "Mythology and the Tolerance of the Javanese," mimeographed. Ithaca, N.Y.: Cornell University, 1965, p. 24.

9

JULIE TAYMOR
From Jacques Lecoq to *The Lion King*: an interview

Richard Schechner

On 19 March 1998 I interviewed Julie Taymor in her studio in Manhattan. At that time, Taymor's production of *The Lion King* was (and still is) enormously successful on Broadway. Taymor's career has spanned continents, venues, and media from Indonesia to off-off-Broadway, from Japan to the New York Shakespeare Festival, from stage to television to film. In fact, when we met, she was busy planning her film of Shakespeare's *Titus Andronicus*. The idea for the film grew out of her 1994 stage version. Shot in Rome and Croatia in 1998 and 1999, the film features Anthony Hopkins as Titus and Jessica Lange as Tamor. It is schedule to open in late 1999. In the interview, Taymor discussed the whole range of her career – with a focus on her work with masks, puppets, and performing objects.

Schechner: What connection is there between your earlier work – the stuff with Herbert Blau, the years you spent in Indonesia – and work like *The Lion King, The Green Bird, Fool's Fire, Oedipus*, and *Titus Andronicus*? Some people just leave their early work behind.

Taymor: No, no, not at all. Quite the opposite. The things that I learned when I was in Lecoq's mime school in Paris at age 16 which had to do with mask work, and then the ideographing work with Herbert Blau have stayed with me. I wasn't interested in being a mime – but I was very intrigued with the use of masks and how the body became a mask. The work at Lecoq's was about getting disciplined with the body. It wasn't just mime. It was work with the neutral mask, character masks, abstract masks.

Schechner: When you say you got connected to your body – I want to explore that because one of the absolutely extraordinary things about *The Lion King* – and about your mask work in general – is the dialogue that takes place between the mask carrier and the mask itself.

Taymor: Really what Lecoq is about is that the body is a complete resource you can use to express anything, including emotions – which we're used to doing as actors. But it's not about "acting" sad. What is it about "sad" that makes the body hard or soft? What rhythm does "sadness" have? So your body becomes a tool. Your body's like paintbrushes. It's completely non-characterological at first. You start with the neutral mask. But then there were other ones that I found really inspiring and interesting. How and when can we be a fat person or a thin person? How do we get rid of what we ordinarily are? What is it about a thin person, what is it about angularity, what is it that makes someone *feel* thin? You should be able to transform your body. That part of Lecoq's work was amazing to me.

Then there was a woman, Madame Citron [Renée Citron, a teacher at Ecole Jacques Lecoq in the early 1970s], who introduced me to puppetry, which was also very great because I wasn't really interested in puppets as an art form then. I had played with them as a kid like any kid, but that was it. Madame Citron animated objects, so it was really about mime, about understanding shape, form, and substance. What is air? What is it to *be* air? What is it to be lead, to be heavy? Ice? What *happens* to a thing when something acts upon it? I might want to use a concrete image like a dripping faucet. (*Taymor's voice imitates the pace and pitch of a dripping faucet*) To (*pause*) be (*pause*) a (*pause*) drip (*pause*) ping (*pause*) fau (*pause*) cet. What does that make you *feel*?

When Madame Citron would use a broom, you'd think about the shape of a broom and what it *does*, and you'd make it come alive. So we'd have dialogues between bottles and brooms and balloons. It was wonderful. You'd start to really see – to anthropomorphize these things.

Schechner: Yeah. I'm smiling because you say "broom" and I'm immediately thrown back to –

Taymor: To Disney!

Schechner and Taymor: *Fantasia*! "The Sorcerer's Apprentice!"

Taymor: Well, what is animation? It's that you can really put life into inanimate objects. And that's the magic of puppetry. You *know* it's dead and therefore you're giving it a soul, a life.

Schechner: But how can you say that's not characterological?

Taymor: It's anthropomorphic. But the stuff with the masks that were abstract wasn't about playing characters.

Schechner: But what about playing an emotion?

Taymor: First, it was just those abstract masks that were rounded, say. Then it was about having the body – purely abstractly – create the same sense of roundness. And when you do that, you feel a certain way. When you put a costume on a person, it makes them *feel* a certain way. So this is pushing that further. Forcing a person to get into a concrete exterior form helps them get out of themselves. That's one of the things about masks.

Another thing we did with Lecoq *before* the masks – remember, I was only sixteen at the time – was acting out concepts. Let's say you wanted to act out a landscape with your body. We would create a concept of the landscape. This I've taken with me up till today. That's the way I explore a piece. When I did *Titus Andronicus*, for the first four or five days I didn't have the actors work on characters. I say, "Okay, let's really look at the themes of the piece, and whether it's violence, racism, blah, blah, blah." And then in an extremely abstract way, I have the actors create ideographs. What I find from those things, whether it's for them or for me, is a visual style for the show that I can use and work in. It also helps them understand. And it brings the actors together without too much competition: who's the star, who's this, who's that? Instead, all of a sudden we're all saying "Why are we doing this piece?" In *Titus*, it got out some pretty *intense* concepts.

Schechner: What exactly do you mean by "ideograph"?

Taymor: An ideograph is an essence, an abstraction. It's boiling it right down to the most essential two, three brush strokes.

Schechner: Can you give me an example from one of your pieces?

Taymor: The best example I can give is from *The Transposed Heads*, which is a piece about friendship. The actors came up with the most spectacular ideograph that I've ever seen. I use it all the time because it's the one that people can get. It takes two people, it's not just a static image. It has a beginning, middle, and end. They came forward and stood with their feet next to each other. Let's do it together because I can't really explain it as well as I can do it.

So, we stand next to each other like this, and then the arms are held up. Put your feet next to mine. And they did this very well. And then you go back until you are totally balanced, like this. Now they worked this out – you can let go now – they went like, "Hi, Joe!", "Hi Bob!" They came in and did a kind of handshake, and then they went into this thing. And what the audience sees is what? They see a *heart*, number one. So this ideograph was a triangle or a heart, depending on how you shape it. But it's also a handshake, it's got that "real" gesture, too. And it's also about balance. If I think, "Fuck you," and give one little push, you're gonna tip over! So in one beautiful, little, sculptural, kinetic move … . It's not *just* naturalism, which we don't need in the theatre, but it's familiar enough to an audience that they'll believe it. It can operate in a naturalistic world, but heighten that naturalism to the point where it adds another layer. Now I was blown away when I saw the actors do it. You know, this was not my idea; this was the *actors'* idea. As a director I file it – knowing that this is going to be a motif. Every time Nanda and Shridaman meet, that's their concept. An ideograph is like a musical motif. And it's the actors' own unique, characterological relationship or thing. So that's one example of an ideograph, very simply, and how it operates both on an abstract and a characterological level.

Schechner: Now this is totally different. You said you were studying at Lecoq's when you were sixteen? Was it summer? Were you taken out of school? Were you living in Paris?

Taymor: I graduated high school early and I'd been in a theatre workshop in Boston with Barbara Linden and Julie Portman. I grew up in the 1960s doing Living Theatre kind of stuff, creating theatre from scratch, from ideas – and I didn't feel I had any training. I knew at that time I was good in movement, I knew I wanted some physical discipline. I was too young for Lecoq's but I got enough out of it. I mean, he usually didn't take people that young. I was there for a year. If I was older I probably would have done the two-year course, but I went to college instead after one year, to Oberlin.

Schechner: Where you met Herbert Blau. What was the connection between the Lecoq work and what you did with Blau?

Taymor: Well, the connection is that Blau, working in the way of Grotowski and Peter Brook, was really also interested in abstraction. In getting to this kind of – *he* might have called them ideographs – that probably came from Blau. What I loved about working with Blau was he was *so* heady. And I was so physical and visual. In Paris I was in mime school, I didn't have to talk. I hardly spoke French, I was very quiet. Then all of a sudden with Blau, I had to do two hours of solo verbal improvisation! So he really got that out of us – me, Bill Irwin, Mike O'Connor. First year we were about fifteen, then it went down, for *The Donner Party*, to seven. And I was the physical visual person in that company. I designed, I came up with the square dance for *The Donner Party*.

Schechner: That was your idea? A great idea. I still remember that dancing after all these years.

Taymor: Blau was extremely good at pulling us into places where we weren't used to going.

Schechner: Now let's shift venue – to Indonesia. Did you study wayang kulit?

Taymor: You know, I studied it before I went, in Seattle at the American Society for Easter Arts, but I didn't go to Indonesia to study traditional arts. I went to observe. This happened a little bit due to Peter Schumann. He said I should just watch and don't assign myself to a mentor. You know I worked with Bread and Puppet one summer at Goddard. Peter saw I could sculpt. So at night I would go into the barn and sculpt and he'd come over and give me some guidance. And then I said, "Well, I'm gonna do this. What do you suggest? Who should I be with?" And he said, "Don't do, just watch." I think he sensed there were a lot of Bread and Puppet look-alikes and he didn't think that was so hot.

   Peter felt if you had your own vision it should show. Don't hook on. Don't go study bunraku and then do bunraku. He told me that if I had the opportunity to travel, I should just travel, take my time, and just watch. "Just watch." That stuck with me. I studied Japanese shadow puppetry a teeny bit here and there, but I had planned to go to Indonesia only for three months. I ended up staying a long time, but that was because I started to create my own work there.

Schechner: Teatr Loh, right?

Taymor: Yeah, but that didn't happen right away.

Schechner: And you had the car accident, came back to the USA, and went back again to Indonesia, right?

Taymor: I had a couple of accidents. And I was there for four years, from around 1974 to 1978 – I can't remember the exact years.

Schechner: All in Java, or –?

Taymor: The first two years in Java and the second two years in Bali. But I didn't start Teatr Loh until I'd been there two years. I'm sure the ideograph stuff was in there at that time. It's with me always.

   I'll give you another example from *The Lion King*. As the director, I hadn't hired the designer yet, but I had to come up with the concept. My deal with Disney had three parts, the first being conceptual. If we all agreed on the concept I'd go to the next part. That suited me just fine because the last thing I wanted was to be enmeshed in something that I couldn't stand behind. Disney felt the same way.

   The ideograph for *The Lion King* was the circle. The circle of life. This symbol is the actual, most simple way of talking about *The Lion King*. It's the biggest song. It's obvious. So before Richard Hudson was hired [as set designer], I already was thinking about wheels and circles. And how, whatever Pride Rock was, I would never do the jutting Pride Rock from the movie. I knew it had to be abstract. You had the sun, then you had the first puppet I conceived, the Gazelle Wheel. The Gazelle Wheel represents the entire concept. You know what I'm talking about? The wheels with the gazelles that leap? With one person moving across the stage you get eight or nine leaping gazelles. Which is a miniature, too. So you get the long-shot and the close-up. I brought the miniature to Michael Eisner [of Disney] and I said, okay, in traditional puppet theatre, there is a black-masking or something that hides the wheels, and you see these little gazelles going like that. The puppeteer is hidden. But let's just get rid of the masking. Because when you get rid of the masking, then even though the mechanics are apparent, the whole effect is more magical. And this is where theatre has a power over film and television. This is absolutely where its magic works. It's not because it's an illusion and we don't know how it's done. It's because we know *exactly* how it's done. On top of that, this little Gazelle Wheel is the circle of life. So then over and over again, with the audience conscious or not, I'm reinforcing this idea of the wheel.

Schechner: Did Eisner immediately go for it?

Taymor: Completely. He said, "Got it!" I knew then that I could do the masks on the heads. I could show the process. There are places where the mechanics are hidden, but they're not very important places. You don't see the machinery under the floor for Pride Rock, but pretty much everything else is visible.

Schechner: One of the things I like very much in *The Lion King* is the tension between what you see, what you imagine, and what you know. I've forgotten the name of the actor, but you know, the guy who plays Zazu –

Taymor: Geoff Hoyle.

Schechner: He's very special. When I first saw him, I said to myself, OK, I'm going to watch him and not his puppet. But that was impossible. I kept slipping into watching the puppet.

Taymor: It's because he puts his energy into the puppet.

Schechner: It was like the bunraku master puppeteer who is so good he doesn't have to wear a black cloth over his face. A double magic: you see the puppet and the puppeteer together. In that universe, God is visible.

Taymor: I've been calling that the "double event" of *The Lion King*. It's not just the story that's being told. It's *how* it's being told.

Schechner: But you did that earlier, didn't you?

Taymor: I first did it in *The Green Bird* where, even though the actor was all in black, I didn't put a mask on his face. I didn't want to hide his facial expression because of the story – a prince *transformed* into a bird. So he wore black, but his costume was the costume of a prince. And he is the *shadow* of the bird. So the personality, the yearning to be a prince again, was always there. I explored the dialectic between the puppet and the human character. So finally the bird flies away and the prince comes down; it's the same silhouette, only now he's got his human face and his green coat.

In *Juan Darién* there's no speaking. There's no speaking in bunraku either; the speaking all comes from the side. *The Green Bird* is the first time where I had the puppeteer both visible and speaking, rather than the neutral puppeteer.

Schechner: The tension in *The Lion King* for me was in the danger that the performance might fail, that the dialectic would not hold. What makes it thrilling for a grown-up is to see if they can all pull it off.

Taymor: Right. Michael Eisner and the other producers, Tom Schumacher and Peter Schneider, were very concerned in 1996 when I did my first prototypes with four characters. Michael Ovitz and the whole shebang of Disney people were there. Things weren't working like they were supposed to work. The main problem was we were working in daylight; we were ten feet away. The actors weren't secure enough to not upstage the puppets. Some of the actors were so nervous in front of this crowd that the puppets were dead. Dead. So everybody said, "Uh, you can't do it for the principal characters." And I said, "But you saw the Hyena and Pumbaa work." "Well, we're frightened about it because you don't know where to look. The actor is more interesting than the puppet." So I said, "Well I agree with you. This didn't work." I knew that.

But I also knew *why* it didn't work and I knew where it could go. See, a good thing about Disney is that they have money to do the next workshop. So I said, "Look, I hate puppets. I'm sick of them. I'm happy to do this with actors, with make-up, Peking opera-style, kabuki. I don't give a shit. I've got nothing to prove. If that's the best way to tell the story, let's do it that way. But I don't think that's why you wanted to work with me." And they answered, "Well, you can do it for the chorus animals, but not the principals." So I said, "All right, what I'm gonna do – and this is as much for me as you, because this is the first opportunity I've had to spend the amount of money it takes do this experiment – I'm gonna do two or three versions of each character. I'll do full make-up and wig for Scar. And for Geoff Hoyle – we'd hired Geoff by then – I'll do it first with the bird and then without the bird. But we have to do it in the New Amsterdam, in a black environment, with all the light, all the make-up, and full costumes. And you have to be 30 feet away."

And that's what I did. A true experiment. And it worked. Michael Eisner said, "Let's do *all* the puppet stuff. Because it is definitely more risky, but the payoff is bigger." So that was it. And there were no more worries about it.

Schechner: Working with Disney gave you the freedom, the money, to really experiment?

Taymor: Yeah.

Schechner: And once Eisner made the decision, did Disney stay out of it?

Taymor: They stayed out of it.

Schechner: They didn't play producer?

Taymor: Tom Schumacher *was* the producer. He was the one who asked me to do it. He was the head of the Olympic Arts Festival in L.A. before he went to Disney. Tom is really one of the best theatre producers I've ever worked with, if not *the* best. He knows theatre from all over the world, so he would sit there and he'd say, "Why don't you try an Awaji puppet?" Because of the Olympic Arts Festival, he's been all over the world. This is a guy who knew exactly one technique from another. And even though he's in California, he was here in New York enough to say, "Do it Taymor style." What he meant by that was, "You don't need all that. Get it simpler." I was interested – because we had the budget – in exploring high technologies. But what happened was that I came back to my beginnings. The most successful stuff is the stuff I've done my whole life, which didn't cost anything. Like the tears coming out of the eyes. Or the silk going into the water hole. Or the shadow puppets of the fish. Or the little mouse.

You have that incredibly big, opening scene and the next thing you have is a little circle of light – just a hand-held light and teeny little mouse that moves along the screen.

Schechner: And the birds, too. The flying birds.

Taymor: Oh, yeah, yeah. You mean the kites in Act 2?

Schechner: Right.

Taymor: Those are the things that I've done since I had no budgets. They have the power. In fact *more* power because they are so transparent, so simple. It is so pleasing to me to hear people say, "My child went home and picked up some fabric and a stick." Do you know what that's like for me? To see a child go home and run around with fabric and a stick instead of creating a bird on a computer where they're given the bluebird head and the bluebird wing, and they get the color. And that means that they haven't really understood air. They haven't understood that silk is gonna work better than velvet, you know? I think it's just shocking what's gonna happen.

Schechner: People say the computer is a liberator, but it's all painting-by-the-numbers, programmed.

Taymor: And it's a very pathetic physical experience. The idea of sitting in front of a little box, minimizing life experience rather than making it greater. Why play on the Internet when you can go outside and ride a bicycle? It doesn't have any air. I can't imagine having a child and having to fight over being outside or working on the computer.

When I was at a tech/design conference two weeks ago, I insulted everyone. I started by saying, "Look at this stage. Look how ugly it is." It was filled with wires and computers. "Don't you guys even think about aesthetics? How unbearable this is?" Now I'm talking to a bunch of Microsoft guys. I mean these were the people who invented all this stuff.

Schechner: Right, there's something whacko about it. It's like the love-affair with the automobile. Everyone thought it was great – you can go anywhere! But where the fuck do people go? To the mall, to the supermarket? The car didn't bring utopia, and neither will the microchip.

I want to talk now about *Oedipus* and *Titus Andronicus*. They seem to be different from a lot of your other work in the sense that these are heavy, bloody tragedies.

Taymor: *Titus* is meant to touch you, and to be emotional.

Schechner: Had you earlier done anything as heavy as this?

Taymor: I did *The Tempest*.

Schechner: But *The Tempest* is a magic show.

Taymor: Yes, but it's got such beautiful, deep themes in it. But you're right, it's nothing like *Titus*. *Juan Darién* is pretty dark in certain places.

Schechner: Yes, *Juan Darién*. But the way you did it was both dark and not. I mean, the very idea that the village was this – the scale was such that a person could literally embrace the village.

Taymor: Right. I'm just saying that it goes to a point where the child is tortured to death and burned alive. I did *Titus* because Jeffrey Horowitz asked me to read it and I was shocked. I'd never been shocked by something I read before. And I thought, "Whoa! If I'm this shocked, how could someone have written this? And it's Shakespeare's first play – people think it's a bad play. I don't really know how I feel about this." People said, "Julie, you know you've done so many things with violence in them." I had. But I'd always stylized the violence. So this was one where I had to say, "You can't stylize this violence because then it becomes too pretty, too aesthetic." I don't like violence. I'm like any other normal person. But I think that the thing that drew me to *Titus*, and that still draws me, is that I've never seen any dissertation on violence as complete as *Titus*. Think *Braveheart* or all those violent Hollywood movies. Or *Richard III* or Jacobean plays. What is it about *Titus*? You don't think about the violence in *Richard III*. It just happens and it goes. There's something else in *Titus* that gets to people, I guess because the violence is so … gruesome. Cutting off hands, and tongues, and rape. It's not just smothering your wife with a pillow.

Schechner: Yes, the violence in *Titus* is celebrated. In *Richard III* he kills the kids because they threaten his claim to the throne. In *Titus*, there's a delight in the torture.

Taymor: By some characters. Yes, Shakespeare chose that aspect. Violence as war. Condoned violence. Ritual sacrifice. Then it has father-to-son violence, which is the patriarch thing. Violence as an act of passion and anger, accepted because it was an irrational act of passion. Then violence as art, which is what Aaron does when he thinks about the art of violence. He's the one who's like the guy in *Clockwork Orange* – that kind of nihilistic violence, violence without meaning. And lust, and sex. Ultimately Titus killing his daughter, which is … Bosnia. Or whatever the latest outrage is. You can't live anymore. You've been raped by the enemy. Your life is over, you are disgraced, you are condemned – so why live?

Schechner: Why did you want to do it?

Taymor: I did it as a play because I found it just so compelling. I am so sick of stories like *Pulp Fiction* where you have a bunch of low-lifes being violent in a stereotypical low-life way. No real story. What I love about *Titus* is that you have a good man, a

Fig. 9.1 Julie Taymor on Saturninus' wolf-head throne for her film *Titus*. (Photo by Elizabetta Catalano, courtesy of Julie Taymor.)

powerful man, your chief of state. You want him to be your president. But he behaves exactly the same as the worst of the worst.

Schechner: And as a movie. How will you translate it, both conceptually and physically into film?

Taymor: In the theatre, my set designer Derek McLane and I took ancient Roman ruins and made photographic blow-ups on plastic and then we scratched it. So what you had was something grand, chintzy, and contemporary. I played with the Etruscan right up to the present. Costume is character, not period. I thought of Lavinia more as Grace Kelly, with the little gloves, a 1950s' character. But Tamora is more like Visconti's 1930s' film, *The Damned*. She's androgynous. And Titus, he starts in black and he moves through grays to white, with a chef's hat. White, where the blood really shows. But, at a certain point when he's been completely reduced to being a pathetic old man, he's like *Father Knows Best*. This was Robert Stattel's idea. He said, "I feel like wearing a cardigan. You know, a frumpy cardigan sweater." Clothing became so much an emblem of status in society and what you think about yourself. I'm doing exactly the same thing in the film.

Schechner: You're mixing time periods?

Taymor: Oh, yeah. It's in two time periods – or maybe I should say we're creating our own time period. I can say I've never seen anything like it in film except maybe *Road Warriors* and *Blade Runner*. We're going to shoot in Rome using both the ancient Roman ruins – they have elements of modernity to them – and then we're going to use Mussolini's government center, which was modeled after the ancients. And we'll take these modern places, which have an incredible kind of minimalist power, and we'll put Roman cobblestones down. And what we'll try to do, if we go into an ancient catacomb where they buried their dead, there might be – like in Mexico – a little photo of the character next to something that reminds you of him.

In the theatre production I used the gold frame and red curtain which is symbolic of revenge dramas. I had the concept of "Penny Arcade Nightmares," all in gold and red. In the film, the Colosseum has become the symbol. It's more cinematic. Everybody in the world knows that the Colosseum is the original theatre of violence and cruelty. The film starts in a kitchen that could be in Sarajevo or Brooklyn. A child is watching TV. As the child's innocent play with his toy soldiers escalates into a palpably thunderous explosion of bombs, the boy falls through an *Alice in Wonderland* time-warp, with the intervention of a Shakespearean clown, right into the Colosseum. Magically, his toy Roman soldiers have become armored flesh and blood, covered in layers of earth – Titus and his armies are returning from war with a triumphant march into the arena. The boy takes his part as Young Lucius, Titus's grandson, and it's through his eyes that the audience will witness this tale of revenge and compassion.

Schechner: And you're using Shakespeare's text?

Taymor: Completely.

Schechner: Nothing added to it?

Taymor: No.

Schechner: And who's playing what? Do you know yet?

Taymor: Anthony Hopkins is Titus.

Schechner: Wow. Who's producing it? Disney?

Taymor: No studio! We're raising the money independently. If we can do it for 12 or 14 million, it will be a miracle –

Schechner: You mean you can have Hopkins in a film for that kind of budget?

Taymor: He's not doing it for the money.

Schechner: To get back to *The Lion King*. It was all miked, right?

Taymor: Body-miked?

Schechner: Yeah.

Taymor: Of course, but it's the best sound designer in New York. With a full orchestra, you have to mike.

Schechner: Ethyl Merman didn't mike.

Taymor: In those days nobody did. But that's why she came right down to the front of the stage. The New Amsterdam was a vaudeville house and we learned that the sound is only really good at the front of the stage.

Schechner: This interview is going into an issue of *TDR* on puppets and performing objects. I wonder if you feel an affinity with American traditions of performing objects – stuff like the Macy's parade, the Disney and other theme parks. You talked about Asian arts. What about American popular arts?

Taymor: I never liked those things. Not even as a kid. I think I always felt that that kind of thing was just goofy, literally. The roundness of everything – the aesthetic of it – never appealed to me. When I was given marionettes as a child, they were more like Czech marionettes. They weren't that four-fingered, big-eyed – I never like the big-eyed types of things. Bread and Puppet was one of the first things I saw that really grabbed me, during the Vietnam War. It was *that* power of parade. I've never seen the Macy's parade.

Schechner: Over the last ten years or so, you've been making movies. Are you changing over from live performance to film?

Taymor: Not really. I did two non-feature films, which I enjoyed, *Oedipus* and *Fool's Fire*. And now *Titus*.

Schechner: Do you have any theatre projects coming up?

Taymor: Elliot [Goldenthal] and I are still working on *Grendel*, that's opera. If Nigel Redden [the producer] can pull it off, we'll do it in 2000. There's nothing more ridiculous than the amount of time we'll have spent to work on what will amount to a non-commercial eight performances. It's ridiculous! We started this in 1988, so it'll be twelve years. And I want *The Green Bird* to come back to Broadway. I'm really gonna try hard to have an open Broadway run. After New York we did it in La Jolla. We made cast changes and cut 20 minutes. It was very good. [Theatre for a New Audience's production of *Green Bird* directed and codesigned by Taymor will be presented on Broadway by Gregory Mosher and Bill Haber in the 1999/2000 theatre season.]

Schechner: But with the fabulous success of *The Lion King*, aren't producers running after you?

Taymor: Not a lot of theatre producers.

Schechner: Why not, do you think?

Taymor: I never had theatre producers run after me. Some people want to make more Broadway shows out of movies. But Elliot and I aren't going to do *Batman: The Musical*.

Schechner: It's interesting – plays from movies. Until recently it was the other way round. Now they think they already have name recognition and a proven box office.

Taymor: And they own it.

Schechner: Right. They own it.

Taymor: Name recognition definitely works. If *The Lion King* hadn't been a movie, there would be nothing like this. You've got children who *know* it. It's like the *Mahabharata* for our culture. These kids have it memorized. And they love it, and they say, "Mommy" – I get these stories all the time – they say, "Don't worry, Mommy, Simba's going to be okay."

You know what I love about *The Lion King*? It's really theatre operating in its original sense, which is about family and society. It's doing exactly what theatre was born for – to reaffirm where we are as human beings in our environment. It's precisely to re-establish your connection with your family, to know what your hierarchy is. And to watch families come and go through that with their children is a very moving experience for me.

Schechner: Greek theatre was that –

Taymor: And Shakespeare –

Schechner: Great popular theatre was always something like that. A ritual celebration, rather than "what's-going-to-happen-next?"

Taymor: When I worked on the story of *The Lion King*, I ultimately knew that this is a classic story. It doesn't have to be so absolutely amazing. What needs to be amazing is the *telling* of the story. The meaning comes in the telling, not in the story itself. It's how you tell it. And everybody always talks about this crying. The most common statement is, "The giraffes came on and I burst into tears." From adults. You know, children don't say that. And you ask, "Why is that?" I remember having a disagreement with Richard Hudson over how to do the sunrise. I won because I'm the director. He wanted to use projected light, which of course you can do. But I said, "Then you might as well use a movie because a film clip can do it even realer." Then I said, "It's the beginning of the show. I can't do that. I've gotta establish the rules of the game at the beginning. I just want it to be flat, and I want it to be clearly pieces of silk, on the floor. So that when the audience looks at it, they go, 'Oh – it's just pieces of silk on flats going up and down.'" And the giraffes were the second thing I designed. I said, "Sure, I could hide those people in a costume with stilts." But then no one would feel anything. The fact that as a spectator you're very aware of the human being with the things strapped on, and you see the straps linking the actor to the stilts, that there's no attempt to mask the stilts and make them animal-like shapes – *that's* why people cry.

Schechner: Earlier in your work, you were your own designer, weren't you?

Taymor: You mean sets? Not always.

Schechner: Well, like in *Juan Darién*, who designed the village?

Taymor: We codesigned the set, Skip [G.W. Mercier] and me. The actual look of the village is Skip's. My concept, his realization.

Schechner: And in the *Lion King* you had a costumer?

Taymor: No, I designed the costumes. The puppets and the masks are codesigned by Michael Curry and myself: I am the aesthetics director. I sculpted everything, I drew everything. He did the mechanics. Sometimes he did the visuals, but our balance together is really technical and aesthetic. Richard Hudson did the sets. I gave him some basic concepts like the circles. I said to him, "You're a minimalist, that's perfect, because the puppets are gonna be so rich. I need a minimal background." He's a white guy from England born in Africa, spent his first seventeen years there.

Which brings me to the only other thing that I want to say about *The Lion King*, something particularly important to me. The production is very interesting when you think about race in America. For white people, *The Lion King* has nothing to do with race. It's beyond race. It transcends race. For black people, it's the opposite. It's all about race.

Schechner: How's that?

Taymor: First of all, when you see the movie of *The Lion King*, unless you're an adult you have no idea that the voice of Mufasa [James Earl Jones] is an African American. In my production you see the actors in flesh and blood. Technically, the entire chorus is non-white – some of them look white, but they are of mixed race. You have a non-white cast onstage for the most part. And for a black child – black papers have written about this – the response from the black audience has been rewarding and moving. In American mainstream theatre, a black king is nowhere to be found.

Schechner: Right.

Taymor: *Never*! To have Mufasa played by a black actor. In the movie, Matthew Broderick was Simba's voice. Okay, so we had a black father and a white son. *Why* didn't they cast a black actor to do the voice of Simba? I didn't intentionally have two light-skinned people playing those parts; they were the best actors for the roles. Our other Simba who's playing it now is *very* black. The black audience sees race onstage. Now I know my work isn't African, but Lebo's music [Lebo M] is African.

The Lion King isn't about racism the way, say, *Ragtime* or so many other plays with black performers are. In this regard, *The Lion King* is totally refreshing – a kind of glimpse of the future. My friend Reg E. Kathay said, "This is like the next century." But no one in the white press ever talks about the race issue in *The Lion King*. I think one article in L.A. brought that up.

Schechner: But the black press talked about it?

Taymor: Oh, yeah.

Schechner: Is the story itself an African story?

Taymor: No. African tales are much more outrageous than this. This is a western story. What is very African about *The Lion King* is Lebo's music. The visuals, too, the textiles. And Garth Fagan's choreography. I picked Garth because I wanted something real cross-cultural, very European and African, or American-European and African. I liked that Garth is a contemporary choreographer from Jamaica. He has the roots and he knows African idioms, but he's doing his own modern stuff.

Schechner: Anything else?

Taymor: You know what, I'd love to make a film of my *The Lion King*.

Schechner: A film of a play based on a film?

Taymor: It's different! First of all, the movie only had five songs. And the faces of the people are very compelling. We're not talking animation.

Schechner: But would Disney do that?

Taymor: Not right now. They don't want to ruin the box office. And then I thought, maybe we could shoot it in Africa. But what I can't quite figure out is this: the whole reason to stylize is because you're not in a real setting. So how do you do the Serengeti in the Serengeti? It would be fantastic to have the Serengeti, and then out of the ground, the land starts rising up, and there are the people. Or take a real cave and literally paint the cave with slashes like we did onstage, so that you stylize the natural. I mean, you literally treat the land and maybe you color the grass. We could film from helicopters, you know, or any angle. It could be amazing to try and figure this out. I don't even know what it would look like to have real giraffes moving by fake giraffes. I know it's completely the opposite of what it's supposed to be, and what its success is in the theatre, but there's something very compelling and interesting to me about having the real, and then having the stylized. It's a musical. I mean, it's not like you're pretending to be really real.

Part III

MASKS
Commedia dell'arte and *topeng*

10

INTRODUCTION TO PART III

Joel Schechter

While stage artists continue to adapt and renew Italian *commedia dell'arte* and Balinese *topeng*, traditional masks have remained a constant in both of these popular forms. Over the centuries one Balinese mask has represented a *patih* – a prime minister – with "plump cheeks and a mischievous grin."[1] This wooden mask handcarved in Bali covers the whole face, unlike the leather Italian half-mask worn by Pantalone in commedia; beneath old Pantalone's long hooked nose, the actor's own mouth can freely open when he advises his daughter to marry a wealthy man as old as her father.

These masks and others in the tradition each hold one set facial expression; but the bodies of the actors express considerable variation and nuance in character. Actors perform with heightened, non-naturalistic physical movement, which includes dancing in *topeng* and slapstick comedy in commedia. In the *topeng* performance described later by John Emigh, one actor plays a series of roles; he wears different masks and transforms his voice and movement to suit the masked characters. The multiplicity of roles assumed here has a western counterpart in Dario Fo's one-man shows, where the Italian satirist versed in commedia and other popular traditions impersonates sixteen different people to retell the miracle of Lazarus' resurrection, and portrays a blind man and a cripple simultaneously in another episode of *Mistero Buffo*.

Usually a traveling troupe of actors, not a single virtuoso, performed *commedia dell'-arte* when it began in sixteenth-century Italy. According to one seventeenth-century commentator, du Tralage, "the theatre [has become] so popular that most of the working men deprive themselves of food in order to have the wherewithal to go to the play."[2] Actors portraying Arlecchino, Brighella, Pantalone, or a zanni wore half-masks and developed detailed physical behavior for their stock characters. Most of the dialogue and comic business (*lazzi*) was not published, and instead, like other forms of popular theatre, orally transmitted and physically demonstrated to new performers. As Robert Erenstein notes, commedia ushered in "actor's theatre," where there was "an absence of authors;" "of their *commedia all'improvviso*, all we have is *scenari, lazzi*, illustrative material and spectators' comments."[3] Most of the primary source materials which survive are fragments of text or brief scenarios (many collected in Mel Gordon's anthology, *Lazzi*).

The poverty of primary sources has not prevented generations of actors from keeping commedia alive, learning from one another and in some cases creating speculative reconstructions of techniques which, if not authentic, are at least lively and provocative variations in the tradition. Twentieth-century stage directors who found inspiration in commedia and revitalized it through innovative productions and ensemble training include Meyerhold, Vakhtanghov, Craig, Strehler, Fo, Mnouchkine, Taymor, and R. G. Davis.

In a memoir about his years as director of the San Francisco Mime Troupe, Davis humorously recalls that when he explored commedia traditions with his actors, and with Carlo Mazonne-Clementi as an advisor, "one important event" occurred after their first outdoor performance in 1962. Actress Yvette Nachmias stepped offstage and yelled to Davis, "The reason for the large movements and gestures is because they performed outside."[4] Her discovery constitutes a small but important footnote in the history of popular theatre. Masked performance outdoors, whether in a rural village or on a city street, benefits from the enhanced visibility conferred on characters by masks and heightened physical movement. While they are not exactly "street theatre," both commedia and *topeng* have often been performed in spaces which have no imaginary fourth wall, or, as Davis notes of the commedia on his outdoor platform stage, "there were no walls."[5] The open space, along with direct addresses to the audience and stylized acting, create theatre that is more presentational than representational, theatre that thrives on direct contact with its audience.

The actors' direct contact with the audience is facilitated by the absence of imaginary and real walls; but it also comes from the non-naturalistic acting that breaks out of narrative and language conventions. John Emigh observes the *topeng* clown character, Se Mata Mata, creating comic audience contact through nonsensical dialogue:

> Se Mata Mata's first "word" is a sneeze … . He then proceeds to string together nonsense syllables that resolve themselves in inanities and obscenities, assuring the audience that even if they don't catch the words, they won't miss the meaning. The "meaning" is to be found precisely in the assault on the elaborate linguistic structure that Kakul [the performer] has himself created … .[6]

Dario Fo's assault on language through *grammelot* is remarkably similar in effect. As the Italian satirist explains it (in a lecture excerpted here): "*Grammelot* is a term of French origin, coined by Commedia players, and the word itself is devoid of meaning. It refers to a babel of sounds which nonetheless manage to convey the sense of a speech."[7] Fo tells his audience that *grammelot* can be understood by those who don't speak Italian, English or French; it represents "the triumph of ignorance." His art thrives on the fact that a great deal can be said and received through body language, through the sounds rather than the sense of words.

The de-emphasizing of conventional speech appealed to Antonin Artaud when he first saw Balinese theatre performed in 1931. He effusively praised "this purely popular and not sacred theater [which] gives us an extraordinary idea of the intellectual level of a people who take the struggles of a soul preyed upon by ghosts and phantoms from the beyond as the basis for their civic festivals."[8] A viewing of Balinese theatre in Paris led the French author and director to pursue his own ideas of theatre with greater enthusiasm; for him it was the discovery of "a theater which eliminates the author in favor of what we would call, in our Occidental theatrical jargon, the director; but a director who has become a kind of manager of magic, a master of sacred ceremonies … " and "the sense of a new physical language, based upon signs and no longer upon words."[9]

Artaud's understanding of the Balinese theatre (particularly its use of words) was not completely accurate; as Bettina Knapp notes, "the meaning of the changed or enunciated words escaped him."[10] The freedom from logocentricity Artaud found in Balinese theatre may have been due in part to his not knowing the language spoken; and perhaps the exoticism of the non-western troupe visiting Paris appealed to him. In any case, the absence of a single or authoritative author in both the Balinese and Italian masked theatre results in an actor-driven event.

While commedia is generally comic and based on Italian stock characters, *topeng* has a more serious side affiliated with religious rituals and celebrations. As Emigh notes of the performance he documents, its stories date as far back as the sixteenth century, when court poets chronicled Balinese history. *Topeng* has sequences in which

> the heroes and villains of the chronicles yield the playing space to the clowns … . The fantastic and eccentric Se Mata Mata yields to the all too familiar Cucul … . It is not that the noble and demonic personages of the chronicles are obliterated: to the contrary, *topeng* performances serve to keep these characters alive … . It celebrates the vitality of the present as well as the grandeur of the past.[11]

Much as Balinese theatre brings ancient demons and topical, modern clown references together in one event, western directors have similarly employed commedia's traditional characters to celebrate – and criticize – present-day conditions and social ills (if not demons) by updating scenarios. The San Francisco Mime Troupe, discussed later in the volume, and California's Dell'Arte Players have developed a series of contemporary plays with commedia-based characters. The Dell'Arte play *Performance Anxiety* featured an Arlecchino who was made pregnant by Pantalone and subsequently advocated birth control. (This is not a commedia scenario which Papal-loyal Italians would applaud.)

In France, under the direction of Ariane Mnouchkine, Théâtre du Soleil turned to commedia characters for *The Golden Age, First Draft*. The 1975 production portrayed Pantalone as a contemporary French real-estate promoter, whose greed contributed to the death of an Algerian immigrant construction worker named Abdullah. The innocent Abdullah, described as "he who falls into every trap," is a new addition to the usual cast of commedia characters: the non-westerner who struggles to survive through his hard labor. *The Golden Age* was created as earlier commedia plays were, through company improvisation. Rehearsals began without a written text, and according to director Mnouchkine, the play had "First Draft" in its title because she wanted: "To show a play for what it is: a moment in the inquiry of theatre in the present tense."[12] The capacity for improvisation and immediacy within commedia performance was fused with a spirit of scientific inquiry and laboratory experimentation, so that the rehearsal process became a means of exploring larger social and political situations, not just character relationships onstage.

Experimental theatre along these lines is encouraged by the absence of complete, original commedia texts. Although commedia troupes left very few definitive documents for scholars to study, the creative methods that made the texts unnecessary have given modern actors and directors a freedom to reimagine and renew the lives of Arlecchino, Pantalone, Il Dottore, and their scenarios. Still, there are documents around for actors and scholars to read, as more is written on the subject each year; the selections offered here are only a starting point.

NOTES

1 John Emigh, "Playing with the Past: Visitation and Illusion in the Mask Theatre of Bali," reprinted in this volume.

2 Quoted by Pierre Louis Ducharte, *The Italian Comedy*, New York, Dover, 1966, p. 19.

3 Robert Erenstein, "Satire and the *Commedia dell'arte*," in *Western Popular Theatre*, edited by David Mayer and Kenneth Richards, London, Methuen, 1977, pp. 32–3.

4 Quoted by R. G. Davis in *The San Francisco Mime Troupe: The First Ten Years*, Palo Alto, Ramparts Press, 1975, p. 35.

5 Ibid, p. 32.

6 John Emigh, op. cit.

7 Dario Fo, "Wordless Speech," reprinted in this volume.

8 Antonin Artaud, "On the Balinese Theatre" in *The Theatre and Its Double*, translated by Mary Caroline Richards. New York: Grove Press, 1958, p. 56.

9 Ibid, p. 60.

10 Bettina Knapp, *Antonin Artaud and the Modern Theatre*, edited by Gene Plunka. New York: D. Lewis, 1969, p. 91.

11 John Emigh, op cit.

12 Mnouchkine quoted by Christopher Kirkland in "Théâtre du Soleil: *Golden Age, First Draft*," reprinted in this volume.

11

COMMEDIA AND THE ACTOR

Carlo Mazzone-Clementi and Jane Hill

Although we can conjecture about commedia in a historical framework, we cannot *know* what it was like. There are no existing scripts, no photos. There are only a few paintings, a few sparse descriptions, and a horde of mostly untranslated scenarios. Yet, a great

Fig. 11.1 Carlo Mazzone-Clementi in the commedia role of the doctor. (Photo courtesy of Dell'Arte International School of Physical Theatre.)

interest in commedia continues. Anyone can open the drawer marked *commedia dell'-arte*, but, having opened it, how does one know what to choose from it? For some, commedia means a dusty reincarnation of the postures and poses of a Callot, charming in print, but deadly on the stage. The magnetic appeal of commedia, for me, has been to rediscover the magic of the performer: how he worked, what he did, and to some extent, why he did it, consciously or not. The only possible approach is an inductive one. We must begin where we are.

One can begin with the stock characters. Actually, I prefer the phrase "comic proto-type." In commedia, there are three levels of characterization that build to the level of this comic prototype. The *caricati* are basically caricatures (the lovers, the noble father, the noble mother, etc.). They wear no masks and are essentially a part of the landscape. The *macchietta*, or "little spot" (e.g. the funny messenger), is the equivalent of our modern "cameo" role. Then, there are the pivotal roles known as *maschere*, the masked characters for which *commedia dell'arte* is famous (Arlecchino, Pantalone, Capitano, etc.). The rules of professional etiquette for these categories are clearly defined in a manner much like burlesque. A *caricato* is not entitled to get big laughs. The *macchietta* has a bit more freedom to "warm the audience up."

The *maschere* were clearly the "top bananas" of their day. They are deeper in the symbolic or mythological sense because they come straight from the archetype, with all the attendant nuances and intricacies. They are distillations of the observable. Their garb and customs may change, but not their traits. We see them in historical plays and on the streets of our home towns. We laugh because they are recognizable, and delight in watching the "known" character contend with an "unknown" situation – one that must be faced intu-itively by the character and inventively by the actor. The characters have been compared to barnyard inhabitants. Hens, chicks, roosters, capons, ducks, peacocks, all the farmyard bipeds make us laugh, their walks absurd parodies of man's own gait. Pantalone, Arlecchino, Columbina, Smeraldina, Brighella, Capitano, Il Dottore and the others are not identified so much by the color and cut of their costumes as by the walk, the gesture, the manner in which each uses his "feathers" to express pride, joy, anger, and sorrow, alter-nately swelling and drooping, preening and ruffling, as he picks his way like a strutting fowl, ever vulnerable, across the stage, before the appreciative eyes of the audience.

Commedia masks are a study in contrasts: the immobile upper half is in counterpoint with the mobile lower jaw of the actor, which somehow becomes an extension of the mask itself. The half-mask of commedia marks an interesting development in the theatre. The Roman performers' masks were often little more than megaphones used mainly to project the voice. As masks evolved in the Middle Ages, they became a tool for characterization. The appearance of the half-mask of the professional commedia performer – the first time a half-mask was used theatrically – freed the voice and returned the body to prominence. Use of the half-mask allows greater physical freedom than a full mask. Made of leather, the commedia masks are light and flexible, permitting rolls, tumbles and displays of skill limited only by the capabilities of the actor wearing it. The choice of leather (i.e. *animal skin)* has a psychophysical effect, which can only be understood when one has compared the wearing of a leather mask to one made of wood, paper, or plastic.[1] Practically, of course, a performance becomes possible at the drop of a hat, when one can take one's "make-up" from a bag, and leap on to the platform in any town square.

The commedia is earthy, fertile, alive, and ready to fly. It is "popular" theatre in terms of what it depicts and to whom it appeals. Large numbers of followers have no signifi-cance for the commedia performer. There is only one audience to please at each performance. When one plays Verona, one does not worry about the reactions of the Romans. The piece is shaped and colored by the local audience, their moods and responses. Traditionally, commedia performers played in more than thirty basic dialects. Each village produced its own dialect and was represented by its own character, an elaborate extension of the village idiot. In some cultures, the afflicted are objects of guilt or veneration, and are not suitable subjects for comedy. But to the Italians, the village fool became a point of departure for understanding mankind. And while the village fool was the object of mirth, it was mirth devoid of malice. At a single commedia performance, the major characters usually came from many different parts of Italy, bringing with them their local heritage. Each performance "on the road" was custom-tailored for a specific audience. Mass appeal was unimportant. In fact, had television existed in the Renaissance, commedia might have died an early death.

How, then, does one approach the study of commedia in the twentieth century? My first approach was through the discipline of mime. Two Frenchmen have had great influence on my work: Marcel Marceau and Jacques Lecoq. I worked with both when I was young. Through them – and through a short period as a scholarship student at the school of Jean-Louis Barrault – I first met mime. I was fortunate enough to travel around Italy with Marceau, performing with him, responding to his creativity. Philosophically, mystically, and poetically, he was a catalyst for me. Practically, however, it was Lecoq's excellent systematized natural method that confirmed my intuition regarding mime – that it was to be the basis of all my theatrical work, and that it was to open many doors in my understanding of commedia. Both Marceau and Lecoq were obsessed by commedia. Witnessing their fascination with it, and later, at the Barrault school, coming into contact with more Frenchmen who were commedia enthusiasts, I felt for the first time a sense of my own national and cultural identity. Through the French, I discovered what it meant to be Italian. In their *pantomime blanche*, I saw an extension of commedia, the legacy of Pedrolino (Pierrot) and Scaramouche. As the French theatre once used Italian commedia for its source and creative inspiration, so I have drawn on the teaching of Lecoq for my work in commedia.

TEACHING COMMEDIA ACTING

At the school of Jean-Louis Barrault, students are taught that the life cycle of an individual and/or an action may be broken down into four parts:

1. instinct of expansion;
2. sense of egocentrism;
3. instinct of conservation;
4. sense of sublimation.

The first natural act of expansion is to be born. The fetus, awaiting birth, is primarily a concentric creature, centered from the cerebellum to the heel, in a direct, curved line. At birth we make our initial great eccentric act. The rest of our life can, if you like, be analyzed in terms of concentric and eccentric actions. Like a human gyroscope, we move to and from our center, the spinal column. A simple action, such as putting on a jacket, is concentric to the dorsal spine; we close ourselves into the object. Removing it, the action becomes eccentric; we expand from the object, from the center, from the spine. The eccentric act is dynamic, the concentric one moves toward a static state. Action must always precede analysis. The first step predetermines the ones to follow. Having made the first eccentric motion at your birth, you can now look around. Birth is a matter of territory; identity comes later, through action. Self-awareness in space and time equals presence. (Self-consciousness leads to immobility and is the enemy of presence.) From presence, one can develop the ability to represent.

Characterization must begin at home: in the body. Some of us are not at home in our bodies. We must discover what that means. Therefore, the main emphasis of my work is physical self-discovery. In his book, *Reflections on the Theatre*, Jean-Louis Barrault speaks of the actor as constantly going "from–to." "How" is a character. Beginning where you are means *really* knowing where you are, from your heels up, and not (for the moment at least) avoiding contact with reality through flights of the imagination, philosophical excursions into existentialism, or even emotional recall.

The most simple act of going "from–to" is the RUN. That is where we start. Running is a primary physical activity. It circulates the blood, activates the heart, exercises the lungs, and drives extraneous thoughts from the mind. The motion of this act is dominated by the contact of foot and floor – inhaling, exhaling, turning, wheeling, sweating, as you follow the leader. Do you run badly? You will discover it in motion. Is your body unresponsive? Thinking about it will not help. The kinesthetic response comes only with motion. Kinesthetic response is not a product of brute energy. Paradoxically, the difficult must be easy. We must break down the RUN, balancing on one foot, then the other. Stretch, reach. Equilibrium: does it desert you when you depend on only that tiny pedestal, your foot? Don't try harder, try less. Tension is the enemy of balance. And what of the foot? How does it function? Walk quickly with short steps, slower with long strides, on the heels, on the toes, the insides, the outsides. By exploring extremes of articulation, we learn to extend our physical range in the same way that the singer extends vocal range. A walk develops one step at a time. The walk is the base that supports the top (eventually, the mask). In the walk we learn to, literally, *under-stand* the character. The nature of any tree begins at the roots. The body must adjust to the foot. There is no choice.

The first adjustment comes in the spine. But what is that? Does it move? How? To discover, we must return to a vertebrate condition. On the floor, then. Belly down. You move across the floor like a reptile. Your useless head cannot pull you. Impetus, again, from the foot, and that motion flexes the spine. I can't emphasize enough the importance to each performer of his *own* body; the wonders of that fulcrum; the greatest leverage ever discovered, the foot. In, around, and through activities that explore the foot and spine, supporting and sustaining it all, is the BREATH. Are you a miser with your breath? Do you fight its natural cycle? Is it working with your motion, or against it?

By this time you should be warmed-up, worn-out, ready to begin "where you are." Accept this condition: you are IN THE DARK – literally. Again, we move "from–to." The character is you. We place a TARGET on the floor. Move to it in the dark. You can not compute this. It is intuitive. You and the target are one. Still IN THE DARK, with eyes fully open, there is a TUNNEL this time. Explore it. A tunnel is not a hole. Do it, don't demonstrate it. And now, IN THE DARK, you are blindfolded; there is a MAZE. There should be intuition, exploration, but also this time, selection of a course. There are obstacles. What is the kinesthetic response? (Psychology comes later.) One does not push one's way through a maze in the dark. Perception must travel from the foot to the brain. In a TUNNEL, even in the dark, we seek visual reassurance of our experiences, if our eyes are free and open. In a MAZE, blindfolded, we have no choice but to work from our own centers outward. We must choose between immobility and action. To choose action involves overcoming fears of the unknown. An actor must be willing to take chances. With relaxation and a clear vision of the goal, we find inspiration, which is fundamental to creation. These rudimentary exercises must not be done superficially. Whether your focus is close to the body or far from it, you must be in touch at the kinesthetic level. Like the perfect swordsman or lasso thrower, you are connected to the target, a part of it. You are a dancer moving toward an always-escaping image, pursuing it continuously, freshly, inspired by the pursuit to new ideas of motion. As this dancer, you might be drawn into a spiritual dilemma: the immobility of perfect motion.

One cannot discuss the body in motion without relating it to the four elements: Earth, Water, Air, and Fire. We must explore each, learning with our bodies what it means to be rooted, fluid, floating, and exploding, by experiencing each condition through mime.

We cannot talk of commedia, or my approach to it, without discussing both mime and silent movies. Charlie Chaplin, Buster Keaton, Mack Sennett, Harold Lloyd, Harry Langdon, Marie Dressler, W.C. Fields were all able to use any fuel for their creative fires. In later years, an anecdote told by a friend reminded me of these comic geniuses. When he was a young comedian, just beginning in the business, a certain "top banana" chose him to replace an actor who was ill. As the time of his routine came closer, my friend became more and more anxious, and kept pressing the comic for information about what he would be expected to do. Finally, a moment before curtain time, in desperation, he asked again. The older comic looked him in the eye. "Here's what we'll do: you'll talk first, and I'll talk next." No matter what the material, the true comedian will know how to use it!

The readiness of the performer is an important element in commedia. The actor, in addition to knowing his character intimately, must be able to accept a proposed scenario, a mere plot-and-circumstances skeleton, and create. His creation must be original, unpredictable, and balanced. At its best, commedia is a *tour de force* for the actor, limited only by his imagination, his skills, and the ability of his partners to respond, interact, and create with him spontaneously. The commedia actor never works alone. His virtuoso excursions must never proceed from his own ego. There must be a constant awareness of the whole. He must know and understand his partners, balancing and contrasting them, working together with such sensitivity and unity that we are caught up in their game before we know what has happened. Nonsense is more important than sense. No comic prototype is governed by the rational; his responses are always instinctual and must come from a deep understanding of himself as an actor, his character, and his fellow actors and their characters. They are thrown together into a wild jungle of unpredictables – the improvised situation, not in today's sense of being "unrehearsed," but in its original meaning, "all of a sudden." Trust and confidence, based on real, existing skills and knowledge of one another, must be present in a commedia company. You are literally all in it together.

Balance and counterbalance with the partner cannot begin in the brain. We must start, once again, at home: the body. The elementary push-and-pull of the WALK is now explored with the partner. These counterweight exercises with a partner ("Push me/Push you, Pull me/Pull you") train you to move together – up, down, sitting, side-to-side, even flipping in the air – with a common fulcrum. Adjustments must be made for varying sizes and weights. There is never an *ideal* partner. There is always and only *this* partner of the moment. When you have learned to share physical space and contend with gravity together, you are then ready to apply the same principles to your comedy relationships. We always proceed from the non-verbal to the verbal. When we play together verbally, the same sense of balance and response must be present. Using simple, one-syllable words, or a limited list of words, or nonsense syllables, we play together, sharing and contributing to the whole.

Only when partners have explored their relationship thoroughly in the area of physics, verbal response, and recognition are they ready to move on to characterization. Then we must realize that you cannot be a fool to play one. The comic prototype sees nothing funny or unusual in himself. He simply *is*. Indeed, the reactions of his partners and the audience are the strange thing. He is normal. We play games related to this. Two characters in UNUSUAL OUTFITS are seated together at a cafeteria table. Each is certain there is nothing strange about himself. How do they respond to one another? If they are honest and create together, the results will be hilarious to us, natural to them.

Moving from work with a single partner to work with a larger group, the exercises become more complex. We learn to create for one another the '*improvviso*' situation, to accept easily a new reality (no matter how absurd), to respond in character, honestly, inventively, and spontaneously. All advanced exercises in collective spontaneity take a spiral form basic to commedia. Commedia is juggling. Two points are never enough. It is the third point that makes things turn and move, in an engineering sense. (In this respect, commedia is the sister of the circus.) Emphasis is more on nonsense and character, rather than sense and psychology. With these basics firmly established, it is time to examine the mask and its use in commedia.

The mask hides and reveals at the same time. To work with a mask one must be aware of its implications. A mask puts one immediately on a tightrope between poetry and prose. In my classes, I work with two types of mask. The first is the metaphysical, or neutral, mask which, by removing the actor's facial physiognomy, leaves the total being revealed. It is in this "persona" that the actor must discover the mystery of the mask itself, the nakedness and truth of his body behind it, the absorption of the mask into himself, and the projection of himself through the mask. When he accepts the neutral mask and is at ease in it, when he has overcome the terror of losing his face and finally accepts the head as what it is – the last vertebra – then he is ready to begin working with the character masks of commedia. He can begin to receive their messages.

These masks of character are metamorphic. Their life, too, must be discovered and united with the life and visions of the actor. When this unification is successful, magic occurs. Behind any mask lies an entity deeply connected to the personality of the performer. The actor must always bring something fresh and personal to his role. No two Pantalones should be alike. The actor must find his own unique characterization without betraying any of the characteristics of the prototype. It is in this challenge that the joy of performing commedia comes. Having found *his* Pantalone, the actor must then weave it into the fabric of the scenario, carefully balancing, counterbalancing, and responding to his fellow company members in a constant tension-elasticity structure. In Bergsonian terms, that is comedy. Contrast is a must.

The commedia actor has a free body with the mask as a natural extension. But to perform commedia properly, you must also have a concept of the levels of commedia style. *Andare a soggetto*, to go with the subject, is to accept a basic premise and, with your team, create in, around, over, under, and through it. *Commedia a braccia* indicates that the physical activity is measurable "at arm's length": in other words, that the actors adapt their movements and positions precisely but spontaneously (after all, arms are different lengths!). *Commedia all'improvviso* or "all of a sudden" means just that: anything goes (or comes!). The *concetti* (concepts) are strong punch-lines that can be applied at any appropriate place, to summarize, comment on or resolve a scene. And, of course, there are the *lazzi* or bits of comic business, perfected by the actors and taken from their bag of tricks like comedic jewels to amaze and delight us. It is wrong to think of the actors' *lazzi* and *concetti* as mere gimmicks or tricks. The beauty of them is that they grow from the character traits and attitudes. They are never cheap or arbitrary. These excursions into invention were, naturally, intended for the enjoyment of the audience. Between the actor, his partner, and the audience there is always a bond. The *aparte* (aside) is a continuous channel between actor and audience. A mutual response must happen for commedia to "take off." Performing the same play before different audiences is always a totally unique experience.

This fact was brought home to me poignantly when my troupe of young commedia players, the Dell'Arte Troupe, toured a production of Gozzi's *The Green Cockatoo*, a satirical fairy tale filled with magic and transformations – and several commedia characters. We first performed for six people in a barn in a rural area of northern California. We then took it to the Firehouse Theatre in San Francisco, where the audience, mostly young intellectuals, were delighted by the play's comments on intellectual pretensions. Our next performances were at a small theatre in Berkeley, attended mostly by college students. They responded warmly to the elements of fantasy and comic business. We then played the city parks of Berkeley, attracting young people, old people, children, and dogs. The play changed considerably, became broader, more directly involved with the audience, as the audience itself became an '*improvviso*' element, shifting, moving, and responding.

Through the ages, everyone has used commedia for his own purposes, from Molière, who openly proclaimed, "I take my best where I can find it," to Shakespeare, Brecht, and the political street theatre groups of our own time. I do not pretend to have rediscovered commedia as it was in the Renaissance. In fact, that seems to me a shallow and limiting approach to commedia. But a kind of theatre that points out our human frailties and foibles in such an honest, unpretentious way, a theatre in which actors are skilful, perceptive, inventive, united, and generous, seems to me to be much needed today. In a world gone mad, who has more to say to us than the zannis? Well, the Venetians have a proverb, "If they aren't crazy, we don't want them." And commedia, after all, is not a theatrical form; it is a way of life.

> *For some I am an emperor*
> *For some I am a master*
> *But for you, beloved audience,*
> *Your humble servant, ever after.*
> Pulcinella

NOTE

1 The art of maskmaking in leather, lost to us since the Renaissance, was revitalized through the work and research of Amleto Sartori, a well-known Paduan sculptor (1915–62). Although some sixteenth-century Venetian masks survive, there are no records of the techniques used to create them. Working from descriptions of certain tools, a few wooden molds and some notes on contemporary bookbinding procedures, Sartori was able to recapture a lost art. The commedia masks of Sartori are highly individualized creations, molded for the actor, expressing his concept of his character, as well as the traditional facial characteristics of the prototype. With Sartori's death in 1962, his son, Donato, took over his work.

12

THE DELL'ARTE PLAYERS OF BLUE LAKE, CALIFORNIA

Misha Berson

The small town of Blue Lake, California is located in Humboldt County, 300 miles north of San Francisco in the heart of coastal redwood country. It has 1,200 residents, three rowdy bars, and an economy devastated over the years by the decline of the lumber and fishing industries. It is also the home of a very unusual theatre company that, through its year-round school and performances throughout California and the Northwest, is reviving sixteenth- and seventeenth-century style *commedia dell'arte*. They have also won over skeptical townspeople by contributing significantly to the ailing local economy.

The Dell'Arte Players, like their Italian counterparts of several centuries ago, are multi-skilled performers trained as actors, musicians, acrobats and mimes who collectively devise original shows. They sometimes work with stock commedia characters who are akin to Arlecchino, Pantalone, and Il Dottore, but their work is also infused with modern sensibilities and rural cultural/environmental concerns.

The choice of living and working in picturesque but economically depressed Humboldt County was a conscious one for the five longtime core-company members of Dell'Arte. None of them grew up in the region; they hail instead from San Jose, Detroit, Seattle, Paris and Washington, D.C. All have had theatre training and professional experience elsewhere. What drew them to Humboldt was the desire to lead a small-town, rural existence, a fascination with Native American cultures and the natural environment of the region, and a hunger to create theatre indigenous to the rustic area.

The theatrical style of Dell'Arte derives in part from the boisterous, outdoor, commedia, agitprop verve of the San Francisco Mime Troupe – a veteran alternative theatre that Dell'Arte member Joel Weisman had worked with, directing such shows as the Obie-winning *The Dragon Lady's Revenge*. But the influence of traditional commedia on the troupe cannot be underestimated.

Carlo Mazzone-Clementi was the bearer of that tradition. An early partner of Marcel Marceau and a colleague of Jacques Lecoq, Mazzone-Clementi is an expert in mime, mask and commedia from Padua, Italy. In 1957 he emigrated to the United States and began teaching in acting schools around the country. In 1972 he and his wife, Jane Hill, moved to Humboldt County to start a summer theatre and the Dell'Arte School of Mime and Comedy, the only full-time training program of its kind in the United States.

The Qual-a-wa-loo Grand Comedy Festival (*Qual-a-wa-loo* is the Wiyot Indian name for Humboldt Bay) mounted professional productions of Shakespeare and musical comedies, and lasted through the summer of 1976. It also provided the meeting-ground for several artists who would go on to constitute the Dell'Arte Players and (after Mazzone-Clementi's involvement ended) take over management of the Dell'Arte School. During the 1976 Qual-a-wa-loo production of *As You Like It*, performers Joan Schirle and Michael Fields, director Joel Weisman, and scenographer Alain Schons (who had recently come to the USA. from working in France with the Théâtre de l'Aquarium) first worked together. The production foreshadowed the style that would become the Dell'Arte trademark of bawdy, commedia-style physicality in a rural setting. The Forest of Arden was transformed into the forests of Humboldt County, the action was highly physicalized and slapstick, and the actors dressed in local hippie/gypsy/army-surplus fashion and made frequent references to local events and personalities. In 1977, these four artists were joined by several others to create a new piece for a new company, the Dell'Arte Players.

THE LOON'S RAGE

The Loon's Rage, Dell'Arte's first show, was created with the help of a National Endowment for the Arts grant, that was awarded to support a play combining Native American mythological characters with *commedia dell'arte* conventions. As Michael Fields notes, "It was one of those grant 'givens' that will sometimes return to kill you."

The piece was designed by Schons to be performed, Mime Troupe-style, outdoors on a portable stage. It was to be easily tourable, with flats that quickly came apart and two painted backdrops indicating the settings of a redwood forest and the inside of a nuclear power plant.

The Loon's Rage established several themes and stylistic choices that the company has continued to work with. The prominent theme was the natural world pitted against modern technology. The characters in the play were anthropomorphized animals (Crow, Panther, Salmon, Coyote, Antelope) based on animals in Indian legends. The creatures are sick and dying, and they don't know why. After meeting Nova, a worker at the nearby nuclear power plant, they grow curious about the relationship between the plant and their health. The plant is run by Nova's Il Dottore-style scientist father and his Pulcinella-esque assistant, Punch. Crow discovers problems and cover-ups at the plant, but dies from being fed poisoned pellets (echoing the Karen Silkwood case, which was then in the newspapers). A melt-down occurs at the plant, but Loon (a bird character that has the gift of prophesy in Native American folklore) enters to halt it, just barely averting ecological catastrophe.

As in subsequent pieces, the acting in *The Loon's Rage* was both broad and naturalistic, comic and serious. The set was illustrative and functionally comic as well. During the meltdown, for example, a cardboard machine in the nuclear plant spit real water, fire and smoke and eventually appeared to blow up. The actors doubled and tripled in roles, and most wore character masks designed by Schons. Topical and local references were frequent, and the complicated plot accommodated songs like "The Nuclear Rag," musical punctuation on woodwinds and percussion, and *lazzi* (comic bits) laced with slapstick.

One aspect of *The Loon's Rage* was not repeated by Dell'Arte. The script was written by Joel Weisman with two "outside" playwrights, Steve Most and Joan Holden, who writes for the San Francisco Mime Troupe. All subsequent shows were collectively scripted by company members.

Fig. 12.1 Joan Schirle as Scar Tissue, Donald Forrest as Deep Trout in *Intrigue at Ah-Pah* from the Redwood Curtain Trilogy by the Dell'Arte Players Company. (Photo by Michael K. Rothman.)

INTRIGUE AT AH-PAH

After successfully touring *The Loon's Rage* and later a repertory of standard one-acts by Thornton Wilder, Megan Terry and others, the Dell'Arte Players were able to secure enough support (through the federal Comprehensive Education and Training Act and state arts funding) to devise a new show that again blended commedia style with environmental issues. This time they used the Raymond Chandler/Dashiell Hammet "private eye" suspense novel genre to tell their story.

Intrigue at Ah-pah was based on extensive research into a hot local issue. In 1978, federal agents tried to enforce tight fishing regulation on the nearby Klamath river, seriously affecting the livelihood of Urok and Hupa Indians who had been fishing the river for generations. Protests, arrests, violence, and legal battles ensued, with environmentalists charging that the decline of the salmon was not caused by over-fishing but by federally sponsored dams and indiscriminate "clear cutting" of redwood forests.

The company (then comprised of Schirle, Schons, Weisman, Fields, Mara Sabinson, Donald Forrest, and dramaturg Steve Most) created an intricate, swiftly moving comic, suspense plot. In Steve Most's words:

> The plot gets away with a lot, but it has a license: by spoofing Bogart movies it triggers laughs that stories of multiple murders don't always get. The genre gave us a structure for the plot. (Female detective) Scar Tissue had to fall for someone deeply involved in the mess on the river, a male Bacall to her Bogie. There had to be murders, suspects, false leads. Early on, we decided that an Indian was to be the fall guy, set up for someone else's crime. The other characters fell into place: some based on people we know, others invented by the actors who played them, drawing from detective novels and the observation of locals. We held long meetings to air our ideas, unravel the complexities of the story, and move toward a workable scenario.

The play opens with the murder of a federal Fish and Game biologist on the banks of the Klamath, and the plot revolves around the attempts of the tough-talking, soft-hearted lady detective, Scar, to find out who killed him. Much of the intrigue of the piece (which was popular locally and in San Francisco and Los Angeles) was in the comic repartee between the broad, colourful, "local color" characters of evil lodge-owner, private eye, small-town beautician, innocent newsboy, and flower-power hippie, and in the precision physical comedy routines.

In one scene, the newsboy unknowingly ingests a hallucinogenic drug and goes on a stomach-rippling, eye-popping, knee-bending trip. A fish informant named Deep Trout (the actor wore a fish-head mask and a detailed full-body costume complete with fin feet) goes into spawning spasms in mid-spiel. There are stylized karate fights and love scenes, and the actors make frequent role changes behind the richly painted forest and fishing lodge backdrops (the show was designed for both outdoor and indoor performance) at breakneck speed.

The dialogue, like this excerpt from a monologue by Scar Tissue, provided both information and opinion about water politics, and a vivid caricature of the hard-boiled Hammet/Chandler prose style:

> Well, those big boys don't like blackmail, and they don't like publicity. They can get their water legal-like by greasing a few palms and writing a few bills. They have time. They can wait. So they sent their messenger boy with the white shoes and dope-tipped umbrella to deliver the bad news to Pops. "Project terminated." He was in town to close shop, to remove all trace of the project, including the Ah-pah File. So Pops never found out that his whole frantic murder spree was for nothing. And I'll bet somewhere down below Watson is having one hell of a last laugh.

To make sure the audience got the point and understood the environmental issues raised, the actors distributed a National Lawyers Guild "Ah-pah File" pamphlet detailing the legal issues in the actual controversy brewing over Ah-pah Creek (which feeds into the Klamath) before each performance.

WHITEMAN MEETS BIGFOOT

In 1980, after performing at the Venice Biennale, the Dell'Arte Players returned to Blue Lake to begin their next project, a stage version of *Whiteman Meets Bigfoot*. In this case, the scenario was already written and the visual style indicated, because *Whiteman* was closely

Fig. 12.2 Joan Schirle, Donald Forrest and Joel Weisman in the Dell'Arte Players Company production of *Whiteman Meets Bigfoot*. (Photo by Peter Canclini.)

based on the comic book of the same name by California artist Robert Crumb. Crumb's story – popular in the late 1960s as a raunchy saga of suburban angst and a paean to the rediscovery of nature – was about a conservative "white man" taking his wife and two spoiled children on a camping trip in their Winnebago camper. On a hike in the redwoods of northern California, he gets lost and finds himself in a pack of *yetis*, giant ape-like creatures of Indian legend.

In the comic book and the play, the man goes from terror to understanding, and soon falls in love with an amorous female yeti. They engage in a torrid interspecies affair in her enormous nest. Just as he grows fond of his idyllic new life, his beloved yeti is captured by scientists eager to study her. Determined not to return to human civilization or allow his love to be victimized, Whiteman frees the yeti and flees back to the woods with her.

Whiteman Meets Bigfoot was Dell'Arte's most technically ambitious show. The stage picture was much larger than usual – intended to look like the frame of a cartoon – and the work required a theatre with flyspace and wings. The large sets were painted in R. Crumb's style (with his blessings), and setpieces included the suspended yeti's nest and a giant cut-out of a Winnebago camper that moved forward on rollers when an actor "drove" it. A bridge suspended above the action accommodated the meanderings of the narrator, Mr. Natural.

The piece also relied heavily on larger-than-life, exaggerated cartoon modes of movement by actors wearing outrageous costumes. Donald Forrest portrayed the 9-foot yeti by wearing tall stable stilts (which allowed him to stand still, walk, dance, and perform acrobatic feats) and a furry head-to-toe masked body costume. Mr. Natural, a stock R. Crumb holy-man character, had a bald pate, big clownish shoes, and a long white beard; he moved in the long strides Crumb calls "trucking." The scientists, in funny glasses and moustaches, resembled the slapstick, buffoon clowns of *The Loon's Rage*.

The one serious departure from R. Crumb's original comic strip was the ending. The group agreed that a *dénouement* resulting in a retreat to an idealized, utopian wilderness was not consistent with their own views. The show ended instead with bitter, angry remarks by the scratchy-voiced Mr. Natural, suggesting that Whiteman's actions had been futile in the face of encroaching civilization.

Whiteman Meets Bigfoot was retired after a short tour because the company did not have funds to remount it and it was difficult to tour. During its tour of Humboldt County, it became the subject of controversy when protesters picketed a performance in Garberville. They objected to its "immoral and unnatural" content – a man loving an ape – as "an abomination to God."

PERFORMANCE ANXIETY

After reviving and touring *Intrigue at Ah-pah*, in 1981 Dell'Arte was commissioned by the Humboldt County Open Door Clinic to construct a theatre piece about male responsibility for birth control. The company took this unlikely theme as an opportunity to work again with traditional commedia scenarios and characters.

Written collectively by the company (then comprised of designer Schons, director Weisman, and performers Schirle, Forrest and Fields), *Performance Anxiety* is the only original Dell'Arte piece that does not focus on environmental issues but deals instead with private, individual responsibility. It is centered around actors and is about actors.

Fig. 12.3 Donald Forrest, Joan Schirle and Michael Fields in *Performance Anxiety*, Dell'Arte Players, Blue Lake, California. (Photo by Michael K. Rothman.)

The set of the first half of the play-within-a-play is dominated by a traditional Rennaissance *architettura* painted scene, with the houses of commedia characters Isabella and Pantalone in the foreground. At the right is a "backstage" area with a payphone, graffitied walls, and a sandbag weight hanging from the rafters.

The action is a complicated marriage of a traditional commedia love-lust-and-money plot involving Isabella, Pantalone and Arlecchino, with a backstage story of egoistic actors performing the piece at a suburban dinner theatre. In the midst of behind-the-scenes bickering, the actor playing Arlecchino receives a phone call notifying him that a woman he slept with is now pregnant with his baby. Confused and upset – additionally so because he has just been fired from the play – he winds up "accidentally" hanging himself.

Act II returns to the commedia scenario, but with a sudden twist: Danny Arlecchino is impersonating a servant girl to spy on the beauteous Isabella for Pantalone. When lecherous Pantalone enters and the two are left alone, the actor realizes he *has* become a woman. Although he pleads to be left alone, he is chased and impregnated by Pantalone in a wild slapstick scene. He becomes pregnant and has a baby instantaneously, only to be impregnated again and yet again, until he is literally juggling three babies that he cannot put to his breasts all at once. The play ends with a quiet dialogue between Danny Arlecchino and Isabella about sharing responsibility for birth control; there is a return to "reality": Danny lies dead, surrounded by his mourning fellow actors. His death was an accident, just as the baby's conception was an accident.

Though the plot shifts between dream, fantasy and reality, playing and not-playing are not always clearly defined, and the dominant force is the highly acrobatic scene between Arlecchino and Pantalone in the second act. Chases, falls and tumbles abound, and for the "pregnancy," Arlecchino (played by the company's most acrobatic actor, Donald Forrest) uses yoga techniques to expand his stomach and a rippling effect to simulate birth. His skills are used in the precision juggling of baby dolls.

Performance Anxiety was Dell'Arte's latest and most blatant attempt to blend old-style commedia with a contemporary theme, using the lechery and bawdiness familiar in the form to consider a modern sexual theme.

13

THÉÂTRE DU SOLEIL
The Golden Age, First Draft

Christopher D. Kirkland

The Théâtre du Soleil, the gaudy and tumultuous star in a rising constellation of French leftist theatre troupes, emerged early in spring 1975 from eighteen months of work to offer a devoted public some contemporary reflections. *The Golden Age, First Draft,* staged by director Ariane Mnouchkine in three warehouses of an abandoned arsenal in the woods of Vincennes on the eastern outskirts of Paris, has succeeded in moving the group in an entirely different direction from their previous work, such as the unanimously acclaimed *1789*. But the current production, unlike its predecessors, is not offered as a finished product or as a concept fully realized. It is rather a public beginning, a point of departure.

Mnouchkine's troupe began attracting wide attention in 1967 with a production of Arnold Wesker's *The Kitchen*. It has grown increasingly popular with an innovative, pre-Brook production of *A Midsummer Night's Dream,* which was performed in a circus hall; with its step into non-literary, collective creation titled *The Clowns;* and with the satirically caricatured historical spectacles *1789* and *1793*. For the last few years, since *1789*, it has been performing at the broken-windowed, mud-or-dust *Cartoucherie* lot where it rents some 36,000 square feet of warehouse space from the City of Paris. With *The Golden Age, First Draft,* which opened on 10 March, the troupe addresses itself more directly than previously to the issues of social contemporary reality – to investigating the everyday struggles, the events hardly familiar before banalities, which fill newspapers and newscasts, that unite and divide all manner of political groups, and which compel the erratic push and pull of government in France.

Topics for the play's episodes originate in a published chronology of events, dating from the 1973 cholera epidemic in Naples to the December 1974 death of forty-two coal miners in northern France; it includes specific instances of strikes, workers' solidarity, factory occupation, injury and fatality in industry and commerce, prison brutality, military indignity, individual rights, over-crowded low-income housing, price-fixing, government repression, bribery, favoritism, and racism.

The actors approach sociopolitical events and issues with the technique of improvisation and the character-types of the three theatrical styles in which they have been working intensively during the last eighteen months – *commedia dell'arte,* ancient Chinese theatre, and circus.

Episodes develop from talks with workers in factories, mines, hospitals, and schools. Generally, according to members of the company, militants dominate the first hour or two of group sessions with abstractions and opinions. Then the performers get the workers to describe the concrete banalities of how they get up every morning, how they get to work, what they laugh about in the coat rooms. Next, the performers improvise, using the masks, costumes, and make-up of the characters familiar to them, mixing elements from all three styles to represent the concrete details they have picked up in conversation. The current production's final episode comes directly from discussions and improvisations with a committee of workers from the Kodak factory in Vincennes, its setting changed to a construction site. A group of high-school students helped the troupe improvise an opium den scene from traditional Chinese theatre into an episode about family television and drugs. A group of young immigrants participated in the development of an episode relating to a rent strike scandal of a year ago, involving 240 workers housed in 26 rooms of a low-income apartment building, each paying a rent of 80 francs (about $17.75) a month.

For the current production, technical director Guy-Claude François conceived, as he described it in the winter–spring 1975 issue of *Travail Théâtral,* "a free space, without definite architecture, modern but not modernistic; a place where people tell each other stories, a place which prompts people to speak and to listen, a sort of agora, an attractive meeting place with an agreeable environment." He removed a wall that separated the two warehouses to open up a space of about 120 by 150 feet, bisected by a row of eight pillars too expensive to remove. He then brought in earth and concrete by the carload to build up a cruciform ridge about ten feet above the floor, which fell gracefully away in a 30-degree grade towards the corners. It quartered the room into nearly identical amphitheatres. Next, he covered the entire, contoured floor with rough, light-brown carpeting, like a brush doormat in texture and color. Seventy-two loud speakers, which worked off of a 16-track tape deck, were set into the walls. He lined the two peaked ceilings in bright copper, and placed thousands of small light bulbs at 8 to 10-inch intervals along every beam and rafter.

The resplendent, warmly hued space prompts youthful spirits to run up one of the hills and to run, roll, or slide down the other side before the performance begins. Performers change into extravagantly padded costumes and chat in one of the flat corners. A dancer-gymnast limbers up while another actor plays bongo drum rhythms, another props his mirror up against one of the 8-inch pillars to paint his lower face in white, and to line it heavily with a black pencil. Savvy spectators, aware of Mnouchkine's tendency to move her audiences around, try to outguess her by perching along the ridge, from where they can sit to see all of one amphitheatre, and stand to see into the others.

In the adjoining warehouse, about 60 by 150 feet, narrow balconies and symmetrical staircases built of dark-stained wood line two of the walls. Colorful banners hang from the rafters. Costumed actors, most with *commedia dell'arte* half-masks pushed up onto their foreheads, sell fruit, sandwiches, wine, and coffee from a stand.

Soon circus music gives way to Renaissance fanfare. The Prince of Naples, 1720, glowers over his noisy, standing public from one of the wooden balconies. Actors move people from their chosen spots in the larger room to the smaller room, where Harlequin appears in a yellow spotlight on a high stage. In animate mime, he begs the public not to smoke so that they can see what they have paid to see, and not to carry bottles into the other room "because it's we who have to sweep and sweep, and we don't like that." The Prince descends to ask Harlequin about life in the city; sickened by Harlequin's lively account about shopping among the corpses, the Prince sends Harlequin to summon

Mayor Antoine Raspi and his businessman friend Pantalone, the two responsible for allowing infectious ships into the harbor of the pest-ridden city. The Prince orders them to produce a culprit in three days, and, just before the stage manager yells them off stage, they pass the charge on to Harlequin. He happens anachronistically upon an amiable, twentieth-century, Algerian immigrant laborer named Abdullah, who is sailing toward Marseilles on the "Mea Culpa." Harlequin, Raspi, and Pantalone will conspire to blame the pest on Abdullah, ignoring his 250-year removal.

The first scene sets the *commedia dell'arte* style of the performance, and introduces the play's major theme – the struggle of the sub-proletariat at the bottom of hierarchies of strength, profit, and power.

The performers funnel the spectators through double doors into the nearest amphitheatre. Two actors, carrying 250-watt, portable follow-spots, settle among the audience. This area becomes the valley of the sub-proletariat, the setting for the story of Abdullah's arrival, life, and death in France, which is interrupted by trips to the other valleys for indirectly related scenes. Abdullah arrives in Marseilles to admire String the Sailor, a character borrowed directly from ancient Chinese theatre, and to moor the ship with a lively dance of busy arms. A group of actors on the ridge provide the rhythms with bongos, sticks, rattles, gourds, and jangles. Then Max, the customs cop, impersonates a new-horizons, see-the-world American tourist who has lost her baggage. Then Max gets to harassing Abdullah.

The narrator Salouha, with Algerian accent, suggests that the audience move to another setting for another story. "This is the best part of the show," she says, "because the rug is very slippery. Help one another!" The audience struggles up to the ridge and skids down into another valley where a Spanish maid, Bernarda, refuses to serve anything but ham sandwiches to an elegant dinner-party during which a real-estate promoter and a dreamy young architect conspire to blame their fallen building and its 100 fatalities on striking, careless workers. Actors sit at the edge of the playing area to watch their colleagues work; they hiss and comment, jump up to enter the scene through a mimed door, and fall out of character among the other actors in the audience. They raise and lower the masks, designed by Erhard Stiefel, as tournament knights raise and lower their visors between engaging and disengaging.

The spectators then get up and back over to the first valley where imaginary droppings of mimed seagulls and a ring-studded, immigrant conman contribute to the miseries of naive Abdullah, "he who falls into every trap," and who survives by ruse as his first and his last resort. He finally manages to get to sleep – on a shoulder and an ear in a pose borrowed from Grotowski – in an over-crowded workers' dormitory.

Then the spectators move diagonally over the center to watch a rag-faced housewife named Irene through her mimed dinnertime routines. She never takes her eyes from an imaginary television set, which puts her through the whole repertoire of soap-opera sentiments. Her husband, shoe salesman Aime l'Heureux, returns from work. Even as he scorns it, he gets caught up in the show. "These two are really good together," he says to the audience; "too bad you can't see them." A cutie-pie daughter named Mimi arrives from high school to boast of the latest factory strike before she too gets caught up in the TV trance, which continues as a spaghetti dinner gets spilled onto the table and eaten while no one notices. The parents go off to bed; Mimi's boyfriends arrive with pot, which induces a bar-room brawl done in the style of a silent film in slow motion.

Then the spectators move back over the ridge's center to Abdullah's valley where grotesquely bulbous Fat Lou, with an orange beach ball of an Afro, delivers a deliberately gratuitous English lesson and ends it with a feminist twist. Two semi-literate workers dodge searchlights to smear walls with graffiti ("Who wastes? Not us!"), and a husband avoids hearing his wife break the news of yet another pregnancy ("One more word and I'm leaving!" "I'm pregnant." "That's it, I'm leaving!").

Now the movement is to the fourth valley where pushy actors, sometimes polite, sometimes brusque, herd the spectators into a new configuration, filling the flat corner and looking up towards the ridge with the rafter bulbs glowing against the copper ceiling. Here by night on the virgin shore, mouthing the surge and hiss of midnight surf, two young lovers meet, play adolescent games, and undress; the Mayor Dussouille, the real-estate promoter Pantalone, and the catastrophically romantic architect Olivier arrive to chase the lovers away before they can "pollute the beach with fornication."

Finally, the movement is back to Abdullah, who is bribed by the promotion-seeking director of a construction project and his slavish crew chief Max into working on a high scaffold in a fierce wind. Abdullah dances his fall to the thundering chorus of Verdi's "Requiem." Even during the mutely screamed laments of Abdullah's wife, Pantalone interrupts to declare the show over: "We're dragging you through all this muck! You didn't come to hear a story like this." But the others persist. Like messengers in Greek tragedy, they run on stage to call Pantalone's attention to vivid examples of social injustice in every direction: "If you want to see men swimming in their own excrement … ." Pantalone leads his establishment characters up rungs in the wall where they fasten themselves, as the lights dim and the theatre fills with primitive noises.

Neon lights in exterior boxes built around the warehouse windows gradually come up to shine through frosted glass, filling the room with a clear, bluish dawn. It is a second and wholly different triumph of atmospheric lighting in a production continuously dependent on original lighting effects and devices. The audience has risen for sustained and rhythmic applause, but Salouha finally quiets them to eternalize Abdullah in the epilog. She says that Abdullah always falls, that Pantalone always covers up the scandal, that the powerful haven't yet climbed the wall. "But, perhaps, you will begin." The sixteen actors take their calls improvising dance to liberating music, then cavort and gambol over the contoured acreage, waving farewells. We go out into the muddy arsenal lot by night with the sense of setting out on a pre-dawn expedition.

In grand design and in small detail, the production seeks to keep its audience mentally and physically alert. Even the ambiguity of the title compels speculation. Is the Golden Age past, present, or future? Is it the point of view of a sarcastic pessimist or of a sincere optimist? Is 1975 an age of ultimate submission to gold, or the dawn of the long-awaited awakening to the golden rule? Might *First Draft* apply to each of the senses of the title as well as to a transient production?

Likewise, the eight scenes of the production, which vary between twenty and thirty-five minutes, cause the audience to shift constantly. Even during the first scene, in the smaller room, Naples 1720, the action draws the standing audience from one playing area to another. Some 450 people climb and slide between valleys so similar that one begins to look hard for the differences. What's changed? The audience. Spectators resettle in a nearly identical theatre with new neighbors and a changed perspective. It would be approximately 450 times easier to change the minimal props (at most a saw-horse table and three or four chairs). Even in the resettling, the performers unsettle the audience, establishing a front row only to move everyone back or forward a few feet minutes later. One remembers army ditches dug to be refilled; we're in their power. In the middle of the fourth scene, the Narrator proposes "a little trip," dividing the house between an annoyed "Oh, no," and a more tolerant and cheerful "Here-we-go-again." "But where are we going?" the Narrator asks after everyone has begun crawling to their feet. "No, no, this time it's a trip of the imagination. So follow me. But don't budge!" The spectators are uniquely tolerant, initially by disposition and soon by training.

During every scene, the performers who are not "working" whisper, talk shop, and gossip. They also watch the audience and pass around observations, one or two balancing a portable spotlight on their knees to focus it or to bounce the light off the ceiling. The Narrator condescendingly explains theatre conventions: she calls on dancer-gymnast Philippe Hottier; "as you may have noticed, he's the specialist at making scenery when there is none;" "a characteristic of our theatre is that the same actors play different roles, and an Englishman plays a Frenchman, a Frenchman plays a Spaniard;" "To play 3,000 we are three or four."

During this the audience is acutely responsive to the details of technique and effect. This theatrical awareness sets up a political awareness. Devices demand a second and a third thought, thus prompting and exercising the extension of thought.

In an article published in the Socialist Party Weekly *l'Unité,* Mnouchkine wrote: "First Draft ! What insolence! To admit that we're still seeking, that we haven't found everything yet. To share our errors before having disguised them as prejudice. To attack before having protected our flanks. To expose what we have but begun, what little we have yet said, to show that much remains to be said. To show a play for what it is: a moment in the inquiry of theatre in the present tense.

Why not postpone the opening, wait until we're ready and confident? Why not let it ripen some more? Why not continue to dream of our great project without daring to spoil it?"

"What a temptation! Happily, we have to eat!!!"

She began the same article by quoting questions posed by Jacques Copeau (1878–1949): "Are we the representatives of an irreparable past? Are we, on the contrary, heralds of a future barely visible at the extreme limit of a declining era?" Mnouchkine rejected the death-wish nostalgia of the first question, and chose to respond affirmatively to the second by using the theatre as a tool to tell the story of our times, " … to give our complex and glutted world a clear and nourishing representation."

She also quoted Copeau's notions about the way toward "a theatre of our times": "I think more than ever that we will have to break the existing mold, and return first to primitive forms, like the fixed character forms in which the characters are all." Although Copeau was scarcely familiar to the company during most of its work ("You know, I don't have any background in theoretical theatre," stated Mnouchkine), he has become a frequently cited reference since last fall, when Editions Gallimard published *Appels,* the first of several volumes entitled *Registres* collecting Copeau's notes, letters, and essays. The company discovered with ambivalent surprise, as Mnouchkine read them selections, how precisely Copeau, in 1916 and '17, had anticipated their work.

In Limon in 1916, Copeau wrote about improvisations:

It is an art which I don't know, and I am going to look into its history. But I see, I feel, I understand that this art must be restored, reborn, revised; that it alone will bring a living theatre – the plays of players. Leave literature … . Create a fraternity of players … living, working, playing together … creating together, inventing together their games, drawing them from themselves and from others. What little I have done leads me there … . Our goal is to create a new theatre of improvisation, with the types and subjects of our times.

In New York in 1917, in his sixth Little Theatre conference, he proposed the clearing of the stage for collaboration with the players on "The complete creation … of an entirely new, modern theatre, improvised, with the character types drawn from contemporary society. A French farce of the twentieth century."

But ten years later, in the absence of theatrical men of genius the likes of Aeschylus, Shakespeare, and Molière, Copeau called for directors with "a sincerity made of intelligence and humility."

> A director's role [he wrote in 1926] is not to have ideas, but to understand and render those of the author … . He doesn't invent them, he rediscovers them … . I think a well conceived play prescribes one, and only one, staging: that which is written in the text of the author, like notes on a musical stave.

Lack of a written text has been debated as both the main strength and the main weakness of *The Golden Age, First Draft*. Several critics have concluded their reviews by wishing the Théâtre du Soleil a writer. But the performers in this instance have worked as corporal playwrights, substituting flesh and blood improvisation for pen and paper. They have been wary of the blindness of cliche and caricature. They have tried to avoid psychology and realism. "We now possess the technique," Mnouchkine commented, "which permits us to play with imaginary objects."

The group seeks not to portray grand events in their populist spectacles, but people. Slender and young, they most naturally portray characters who are fat and old and who speak in cartoon-character voices. They work from the basic theme of corporate director Pantalone versus immigrant laborer Abdullah. They have given up history for social reality. They stick to problems within a practical range, focusing exclusively on national problems, exposing areas where theatrical insight and power might have a fundamentally constructive effect. The present draft contains no reference, for example, to world famine or war. Above all, in every way they can devise, they try to demystify theatre. According to a program note by Catherine Mounier, a scriptwriter who has been following their work, they wish "to advance as much as possible the role of theatre [as] an encouragement for changing the conditions in which we live."

The Théâtre du Soleil currently gets an annual government subsidy of one million francs (about $220,000). They oppose the "supersubsidy" which underwrites France's National Théâtres. They are trying to persuade the government to disclose who in the arts gets what and why. Members of the company currently earn 1,750 francs (just under $400) a month. During ten of the eighteen months between productions they were on unemployment compensation of about 800 francs (about $175) monthly, and working alternate days outside of the company to support themselves.

Last year, to help the company, some 5,000 people bought tickets, sometimes for five or ten times the face value, for the next production. A hundred artists also sold their paintings and sculptures, contributing the proceeds.

The theatrical manifestation of 21 June 1973 was initiated by the Théâtre du Soleil in response to the now mythical remark by Minister of Culture Maurice Druon about groups who carry "a collection plate in one hand and a Molotov cocktail in the other." Some forty theatre companies organized a full dress cortege led by thirty, black veiled drums, with three truck-mounted orchestras playing dirges, a hearse drawn by four horses, and 10,000 mourning demonstrators all dressed in black and with black gags tied over their mouths. Although the organizers asked participating political parties not to carry identifying banners, they brought them anyway. After a few moments of tension, all the parties marched with their banners hidden but ready, behind a single banner quoting Diderot: "Awake! This nation is falling into a sweet sleep, but it is the sleep of death!" The procession marched from the Bastille to the Place de la Nation, where they buried Free Speech. At the final moment, the political parties simultaneously raised their standards. After the demonstration several avant-garde theatre groups attacked the Théâtre du Soleil for mixing politics with theatre *outside* the theatre.

Some in the group want to define current political issues more precisely. For them, *The Golden Age* is a much more political piece than *1793*. Virtually everyone in the company of forty is a leftist: two belong to the Communist Party, three are Trotskyists, one is an Anarchist, and two are Christians, though leftist Christians. They begin with banalities. They do not politicize them intentionally, yet everything they do is political. What they say gets across by how they say it, and by the rapport they establish with their audience. Essentially, in the final analysis, the Théâtre du Soleil is trying to make contemporary issues clear, amusing, and grand.

14

WORDLESS SPEECH

Dario Fo

Translated by Joe Farrell

I would like to begin with a discussion of *grammelot* and this will provide a means of dealing with the history of *commedia dell'arte*, and also with a very special problem – the problem of language and its application in practice.

I will give a demonstration of *grammelot*, using a piece from the classical repertoire to show how it should be done. *Grammelot* is a term of French origin, coined by commedia players, and the word itself is devoid of meaning. It refers to a babel of sounds which, nonetheless, manage to convey the sense of a speech. *Grammelot* indicates the onomatopoeic flow of a speech, articulated without rhyme or reason, but capable of transmitting, with the aid of particular gestures, rhythms and sounds, an entire, rounded speech.

Granted this standpoint, it is possible to improvise or articulate *grammelots* of all kinds in the most diverse lexical registers. The prime form of *grammelot* is that devised by the incredible imagination of children, when they believe their babbling (which among themselves they understand perfectly) is ordinary speech. I once overheard a Neapolitan and an English child chattering away to each other, and I noticed that neither of them hesitated a moment. For communication, they did not use their own languages, but another, invented one – a *grammelot*. The Neapolitan pretended to speak in English, and the English child pretended to speak Southern Italian. They understood each other perfectly. With the help of gestures, tones and infant prattle, they had constructed a code of their own.

As for ourselves, we can, after a minimum of application, of study and practice, speak all the *grammelots*, be they Spanish, French, German or English. I will have a few technical suggestions to make, but in this context it is impossible to lay down or endorse rules. The only way to proceed is by intuition and by an almost subterranean knowledge, for in this field no definite, comprehensive method can be prescribed. However, by observation you'll get the idea.

Let's take as an example Aesop's fable of the crow and the eagle, which many of you will know. First frame: the eagle soars through the skies in huge circles, when, second frame, all of a sudden, it notices a lamb, slightly lamed, a short distance from the rest of the flock. Third frame: it circles round, swoops down, seizes the lamb in its claws and carries it off. Fourth frame: the shepherd comes running up, shouting at the top of his voice, throwing stones; the dog barks but it makes no difference, for by now the eagle has flown off. Fifth frame: a crow perched on the branch of a tree. "Ha! ha!" it screeches in excitement. "I never knew it was as easy as that to snatch a lamb. All you have to do is swoop down on it! What's stopping me doing the same? I'm as black as the eagle, I've got claws too and they're every bit as strong, my wings are nearly as big as hers and I can circle and swoop just like her."

No sooner said than done. Sixth frame: the crow starts circling and is about to swoop down on a lamb standing on its own, as he had seen the eagle do, when he espies a flock of sheep feeding a little further on. "What a brainless fool that eagle was! With all these fat sheep around, what's the point of going for a mangy lamb? No flies on me. I'm going for the biggest, juiciest sheep of them all, so that in one go I'll have enough to keep me going for the rest of the week." He swoops down, sinks his talons into the sheep's fleece, only to discover to his dismay that making off with it is harder than it looked. At that moment he hears the shepherd yell out and the dog bark. In terror he flaps his wings wildly but cannot raise the beast, nor can he even disentangle himself from the animal's hide. He pulls and tugs but all to no avail. It is too late. The shepherd arrives on the scene, strikes him a blow with his wooden club, the dog pounces on him, seizes him by the neck and throttles him. Moral: black feathers, a firm beak and a wide wing-span are not enough. If your trade is lamb-snatching, you have to be born an eagle. A further moral is this: the real problem is not getting hold of your prey – making a getaway without getting a knock on the head is. So, make do with the underfed lamb and leave the succulent sheep for the day when you have a jet engine attached to your hindquarters. This variant does not feature in Aesop.

Let's now consider how one would set about recounting in *grammelot* the parable in question. I am doing it off the cuff, so improvisation is of the essence. At this point, I can reveal some details of method. To perform a narrative in *grammelot*, it is of decisive importance to have at your disposal a repertoire of the most familiar tonal and sound stereotypes of a language, and to establish clearly the rhythms and cadences of the language to which you wish to refer. It may be that we wish to use a pseudo-Sicilian–Calabrian dialect and to construct a *grammelot* on the basis of that sequence of sounds. What are the fixed or decisive points that need to be established to make this possible? First and foremost, it is important to inform the audience of the subject that will be discussed, as I have just done, then it is vital to elaborate, through sounds and gestures, the key elements that characterize the crow and the eagle. Obviously I will only be able to hint at the dialogues, allow the audience to guess their nature, rather than set them out in their entirety. The greater the simplicity and clarity of the gestures which accompany the *grammelot,* the greater the possibility of comprehension. To recapitulate: onomatopoeic sounds, clear and clean gestures, the correct timbre, rhythm, coordination and above all a firm grasp of the techniques of summary.

His performance begins with small gestures and the conversational tone, but increases in rhythm and incisiveness. He conveys stage directions in 'throwaway' lines of babble. He widens out the gestures, passing rapidly from one frame to the next. He accelerates the dramatic pace by raising the tone of voice and the cadences.

Every so often, in the course of the delivery, I was careful to throw in a couple of easily recognizable terms to assist the listeners. Which words did I pronounce clearly, even if with some distortion? Eagle, shepherd, crow, and then, with the aid of gestures, I picked out certain verbs like howl, bark, run. The key to the whole exercise resides in that connection with one decisive, specific word that we have agreed on together. "The eagle circles in the skies," or else "the dog barks and growls" – these are images that must be conveyed clearly and precisely. This is the key phase of exposition in the onomatopoeic procedure that is *grammelot.*

Another important means of communication is the correct use of gesture. When portraying the flight of the bird, when attempting to reconstruct the efforts of the crow to rise from the animal's back, I must stand side-on towards the audience in the stalls, because it is vital to present the exertions of the subject as it beats its wings, and this is more evident when my body is entirely visible, in silhouette, rather than when it is turned directly towards the audience. I could perform the same scene facing the audience, but the results would be substantially different.

The positions of major impact should be repeated, using the identical image on the occasions that are decisive for one of the variations of the theme. To explain: first frame – the eagle: I take up position side-on, lean forward, wave my arms, spin round as though about to soar off. Second frame – the crow: the important thing is to repeat everything in the same way, but bringing out the clumsiness of the operation. In the first case, the spectator will be invited to note the ease with which the eagle takes off and flies through the skies with the lamb in its claws, whereas on the second occasion he will witness the bungling efforts of the crow as, all ungainly and maladroit, he struggles to extricate himself from the sheep's fleece. The repetition of the terms of the action in both cases must be, if it is to work, meticulous, almost as though the one were overlaid on the other. This focus on a few central points conveyed by stereotypes and clear variants constitutes one of the techniques used in the narratives recounted on Greek and Etruscan vases, as well as in Giotto's frescoes for his sequences of images on the life of St Francis or of Jesus – sequences which some people consider the finest cartoon strips in the history of art. Similarly, the sequence I have just executed could be easily translated into comic strips.

In this context, one other observation may be of some value. Many people will have gone to see an opera performed in a foreign language, and will have been surprised to discover that they could follow much of what was going on, and that at certain moments the whole thing was absolutely clear. Plainly gestures, tone, rhythms and, above all, simplicity all play a part in ensuring that the foreign language does not become an overwhelming obstacle, but of itself that is insufficient as an explanation. It is impossible not to become aware of something subterranean or magical which goads the brain to grasp, by a kind of instinct, matters that are not completely and clearly expressed. Who has not had the experience of being dimly aware of acquiring, over a period of time, a number of vague linguistic notions, with variants that stretch towards infinity? The hundreds of tales stored in our minds, from childhood nursery rhymes to stories garnered from cinema, from theatre, from cartoon strips, from television all contribute to enabling the brain to make sense of a new story, even when recounted without intelligible words.

15

PLAYING WITH THE PAST
Visitation and illusion in the mask theatre of Bali

John Emigh

What follows is a detailed account of a single performance of *topeng pajegan* performed by I Nyoman Kakul in the village of Tusan, Bali, on 6 February 1975. *Topeng* is a popular form of masked theatre in Bali, and *topeng pajegan* an old and particularly demanding version of that form, in which one man portrays all of the characters – dancing, telling stories, making jokes, and performing rituals.

When we met in January 1975, Kakul checked a calendar, found it to be a particularly propitious hour to begin study, gave me my first lesson, and invited me to live in his family compound for the next several months while I studied masked dance. In the months that followed, as I watched Kakul teach and perform, daily had him wrench my resistant body into something approximating the proper shapes for Balinese dance, and met with other performers and mask makers on the island, I came to understand *topeng* as a form that mediated between rituals of ancestral visitation I had recently seen in New Guinea and the theatre of character and illusion that I had studied in the west. I also grew to have a great respect and liking for the form itself and for the men who practice it.

Kakul had a stroke soon after I left Bali. He no longer performs. I hope that, along with its other purposes, this account will serve as a testament to his artistry.

PERFORMANCE AND OCCASION: THE CLUSTERING OF EVENTS

Topeng is usually performed as part of the festivities accompanying a wedding. a crema-tion, or an *odalan* – a yearly occasion when the gods come down to their appropriate temple shrines. Sometimes the performers will be drawn from the villagers themselves. At other times a specialist will be hired from outside the village. In February 1975 at Tusan, Kakul was hired to perform *topeng pajegan* as a part of the ceremonies leading up to the cremation of a *brahmana* (high-caste priest). Kakul himself is a *sudra* or *jaba* – born outside the caste system of privileged status. As usual, Kakul travelled to his work by public conveyance, his baskets of *topeng* masks and costumes competing for space with the chickens and goods that other passengers were bringing to market. As the bus approached Tusan, the road wound around a bend in the River Unda. On one side were green hills and a huge gnarled banyon tree that marked the entrance to the village. On the other side, across the river, a vista of terraced rice fields stretched out toward the sea. A parade of villagers, dressed in brilliant reds and greens and yellows, with white cloths tied around their heads, came flooding out onto the road from the village. The cremation itself would not be held for three days, but already much of the village life was given over to the activities surrounding this event; the sense of holiday contrasted sharply with the mundane world of the bus and its passengers. Many of the villagers were carrying brightly colored gilded umbrellas. Others wore striking small gongs of different sizes to create a joyful interplay of pitches and rhythms. Rice cake offerings of pink and yellow and white were piled high on silver trays perched on the heads of several of the women. As the bus stopped, Kakul opened his eyes and reached for a basket of masks.

By the time the baskets of masks and costumes had been carried to a central courtyard, the procession was returning. The rice offerings were set down. Kakul was greeted as visitor, guest, and hired expert. The manner of greeting was determined by caste and conditioned by his renown as an 'entertainer.' A group of priests sat in a pavilion – laughing, trading stories, chewing beetle nut. They greeted Kakul with enthusiasm and he returned their greetings, maintaining the extreme attitude of respectfulness that befits a *jaba* in the company of *brahmana* priests. This behavior was in marked contrast to the demeanor he exhibited a short time later apart from the priests, at a huge feast of turtle meat and hotly spiced rice. Here Kakul was animated and filled with expressive energy – an extraordinary storyteller set down among friends.

Before the feast had finished, perhaps a hundred village men poured into the center of the village in answer to the sound of beaten wooden gongs, or *kulkuls*, and took up a huge structure of thick, crossed bamboo trunks that supported an enormous, larger-than-life image of a white cow, decked with gilded embellishments. This figure would become the burning sarcophagus of the deceased *brahmana* in the cremation to come. A strident and boisterous gong ensemble formed and the cow was borne aloft by the villagers. The entire structure was spun about in the main square and then carried at a breakneck pace down the dirt road, accompanied by gongs and a cacaphony of shouts and laughter.

This clustering of activities is typical of the occasions when *topeng* is performed. Processions, feasting, beating of gongs, shouts and laughter are deliberately overlapped, creating an event of great density. While the particular events were appropriate for a cremation, a similar overlapping would precede a wedding or *odalan*.

A Balinese actor prepares

As the villagers returned up the road, sweating under the burden of the white cow, Kakul moved to a relatively isolated area and began preparations for his performance. An offering had been prepared for his use. Standing over the offering, he spoke formulaic mantras in Javanized Sanskrit, invoking earth, air, heavenly ether, and the nine manifestations of the Hindu godhead to bless his actions as performer. He did not make any effort to hide this ritual of preparation; neither did he make any effort to display it. The mantras were spoken quietly, in plain view, away from the main areas of activity. While the mantras concentrated Kakul's energies on the performance to come, the use of Sanskrit placed him in touch with a traditional path of access to a divine world. In employing the language of the *brahmana* priests. Kakul stepped out of the vernacular and, in so doing, stepped outside of the caste-based linguistic conventions that would define him as a *sudra* in the social structuring of Balinese life. By using the language of the priests and of the distant past, he began to assume the position of a mediator between history and contemporary realities – a role in which the day-to-day social obligations and caste-based rules of etiquette could be suspended.

Following the speaking of these mantras. Kakul headed for the performance area. A curtain had been set up in a large courtyard, and a temporary structure of woven mats was set behind the curtain to provide a changing room. There, behind the curtain, Kakul changed into his *topeng* costume, with help from an assistant. This is an elaborate procedure. The *topeng* performer wears only one costume for all of the characters that he portrays; only the masks and headdresses change. Composed of many layers, the costume is hot, uncomfortable, and spectacular. Over white pants and a flowing white cloth that falls between the legs, a brilliant assortment of bands, cloaks, and tabards are arrayed. The green, red, blue, purple, and black expanses of material are all embellished with gold ornamentation, while fringe drips from the tabards and glittering sequins dot leggings, wristlets and collars. At last, a ceremonial sword, or *keris*, is wrenched into position, its handle poised over the dancer's right shoulder and its sheathed blade forcing the whole costume to billow out to the left.

This costume is unlike the ordinary dress of the Balinese. Although *topeng* stories are drawn from chronicles detailing ancient wars and the dance vocabulary has its roots in the martial arts of the Indonesian archipelago, the relationship of the costume to the court or military dress of the fourteenth and fifteenth centuries is obscure. The costume is designed to evoke and exalt that period, not duplicate it. It belongs to the marginal performance time between the past and the future.

His costume in place, Kakul then turned to the unopened basket of masks and spoke the following words:

> *Om, honored grandfather,*
> *Om, honored grandmother,*
> *Please wake up in order to dance.*

He knocked on the basket three times, then opened the basket and arrayed the masks in the order they would be used. After the performance, upon closing the basket, he would speak to the masks once more, give them an offering, again calling them "honored grandfather" and "honored grandmother," and bid them return to their "heavenly homes." Using a flower, Kakul sprinkled "holy water" onto the masks and onto his own face. He then held a burning stick of sandalwood incense up to the nostrils of the masks, breathed in the incense himself, and spoke further mantras in Javanized Sanskrit, asking divine blessing for his performance. The flower is emblematic of Siwa, the water of Visnu, and the burning incense of Brahma. The holding of the incense up to the masks is strikingly similar to the "smoking" of a trance dancer.

There is a long and still vital tradition of trancing and spirit visitation evident in Balinese theatre and life. In deep trance, untutored spirit mediums are said to speak in ancestral languages and transformed voices, prescribing ways to propitiate neglected spiritual entities. Pre-adolescent girls in trance, *sanghyang dedari*, perform dances they have never rehearsed, in unison, their eyes closed. In the small village of Trunyan, a pre-Hindu enclave in Bali, a set of masks may be found bearing a remarkable similarity to ancestral *tubuan* masks of New Guinea, complete with a costume made of padandus leaf hoops. As in the New Guinea dances of ancestral visitation, the *berutuk* mask seems to function as a conduit for visiting spirits. The existence of the *berutuk* ceremonies may point to a Papuan underlay in Balinese culture. Both the *sanghyang dedari* dances and the *berutuk* ceremonies can be traced to pro-Hindu practices, antedating the influence of the Javanese courts on Balinese life and theatre. But the Bali Hindu religion has embraced this tradition of visitation.

At the *odalan* ceremonies that often provide the occasion for *topeng* performances, gods and ancestral spirits are called down to visit their shrines, thus activating a temple. Called forth by the same sandalwood incense used to "smoke" trance dancers and mediums and to prepare the *topeng pajegan* dancer and his masks, these ancestral spirits are also depicted as leaving from their "holy mountain," Gunung Agung, the volcano that dominates the Balinese horizon – providing a fixed point for the Balinese sense of direction as well as a home for both the Hindu deities and the ancestral host from Majapahit. Majapahit was a feudal Hindu empire of East Java from the twelfth to the fifteenth centuries. Most Balinese trace their ancestry from Majapahit – its chronicles are very important in the *topeng* repertory. The entrance of the *topeng* dancer is always made from the direction of Gunung Agung, and it is here that the *topeng* masks may be thought to have a "heavenly home." The brilliant-colored "fiery raiments" of the ancestral host, along with their sportiveness and love of display, remind one of nothing else in Bali so much as the *topeng* performer. Indeed, the Balinese word for an actor's "presence" is "*taksu*" – the same word used for the ancestral spirits. *Topeng* draws from the tradition of visitation – but in *topeng* the tradition is theatricalized. The *topeng* dancer does not show any evidence of performing in a trance.

The *topeng* actor seeks inspiration, not possession. But his approach to characterization through the mask is informed and supported by the tradition of visitation. Occasionally, when I would bring a new mask home, Kakul would take hold of it with his right hand, supporting it on his palm from behind so that it was fully visible to him. He would turn it first one way, then another, and make it look up and down. He would play with the movement, adjusting the speed and the sharpness of definition, until he was satisfied that he had found how the mask moved best; how *it* wanted to move. Only then would he put it on his face and begin to move his body, bringing the mask to life, making an amalgam of mask and movement that, for lack of a better word, can be called character. Always, his words would be about the demands of the mask. When he liked a mask, he would say, "This one lives." When he didn't like a mask, he would disparage it as having no life in it. This method of seeking out the will of the mask is typical of *topeng* performers.

Unlike the *sanghyang dedari* dancer, the *topeng* performer first learns dances by rote, his body being pushed and pulled into the proper shapes by his guru. Bit by bit, by imitation and by direct manipulation of his limbs, he assimilates the dance vocabulary he will need to perform a range of masked characters. The masks themselves are not used at all at this stage of the training. Yet, to my surprise, when I was studying with Kakul, he would repeatedly criticize my facial expressions as I grimaced while awkwardly trying to make my feet, arms, and body work together in excruciatingly unfamiliar ways. The mask was not a disguise. If the face of the actor behind the mask did not register the character of the figure dancing, the body would move wrong, and the mask would be denied its "life."

After I left Bali, W. S. Rendra, the Javanese poet, playwright, and director, told me of the way his grandfather prepared to perform with a new mask. I don't know if this exact procedure has been followed in Bali, but the procedure Rendra describes is entirely in keeping with what I know about attitudes towards masks in Bali. When Rendra's grandfather acquired a new mask, he, like Kakul, would take it in his hand and turn it this way and that, trying to sense the spirit suggested by the mask – its life. He then placed the mask on his bed, by his head. As he slept, he purposefully interjected the imagined spirit of the mask into his dreams. In these controlled dreams, Rendra's grandfather asked the spirit of the mask to appear as a witness to important events drawn from his waking life. Working backwards in time, he finally dreamt his own birth. In that dream, the embodied spirit of the mask took the "brother" placenta in his hands. After this dream, the dancer was considered able to let the spirit of the mask enter his body; and, through his body, the life of the mask was able to find expression, animating dance movements previously learned by rote. The dancer was not possessed; but his behavior was transformed.

INTRODUCTORY DANCES: THE SHAKING OF THE CURTAIN AND THE ENTRANCE OF THE ANCESTOR

As Kakul arranges his masks in the order they will be used, the *gamelan* orchestra begins to play. Brightly, quickly, gaily, wooden hammers fall on the bronze keys of the metallaphones with perfect and seemingly effortless precision, forming intricate interlocking patterns that are embellished by the striking of several small bronze pots and the playing of sweet-voiced flutes, marked by the regular sounding of a large gong, and urged on by the rapid play of drums. Attracted by the music, the audience has begun to arrange itself in a large oval in the courtyard. The orchestra is at one of the small ends of this oval; the decorated curtain that hides Kakul's preparations is at the other. At either side of the curtain, gilded ceremonial umbrellas have been stuck into the ground. There is no other "scenery," no further isolation of the dancing space from the space outlined by the audience.

Children gather first, sitting cross-legged or stretching out on the ground, their faces bright and expectant. The performance had been "scheduled" to begin at four o'clock. It is now seven o'clock and pressure lamps are being stoked and hung overhead to provide illumination as the daylight dwindles. No one seems to mind. Things happen as they are ready on ceremonial occasions, or when the time is propitious. Clock time is regarded as a relatively unimportant convention on these occasions and has little to do with when things begin or end. Gradually, adults begin to fill in behind the children forming several more or less attentive "rows" of people sitting cross-legged, squatting, and standing, while others look casually on from a distance. Casual banter blends with the music.

Behind the curtain, arrayed in his colorful and gilded assortment of tabards and cloaks, his *keris* handle poised over his right shoulder and his costume billowing out behind him, Kakul makes a final check of the masks to be used – an extraordinary assortment of kings, beasts, heroes, rogues, and buffoons. He takes the smiling, red mask of a proud *patih* (prime minister), I Gusti Ngurah Lepang, in his hand, regards it for a second, then sets it in place. A partial wig is slipped on so that the black hair falls to Kakul's shoulders and an elaborately carved and gilded leather headdress, studded with flowers and sticks of burning incense, is placed over what remains of Kakul's grey hair. Leaves are fixed along the sides of the mask, blurring the dividing lines between mask and face. Kakul sets himself in position for his entrance. A guttural sound emerges from his throat. One hand gives a quick shake to the curtain, while the other makes last minute adjustments. Signalled by the lead drummer, the *gamelan* starts to play the 8-beat, cyclical melody of *baris gilak*, traditionally associated with the dancing of warriors. Kakul shakes the curtain harder. A rush of sound from a set of over-lapped small cymbals attends its movement. Again the curtain shakes, more violently this time; again the shaking of the curtain is accompanied by a rush of percussive sound, bringing to mind the auspicious shaking of the world that accompanies the coming of the ancestral host in invocatory songs used in temple ceremonies.

Kakul parts the curtain in the middle and, as the red-faced *patih*, enters into the space defined by the expectant audience. His head makes small, sharp and sudden movements.

111

His legs are bent, the feet set wide apart and firmly planted on the earth in a position derived from martial arts. The fingers move quickly in multiples of the musical pulse, as though they are antennae testing the air of an unfamiliar world. The warrior alertly scans the new space, his hands elegantly moving up to the gilded lacework helmet as he glances about him. Ominously, perhaps suspiciously, with a sense of great strength and consummate control, he moves forward. The walk is extremely "unnatural." The body seems coiled and tense. The feet pivot out on each step, maintaining balance and readiness. The hands sculpt the air in graceful, smooth lines. Suddenly, the *patih* focuses his attention on a ceremonial umbrella. With a quick cross-step, he moves towards the umbrella and raises up on one foot, remaining poised in the air as the orchestra dramatically halts for two beats. Kakul seems to be immense. The music resumes and Kakul lifts his gilded cloak in a display of grandeur and pride. He walks more quickly now, claiming the oval as his own, dominating the space, his rapid moving fingers still testing the air. Occasionally, he will suddenly shift focus and react to an unseen enemy. Or is he reacting to the presence of the audience?

Kakul has never danced with this orchestra before. Still cymbals and drums seem to extend the movement of his body into sound, creating an experience of synesthesia in which sound and movement are one. A small, flashing movement of a knee or elbow signals Kakul's intentions to the lead drummer and the drummer signals the rest of the orchestra in turn by a rhythmic code. As Kakul suddenly pivots full around and stops in a pose of arrested motion, the full *gamelan* once more stops with him. Eventually, the space claimed, the display completed, the proud *patih* disappears through the split curtain and it closes behind him.

Behind the curtain, Kakul takes off the mask and headdress of the *patih* and takes up another mask, This mask is tinged an odd greenish-blue and features plump cheeks and a mischievous grin. It has a distinctly comic cast and belongs to Pasung Grisgris, a *patih* who once in fourteenth-century Bali grafted a pig's head onto his King's body. The new mask in place and another headdress set above it, Kakul draws up a chair to the curtain, takes the folds that form the opening in his hand, and gives them a shake. Again, the cymbals and drums accompany this motion with a rush of sound. The *gamelan* is playing another variation of *beris gilak*, the warrior's tune. After teasing the audience by playing with the curtain, Kakul throws it open and reveals the mischievous *patih* perched on top of the chair.

The gestures that he makes now are quite different in effect from those of the proud red-faced *patih*. Rather than dominating the space with the alertness of a threatened warrior, he plays with the dynamics of the performance situation, openly toying with the drummer, daring him to follow his rapid gestures, teasing the musicians and the audience, and occasionally even punctuating the *gamelan*'s music with a scabrous gesture. The dance follows the general outlines of the previous display, embellishing the same basic dance vocabulary, but the tone is lighter, more playful, with a touch of parody. The audience responds to the playful antics of Pasung Grisgris with howls of delighted laughter. His antics completed, Pasung Grisgris, too, returns to the unseen world behind the curtain that opens, lets him through, and swallows him up again.

The *gamelan* changes melodies. This time the sound is gentler, not so insistent, or manic, or forceful; there is an almost seamless 32-beat cycle marked by two gong strokes. Kakul takes up the mask of an old man and regards it for a moment. This is the only one of his masks that he himself carved. He fixes the mask on his face and sets a flowing mane of white hair upon his head. The character is I Gusti Dauh Bale Agung, aged minister of the Royal Court of Gelgel in fifteenth-century Bali. The curtain shaking is again repeated, as it will be for each new character. This time, though, the shaking is less vigorous and Kakul parts the curtain to reveal himself as an old man sitting on a chair, surveying a new space, taking in the audience, hearing the music, adjusting his costume, and gathering energy for his dance. First one hand, then the other begins tentatively to move to the gentle music. Gradually, energy and confidence seem to return to the aged courtier and he takes a standing position. After further adjustments, the sight of the ceremonial umbrellas seem to awaken a sense of pride in battles waged long ago and lodged in an old warrior's memory of his past.

The old man begins to dance, slowly at first, then faster and faster. The music keeps pace and grows louder as the aged dancer grows more and more energetic, finally overextending himself, carried away in his proud enthusiasm. A series of rapid turns leaves him off-balance and he stumbles toward the audience, barely managing to stop himself from falling into its midst. The audience roars with laughter. Slowly, the ancient courtier collects himself, breathing slowly. He reaches out to shake the hand of a small child who is looking up at him with an enraptured smile. He seems about to resume his dancing, but instead reaches suddenly up to his flowing mane of hair and grabs hold of an imaginary head louse. He looks at it and the audience laughs. He pinches the imaginary pest and tosses it in the direction of the delighted audience. Twice more, he hears the music playing and starts to resume his dance. Each time he reaches instead for lice – once on his leg, another time on the back of his neck. Finally, he shakes off these distractions and begins to dance. He is more careful this time and there are no more stunning turns, but he manages to recapture a sense of human dignity and authority before exiting through the curtain. The obligatory set of introductory dances, or *pengelembar*, is over. No words have been spoken and none of the characters portrayed will reappear. But a world has been introduced, and a range of human response demonstrated. Perhaps a third of the performance time has elapsed.

Accompanied by an elaborate interplay of movement and sound, the *pengelembar* characters enter through the curtain from the sacred direction of Gunung Agung and return in that direction after their dances are over. Behind the curtain lies the abode of the gods and the ancestors. In front of the curtain is a neutral space created from unadorned Balinese earth and demarcated by a ring of spectators. As Kakul enters from the direction of the ancestors as the proud *patih*, I Gusti Ngurah Lepang, his brilliant costume, his mastery of a special vocabulary of movement, and his concentrated energy set him apart. The audience regards him as extraordinary, but the hypersensitive, abrupt, and prideful display of the *patih* may indicate that the world of the audience is as challenging to him as his world is to them. A distance is established between a character emerging from a world dominated by the ways of the past and the audience living and watching in the present. The actor moves as a character from the world of the past into the world of the present in a sort of foray across boundaries of time and association.

The pattern is that of a rite of visitation, but the playing out of this pattern has been theatricalized. The audience knows that behind the curtain lies not only a sacred mountain where gods and ancestors dwell, but Kakul's basket of masks and changing table. Kakul himself is not a man entranced or possessed, but a performer in triumphant control of his actions, choosing to portray first one character, then another, adjusting his costume, signalling to an unfamiliar orchestra his intentions as a dancer, determining the dynamics of the performance.

The first dance uses the esthetics of ancestral visitation to establish a division between the world of the past and the present. The next dance plays with that sense of division. Pasung Grisgris's teasing and playing with the orchestra and audience is as direct and immediate as it is mischievous. As the boundaries between worlds are violated, laughter occurs. The third character presented in the *pengelembar*, I Gusti Dauh Bale Agung, is far more "human" than either of his predecessors. He makes further excursions across the boundaries separating the storied world of the past and the mundane world of the present. When the old man reaches out and touches a child in the audience, he is engaging in a form of contact that would be unthinkable for either the proud *patih* or his antic opposite. The order of appearance of these characters is not arbitrary. While the number of *pengelembar* characters varies from performance to performance and the choice of middle characters is up to the discretion of the dancers, a proud *patih* invariably comes first and a somewhat eccentric old man invariably enters last. By playing with the theatrical possibilities inherent in the representation of visitation, a framework for performance is established that will allow for a playing back and forth between the world as it is imagined to have been and the world as it is known to be.

Storytelling: the languages of *topeng*

Topeng is not only a dance theatre; it is also a storytelling theatre, rich in verbal interplay. The introductory dances stake out the means of playing back and forth between the distant past and the immediate present through modulation of the degree of artifice used, through control of the directness of contact with the audience, and, most importantly, through the use of humor. This play between the past and the present, the distant and the immediate, the grand and the mundane is at the heart of *topeng*.

The stories of *topeng* are drawn from the *babad dalem* or *Chronicles of the Kings*. These chronicles are not contained in one central and authoritative collection. They are the work of numerous court poets, *brahmanas* employed to glorify the ancestral heritage of their various *ksatriya* lords – drawing from inscriptions on copper plates (*persasti*) and from oral tradition. Beginning in the sixteenth century and continuing into the early years of this century, these court poets wrote out their semi-historical chronicles on sheets of dried and boiled palm leaves, known as *lontars*. The quasi-historical works that were produced by this process tell stories pertaining to the royal courts of the Majapahit Empire. They report the coming of the Majapahit expeditionary force to Bali in the fourteenth century, and relate incidents centered around the often warring Hindu princedoms that were established in Bali during the years that followed. The story used by Kakul in Tusan relates to an invasion of Blambangan, Java by an expeditionary force sent in approximately 1500 by Dalem Waturenggong, who ruled the Balinese Kingdom of Gelgel, now located in the province of Klungkung.

Kakul's immediate source is contained in a small notebook of stories, drawn from the *lontars*, that he often refers to while choosing and preparing a performance. As with many of the *babad* stories, variants exist, stressing the roles of different historical figures. Kakul thus has a wide range of interpretations available to him and he can shape the stories in any one of a number of ways. He does not quote from the *babad*. Instead, he creates various storytelling *personae* and, through them, improvises on the *babad* storyline.

The first such storyteller to enter is the Penasar Kelihan. His entrance, accompanied by the usual shaking of the curtain and flourishes of cymbals and drums, reveals him to be proud, flamboyant, and commanding. He has the hearty laugh of an enthusiast and dances in an exaggeratedly macho fashion that pushes the dance to the edge of parody. The mask of the Penasar Kelihan covers the face only as far as the upper lip, leaving the jaw free to move. Huge wide eyes bulge out of the purple mask and impart a look of perpetual exaggeration.

After performing for approximately half an hour, Kakul now speaks for the first time. The words that he utters are half sung, half chanted in Middle Javanese, a literary language used by poets in Bali from the seventeenth to the nineteenth centuries in composing *kidung* – romantic epics set in Majapahit to be sung in groups or used in the courtly *gambuh* drama. The particular words used begin the *kidung tantri*, a Javanese version of the *Tale of A Thousand and One Nights*: "A story is told of the King of Patall, rich, proud, and full of dignity." The use of the ancestral language is more important than the content of the words here. Indeed, the words are unintelligible to the vast majority of people in the audience. Most audience members would simply identify the language and style of singing as *ucapan gambuh* speech of the courtly *gambuh*, theatre. The audience would also be cognizant of the theatrical associations of this mode of speech with the Majapahit Empire.

After playing with the *gamelan*, with the audience, and with his own sense of presence – combining the *topeng* dance vocabulary already defined as belonging to the world of the past with exclamations and hearty laughter that place him in a most immediate present – the Penasar Kelihan stops short and speaks in yet another ancestral language, Old Javanese, or Kawi. The mode of delivery is guttural, authoritative, chanted. The themes and characters associated with this mode of delivery originate in the Indian, epic tradition, notably in the *Ramayana* and the *Mahabharata*. From 900 to 1500 these epics were translated and reworked in the Hindu courts of Java, becoming Javanized in the process. Kawi began to appear as the language of Balinese courts as early as 994 and passages from the Javanized epics still serve as sources of ancestral wisdom.

The first words that the entire audience can comprehend are immediate and personal. The Penasar Kelihan is happy to be here, strutting, dancing, and telling tales. He is especially happy, he says, because he has just become a bachelor again – inviting the audience to laugh at the age-old joke with his own infectious laughter. Once again, the mode of address is more important than the information being given. The use of colloquial Balinese recontextualizes the present in the potential space thus far dominated by the languages of the past. The encouragement to laughter grants the audience permission to participate playfully, if vicariously, in the leaps from past to present and back again, licensed by the occasion of performance.

This is a mode of play that a Balinese audience is particularly well prepared for by skills in communication unnecessary for their daily lives. I have referred to the Penasar Kelihan as speaking "colloquial Balinese." In fact, the nature of "Balinese" is far more complex than this would indicate. Writing in the 1930s, Miguel de Covarrubias in *Island of Bali* described language practices as follows:

> When two strange Balinese meet, as for instance on the road, they call each other djero, a safe, polite way of addressing someone whose title is unknown. Since there are no outward signs of caste … strangers talk in the middle language, a compromise between daily speech and the polite tongue. Should, however, one be of low caste and the other a nobleman, it would be wrong for them to continue talking in this manner, and one of the two, probably the highcaste man, will ask the other, "Antuk linggih?" "Where is your place (caste)?" which is answered by the other man's stating his caste. Then, the usual system is adopted; the low man speaks the high tongue and the aristocrat answers in the common language … two distinct, unrelated languages with separate roots, different words, and extremely dissimilar character. It was always incongruous to hear an educated nobleman talking the harsh, guttural tongue, while an ordinary peasant had to address him in the refined high Balinese.

Even with the tendency in Bali today to use the status-marking modes of language less, it is still an insult to be termed "*sing nawang basa*" or one who doesn't know the language. The Balinese are very sensitive to relationships among context, speech, and action. The theatre plays with this consciousness, both reinforcing the sense that different words and actions properly belong to different contexts and delighting in the leaps from context to context provided by an expert performer.

As Penasar Kelihan, Kakul abruptly shifts to the respectful vocabulary and mode of address appropriate to High Balinese in order to address humbly his Lord and King, Dalem Waturenggong, and to pay homage to the Hindu deities and consecrated ancestors. For the first time, he places himself as a character within a world of illusion with interconnected social relationships and the capacity to sustain a "plot." At first, this world of illusion is referred to as "here in ancient Bali;" it is then particularized as being "here in Gelgel," invoking the nearby ancient capital. The Penasar Kelihan identifies himself as a servant to Dalem Waturenggong, thereby specifying the time of the story as being approximately 1500.

This world of illusion, though, is abruptly shattered almost as soon as it is stated. After a vigorous bit of dancing and a mischievous *kekawin* refrain from the *Ramayana* describing the young monkey Angeda rising high on his tail in order to insult the demon King Rawana, Kakul momentarily drops the story and even the character of the Penasar Kelihan altogether and speaks of a "here" that is definitely Tusan at the present moment of performance. His use of the "crude" low Balinese is made even more immediate by deployment of the local Klungkung dialect as he chides the *ksatriya*-led *gamelan* for rushing during the dance and makes fun of himself as a mangy "old dog." The contrast between the behavior of the new *persona* and the humble pleadings of the Penasar Kelihan as he tries to avoid his King's curses could not be greater.

So far, the audience only knows the historical time and locale of the story to be told; yet Kakul has deployed Middle Javanese, Old Javanese, and high, low and medium Balinese and has given to each its own sense of decorum, its own mode of being. Before the performance is over, he will also deploy Modern Indonesian and Archipelago Sanskrit. What A. L. Becker noted about *wayang* is true also of *topeng*: it includes within it, in each performance, the entire history of the literary language. *Topeng*'s "content" can be seen as the presentation and contextualizing of the languages of the past and present.

These various linguistic worlds established one by one and the process of contextual leaps set in motion, Kakul, as Penasar Kelihan, begins to concentrate on the story itself, providing expository information, freely dropping into crude dialect for immediacy and humor, soaring into recitations from the *Mahabharata* in Kawi to invoke an ancient warrior's *ethos*, and singing sections from the *kidung malat* in Middle Javanese to invoke images of courtly grace and elegance. As Kakul leaps from frame to frame, he assumes three essential roles while still wearing the mask of Penasar Kelihan: he is servant in an illusionary world of ancient Gelgel, the proud reciter of epic poetry, and the mangy "old dog" of a performer. Alternating among these, Kakul manipulates the flexible vehicle chosen from the *babad* stories recorded in his notebook. As Penasar Kelihan, he quotes kings and ministers as the story unfolds, ever sensitive to their bearing and manner as language shifts appropriately in the caste-conscious world of ancient Gelgel.

ANOTHER STORYTELLER: COMMON SENSE AND EXTRAORDINARY HAPPENINGS

For all the textual and contextual leaps, the world of "ancient Bali" invoked by the Penasar Kelihan is coherent in its formulation and rigorous in its demands. The singing of the *kidung* selections in Middle Javanese evokes an image of elegance and courtly grace consciously derived from the Courts of Majapahit. As the King is about to enter, "the air is transformed. It is all gentleness and prettiness." The recitations in Kawi of lines from the Javanese *Mahabharata* and *Ramayana* give a sense of divine purpose to the power and elegance of the Court. In this world, every man has his place in a hierarchical chain. The King humbles himself before the gods and holds his dignity among men inviolate. Warriors pledge their lives to their Kings and command the service of their men. Thus, the Penasar Kelihan, though low on the chain, humbles himself before his King and commands his lackeys without ceremony to "Pack up! Get ready for a fight!" "A small ring is a bracelet for the finder," sings the Penasar Kelihan. By extension, the implication is that the King is a god on earth. This sense of form repeating form is given its most elaborate expression by Jelantik, the eventual hero of the story, when he likens the "macrocosmos" of the spiritual world to the "microcosmos" of the physical world and states that "the microcosmos finds expression in the body of every man."

The world of ancient Bali as presented by the Penasar Kelihan is one that needs vigilant defense. He recites from the *Mahabharata* that "since time immemorial, the warrior's path has been one of action." In this story, the order of the world is in jeopardy, because of the disfigurement of an image of the King. While such shocks to the world's ordering demand redress and give rise to drama, they also open the way to humor. The Penasar Kelihan himself, though, cannot truly exploit the humor latent in the instability of such a world. With his love of epic verse, his exaggerated dance posture, and his hearty, enthusiast's laugh, he is quintessentially advocate and advertiser for the ethos and splendor of "ancient Bali." But this Penasar does not tell this story alone. He alternates storytelling functions with the Penasar Cenikan, or younger storyteller.

In *topeng panca*, the company form of *topeng*, these characters work in pairs and are understood to be "brothers." They are invariably in the service of the kings, heroes, and adversaries whose deeds the chronicles relate. They are also, most importantly, mediating characters between the heroic world of the past and the mundane world of the present. Coming from the past into the world of the present, these characters may talk about anything from esoteric Hindu mythology to birth-control programs or tourists falling off motorcycles while they provide exposition for the "plot." More often than not, their talk is humorous and their characters are designed to maximize the use of humor as they assume their roles as mediators.

As with any good comedy team, the "brothers" have contrasting styles. The Penasar Kelihan is the straight-man, full of self-importance and bound to the world of the past by word and gesture. The Penasar Cenikan, on the other hand, has the freedom from constraints of a comic innocent. He walks upright, arms by his sides, in a casual manner that violates all of the carefully established decorum of the legendary world. His speech is almost always in contemporary Balinese. When he does sing a *kidung* selection or quote *kekawin* poetry, the result is often parody. In his light, nasal voice, he often makes light of the pretentiousness of his older sibling. Like his brother, he wears a half-mask; but his is of a far more "natural" appearance, the performer's own mischievous eyes showing through the empty eye sockets. Unlike his brother, he has a proper name, a very common and undistinguished one: I Ketut Rai.

In Kakul's *topeng* there is a marked difference in tone as the Penasar Cenikan takes over the storytelling. As in the introductory dances, the tendency is toward the human and the contemporary. Speaking almost entirely in Balinese after a self-deprecating passage from the *kidung malat*, the Penasar Cenikan does not mock the heroic values espoused by the Penasar Kelihan – he speaks as an outsider to the heroic world that supports those values. His speech is full of expletives revealing an attitude of wonderment toward the events he must relate: "Pih!" "Beh!" "Aduh!" The idea of becoming a great warrior himself amuses and pleases him, but the assumption of the role of "Ketut Rai the Invincible" is not convincing and it is with a sense of surprise at his own words that he recounts his noble reply to his Lord's suggestion that he stay at home with his wife rather than go off to war – a report that draws the audience's laughter as well.

And yet, this simple man of common sense must report the most extraordinary happening of the story: the appearance of Jelantik's accursed father in the form of a giant leech who can be restored only by his son's death on the field of battle. The Penasar Cenikan does not pretend to understand the workings of such curses as they fall upon those who disturb the fixed order of the world. He can only relate what he saw and heard, improbable though it might be. He tells the audience that the leech was hairy. He compares it in size and shape to familiar objects of the day-to-day world: a roofing mat, a beetle nut canister. He interjects mundane details concerning a fishing pole and bait. He is an unlikely chronicler of extraordinary events.

Rather than disguise the distance between the fantastic world of the ancestral heroes and the mundane world of the ordinary man, his wondering presence emphasized that gap; but, as he plays across that gap, the telling of the story becomes more recognizably human. With his addition as human witness, the past contains something more of the present and the audience's own response to such fantastic happenings finds expression. By alternating the Penasar Cenikan's wonderment in the face of the extraordinary events that he has witnessed and must describe with the Penasar Kelihan's boldly assertive reactivation of the languages and attitudes of the ancestral past, the audience is afforded contrasting ways of approaching the stories that define their history as a people.

The dancing of the principals

During Kakul's performance, each of the principal characters within the story is accorded a dance. Framed by the alternating voices of the two Penasars, King, hero, and antagonist, all make their separate appearances. The King is first and the manner of his invocation is interesting. As Dalem Waturenggong, King of Gelgel, is called into the playing space by the Penasar Kelihan, and the rate of change from language to language undergoes a rapid acceleration: Kawi, Middle Javanese, and Balinese follow each other in rapid succession as if all times are dramatically merging into one in order to accommodate the King's entrance. An interplay is established between expectations appropriate to the rival esthetic modes of dramatic illusion and ancestral visitation. The king's entrance is embedded in an unfolding story and is partially anticipated in the terms of dramatic illusion. He is bidden to come forth among his ministers and his people, asked to enter the "hall of justice" in "ancient Bali." He is quoted as preparing his loyal followers for his entrance, establishing protocol among imagined ministers gathering in an illusionary world. The King is arriving on business. Yet the Penasar Kelihan also sings of his imminent entrance through the curtain in terms of performance and display. He tells the audience that the King will come forth "dancing beautifully." The use of ancestral languages, the deployment of music, the shaking of the curtain, the lack of illusionistic scenery, the placement of the curtain itself, and the promised emphasis on display all combine to relate the King's entrance to the traditions of ancestral visitation already theatricalized in the introductory dances.

A similar shuffling back and forth between these rival esthetic modes is evident in the other two appearances of principal characters embedded within the telling of the story. As the

Fig. 15.1 I Nyoman Kakul without mask, and masked as Patih Jelantik. (Photos by John Emigh.)

Penasar Cenikan calls upon his master Jelantik, he urges him to "come forth" and "reveal" himself, employing terms of visitation, performance, and display. The hero's imminent appearance is also talked of as "going forth," as a departure for Blambangan – the next stop along the line in a developing dramatic "plot." The audience is asked to regard Jelantik's entrance and dance both as an act of revelation – a coming forth into their world – and as an event within the dramatic line of action – a going forth to another illusionary locale.

As the King of Blambangan shakes the curtain, thereby cueing a frenzied rush of percussive sound, he cries out in Kawi, "Behold, here I come, the King of Blambangan," and warns the audience that preparation is necessary to witness his powerful counte-nance. The curtain is yanked open and the King thrusts his animalistic hands forward, looking through the opened curtain into the performance oval, demanding to know whom it is he is facing. Is he talking to the warriors from Gelgel who have invaded his territory? Or is he speaking to the audience he sees revealed to him on the other side of the curtain, demanding information from them in a language which is no longer theirs? The ambiguity is deliberate. By shifting back and forth between the modes of illusion and visitation, the performer can playfully toy with the vantage-point of the audience. The display format of the introductory dances is now loosely embedded within a devel-oping line of action or "plot" and the result is a theatrical form rich in its ability to awaken wonder while it mediates between the world as the audience ordinarily experiences it and the world as the audience can imagine it to be.

In appearance and movement, three principal characters of the central story are delib-erately fashioned as contrasting figures. Their dances do not advance the story itself. Rather, their entrances are presented as acts of revelation highlighted within the narrative structure. Dalem Waturenggong appears in a white mask with almond-shaped eyes and a

119

fine black moustache. His headdress is covered with flowers. The gestures used by the Dalem are flowing, graceful, and delicate, with a sense of inner strength and great pride. Jelantik's mask is of a more earthy, natural color. The eyes are wider, the smile larger. The stance accompanying the mask is wider, the movements sharper. The debt to the martial arts is clear. As Jelantik, Kakul presents a figure of great dignity and strength, alert to everything about him, but without the hypertension that the red-faced *patih* exhibited in the *pengelember*. As Sri Dalem Blambangan, King of Blambangan and "villain" of the evening, Kakul wears a red demon's mask with bulging eyes, large boar's tusks, and a protruding tongue over which there is an opening to allow for speech. Covering his hands are white gloves equipped with six-inch fingernails made of water-buffalo horn and tufted with animal fur. He is revealed perched on the back of a chair, legs wide apart, hands thrust aggressively forward and to the side, with fingers spread apart and trembling.

These masks and the postures and movements associated with them do not derive from descriptions in the historical chronicles, but, rather, from performance tradition and typology. Indeed, the mask used for Dalem Waturenggong could also be used for any other refined king; and the mask used for the Sri Dalem Blambangan can also be used for the god Mahadewa in his terrible aspect. The point is not to present these figures "as they were," but as they ought to be imagined. The story is a scaffolding used to show essentialized images of human capabilities.

Bondres: joking and reflexivity

The dramatic line of action comes to an end with the report of Patih Jelantik's death on the field of battle. With that event, a successful synthesis of the thematic lines enmeshed within the dramatic "plot" is achieved, Jelantik's father is freed from his curse and the honor of Gelgel is preserved in a single heroic action. Yet the performance continues; indeed, the Penasar Cenikan's report of the resolution of the dramatic themes seems perfunctory and the audience's interest intensifies and quickens rather than dissipates with the entrance of the next character. It is time for *bondres:* a parade of clowns offering jokes that seem ever so loosely connected to the dramatic action. For the Balinese audience, this is a happily anticipated part of any *topeng* performance. In Kakul's performance, the jokes bear a direct relationship to the themes and actions of the dramatic "plot": the jokes work reflexively, by turning the audience's attention back in upon those themes.

The Penasar Kelihan touts the ethos of "ancient Bali." The three dancing principals of the dramatic plot embody that ethos. Cenikan stands in awe of it. King, hero, villain, and servants all function in their given orbits within this ethos. The next three characters to appear, however, offer alternative modes of behavior that cannot be assimilated within the structure of values shared by the warriors, courtiers, and kings of "ancient Bali." Through these *bondres* characters, Kakul is able to position himself outside of the realm of punctilious behavior and heroic self-sacrifice. The truths of this realm are revealed as partial.

The first in this succession of clowns, jokesters, and outsiders is named Se Mata Mata. His very name – loosely translatable as One-Who-Looks-Out-For-Himself – is an affront to the noble values of Jelantik, who sacrifices his life for the restitution of his country's honor and the salvation of his cursed father's soul. Se Mata Mata's first "word" is a sneeze, immediately violating all of the elaborate linguistic protocol thus far used to narrate the *babad* episode of Jelantik's mission to Blambangan. He then proceeds to string together nonsense syllables that resolve themselves in inanities and obscenities, assuring the audience that even if they don't catch the words, they won't miss the meaning. The "meaning" is to be found precisely in the assault on the elaborate linguistic structure that Kakul has himself created, composed of layers of language drawn from the distant and honored past, as well as the "high" and "low" levels of speech used in the status-conscious present. Se Mata Mata performs acts of linguistic vandalism and the audience roars with laughter.

The range of the assault broadens as Se Mata Mata proceeds to sing an "Indonesian national anthem," repeating the phrase "defend the country" over and over again in Modern Indonesian. Each time the phrase is uttered, the audience laughs. The joke here seems to be concerned with the awkward fit of the values extolled in Jelantik's story to the ambiguous loyalties that the Balinese feel towards the contemporary nation state of Indonesia. Kakul forces this comparison by insisting that he, Se Mata Mata, began the fighting on the beaches of Blambangan by singing this Indonesian refrain. The claim is preposterous of course, and the audience's laughter reveals that they are in on the joke, knowing Se Mata Mata to be a braggart and a liar. I believe that the joke goes deeper, though, and that the audience's laughter may also reveal an awareness that the "truths" associated with the chronicles of the feudal past can lose their certainty when applied to the realities of the present.

Jumping from his transparently vainglorious claim to be the true hero of the dramatic events at Blambangan, Se Mata Mata next acknowledges the laughter that he has generated and points out one laughing member of the audience as "his girlfriend." The mask of Se Mata Mata makes this joke doubly funny; it appears to represent something between a pig and a man and is hinged so that, when the character talks, it opens to reveal a set of wonderfully hideous crooked teeth. The aspect of this mask is as far from the heroic countenance of Jelantik as it could possibly be; and to think of this mask as the object of romantic attachment is to engage in delicious nonsense. Wearing this mask, Kakul does not simply portray a piggy man: he presents a laughable embodiment of human swinishness.

In this anti-heroic mask, Kakul proceeds to dance *baris*: the warrior's dance related historically, musically and choreographically to the heroic dance of Jelantik. The performance is a hysterically funny parody. The audience delights both in Kakul's making fun of his own mastery of dance and in the violation of the dignity and grace he brought to Jelantik's appearance in the performance oval. The effect is not, finally, to make fun of Jelantik or to negate the importance of his presence; rather, it is to amplify the scope of the world represented in performance so that it can contain both the feudal hero and his contemporary antithesis.

The next character to emerge, Desak Made Rai, further expands the scope of this world. Up until her entrance, the play has been all male. The first vernacular words spoken by the Penasar Kelihan express his happiness at becoming a bachelor once again. The Penasar Cenikan takes Jelantik's suggestion that he might wish to stay with his wife rather than march off to war as an insult and draws the audience's laughter as he mentions the "sacrifice" of leaving home. Jelantik's heroic dance, accompanied by an all-male orchestra, is derived in part from the male skills of martial arts and a blustering macho pride pervades the movement and speech of the Penasar Kelihan. Into this world, Desak Made Rai enters: flirting, teasing, cajoling the orchestra, and accusing *brahmanas* in the audience of trying to pinch her.

Kakul's female impersonation is funny, to be sure; but the jokes here do not at all play upon womanly ways. The masculine world that Desak Made Rai intrudes upon is made fun of as well. When Kakul performs dances intended for women, they are not parodied.

In other dance forms in Bali, the ideal male heroes – Rama, for example, or Arjuna – are often performed by women. The understanding seems to be that in the ideal person, male strength is combined with feminine grace. The world of traditional *topeng* is essentially masculine in its conventions and concerns, but the entrance of Made Rai partially redresses an imbalance.

The appearance of the final *bondres* character creates an even more startling intrusion into the world of warriors, kings, and courtiers. Pulling his brightly colored and gilded cape up over his head and shoulders so as to reveal the stained white lining, Kakul emerges as Cucul, a shivering, whining peasant, far too caught up in his own domestic problems to feel himself a part of history. As a *jaba*, or *sudra*, Cucul's concerns are not those of the kings warriors, courtiers, and merchants who comprise the *triwangsa* or upper three castes. His deeds and concerns will not be chronicled. Jelantik's noble self-sacrifice and the defeat of Sri Dalem Blambangan mean far less to him then the fact that his wife has left him.

There is a circularity about the dialog of the story. The first line of vernacular dialog forms a joke about a man's happiness at being rid of his wife. The last line of vernacular dialog is spoken by a man who is desolate because his wife has left him. The very first lines of the play tell in an almost forgotten language of "a King, rich, proud … full of dignity" and "truly magnificent" – a king, by the way, who was in the habit of killing off his brides. The last lines of the play are spoken in plain speech by a poor man who wishes his wife would come back home. Having created a world dominated by kings and warriors, Kakul, the *sudra* performer, ends the story with the image of a common man, at once comic and pathetic, caught outside of the glorious world of noble heroes and demonic villains.

Once again, and in a far more elaborate manner, the movement has been towards the human and the contemporary. Within each section of the performance, the same pattern is discernible. In the introductory dances, the arrogant red-faced *Patih* yields to the lovable old man. The Penasar Kelihan yields his role as narrator to the far more prosaic Penasar Cenikan. The high-flown, sung and chanted languages of the ancestral past yield to Balinese vernacular speech. The heroes and villains of the chronicles yield the playing space to the clowns of the *bondres*. The fantastic and eccentric Se Mata Mata yields to the all too familiar Cucul. This pattern is cyclical. Fantastic and extraordinary figures keep appearing from the remote past; but, time and again, these figures are supplanted by other figures far closer to human life as experienced in the present. It is not that the noble and demonic personages of the chronicled past are obliterated; to the contrary, *topeng* performances serve to keep these characters alive. The performances also serve to contain these figures, though, and this playful process of reciprocal revitalization and containment is finally what *topeng* is all about. In the process, it celebrates the vitality of the present as well as the grandeur of the past.

Topeng and caste

Clifford Geertz notes in *Politics Past, Politics Present* (1967) that Balinese ceremonials provide "public dramatization of the ruling obsessions of Balinese culture: social inequality and status pride." Certainly caste roles are important in the "drama" enacted by Kakul: Jelantik is aware of himself as an exemplary *ksatriya* warrior; and the kings and servants who provide the occasion and support for his actions within the dramatic world of illusion all see themselves as acting within a matrix of values and possibilities that are largely caste-determined. In Kakul's performance at Tusan, though, much of the humor of the *bondres* section seems to play *against* this caste-consciousness, and in each section of the performance, there is a movement away from the rigors of caste-conscious behavior towards more all-embracing images of humanity.

Caste, though sometimes an important determinant of behavior in Balinese life, does not determine whether or not a man may be a performer nor what roles he may perform. Kakul, though a *sudra*, is particularly well known for his depiction of refined kings as well as his *bondres* characters. There are *brahmana* performers in Bali who are particularly well known as Penasars. In *topeng* forms using more than one actor, it is not unheard of for a *brahmana* or *ksatriya* performer to be playing a cringing servant to an overbearing prime minister played by a *sudra*. After the performance, the language conventions will be reversed, and the protocol appropriate to the caste distinctions outside of the theatrical roles will be reinstated. This dispersal of roles across caste lines can be played with, as when Kakul teases the *brahmana* for "trying to pinch" Desak Made Rai, and, most notably, when he steps out of the role of Penasar Kelihan to joke about himself as an "old dog" without much hair left, or when he chastises the leader of the *gamelan* (who happened to be a *ksatriya* in Tusan) for playing faster than he wished.

It would be far too pat to call *topeng pajegan* a "ritual of status reversal;" but it is necessary to point out that, while *topeng* performances do dramatize situations based on "social inequality and status pride," the range of attitudes portrayed in handling these dramatic themes is complex. The most startling instance of this complexity comes in Kakul's last appearance in the playing space.

Sidha Karya: the performer as priest

The performance is not over. Although there will be no more mention of Jelantik and his mission, and no more jokes reflexively playing back upon the contextual world of his heroic actions, Kakul will enter through the curtain and into the playing space one last time. He wears a white mask of hideous aspect, with a gaping mouth and protruding teeth. On his head is an unkempt wig made up of horse's hair. The character is Sidha Karya, and his appearance is necessary in every *topeng pajegan* performance.

Sidha Karya is a character from the *babads*, recorded as having lived during the reign of Dalem Waturenggong. But his story is independent of Jelantik's and he would appear whether or not the *topeng* story was "set" in Dalem Waturenggong's reign. As he himself states, his appearance is required if the event is to be "successful." Indeed, his name means One-Who-Makes-The-Ceremony-Successful. The story of how he got that name is worth relating here, even though there is only a single oblique reference to that story in the performance "text."

After the Hindu migrations from Majapahit, the god Mahadewa came to be associated with the "mother temple" of Basakih, high on the slopes of Gunung Agung. During the reign of Dalem Waturenggong, Dewa Mahadewa summoned a priest known as Brahmana Keling, who was still living in East Java, to come to Besakih. Dalem Waturenggong was preparing for a great ceremony to be held at Besakih at that time and, as preparations were being made, Brahmana Keling arrived. He told the sentries to deliver to Dalem Waturenggong the message that his brother, Brahmana Keling, wished to be received. Upon hearing this message, Dalem Waturenggong was puzzled and angry. He denied having any such brother, and refused to meet with the wandering priest. Summarily dismissed, Brahmana Keling warned that Dewa Mahadewa would be displeased at the King's actions. Soon after the priest's departure, a swarm of locusts descended from the sky and a horde of hungry rats came out of the irrigation ditches of the rice fields. Together, the locusts and the rats devoured the rice in the fields. Famine swept the land and many died in a terrible epidemic. Without the rice, offerings could not be made and the great ceremony had to be postponed. Realizing that he had been in error, Dalem Waturenggong summoned Brahmana Keling to him and publicly received him as his "brother." Soon the locusts and rats vanished. The spread of disease was stayed and the rice fields once more turned green. The great ceremony at Basakih was held one year after it had been originally scheduled; and this time, Brahmana Keling officiated as high priest. Dewa Mahadewa was pleased. Brahmana Keling became known as Sidha Karya in memory of the successful event and was appointed the high priest of a temple in Denpasar, the current capital city of Bali.

The story of Sidha Karya is formed around the uneasy sharing of priestly and secular power between the *brahmana* and *ksatriya* castes in Hindu Bali. The name of Brahmana Keling hearkens back to the ancient Kalinga empire of India and probably places the roots of this story in the early encounters between Hindu priests and the feudal lords of Sumatra and Java. Much of the appeal of the story is in its patterning: a mysterious, threatening, and potentially destructive force is turned into a force for wellbeing by a process of recognition and inclusion.

In the *babad* story, Brahmana Keling, the potential destroyer of Bali, becomes Sidha Karya, the principal intermediator with the gods, once his divinely arranged place in the scheme of things is discovered and acknowledged. The ceremony that ends a *topeng pajegan* performance does not refer directly to this story, but the treatment of Sidha Karya is patterned around a knowledge of it. Sidha Karya's aspect is awesome in its ugliness and otherworldliness; yet, he is called forth as the emissary of Dewa Mahadewa, manifestation of the Holy Presence, incorporating all divinity within his person. The performance model is again that of visitation, but this time without the wrappings of dramatic illusion.

As Sidha Karya, Kakul will alternately take on the functional roles of ancestral character, emissary of the gods, embodiment of the godhead itself, and intercessor for the assembled audience. In short, he is a mediating figure, adjusting his role within the ritualized proceedings so as to deliver "successfully" the offerings of man to the gods and the blessings of gods to men. The languages used now are Sanskrit and Kawi – the first being the medium of exchange used by the priests when addressing the Hindu deities, and the second being the language associated with the ancestors of Majapahit who brought those deities with them to Bali and who are still understood to accompany the gods on their occasional visitations "into this world" and "upon this earth."

It is common in Bali for performance genres regarded as "secular" to be given as offerings of religious occasions; stories are enacted to please and amuse the divine as well as the secular audience. It is also common in Bali for acts of offering to be ritually performed with an emphasis on style and grace; the presentation of food offerings is often danced to the accompaniment of music. *Topeng pajegan*, also called *topeng wali* (ritual *topeng*), combines these two traditions. Ritual and theatrical frames cannibalize each other. Ritual patterns of visitation are embraced and subsumed by theatrical presentation, and a theatrical world of illusion is, in turn, embraced and subsumed by ritual ceremony. The pervasive traditions of visitation pave the way for the introduction of a dramatic world and this world is then supplanted by an act of visitation. Throughout, a playful tension is maintained between these two esthetic traditions. In the dances, Kakul alternates, including and excluding the audience. As Penagar Kelihan, he leaps from the role of character to the role of performer and back again. As Sidha Karya, a jumping of frames occurs as Kakul alternates between being a priestly mediator and portraying an embodiment of the godhead. In the overall shape of the performance, a transformation takes place: in the introductory and "dramatic" sections, the performance is to be regarded as an offering; in the Sidha Karya section, an offering is performed. Kakul's private ritual of preparation asking for the gods' blessings leads to the performance of a public ritual in which these blessings are conferred on the community.

Kakul can only take on the role of priestly mediator because of his skills as a dancer and storyteller. A priest cannot perform the Sidha Karya ceremony himself and Kakul would not perform it without previously doing the rest of the performance. We are left with a bewildering and intriguing paradox: the village of Tusan, with a large *brahmana* population, must bring in an outside performer, a *sudra*, in order to complete successfully a ceremony attending the cremation of a high priest. Within the context of performance, Kakul becomes what he plays. For a time, within the mask of Sidha Karya that he is privileged to wear, he functionally *is* the "priest of *dharma*," emissary from the gods and intercessor for mankind.

Kakul's last actions as Sidha Karya constitute what may be the most startling event of the whole performance. The "priest of *dharma*" takes the coins from Dewa Mahadewa's offering, throws them towards the children who line the inside of the audience oval, and calls to them in Modern Indonesian – the language of the schools. The children scramble to pick up the coins and then run screaming as the terrifying and otherworldly Sidha Karya chases after them. Their faces register fear and thrilled excitement. Sidha Karya, who is also known as the Pengejukan, or One-Who-Takes-People-Up-In-His-Arms, then grabs hold of one of the children and bears him aloft. He sets the child down next to the offering prepared for Dewa Mahadewa himself and gives the child some of the food, whereupon the excited child returns to the smiling audience. The performer takes one last turn of the playing space and, still in the mask of Sidha Karya, he exits for the last time through the curtain. There is no curtain call. The music stops and the audience slowly disperses.

Returning home

Behind the curtain, Kakul removes his last mask. He has performed at an extraordinarily high pitch of energy for an hour and a half and is thoroughly exhausted. His face and body pour sweat. I am amazed to rediscover how tiny and vulnerable this man is who has just embodied a whole universe. The masks are blessed and put away. Layer by layer, the costume is removed. There is time for resting, joking with friends, polite exchanges with the *brahmana*, and *ksatriya* patrons, the drinking of a strong, clear, distilled liquor called *arak*, and the eating of another big meal. Two of Kakul's sons and several more performers arrive. There will be another *topeng* performance later that night, this time a secular performance (without Sidha Karya) involving nine actors, including Kakul. A rain squall moves past, causing a delay, and this performance does not start until well after 11 o'clock and it lasts until about 4 o'clock in the morning. The rows of children are often asleep now, lying upon one another and waking to appreciate bits of *bondres*. In between appearances, the performers catch naps behind the curtain. Despite the hour, the audience remains large and appreciative, sometimes chatting as the story slowly unfolds, other times caught up in the antics and entanglements of the story's characters or arrested by the virtuosity of a dance.

After the last character swirls through the curtain, the actors sit together talking, joking, resting, waiting for dawn and the first mini-truck for Batuan. It comes and all pile in, crowding two-deep amidst the baskets of costumes and masks. Some of the performers will go directly to the rice fields, while others are free to go home. In a corner of the jouncing mini-truck, Kakul lies with his head against a basket, his work finished, his face serene in sleep.

ACKNOWLEDGMENT

I Ketut Kantor, I Made Regug, and I Wayan Tedun all taught me a great deal about the Balinese use of masks and masking while I was in Bali. In this country, Amy Catlin, Fritz DeBoer and Andrew Toth have all made helpful suggestions, as have I Nyoman Sumandhi, I Nyoman Wenten, and, especially, I Made Bahdem. Richard Wallis lent me a copy of his 1978 University of Michigan dissertation which helped me a great deal in writing the section on the languages of *topeng*, as did A. L. Beeker's forthcoming article on Javanese *wayang kulit*. Finally, there is a pervasive debt to I Wayan Suweca, who I worked with for three years.

Part IV

CIRCUS, CLOWNS AND JESTERS

16

INTRODUCTION TO PART IV

Joel Schechter

Circus arts have existed for thousands of years; but clowning, juggling, acrobatics, high-wire walks, feats of strength and acts with trained animals were not exhibited together in one theatre or one ring before the eighteenth century. The invention of the modern circus dates from 1768, when Sergeant Major Philip Astley in England designed a ring 42 feet in diameter to display equestrian acts. Horses and their riders were the main attractions. Rival exhibition spaces followed, along with other acts housed in amphitheatres and circus tents with one, three, or as many as five rings.

In ancient Rome, the "circus" (which means "ring" in Latin) was an arena for chariot races and gladiator combats. It anticipated modern circus acts which feature daring Cossack horse-riders instead of charioteers, and lion-tamers instead of gladiators. Other arts practiced in ancient times have modern circus counterparts too: rope-walkers, jugglers, acrobats and mimes entertained pre-Christian Romans, and, as noted earlier in Arnold Hauser's discussion of Greek mimes, these artists were popular because they "received no subvention from the state, in consequence did not have to take instruction from above, and so worked out artistic principles simply and solely from [their] own immediate experience with audiences."[1] Modern circus artists continue to be "popular" in this sense, as box office profits, not the state, pay their wages, although since Russia nationalized the circus after its 1917 revolution, states have subsidized clowns and animal acts. Circuses always have been popular in the sense of being crowd-pleasing, too. With the rise of mass media – film and television competition – big-tent circuses experienced a decline in popularity; but that was followed by a resurgence of public interest, as audiences flocked to see Cirque du Soleil and other "new wave" circuses.

The "new wave" in circuses began in the 1970s. This movement away from large expensive spectacles such as Ringling Bros., Barnum & Bailey's "Greatest Show on Earth," toward smaller, more intimate one-ring shows arrived in North America with the Pickle Family Circus (founded in 1974–5), the Big Apple Circus (founded 1977), and Cirque du Soleil (first season: 1984). In England and France the new circus movement has also thrived, with the Circus Space in London and a wonderful circus school at Chalons en Champagne.

Leading the new wave in the United States, the Pickle Family Circus featured entirely animal-free acts, and in its early years the clown-centered cooperative performed outdoors without a tent. Cirque du Soleil also chose not to include animal acts; it added expensive moving lights and high-tech sound equipment for effects first popularized in rock concerts. To some extent the movement of Cirque du Soleil's gymnastic performers resembles that of dancers, although their flying leaps and contortions to musical accompaniment are not usually seen at modern dance concerts.

The Pickle Family Circus and Cirque du Soleil also developed a new "narrative circus" form which incorporates variety acts into a story, usually an allegorical journey where trapeze flight, contortionist ballet, and clown gibberish become metaphors for a new and strange world. This represents a significant departure from traditional circus, in which different acts are self-contained displays of skill and daring.

Most popular acts performed in the modern European and North American circus can also be found in non-western countries. Peking Opera, for example, has a longstanding tradition of virtuoso acrobatics. Clowning has thrived in Asia, through forms such as *topeng* (discussed elsewhere in this volume) and the wandering minstrelsy of India's *bahurupiya*, introduced here by John Emigh. The wandering jester Hajari Bhand is in some ways an Indian counterpart to the Italian satirist and clown Dario Fo (also discussed in the volume), and it is intriguing that two performers from such different parts of the world could have so much in common as popular theatre artists. Both of them have sustained a life like that of "the unchronicled jesters who worked at court and on the road in medieval Europe," as Emigh notes of Bhand.[2] Both of them excel at satiric impersonation. Both have now had their lives chronicled, as their unwritten, oral tradition of clowning attracted scholars among their following.

While they may have specific cultural references within their acts, many clowns and other circus artists have achieved an international following (including scholars) in recent years. Their popular flights through the air, pratfalls, highwire walks and animal taming require no translation and have worldwide appeal. The universal language of circus arts allows one show to feature Russian clowns, Chinese acrobats, Thai contortionists, Mexican trapeze artists, and a Canadian ringmaster. While nations still compete with one another for armaments, oil and advanced technology, circus artists offer models of international collaboration and peace within one tent. There was even an International Congress of Clowns held in Philadelphia in 1991. Fred Siegel's report on the event, reprinted here, confirms that circus acts can address political topics such as the dangers of nuclear power and toxic waste, and can amuse people in the process. The kind of political clowning described by Siegel is more likely to be seen in alternative venues – "new circus" tents, experimental theatres and festivals – than in traditional circus rings.

The history of clowns and jesters is far older and more complicated than that of modern circus. For centuries, powers of healing and shamanism have been attributed to clowns, including Native American tribesmen. In recent times, scientific findings by scholars like William Frye have affirmed the medicinal value of laughter; and the Clown Care Unit of the Big Apple Circus in New York has brought its version of curative clowning into urban hospitals.[3] There has also been increased practice of clown ministries, comic religious services which recall the "Feast of Fools" that convened in medieval churches and Erasmus's praise of Christ's folly. Here clowning might qualify as a form of the popular drama to which David Mayer attributes "utility in that it serves social needs through public rites or through plays that reinforce desirable social and moral conclusions."[4]

But clowning is just as likely to question social and moral conclusions, or parody them, as it is to reinforce them. One of the most popular features of older circuses in Europe was the clown *entrée*, a self-contained playlet which usually lasted 10–25 minutes, and enabled clown duos and trios like Grock and Antonet or the Fratellini to set their finely-formed characters against one another, and against social order as embodied by the circus ring-master, in a dramatic plot. Although the traditional *entrée* form has not been widely seen in American circuses, even in Europe it has been reconsidered, as Kenneth Little explains in his essay, "Pitu's Doubt." At a time when new clowns like those in the Pickle Family and Big Apple Circuses were drawing on mime, dance, and actor training, rather than simply copying traditional European *entrées*, the whiteface clown Pitu faced an identity crisis. His father, also a whiteface clown, at one point advised his son not to pursue a career in the circus, because "the circus was dead".[5] A similar exaggeration of the death of the circus and its great clown tradition was offered in Fellini's film, *The Clowns*. But Pitu was able to adjust and renew the *entrée*. His innovation, much like Hajari Bhand of Rajasthan's transition from the role of court jester to village entertainer in India, shows popular comic tradition's resilience in response to new social and cultural conditions.

The *entrée*, with its highly physical comedy of characters, may be the form in which circus comes closest to conventional theatre. But as Hovey Burgess asserts in his interview, "Circus and the Actor," many circus skills are quite beneficial to stage actors: "If only people who could leap through the air were actors, the theatre might be more exciting."[6] In fact circus arts, including trapeze artistry, have been brought into the theatre by some of the past century's most innovative directors – Meyerhold, Eisenstein, Brook, Mnouchkine, Woodruff, Fo and Rame.

The Bindlestiff Family Cirkus, introduced here by Hovey Burgess, takes contemporary circus arts in another direction – toward the culture of punk rock, piercings and self-mutilation. It also revives the vanishing species known as the sideshow. Archaos in the UK has a somewhat similar bent, with its chainsaws, highwire motorcyclists, and "Circus of Horrors." Sideshows at older circuses were never far from exposing the body to dangers either, as fire-eaters, sword-swallowers, and swamis on beds of nails risked – or at least appeared to risk – their lives in sensationalistic acts. Big-tent circuses have also thrived on death-defying entertainments: trapeze artists who fly without nets, or motor-cyclists who drive in a fire-filled cage. But they do not usually display the humorous, self-parodic dementia of Archaos or Bindlestiff.

The comic speeches which build up Bindlestiff's feats are part of the amusement, and bring back to circus the popular art of the *spiel*. Convincing the listener of an act's danger or miracle is half the feat. Self-promotion by circus artists advanced by leaps and bounds during P. T. Barnum's creation of "the greatest show on earth." Audacity and bluff on a smaller scale are still alive today in circus arenas like Bindlestiff's. But their bluffs, while works of art, are small stuff compared to statements from leaders of religion, politics, and industry who think the world of themselves; corporate and official government audacity, bold distortions and boasts on a global scale, have initiated the "circusization" of the world – a difficult act to follow.

NOTES

1 Arnold Hauser, *Social History of Art,* Vol. I. Baltimore: Penguin, 1951, p. 86
2 John Emigh, "Hajari Bhand of Rajastan: A Joker in the Deck," reprinted in this volume.
3 William Frye, "Medical Perspectives on Humor" in *Humor and Health Letter*. Jackson, Mississippi, January / February 1993, pp. 1–4.
4 David Mayer, "Towards a Definition of Popular Theatre," in *Western Popular Theatre*, edited by David Mayer and Kenneth Richards. London: Methuen, 1977, p. 265.
5 Kenneth Little, "Pitu's Doubt: Entrée Clown Self-Fashioning in the Circus Tradition," reprinted in this volume.
6 Hovey Burgess, "Circus and the Actor," reprinted in this volume.

17

CIRCUS AND THE ACTOR

Hovey Burgess

Hovey Burgess, intrigued by an article entitled "Juggler's Jargon" in Tops – The Magazine of Magic, took up juggling at the age of 15. The year was 1954, the start of his multi-faceted career in the circus. By 1958, he was a member of the International Jugglers' Association, having made his professional debut in the Patterson Brothers Circus. Later that year he joined the Hagen Brothers Circus as a fire juggler in the sideshow. He was billed as "Danish Dan from Denmark."

Burgess studied at Florida State University in 1960, performing in the FSU circus. In 1961, he was elected President of the International Jugglers' Association. The following year he worked for the Hunt Brothers Circus in the property department, and was assistant to the animal trainer in the Toledo Zoo Wild Animal Show. Burgess then spent two years studying at the Pasadena Playhouse. Work for his bachelor's degree in Theatre was completed at NYU and Columbia. During this time, he was assistant to the Curator at the Brander Matthews Dramatic Museum.

New York University hired Burgess in 1966 to teach the first circus course created specifically for actors. They sent him to Stratford, Ontario that summer to observe the mime techniques of Jacques Lecoq. This experimental program at NYU's School of the Arts attracted the interest of other schools. Burgess was hired by Juilliard's Drama Division in 1968, and by Sarah Lawrence in 1969. Concurrent with his teaching, he performed an act at the Electric Circus for 16 months, and created his own troupe, the Circo dell'Arte, in which he and his student actors performed in parks and in his Bowery studio. Today, Hovey Burgess is unique in his field. He is the only professional circus performer teaching his skills in theatre training programs. He has developed a method of instruction that makes such techniques vital to the actor's craft.

Question: Since you are teaching in theatre departments, there must be a specific value in circus techniques for an actor. Can you describe the nature of the link between these disciplines?

Burgess: The union is at a basic level. There is a great benefit to the actor because he can learn about his own body movement, about himself – his courage, fears, physical potential, how he can change it, where he can go. Circus enables an actor to trust his physical instincts. It is not important for an actor to juggle before an audience, but he must be able to do so if the play requires it. Talented actors have a theatrical feeling for circus. Historically actors have had access to these techniques. Sophocles was a juggler and an acrobat. It is not a new thing.

Question: What is the dividing line between the actor and the circus performer?

Burgess: Circus is useful to the actor up to a point. An actor lives through an emotion to create a specific impression. The circus performer is called on to physicalize certain things. He may try to create an emotion, but not through emotion. He works alone, while the actor works with a director. In contemporary theatre, where there are no strong character roles, the actor becomes much more like a circus performer. Drama schools, realizing this, have added circus to their curriculums. Mime and fencing are valid, but they fragment the actor. Circus gets at different problems and covers a broader spectrum. It demands a physical excellence like athletics, only it is theatrical.

Question: The goals of the actor are different from those of the circus performer. How does your method of instruction deal with the actor's specific needs?

Burgess: A circus performer must have a gimmick in order to make an act work. He must be either very good or very original. Therefore, when I am dealing with circus performers, I go after the original well-done trick. I try to find out what they could do better than anyone else in the world and develop that skill to a very high degree. It's a very different thing when working with actors. It's a little ironic, but I'm actually interested in what they don't do well. I try to give them a progressive circus approach

Fig. 17.1 Hovey Burgess and Judy Finelli juggling in New York's Washington Square Park. (Photo courtesy of Hovey Burgess.)

toward self-improvement. If they are not flexible I go for that. It doesn't mean they'll be able to do a number as a contortionist. I try to give them simple exercises that will affect their whole range of movement. The development of things they're good at is a side issue. It is done only because it might be commercially valuable for an actor. I make no discriminations among my students, and never make exclusions on the basis of sex. An actor or actress must learn the entire range of movement. It is important to know the way men move as opposed to women. This helps the actor facing a character role. No one can effectively portray a character whose range of movement is outside his own. It is therefore necessary for each student to develop a wide range of possibilities for himself so he can make good choices for the character. One is never required to use everything, but the freedom of choice must exist. An actor who plays a clumsy character, for example, must have the balance and coordination necessary to fall, or else you'd need a new actor every night.

Question: Would you classify the basic circus skills and the principles used in the learning process?

Burgess: The basic techniques fall into four categories: (1) contortion, which is flexibility; (2) juggling (the manipulation of any object); (3) equilibrium, which can include things as simple as sitting in a chair; and (4) jumping, which leads to tumbling. Sometimes these things overlap. This year, I'm working on spinning a rope. The ultimate is to spin a rope in such a way as to jump through it. This is both juggling and jumping. The element of contortion comes into the pulling up of the knees and the working of the wrist. Equilibrium means staying in balance as you jump in the air and come back down.

Relaxation in activity, economizing energy, and repetition are used to learn motor skills.

Question: You start every class with a warm-up. How does this relate to the training program?

Burgess: Some circus techniques are covered in the warm-up. Flexibility, balance and tumbling can be learned with everyone doing everything at once, or in rapid succession. Through warmth, the body becomes more flexible. This enables me to ask people to do harder things without hurting themselves. It also is a conditioning process that tones up the lungs, heart and muscles, enabling students to do things months later. The warm-up resembles more a conventional theatre movement, or dance technique.

Question: Where do your exercises come from?

Burgess: I borrowed freely from a great number of sources. There are three men who taught in the idiom of mime who influenced me – Jacques Lecoq, Carlo Mazzone, and Arne Zaslove. Mazzone and Zaslove are both students of Lecoq. I usually modify their exercises, sometimes beyond recognition, in order to present them in a circus idiom.

Question: How does your work differ from Lecoq's?

Burgess: Lecoq has said that he is interested in the range of expression between mime and theatre. I am concerned with circus as it relates to theatre. Lecoq is in touch with basic principles of movement that are also circus. He tries to capture movement in a time-exposure way, attempting to get people from uninspired to inspired physical states. Breathing is an important part of movement. It is vital for the actor's voice production. It can also affect gesture. The same gesture on an inhalation means something different on an exhalation. This categorization of gesture is Lecoq's work, and I admire it, but it is not my emphasis. I do use this when I teach commedia, then everything is grist for the mill. Everything I know about life, circus, mime and theatre is necessary for that kind of expression. If the student doing my work should get the benefit of some of Lecoq's ideas, I'm happy about it.

Question: Could you expand on the skills you teach, explaining why and how they are taught, and the benefit to the actor?

Burgess: One of the first things I teach actors is how to balance an object – a broom, or a cue stick. The technique requires keeping the top from moving. I start with that because it is simple, and most people have done it. Balance is the basic necessity for all exercises. The actor needs gesture for expression. This skill can break through limitations in movement by indicating a way to re-educate all the muscles of the body. Most people can balance on the right side of their body if they are right-handed. I turn the tables on them and make them switch sides. This awakens an awareness of the lack of control on the unfavored side. Most people know they are right-handed, but they don't know *how* right-handed. This is especially important when the actor is in a proscenium situation and is facing stage right. The left side of his body is facing the audience, and he must find a way of making it expressive.

I then add more difficult objects, or ask that they be balanced on the shoulders or forehead. Sometimes, I request that two objects be balanced simultaneously. This is incredibly difficult. There is always a synthesis. I am always making things harder. I try to find the optimum difficulty that can be attempted.

Through the warm-up and other exercises I try to develop balance and flexibility of the human body. Later on, I get to the manipulation of objects with the body. Tumbling and juggling come later because some of the people I teach are so stiff, so unacquainted with movement that they require something very simple in order to attain a degree of success, to be interested in going on.

Once the student can balance a cue stick in either hand, I introduce juggling. The first step is to juggle two balls in one hand on a flat plane in front of them. The balls are diametrically opposed, forming an ellipse. When one ball reaches the top of the ellipse the next is thrown. This is done next with both hands and then with more balls. Juggling involves use of the left and right hand, as well as valuable hand and eye coordination. There is concentration on the objective of trying to keep the balls going while remaining as relaxed as possible. Actors, therefore, improve their movement without becoming self-conscious about it. They gain an awareness of how they can change their patterns. It isn't the juggling that is important, but what the actor learns in the process. The actor then goes on to juggle with other people, which requires not just an awareness of his own body, but of the movement of his fellow actor. In the case of two actors doing a scene together, I have seen them develop a rapport through juggling. In *Alice in Wonderland*, Gerry Bamman did a flash of juggling. How marvelous to have that choice available.

Concurrent with juggling, my students work on balance on the bongo board. Once they learn to balance with their feet they juggle simultaneously with their hands. That is a classic circus thing. If you have anything free, do something with it. The bongo board is very important to the actor. It gives him a sense of where his center is. The head, shoulders, torso, and spine are floating in air. The legs swing like a pendulum, while the rest of the body is fixed. The strong sense of center achieved is valuable to the actor in terms of where he is, what he is and in relating his movement to the stage and to other people. This also relates to voice work in bringing breath from the center.

The trapeze is used to develop courage and self-confidence, and comes quite early in the work. The basic ways of hanging with tension in only the fingers require several lessons. The trapeze, in its own way, is treacherous. I am not interested in treachery. I try to teach other aspects of it and make people use it safely with minimal danger. It is a calculated risk, which I feel is worth taking. I relate the trapeze to flexibility, giving back stretches, and doing "bird's nests." From the catcher's lock, the student learns to take the weight of other people. I then go on to more difficult things such as ankle hangs. Only once in a project have I had people going from one trapeze to another. This goes beyond the equilibrium of the trapeze to its use as a catapult. Some people are afraid of being upside down or hanging from things. This is a fear to be conquered. I don't ask students to do things they are not physically capable of doing, but when the block is psychological, or emotional, I try to break the fears down. I do not make actors more talented, but try to liberate the talent they have by enabling them to use their physical body more effectively. Physical problems usually relate to acting problems and much insight can be gained in working on the acting problem through movement.

Stilts are an extension of the work on balance. They have many theatrical uses, and were used in Greek and Roman tragedy in order to depict gods or to enlarge characters. They are often used in burlesque in ladder routines.

I find tumbling difficult to teach. I start with a forward roll, which is predicated on flexibility. I add dives over obstacles and through hoops into the roll, working into aerial somersaults. Ted Hoffman, a professor of Drama at New York University, once said that when someone is ready to fly through the air and do somersaults they are ready to start acting. There is great truth in that. Circus skills enable the actor to understand the vitality, intensity and freedom that must exist under the spoken lines if the audience is not to be bored. If only the people who could leap through the air were actors, the theatre might be more exciting. Meyerhold understood this.

Falling is a valuable technique. The main objective is to break the fall so that it looks effective but does not injure the actor. Tumbling and balance are the prerequisites. A fall is broken by not hitting directly into it through sliding and rolling. It is important to know which parts of the body to tense and which to relax.

Relaxation is very important for the actor since it enables economic movement. Circus is good for relaxation as most of the activities are impossible to do unless you are relaxed. I try to make my exercises so progressive that I am aware of my students' optimum abilities and can control frustration and tension. If an actor is tense, he can ruin his voice or injure his body.

I do a minimum of double acrobatics because I like all my students to be involved in everything, and this requires that strong people do some things and light people do others. This kind of work establishes a rapport between actors.

Question: Would you discuss your student projects, explaining what is done and why?

Burgess: My student projects are improvised. The actor is aware of his technical limitations, yet I make him do things that are hard for him and he must try to make it interesting on the stage. The projects are demanding for the actor in the Grotowskian sense. The actor has to be aware of the reality of what he is doing without knowing the result. The actor doing circus before an audience tends to develop a character. When the circus performer has a character it is a self-conscious personality, showmanship thing. My projects are based on the premise that the actor can learn to give life to dull things. The audience may be disappointed by the lack of skill, but they are always excited by the improvised approach.

Question: Did the Circo dell'Arte work on a similar basis?

Burgess: Yes, it did. The troupe was made up of my acting students. The improvisational technique was used especially when we performed in parks. It became a sort of "guerrilla" street circus. We went out and found someone to perform for. We would start rehearsing as one would for a theatrical event. When a crowd gathered, it became a performance.

Question: How did the Bowery performances differ from outdoor events?

Burgess: Our Bowery performances were less successful. We were better equipped and our lack of skill was more evident. We were equipped to do everything, but we didn't do it. In the park, we didn't have the means to do anything and it looked as though we could do everything. We took advantage of our impromptu circumstances. The Bowery's specific space defined things more and the improvisation did not look as clever.

Question: How do your teaching methods compare with those used at the Moscow Circus School?

Burgess: The Moscow Circus School teaches the same thing I do. In some areas, they are more sophisticated. Because acrobatics and gymnastics are taught in the school system, they do not share my problem of inflexible students. The basic similarity is that we both see circus as a very high art.

Question: Has the work of Grotowski influenced you?

Burgess: His early writings influenced me a good deal, but more in terms of directing than in terms of training techniques. His teaching of physical and acrobatic exercises is not done progressively; he asks actors to do things that I consider dangerous. Knowing how the human body works, I do not put such demands on my students. He accomplished a great deal in doing this, because he is quite right that the mind and body are one; that through confronting people with things they are capable of doing but cannot do and making them do it they can learn a lot about themselves. But he is notorious for putting people in the hospital, and that is not my intention. When you don't know how to do an exercise you get hurt. I have been greatly influenced in my teaching by Joe Price, and he deals with slow progressions. Grotowski, when he watched my class, seemed upset with the progressiveness. He felt that the actor should be pushed further for the work to be relevant to his idea of theatre.

Question: In the theatre, the actor never dies with the character. In the circus, the performer and the character die. There is no division. Would you comment on the role of illusion in the circus?

Burgess: In this respect, the theatre is more artistic because it creates an illusion. Circus is quite real. Contemporary avant-garde theatre is going towards this reality. At Richard Schechner's Performance Group I expect to see something really happen. This is the opposite of Stanislavski's sense of reality. One is authentic, the other is authenticity. Everything that happens in the circus should really be happening.

Question: What is the role of imagination in the circus as compared to theatre?

Burgess: The imagination is used differently in each. The audience in the theatre must imagine objects and relationships. The trapeze in *A Midsummer Night's Dream* is a creation of Peter Brook's fantasy. In the circus, there are *real* relationships to people and objects, but it is also a fantasy world, where the audience imagines that it can perform these techniques. The reality of the circus ties in with the fantasy it creates.

Question: Do you foresee the "new" theatre as moving toward circus?

Burgess: Yes, that is fair to say. But it comes from a new emphasis on the physical in the world today. Grotowski revitalized it in the theatre. I hope that the actor, capable of performing circus techniques, stimulates this feeling of physical re-awakening in the public.

18

PITU'S DOUBT
Entrée clown self-fashioning in the circus tradition

Kenneth Little

The modern European circus clown is facing an uncertain future, the result of crumbling boundaries between the world of the circus and that of everyday private life. Circus people call this process "going private." The terms "circus" and "private" have been part of the circus vocabulary for generations, drawing sharp semantic distinctions between circus society and the European public. But in the second half of this century, these terms have come to take on a more than common significance for circus artists because of the increasing involvement of private commercial interests in traditional, family-owned and operated circuses. This growing privatization of the European circus has forced many artists to rethink or confront their place in circus tradition and history.[1]

Pitu, a 33-year-old French whiteface clown, has attempted to redefine the circus tradition so that it makes sense to him today in terms of what he understands as the future of clowning in Europe. Pitu (a pseudonym) has consciously fashioned his entrée clown persona in much the same way that human identity has been self-consciously constructed as a manipulatable, artful process since the sixteenth century (Greenblatt 1980). Though Pitu's whiteface clown has been fashioned with respect to its tradition, his clown image is not simply a set of traditional symbols through which he finds meaning and purpose for his clown work. Rather, entrée clown self-fashioning is the play of a particular difference that is established when Pitu attempts to make sense of his past in the context of an endangered tradition.

While the traditional circuses have to contend with the "private" circuses that do not play by the same rules of finance, family concerns, and artistic sensitivity, circus artists must compete with a growing number of highly motivated private artists who are not influenced by traditional circus practices. These "private" artists have either learned their skills on their own or in private or state-run acrobatic or clown schools. The quality and definition of circus acts are being redefined in terms of these new forms as they develop independently of the western European circus.

Nowhere has this trend toward private artists been more successful and apparent than with clown acts. The definition and role of the clown act in the European circus is changing as it becomes strongly associated with images and styles that are not at all part of the traditional circus clown sketch, the *entrée*.

The entrée is a 25-minute circus act. It is a routine grounded in a basic opposition of comic characters between the authoritarian, exacting, and sophisticated character of the whiteface and his[2] rather clumsy and disheveled partners, the augustes. Most entrée stories are set up as a comic tension between these characters. The whiteface clown attempts to accomplish some fantastic task for his audience, but his plans are forever interrupted by the intruding grotesques, the augustes. Either by the whiteface's invitation or simply by his own desire to participate in the plan or dream of his formal friend, the auguste dissolves the whiteface's carefully articulated endeavors into chaos, thereby disarranging conventional authority, meaning, and control. Disorder rules as the white-face's dream plan is shattered.

The whiteface clown and his auguste partners cannot be defined separately. It is only through their relationships that their comic characters make sense. An entrée could not be performed on the merits of just one clown or the other working alone in the ring. For example, the authoritarian whiteface, who simply wants his plan to be accomplished properly, defines the bad manners, incompetence, and lowly status of his auguste part-ners, who never seem to be able to provide their elegant friend with the necessary help. Of course, the opposite is also true: the augustes define the character of the whiteface.

The relationships between these clowns are always developed around proper plans and manners that are worked out of their guise of order only to reveal the chaotic charac-teristics of culture that are veiled by our habits of thought and action. The relationship always results in the comedy of illogical necessity, reconstituted language, and disor-dered social hierarchy. Under the authority of the whiteface–auguste relationship, cultural semantics is disarranged and kicked into the realm of "free play." Symbols become disengaged from the perishing strength of their meaning and significance, and chaos proceeds to rule. The dialog created between the augustes and the whiteface – like

Fig. 18.1 Pitu (in whiteface) and his circus partners. (Photo by Kenneth Little.)

the one between the circus and the village it carnivalizes – is an open-ended play of differences. No one element of these differences can possibly be assigned as the fixed and established meaning of the entrée or the clown characters themselves, because the surplus of clown mockery in the entrée calls into question any privileged meaning.

Entrée clowns usually learn their art in the circus ring. Pitu's story is by no means unique, and it provides a good example of how those born into the circus decide to develop their interests.

Pitu did not simply decide one day to become a whiteface clown. The idea seems to have been with him ever since he can remember. He is convinced that the circus clown tradition in which he grew up eventually, as he put it, "reached out and took me." From a very young age Pitu watched his father, a very famous whiteface clown himself, and his clown partners work in the rings of almost every well-known circus in Europe. He was still very young when his parents and a few close friends first took notice of his interests in clowning and he was encouraged to develop them. He had a recognized talent for clowning, a comic spirit that it would be his responsibility to mold into a circus clown character. At 14, he began to perform in the ring, doing bit gags as an auguste with his father's entrée group. With the aid of his father, he began learning the techniques of the clown entrée.

Like almost every whiteface clown (his father included), Pitu began his clown career as an auguste, through which he gained considerable experience as an entrée clown. Here he learned the entrées, the gags, the language, as well as the skills of comic improvisation that are so necessary to entrée clowning. After his father's death, and for the next nine years, Pitu worked in the ring with a number of whiteface partners. Finally, in 1980, two young Swiss augustes asked Pitu to join them as their whiteface. He accepted and made his debut in the large Swiss Circus Knie as a whiteface clown with two very "original" auguste partners. He began to explore his art more deeply so that he could learn to "bring out" and fashion a unique clown character.

In his clown work, Pitu, like clowns of other generations, relied on the authority of the entrée tradition. Circus artists invented the whiteface and the auguste, the forms of their opposition, their sartorial and behavioral conventions, and the occasions for their use. Entrée groups fashion a repertoire of comic sketches by uniquely combining a common stock of comic themes, gags, sketches, elements of costume, contraptions, gestures, and language according to their own imaginations and performance contingencies.

Since the late 1950s, however, a new private form of clowning has found its way into the circus ring from the streets, the folk and mime festivals, the theatre, and clown schools throughout Europe. And, while it has not replaced the traditional clown entrée altogether, this "new" clowning has gained almost equal billing and ring time in some of the best European circuses. If the great amount of media space and time and public response are any indication of its popularity, then this new form is definitely on the rise. Its comic style is not that of the entrée form. It is variously referred to as Clown Art, Clown-Miming, or Theatre Clowning. In the United States, such clowns are known as the New Vaudevillians, Postmodern Clowns, or New Wave Comics. Some circus artists disparagingly call them "school" or "private" clowns. In Europe, they have developed their work as a counterstatement to the traditional circus clown entrée, which, some new clowns argue, is dead (Lecoq 1973: 119–20). They have made a conscious effort to stay clear of the physical comedy, the costume styles, character developments, and make-up of the entrée clowns. New clowns voice a common observation that the public is tired of the old, traditional circus clown sketches that are based on the authoritarian nature of a whiteface dominating his subordinate auguste partners and on their slapstick relationship.

mance and his clown costume and make-up. These are the vehicles of his comic self-fashioning. It was through his entrée work and his physical clown character that Pitu attempted to "re-cognize" his tradition.

Reinventing the entrée by opening it up to new ideas and practices is an integral aspect of Pitu's notion of going inside. He and his partners are not concerned with fitting into the restrictive world that entrée clowns have constructed for themselves. Instead, they say they are reaching for something that was characteristic of the very earliest entrée clowns. It might be called a technique of playful speculation or semantic impertinence. These entrée clowns eschewed any attempt to close off entrée discourse with the real world, holding the real world, as an established order of things, in suspect. The world is nothing but playful resource, fragments of which may be rearranged and ordered into confusion. The earliest entrée clowns, Pitu argues, would never have stood for the indignity of a closed system of comedy, especially coming from their own tradition.

For Pitu, part of what it means to go inside is to assemble, as the early clowns did, combinations of comic material taken from traditional circus sources, from the cinema, from literature, from the real world, and from other clowns, as well as from on-the-spot imagination. Pitu and his partners are forever rearranging, adding, and dropping material, and they are never fully satisfied with their final results. Even after they have made decisions about their material and practiced their routines, they will undoubtedly reinvent sections of the entrée once in the ring. Pitu explained to me that entrées are works in progress; clowns are always planning different courses for their action and language as they discover what it is in the entrée that does and does not work for each particular audience.

A clown character must also remain as open as the entrée, through which it takes on both meaning and significance. The biography of a single clown character should be a story of endless refinements as new subtleties of humor and nuance of character are discovered and developed. Pitu's character development took place in the ring and over time as he learned to fashion a unique variation of the traditional whiteface character. Pitu's role as a whiteface developed as a *bricolage* of clown elements. In his costume Pitu tried to personify the "clown debonnaire." His standard costume was well within the tradition. He often wore a beautifully decorated, blue velvet jumper, a pointed white felt cap, nylon stockings, and yellow slippers. He displayed and demonstrated elegance, authority, and firmness on the verge of looking hard and stiff; he exhibited and revealed strength and intelligence to the point of appearing heartless and mechanical; he dressed expensively, in the best of taste, verging on the ostentatious. The ideal was to fashion a clown who exhibited those qualities of cultural refinement and sophistication bordering on narrow-mindedness, authority, and intolerance. Pitu, however, plays on these themes of opposition to reveal a clown whose behavior slowly seems to fall apart, as strength, sophistication, and intelligence dissolve into snares of confusion and perplexity. Unlike many of the whiteface clowns now working, Pitu developed such a clown character to work in the center of the comic action, where he is useful and necessary to the comedy itself. He is a clown closer to the conception of the developing laughter, full of action, still retaining a touch of physical slapstick in his work, and changing with the development of the comedy.

It may be possible to contextualize this particular aspect of going inside in more detail with an example from Pitu's clown work. This example is taken from the Balloon Entrée, a recognized, standard comic sketch that was performed by Pitu and his two auguste partners during the 1983 season of the Circus Knie.

The entrée begins when Pitu the elegant whiteface attempts to entertain his audience with a short magic trick. He succeeds in sticking a long steel needle through an inflated balloon without breaking it. The audience is charmed by this little trick, and they reply to it with enthusiastic applause. Pitu's partners, fascinated with the audience's reaction and eager to try out the trick for themselves, grab the balloon and needle from Pitu's hands. One auguste awkwardly holds the balloon between his hands while the other takes an elegant leap and a thrust toward it, piercing the balloon and breaking it. The augustes are shocked by their failure as the audience looks on with laughter. They blame each other for not having followed Pitu's instructions, and finally they begin to fight. Pitu hurries to them and breaks them up by suggesting that the two misfits help him with yet another, much more sophisticated trick. This time, Pitu explains, he will perform a very dangerous and mysterious feat of archery. Pitu will shoot an arrow from his crossbow (he picks it up and shows it to his partners and to the audience) through a balloon (he places the balloon in the hands of one auguste) and into the bull's-eye of a target (that he places in the hands of his other partner). In a very dramatic voice, Pitu stresses the fact that he will do all of this without breaking the balloon and at a ten-pace distance from the target. Both augustes are excited and fascinated by the trick and are now ready to assist their clown friend.

The rest of the entrée centers on Pitu's increasingly unsuccessful attempts to get his auguste helpers to follow even the simplest instructions. Through naivete, clumsiness, misdirection, or fear, the augustes lose or break one balloon after another. Everything seems to get in the way of the easiest tasks. If it is not their own stupidity or physical awkwardness that get in their way, then it is the malice of inanimate objects and invisible forces that thwart them. As Pitu's archery performance dissolves into chaos, he becomes increasingly exasperated with his helpers and their incompetence. Finally, and at long last, Pitu gets the augustes to follow his instructions. Everything seems to be set as one buffoon nervously holds the balloon above his head and the other holds the target. They face Pitu, ten steps away, as he steadies his crossbow, takes final aim, and begins his countdown. Pitu's concentration is so firmly set on his task that he fails to detect yet another distraction across the ring. The two misfits have found something else to fight over.

Pitu continues his count, oblivious to the fact that the augustes have begun to argue. The one holding the balloon has turned his back on Pitu and is shoving the balloon behind his back outside of the reach of the other auguste. With the balloon still firmly in his sights, Pitu shoots and scores a perfect hit. The balloon breaks and the arrow settles in the rear end of the unfortunate buffoon. Pitu looks up to see where his arrow has landed as a great scream fires from the mouth of his poor partner. Pitu looks on in shock and embarrassment as his wounded helper frantically hops around the ring in excruciating pain. By now Pitu is reduced to incoherent grunts and groans as he unsuccessfully attempts to explain to his audience just what went wrong and the awful treatment he has had to endure at the hands of the augustes. Mortified, he has no alternative but to run from the ring on the heels of the characters who were the original source of his problems.

One of the obvious themes of the entrée develops around Pitu's increasing exasperation, annoyance, and irritation with his disruptive auguste partners. Pitu begins his act with every good intention toward his partners and with the situation well in control. Pitu is self-possessed. He is the elegant clown who is willing to meet the ineptitude and naivete of his partners with patience, good graces, and friendly understanding. He does not start out as an authoritarian taskmaster, but he turns out to be one as the opportunity for a successful act becomes less of a sure thing for him. As it becomes clear that his partners are never going to accomplish the trick correctly, Pitu becomes more of a rough and arrogant bully. The most elegant and graceful of clowns is driven to the brink of irrationality: harried, dictatorial, embarrassed, and speechless. Pitu's character dissolves along with any chance of a successful archery act. He is not the same clown at the end of the performance as he was at the beginning. It is this changing character, evolving along with the comic action, that Pitu considers one of his innovations to the art of entrée clowning.

Most contemporary whiteface clowns conceive of their work in more unidimensional terms. For the most part, they see the whiteface solely as the invariable, dominating, and elegant master whose job it is to establish the predicament's comic theme and purpose and a normative guideline for its development. This is a basic rule for whiteface clowning today. As one clown put it, it is really the role of the *faire valoir*. This term means "to make value," or, in the stricter context of entrée clowning, it means "to bring out." In other words, the chief purpose of the whiteface clown, above all else, is to bring out the comedy and humor of the augustes.

The earliest faire valoir was a straight-man, usually a formally dressed comic artist. Many whiteface clowns more or less conform to this ideal. Such a clown is responsible for establishing the theme and order off which the augustes play. He never deviates from this role, and nothing happens to upset the otherwise stable development of his overbearing, authoritative, and elegant personality. As such, the clown highlights the augustes' funny predicaments, actions, and language, and then fades into the background until the buffoons have exhausted the comic situation and the whiteface is needed to set up another gag. The clown is the never-changing undertone to the comic theme and intention.[3]

Although there are circumstances when Pitu must set up a situation for his partners to transform into a comic event, he is not simply a comic feeder to the augustes. He does not stand on the periphery of the action. As the comedy of chaos develops with the augustes, so too does Pitu's clown change and mold itself to the situation. It is not just that his authority, overbearingness, and elegance are called into question or ridiculed by the augustes; more than this, Pitu the clown becomes undone along with his archery act. He too dissolves into a sorrowful and, at times, even a funny character. In this way Pitu has added something novel to whiteface clowning.

Pitu's physical character is not composed and defined only by his costume and action but also by his *maquillage,* or make-up. Certain aspects of clown maquillage are standard for all whitefaces. The face and neck are always painted white; the ears, lips, and nose, although specially considered and painted differently by each clown, are red. Black eyeliner and mascara are added to the eyelashes. The eyebrow markings, however, are distinctive. They are symbols of whiteface uniqueness, and no two clowns ever share the same marks. A clown must try to find a set of marks that easily adapts to the physical characteristics of his actual face as well as to the persona of the clown.

In this context Pitu's maquillage makes an interesting statement. His is a unique case, because he took his father's clown face rather than developing something new for himself. He explains that he first used his father's face for sentimental reasons; it established an important emotional link between Pitu, his father, his father's clown style, and circus tradition. Pitu's father, a teacher completely immersed in the best of the clown tradition, was an inspiration to his son. Wearing his father's face and using his father's clown name gave Pitu a much greater personal self-assurance as he started out in a career whose future looked grim. Physically, Pitu is very much his father's son – especially in the shape of his face. He says he finally decided to use the maquillage because the marks seemed to fit; they "worked" well on his face. The long black line that runs down the center of his forehead, continues on to the bridge of his nose and then swoops in a large arch over his right eye is strong and unbroken. It serves to emphasize his range of facial expressions. There are other small embellishments: the beauty mark on his chin; a set of extra-thin black lines that extend out from the corner of his eyes; and a pair of red dots located just inside the eyes, against the bridge of his nose. These markings, Pitu argues, emphasize the image of sophistication he is trying to present in the ring.

Pitu's clown face and name are the externalized products of his own spirit molded by circus tradition, in the guise of his father. As such, they are symbols of past stability and present demise on which Pitu had no choice but to depend for the meaning of his clown art. Pitu had recourse to the playful openness of the earliest whiteface style as well as to the more personal inheritance of his father's name and clown face. Together, they are what Pitu means by "going inside".

The entrée tradition's power to impose a shape on Pitu's art is an example of the more general power that tradition has to control identity. Pitu had little choice in the matter of his career as a circus artist. There was little else he could or would do, or even thought of doing. His life was inextricably tied to the circus, and he referred back to it for meaning and example. This is true even in light of the fact that his father, late in his life, told Pitu not to stay with the circus – that the circus was dead.

Pitu did attempt to get inside his tradition and fashion for himself a unique whiteface clown. He refused to accept the very restricted definition of the whiteface as it is characterized by current practitioners, but realized that his clown was being molded by forces outside his control. To be a whiteface clown meant at least accepting the constraints of its character, comportment, dress, and make-up. In this respect, he became his father's clown. To others within the entrée tradition, Pitu's decision was generally considered unorthodox, as were many of the very oldest comic materials and styles that Pitu adopted. Considering the exacting precision with which entrée clowning is now carried on and the conservative spirit that sanctions it, Pitu's work was rather irreverent and undutiful to the tradition. He discounted many of the modern entrée rules, and to many circus clowns this suggested hypocrisy – if not subversion.

In a sense, this is exactly what Pitu wanted to accomplish. The entrée tradition, by its own foolishness and narrow-mindedness, had become nothing more than equipment for living. The entrée form and the characters from which it grew had become dead metaphors in an art that had become simply mechanical reproduction. The whiteface–auguste distinction was no longer rude, disrespectful, or impudent. It no longer created resistance to the ordinary world as semantic impertinence. It was precisely this trend toward the literal and mechanical that Pitu was objecting to, for its effect created audience disaffection and indifference. Instead of creating parodies of life as mechanical and harsh, entrée clowns were more closely copying such a life. Add to this the rising popularity of the new clowns, and it rang the death knell for the entrée as a significant circus act.

In this context Pitu's clown self-fashioning is a "grasping together." Janus-like, he glances in opposite directions at once, back to a refigured past, into which he moves ever deeper in search of an authentic form, and forward to a prefigured future, which has come ominously into focus. He refigures his past out of his father's whiteface clown and the earliest of the entrée styles, against the flow of the authority of entrée tradition as it is now defined and practiced. Such an endeavor is undertaken in the face of a tradition that seems to be coming to an end at an ever-increasing speed. Pitu's clown self-fashioning occurs at the place where the authority of a past tradition encounters a sense of its ending. Ironically, then, it is an achieved clown identity which contains within itself the signs of its own subversion and demise.

It is not that Pitu thought that his life as a whiteface clown was in vain, but rather that the center of his world – the one in which he was born and raised, the one in which he could speak the language – was becoming increasingly unfamiliar to him. It would be like passing on a vocabulary much of whose lexicon seems out of date. The discourse does not make sense, although you can understand the words. It is at this point that his tradition, his clown face and entrée style, looks at him and he reads its ambiguity. But it is also at this point that Pitu is decentered, as he finds himself out of place with his past and future. It is here that he recognizes his own finitude by accepting the fate of living in a world in which he acknowledges the contingency of place and time. The symbols of his own self-fashioning keep telling Pitu that he is more than just this, that his history and future must articulate an ulterior purpose, while at the same time he is forced into a recognition that there is no such thing. The difference between a circus history and its future is the structure of existence that reaches discourse in Pitu's self-fashioning. Pitu plays the difference.

Performance ethnographers have too often misconstrued the subjects they work with as generic artifacts, bundles of symbolic relations that are the social facts of an already constituted world. This is part of the ideology of ethnographic realism where the ethnographer's counterpart appears as a representative of her/his culture – a type, in the language of traditional realism – through which general social processes are revealed. In such cases the meaning of a self, however it may be locally fashioned, is already constituted. It is simply the job of the ethnographer to collect these symbols and ferret out their meaning as ready-made facts of cultural life. Such a portrayal invests the interpretive authority with a synecdochic function by which the ethnographer reads cultural symbols and meanings in relation to a context, thereby constituting a meaningful "other".

On the other hand, if the discourse I am writing into a text is "a tissue of quotations," as Barthes (1977: 146) suggests it is, drawn from innumerable centers of different cultures, then the text's meaning lies not behind it but in front of it. As such, it cannot be construed as an authoritative statement about an abstracted reality. Circus tradition, as a set of symbols by which Pitu gains meaning, is only half the story of his self-fashioning. Pitu is not only a participant in the tradition but also a critical and keen-eyed observer of it. His clown self-fashioning is actually the ironic stance of a participant-observer. He stands, as does the ethnographer, on uncertain historical ground, in the late twentieth century, as a decentered subject simultaneously "in" culture and "looking at" culture. It is the play of this difference, along with his long gaze into circus history and the short glance over his shoulder at his future, that is constitutive of his life as a clown. Through Pitu's clown self-fashioning, we fashion for ourselves an image of the contingent status of all late twentieth-century cultural descriptions.

NOTES

1 Many people have contributed to this paper. I would like especially to thank J. David Sapir, Teresa Holmes, Christopher Taylor, Roy Wagner, Barbara Babcock, and Richard Schechner for useful comments and criticisms of earlier drafts of this work. Various sections of this paper were read at the weekly proseminar in the Department of Anthropology, University of Virginia, at the 84th Annual Meeting of the American Anthropological Association, December 1985, and at the Department of Performance Studies, New York University. The research for this paper was undertaken while traveling with four European circuses in Switzerland, France, and Italy with grants from the Social Science and Humanities Research Council of Canada, the Wenner Gren Foundation for Anthropological Research, and from Circus Knie. I gratefully acknowledge the special help of both Circus Knie and Circo Medrano for their permission to do extensive research while with their circuses.

2 For the most part, entrée clowns are men.

3 This has had a remarkable consequence on the popularity of the whiteface clown with his European audience. With a few exceptions, it has always been the augustes who have claimed most of the public fame and, in some cases, fortunes. The whiteface's reputation has been evaluated mostly as a sideman.

WORKS CITED

Barthes, Roland, 1972 *Image, Music, Text*. New York: Hill and Wang.

Greenblatt, Stephen, 1980 *Renaissance Self-Fashioning, From More to Shakespeare*. Chicago: The University of Chicago Press.

Lecoq, Jacques, 1973 "Mime–Movement–Theatre." *Yale Theater* 4 (1): 119–20.

19

HAJARI BHAND OF RAJASTHAN
A joker in the deck

John Emigh with Ulrike Emigh

Hajari Bhand of Chittorgarh is renowned throughout the Mewar region of southern Rajasthan as a *bahurupiya* – a wandering mimic and comic. For two months in 1982–3, he graciously gave up semi-retirement so that we could document his work. He took to the road again, visiting some of the 460 towns and villages that have comprised his circuit and performing twenty-five different roles, which included some routines with his son, Janakilal Bhand. In the months that followed, we visited his home to share raw footage from the film we were making and to interview him about his life as a bahurupiya and – prior to Independence – as a jester, praise singer, and wit in the Mewari courts.

Using Hajari Bhand's life and work as an example, this essay is an inquiry into the art and function of the now vanishing bahurupiyas and Bhands of Rajasthan. In *The Fool and His Scepter: A Study in Clowns and Jesters and Their Audiences*, William Willeford notes that "Fools have generally lacked the kind of fully established personal and social identities that can be made the subjects of biography and history" (1969: xix). In some ways, Hajari Bhand's life has followed a scenario of trials and choices that we might think of as typical of the unchronicled jesters who worked at court and on the road in medieval Europe. For western readers, an account of his life and art may also provide an imperfect window to an irrecoverable past.[1]

The term *bahurupiya* derives from the Sanskrit *bahu* (many) and *rupa* (form). Over the past forty-five years, Hajari Bhand claims to have portrayed several hundred characters, a vast assortment of Rajputs and holy men, professional men and tribals, gods and goddesses, tradesmen and rogues, and beggars and fools. As one who assumes many forms and playfully takes on different identities, he is aided by the fact that, in Rajasthan, a great deal about a person's occupation, social standing, expected behavior, and speech patterns can still be predicted by the clothing he/she wears. Great emphasis is placed on a bahurupiya's skill at costuming and make-up. A bahurupiya's disguise is known as a *vesh* (Sanskrit for clothing or dress), and the art of presenting himself in make-up and costume is referred to as "doing a vesh." The usually comic actions that accompany the wearing of a vesh are known as *sangs* or *swangs*. Derived from the Sanskrit *svanga*, "having graceful action" (Dash 1979: 14), this term now signifies a comic routine.

One may refer almost interchangeably to a bahurupiya's vesh or sang, with a slight shift of emphasis from his appearance to his actions. Using the streets, courtyards, and

Fig. 19.1 Hajari Bhand at home in India. (Photo by John Emigh.)

marketplaces of Mewar as venues for his veshes and sangs, Hajari Bhand imitates, exaggerates, and sometimes violates stereotypical expectations for comic and dramatic effect. He drops old roles, adds new ones, and frequently changes his patter as the times, his changing interests, and those of his audience require. His art is fashioned from a detailed knowledge of the dress and behavior patterns appropriate to the castes, character types, and mythological figures that have traditionally comprised the Rajasthani world. His playful portrayals reflect and help to shape the Rajasthani public's sense of identity in its most human terms.

BHANDS AND BAHURUPIYAS

The known history of the Bhands in India is sketchy. The Sanskrit *bhana* denotes a jester or a comic monolog (Russell and Hiralal 1915 1: 349; Ragavan 1981: 40). Historical connections with the pot-bellied, irreverent Brahman *vidusakas* of Sanskrit drama, as well as with the witty parasites mentioned in the Vatsyayana's *Kamasutra*, may well be valid (Welsford 1948: 63–4), but ancestors of the present-day Bhands are said to have entered India from Persia with the Muslim courts and are especially associated with Timur-leng (Tamburlaine), who invaded India in 1398 (Russell and Hiralal 1915 1: 349). There is still a substantial concentration of Bhands in Kashmir, where a form of farcical drama, Bhand Pather, is performed on Islamic saints' days and other festive occasions; many of the Bhands presently in north India seem to have come down from Kashmir at a later date (Russell and Hiralal 1915 1: 349; Motilal Kemmu 1980, personal communication). Like the Kashmiri Bhands, most Bhands in north India are Muslim. Thus, in 1896, Crooke (1: 259) cited figures for Uttar Pradesh, Punjab, and Haryana showing more than fourteen thousand Muslim Bhands living in these areas and only fourteen Hindu Bhands. In Rajasthan, however, because of the successful resistance of the Mewari courts to the spread of Islam, a separate Hindu caste arose, including the ancestors of Hajari Bhand, who served these courts as jesters.

The existence of Bhands in the region seems to be of considerable antiquity. G. N. Sharma (1968: 149) quotes the *Samyaktva* of Taruna Prabha Suri, written in 1354, as already mentioning "Bhands and troupes of professionals of both sexes performing buffoonery and farce, accompanied by music, dance, and dialogue." In a 1983 conversation, Sharma expressed his belief that Bhands played a vital role in developing the dramatic aspect of the Bhavai theater in Gujarat, as well as much of the popular theater of Rajasthan. The *A'in-i Akbari* of Abu'l Fazl 'Allami makes note of Bhands playing percussion instruments and "singing and mimicking men and animals" in sixteenth-century India (Jarrett 1978 3: 272).

Up until recently, Bhands have corresponded closely both in their function and in their activities to the professional buffoons and "artificial fools" of medieval Europe. The *Ethnographic Atlas of Rajasthan* (Mathur 1969: 60–1) states that "known for their ready wit and humor, their art of storytelling, jokery and buffoonery, the Bhands provide entertainment and fun to the people of festivals and feasts with the aid of their exciting fables and satires." A traditional Hindi proverb has it that a Bhand is "as essential at an entertainment as a tiger in a forest" (Crooke 1896 1: 258). Within the *ksatriya* courts, Bhands entertained in the evening hours in military encampments or on hunting expeditions, singing out praises for a good shot or jibing at a missed one. Similarly, they accompanied Rajas into battle – sometimes dressed as a Rajput ancestor – praising brave deeds or making jokes at the expense of both sides. Tulsinath Dabhai of the palace at Udaipur puts the case simply: "Their main function was to make the Raja laugh" (1983, personal communication).

Rawat Kesari Singh, a patron of Hajari Bhand since the days before Independence, stresses that "financially (Bhands) were completely dependent on Rajputs. They were given food, grains, and clothes, and at the marriages and deaths of their family members all the expenses were paid by the Rajas and Jagidars." To earn this support, the Bhand provided his royal patron with amusement, flattering praise, and at times witty stinging criticism. "It was," says Singh, "a very necessary part of court life" (1983, personal communication).

Like medieval jesters, the Bhands were privileged men, but such privileges have limits. Like their European counterparts, the Bhands were in constant danger of losing their livelihood by failing to amuse or overstepping the boundaries of royal humor. K. S. Ada of the Bharatiya Lok Kala Mandala tells a story that illustrates the skills required for survival (1982, personal communication). A Bhand in Jaipur had fallen out of favor with his Raja and been told never to show his face to the ruler again. After he departed in shame, a great procession was scheduled out of Jaipur. The Bhand coated his buttocks with wheat powder, stationed himself on a hill at the front of the crowd, and bent over, exposing his rear as his monarch paraded by. When asked to explain this extraordinary behavior, the Bhand said that he felt an overwhelming desire to present himself and pay proper homage to his king, but alas, since he was forbidden to show his face, what else could he do? He was immediately restored to favor.

The practice of performing as a bahurupiya is now associated with Bhands, but formerly members of various castes, including Brahmans, practiced this art in villages as well as at the courts. The *A'in-i Akbari* lists the "Bahurupi" as separate from the Bhands and notes that in their daytime mimicry, "youths disguise themselves as old men so successfully that they impose on the most acute observers (Jarrett 1948 3: 272). The term denotes a professional activity rather than a caste, and not all Bhands have been gifted at this particular set of skills. "It is an art, and a gift. Not all can do it," says Hajari Bhand (1983, personal communication).[2]

Central to the art of the bahurupiya is the ability to create convincing impersonations of identifiable types. Impersonations of deities at Hindu temple festivals may have led to performances involving the comic mimicry of social types among such castes as the Rawals by the end of the fourteenth century (Bhanawat 1979: 26–7). Bhands may have adopted these skills to increase their repertory as jesters, for in Orissa, where the Muslim courts had far less influence, the term bahurupiya is applied exclusively to those impersonating Hindu deities (Dash 1979: 15 and 1983, personal communication). Furthermore, both Hindu and Muslim Bhands who act as bahurupiyas in Rajasthan now sometimes represent Hindu deities. The combination of mimicry with court jests is a natural one, with or without evolution from divine impersonation. The fourteenth-century Italian buffoon, Gonello, for instance, is said to have "carried various disguises about with him" and to have depended upon his gifts for mimicry and impersonation for the success of many of his jests (Welsford 1948: 14). Whatever their religion, their caste, or the origins of their art, bahurupiyas from Gujarat to Bengal have traditionally prided themselves on the accuracy of their impersonations of men and women from all walks of life and on their ability to deceive even those who know them well.

> One of their favorite devices is to ask for money, and when it is refused to ask that it may be given if the Bahurupia succeeds in deceiving the person who refused it. Several days later, the Bahurupia will again visit the house in the disguise of a peddler, a milkman, or what not, sell his goods without being detected, throw off his disguise and claim the stipulated reward.
>
> (Ibbetson 1881: par. 529)

Enid Welsford summarizes the conditions that made possible the professions of court jester and wandering buffoon in medieval and Renaissance Europe:

> It was the existence of the small cultivated court, the sharp distinction but close connection between all classes of society and the comparative rareness of books which made buffoonery so lucrative and popular a profession. The jest books of the sixteenth century depict variegated but compact little societies, where king, burgher, priest and peasant are perpetually jostling one another, and the buffoon slips in and out licking up something from them all.
>
> (1948: 22)

This description applies as well to the princely states of Rajasthan before 1947. With Independence, the social and political system that had sustained the Bhands as court jesters was significantly altered, and the capacity of the courts to offer patronage drastically weakened. For a time, Bhands skilled in the art of the bahurupiya could earn their living through public performances, but the popularity of films and now of television has undercut the support available from the general populace.

Bahurupiyas are becoming more scarce, but they have not vanished. Babulal Bhand of Gauri in the Swayambhadpur district travels with two younger members of his family throughout the Hindi-speaking region of north India, following "his own sweet will" and earning 5,000 to 10,000 rupees a year. Babulal claims that 2,000 to 4,000 people – most of them Bhands or Naqqals – still earn a substantial part of their income as bahurupiyas (1982, personal communication). Of the more than 4,000 Bhands in Rajasthan listed in the 1961 census, R. S. Ashiya of the Bharatiya Lok Kala Mandala estimates that fifty or sixty families still make a substantial part of their income through their traditional skills (1983: 14). Bhands have taken up agriculture, government services, and many other walks of life in order to survive. As members of a scheduled caste, younger Bhands receive educational aid, and Kesari Singh notes a tendency among the educated youth to despise the traditional work of their caste: "They regard it as a shameful profession and feel they should give it up." This attitude is reinforced by those who regard Bhands and bahurupiyas as beggars.

In response to the tendency among townspeople to regard the Bhands as mendicants, Hajari Bhand speaks with dignity, pride and unconcealed anger:

> I am the Bhand of Rajas and Maharanas. We have been Bhands for a long time. All my fore-fathers were Bhands … . I have an allotted area of 460 villages, and I am respected in all these 460 villages. Everyone greets me with respect and I greet them with respect also. I am not a beggar. I am a Bhand. I live in Chittor … . Now, after the death of the Maharana, I have created my own patrons, and I am recognized and respected by all of these people.

A BHAND'S LIFE

Hajari Bhand was born in March 1922. He does not know the exact date. His father, Kaluji, was 46 years old when Hajari was born, and Hajari's elder brother, Mohan, was seventeen years his senior. His father performed four or five roles, which he taught Hajari, and his brother taught him more. He has been largely self-taught, though, and unlike other bahurupiyas, he has never studied under a guru. Both Kaluji and Mohanji were better known as experts at *bhandai*: praising the patron by reciting verses in his honor, or else, if the occasion called for it, criticizing, exposing, or ridiculing him in verse. Kaluji was also head (*patel*) of the Bhand community in the Chittorgarh area, and his responsibilities included keeping discipline within the community and organizing ritual functions.

As Hajari recalls, "Wherever he went, whatever he did, every sort of work, two or four hundred people would gather. He would hold council and they heeded his word. He would treat everyone with respect."

Hajari's grandfather was Moraji Bhand, who originally lived with his brother Jhoraji in Bhandakakhera – on lands ceded to the Bhands after one of their number had posed as a holy man and tricked Maharana Sajan Singh of Udaipur himself into becoming a disciple (Bhanawat 1974: 15). Family legend has it that Jhoraji became a particular favorite of Maharana Svarup Singh when he appeared dressed as a golden lion at a *shikhara*, or hunting expedition, held by the ruler. Seeing the "lion," Svarup Singh shot at Jhora Bhand, who was wearing iron plates on his chest for protection. As Hajari Bhand tells the story, "The Maharana fired, and the lion stood up on two legs. As soon as he was hit, he fell to the ground. After five minutes he stood up again. Then he declared, 'I am Jhora Bhand!' The Raja cried out, 'He is killed' How did he get here as a lion?'" Jhora Bhand was smeared with animal blood. He had a glass bullet in his hand and showed it to the hunt master. Finally, he removed his disguise and revealed himself, saying, 'I fooled you, and now I am your Bhand.' He was given more than 200 *bighas* of land (about 120 acres) near Mandal in the Bhilwara district."

This event took place in the mid-nineteenth century, beginning a long association of Hajari Bhand's family with the highest courts of Mewar. During the rule of Maharana Fateh Singh, Moraji brought his family to Chittorgarh, while Jhoraji's family moved to nearby Bassi, where the local *zamindars* gave them more fertile land. Every year during the Navaratri festivities preceding Dasahara, members of Kaluji Bhand's family, along with other Bhands, would appear at the *darbar* of the Maharana of Mewar at Udaipur – a custom Hajari continued until recently. During the rest of the year, ten families of Bhands would alternate attendance at the Maharana's Court, but the Bhands of Chittorgarh were regarded as particular favorites of the Maharana (Bhanawat 1974: 15–16). Silver coins were placed on lances and given to the Bhands as payment for a good joke or comic routine. During the Navaratri visits, Hajari would receive up to 1,000 rupees in addition to costumes, food, emergency funds to meet specific needs, and, occasionally, more land. At other times, the Maharana would visit their area and the Chittorgarh Bhands would come to entertain. They also worked under the patronage of the local Rajputs of the Bassi and Chittorgarh areas, gave occasional public performances, and were engaged by temples to play gods in religious processions.

In 1936, at the age of fourteen, Hajari was married to the daughter of a Bhand from Indore. He had started living with her when he was fifteen in the house where he still lives. At about this time, Hajari began to perform as a bahurupiya, first in supporting roles and then for a year under the patronage of the Thakur of Bhatyankakhera. Each day he would go to the Thakur's house to eat, and while there he also started to learn from the Thakur the art of bone-setting, which he still practices.

When he was seventeen, Hajari Bhand came to the court of Maharana Bhupal Singh at Udaipur. While at the court, a famous bahurupiya from Jaipur, Ramchandra, arrived. Ramchandra was not a Bhand, but a Brahman who went from court to court practicing the art of the bahurupiya. His paraphernalia and costumes filled an entire railway baggage car. At Udaipur, Hajari saw him win great favor and two hands full of silver rupees by pretending to be a crocodile in the palace lake, frightening and delighting the Maharana. This is how Hajari tells the story:

> The bahurupiya Ramchandra dressed up as a crocodile and plunged into the lake. Someone cried: Oh, where has this beast come from? Bring a gun, someone! By the time they brought the gun the crocodile had dived back into the lake, letting only its snout stick out. As soon as the people handed the gun to the Maharana, the crocodile said: I am the bahurupiya Ramchandra from Jaipur!

The officer in charge of entertainment praised Ramchandra's bravery, derided the Bhands of Chittorgarh as having little talent or imagination, and challenged them to appear in a novel disguise or return to Chittorgarh in shame.

Owing to his evident skills in mimicry, young Hajari was chosen to represent his family. "The next day, I disguised myself as a demon (*raksasa*) first of all. I went among the crowd and many men and women were really frightened. Next, I dressed as a pregnant Pinjari (a woman who cards unspun cotton). I went before the Raja and said, 'Oh, what has happened to me! You, Bhupal Singhji, you have deprived me of my honor!'" As Bhupal Singh tried to conceal his laughter with a handkerchief, Hajari pointed to the Maharana, who had been crippled by polio as a youth, and addressed the crowd: "That one, sitting there, even though he can't walk a step, he still got me pregnant!" Bhupal Singh seems to have been delighted at this flattering abuse. "So Bhupal Singhji gave me 125 rupees and said, 'You did a *sang* which made us convulse with laughter. Now don't do this any longer.' The Maharana was choked with laughter, and he told them, 'Give them 125 rupees and give them good food and treat them well.'"

Young Hajari was not through, however. He disguised himself next as a Gaduliya, an itinerant maker and vendor of ironwares whose caste claims descent from Rajput blacksmiths and swordsmiths of ancient Chittor – a claim that the ksatriya castes deny and resent. His account of his work in this disguise further illustrates how a Bhand exercised his privilege and flirted with disfavor in order to gain greater favor. After many obscene puns about furnishing the assembled lords with iron tools, Hajari shouted out,

Fig. 19.2 Hajari Bhand as itinerant seller of ironware. (Photo by John Emigh.)

I am a Gaduliya. I am one of your ancestors. [As he continues the story] I said I was a Rajput and shouted all the time. Some two, three people tried to stop my mouth, but the Maharana was very pleased. They said, 'Don't shout! We'll give you whatever you demand.' The next day the Maharana gave me a reward of 250 rupees. He said the Bhands of Chittorgarh may freely come to the court.

Hajari had successfully gauged his patron's sense of humor, and his daring had won him favor. Before the stay was over, he had also performed as a washerwoman, an Afghani aphrodisiac salesman, a shepherd, and a dancing girl. Ramchandra, defeated in competition by the young Bhand, offered Hajari's father 300 rupees a month if he would turn the boy over to him. Kaluji Bhand refused this offer, and Bhupal Singh gave Hajari 600 more rupees in appreciation of his skill and heaped gifts of clothing upon him. "Then he told me to come to the palace dressed in those things. I went dressed in them and he said, 'Now you look like a Rajput.' Then I said, 'Kama dhani – excuse me, Your Highness,' and went back home." Hajari remained a great favorite with Bhupal Singh, and, over the years until his death in 1955, Bhupal Singh rewarded and encouraged Hijari's talents by giving him money, a ceremonial sword, and costumes valued at over 20,000 rupees.

Hajari still visits some of his former patrons, such as the Thakur of Orli, Kalyan Singh, and Rawar Kesari Singh, now the elected mayor of Bassi. They express great affection for him and invite him to perform at family weddings and other gatherings. As recently as 1971, Hajari dressed his large family as a group of Bhil tribals and entertained the present Maharana Pramukh of Udaipur, Bhagwat Singh. The grateful descendant of the Maharanas rewarded Hajari with 400 rupees. Still, Bhagwat Singh does not share the passion of his ancestors for the Bhands' jokes, disguises, and comic turns, and in any case, he does not command his ancestors' treasury (G. L. Sharma 1983, personal communication).

With the dwindling of royal patronage after Independence, Hajari Bhand has had to rely more on village audiences and especially the merchant castes for support. Despite the spectacular success at Bhupal Singh's court, the Bhands of Chittorgarh had anticipated this problem, and by the time Hajari Bhand was 20 years old, he, his brother Mohan, and a neighbor, Champalal Bhand, had begun to perform publicly in the villages. Eventually, their travels included villages in the Udaipur, Kapesan, Bhilwara, and Chittorgarh areas and ranged as far as Bhanswara, 120 kilometers away, creating a circuit of 460 villages. These villages were shared out among six families of Bhands working out of Chittorgarh, while another 250 villages were allotted to a group of Bhands from Devli. Sometimes, villages would be alternated from year to year between cooperating families, and family members would be assigned to play their veshes at specific villages. In the event that a bahurupiya performed his veshes in a place assigned to another, he would have to pay a share of his earnings to the person whose territory he had infringed upon. This practice seems to be less in force now, as fewer Bhands are working in the villages. In any case, Hajari did not need to seek permission to enter the villages we visited, since his high status within the community exempted him from these restrictions.

As Hajari grew older, sometimes one or two children from his growing family would accompany him for veshes involving more than one character. Other times, he would perform with his brother, Mohan. Most of the time, however, he traveled alone, leaving bundles of costumes at relatives' houses scattered throughout the district. When arriving at a new place, he found accommodation at a caste member's home, a *dharamsala* (public guest house), or sometimes with the local nobility. In a small village, Hajari Bhand usually performed two veshes a day, one in the morning and one in the afternoon.

In large towns, a single vesh might take all day. His stay in a village would ordinarily last one or two weeks.

As he performed from shop to shop and door to door, he accepted payment offered by onlookers, and also kept a ledger recording the names of shop-owners and householders he entertained. At the end of his stay, he usually appeared in the disguise of a money-lender, or Bania, and collected from those he had entertained, marking the amounts of payment in his record book. Those entertained are expected to give something, be it money, rice, wheat, corn or other in-kind payment according to the season. He estimates that the income from touring half the year amounted to 3,000 to 4,000 rupees.

During his travels, Hajari kept expanding his repertory, picking up ideas from other wandering mimics and inventing new roles based on people he observed in the courts, towns, and villages. "Where I could, I learned, and where I couldn't learn, I taught." Often, he built up characters by observing real-life models over extended periods of time. He tells of attaching himself to a Muslim Fakir for two weeks in order to study his ways. The lengths he might go to in order to master a new role, as well as his adventurous spirit, are shown in his acquisition of the costume of a Behru Jogi, a mendicant Hindu holy man. After approaching a Behru Jogi about obtaining the costume, he was told that he must wear it for one hour a day for twelve years without accepting money before he could earn the right to use it in his work.

> Twelve years long, I wore the costume every morning for one hour. While I was acting the role, people would give me flowers and money, but I didn't accept anything from them. If a flower was given, I gave it to the dogs, and if money was given, I distributed it to children.

After this long apprenticeship, Hajari Bhand not only acquired the right to use the costume as a bahurupiya but also "the spiritual powers (*siddhi*) of a Bheru Jogi." Hijari once put on the costume to face down a local practitioner of black magic who had threat-ened a relative of his, drawing a protective circle around the intended victim. He believes that the powers accruing from his disciplined apprenticeship with this costume have helped him gain respect and relative prosperity. "In its name, I am earning my living and working as a bahurupiya."

Hajari Bhand's life has not been spent entirely on the road or at royal courts. He is a leader of the Bhand community in Chittorgarh, has been married twice, and has fathered thirteen children – the youngest being four years old. Hajari's first wife died when he was 24. He was remarried to a daughter of Ambalalji Bhand of Jaipur, a Bhand noted for his poetic skills. Of his two children by his first wife and eleven by his second, nine sons and one daughter are still alive. To support this large family and supplement his earnings as a bahurupiya, Hajari Bhand supervises cultivation of the family lands (now ten bighas). He also earns additional income from assisting with make-up at school plays and "fancy-dress" competitions. Most importantly – and quite apart from his work as a bahurupiya – he also practices as a bone-setter, and his house is frequently visited by people who have broken, sprained, or dislocated a limb. After being introduced to this skill by the Thakur of Bhatyankakhera, he developed it while achieving distinction as an amateur wrestler. He does not accept cash payments for his services, but through the years grateful patients and their parents have given him goats, cows, and building materials. He also performs frequently in the streets of Chittorgarh. Here, Hajari Bhand does not need to keep a record book. Well-known by the local merchants, he collects his fees twice a year, at the holidays of Divali and Holi.

Festival occasions are important workdays for bahurupiyas. Bhands may be hired by temples to represent gods and goddesses, or they may appear of their own accord. As a younger man, Hajari appeared on Divali as the goddess Lakshmi. He now considers himself too old successfully to perform this vesh, and during our stay he substituted portrayals of Hanuman and Shiva. On the Muslim holiday of Id, Hajari dresses as a Muslim Fakir, and gently satirizes these holy beggars, collecting at least 500 rupees from the amused celebrants. Both Muslim and Hindu Bhands often perform this vesh on Id; there seems to be no sacrilege or resentment felt by the Muslim community regarding Hajari's comic portrayal nor by the Hindu community when Muslim Bhands portray Hindu deities.

In addition to performing from shop to shop in towns and villages. Bhands appear as invited or uninvited guests at the weddings of the wealthy merchant castes, which have taken over (to an extent) the patronage of the Bhands. While Babulal Bhand most frequently appears at such an occasion as a Bania, making jokes about the merchant caste's historical involvement with usury and about the new couple's coming economic plights, Hajari usually goes dressed as a policeman. He starts from his home already disguised as an officer, often commandeering bus rides along the way. "Sometimes a policeman shakes hands with me. Sometimes even a police inspector shakes hands. 'Where have you come from?' he says, 'Where have you been transferred from?' 'I've been transferred from Durgapur.'" In this manner, he makes his way to the wedding festivities, sometimes revealing the joke and sometimes not. "Then I address the people of the wedding party. I frighten and threaten people. 'Hey mister! What do you think you're doing?' 'Oh no, Sir. I'm not doing anything.' 'Remove this bus from here! Ho, where is the license for this vehicle?' 'We don't have all of the necessary papers.'" At times, Hajari Bhand will encounter a real policeman at the wedding. "I tell him, 'The number on your belt is upside down.' He corrects the belt and salutes me." At large receptions, he may invoke a public law designed to control rebellious political gatherings and order the reception disbanded. "I call the bridegroom's father and ask him: 'How many persons have you assembled here?' '150 persons, Sir.' 'Why did you assemble 150 persons? The government's law does not allow that. The law allows only 51 persons to assemble for a feast. Why have you done this?' 'Oh Sir, we'll never do it again.'" As protests mount, angry words are exchanged and bribes offered, he reveals his disguise and collects liberal fees from the relieved relatives.

Hajari recognizes that fewer and fewer Bhands are now able to sustain themselves by the traditional skills of their caste, and he has exerted no pressure on his children to take up his work. Although many of them are still quite young, so far only one of Hajari's sons, Janakilal, has taken up the work of the bahurupiya, and his activities are limited to festival days. In Bhilwara, where he works in a flour mill to make ends meet, Janakilal Bhand usually performs for twenty days during the Divali season, six days during Holi, and occasionally travels to Maheshvari weddings.

Although he sometimes regrets the drying-up of royal patronage, Hajari enjoys working the village crowds. He is regarded with great affection, and mentioning his name evokes smiles, anecdotes, and words of appreciation for his skills as a comic artist and his standing in the larger community. Hajari says that when he was a young man he was offered a contract for performing in Bombay's then fledgling film industry. Taking his father's advice, he turned down the offer. He has no regrets.

The ability to give both flattering praise and stinging abuse was central to a Bhand's skills. Both the praise and the abuse are referred to by the generic term, *bhandai*. Bhandais praising a patron might be given as a salutation or as an expression of gratitude. The formula for these bhandais involves naming valued ancestors, praising the patron's worth, and proffering blessings on the patron and his family. These encomiums are often lavish in hyperbolic praise. This is a bhandai Hajari Bhand composed and recited in our presence of one of his traditional patrons, Kalyan Singh, Thakur of Orli:

> Oh Sir, you are the protector of the earth, like Chhatrapati Shivaji! The whole earth becomes free and their bonds are broken the moment they look at you! You are like Mahadev in appearance, and all baseness flees at a single glance from you! You are more liberal in charity and braver in warfare than any other! You can transform a worthless shell into a jewel worth hundreds of thousands of rupees, such is your worth-enhancing power! This village of Orli where you Rathors rule is like heaven on earth. May God keep you happy forever!
>
> The whole world knows that you are like an incarnation of God. Your name is known everywhere in the universe … . May your illustrious Rathor family shine like the sun! Hajari Bhand will go on singing your virtues forever.
>
> Your household estates are like those of a Lord of the Earth. Your heart is large and generous. Oh Kalyan Singh, you are peerless on this earth. Many people come to you with prayers for help in distress and thousands stand in attendance for you. You are lord of the earth, ocean of mercy, and giver of food to us all!

While these paeans of flattering praise could be extreme, the abuse of a Bhand who had been offended was to be feared. A Hindi proverb singles out "the rage of a widow, a Bhand, and a bull" as being awesome to behold (Crooke 1896 1: 258). Sometimes, this anger could take the form of withering curses aimed at an offending patron. Hajari gave this example:

> Oh patron, may you have a long life. But may you be blind in both of your eyes. May you travel forth to foreign lands and be set upon there by thieves and robbers. May all your 32 teeth get broken, just as you near your door. May you be sent to jail and rot there for life after life. May the ominous swallow-wort and acacia trees grow outside of your home. Oh my lord, may I never again seek even a grain of corn or a bundle of grass from you!

In these appeals to magic power for vengeance on an ungrateful patron, the Bhands stand as living examples of a satiric tradition that stretches beyond the wandering bards of Ireland (who were credited with rhyming rats and, sometimes, kings to death) all the way to Archilochus, whose poetic invective was said to have driven King Lycambes to his death (Elliott 1960: 3–48). It is interesting to note that while the Bhand's identity and profession are usually defined in secular terms, Hajari Bhand – in learning the skills of bone-setting and in earning the right to the Bheru Jogi's spiritual powers – has independently taken upon himself some of the functions and qualities of the shaman or wizard. Paradoxically, still another link with the traditional procedures of sacred magic may be seen in the use of blatant obscenity in the imagery of this bhandai that Hajari once used to upbraid a Thakur for his lack of generosity:

> Thakur saheeb, rajputi (the courage and benevolence of the Rajputs) is no more. It has gone far beyond the seas. All virtuous Rajputs have been cooked to death in a whore's fart. Poor rajputi moves about, crying, "Where should I go now? Everywhere I wander, I see nothing but prostitutes' legs spread wide!"

The use of graphically obscene imagery is made all the more shocking and effective by its juxtaposition with rajputi, a chivalric code of values that traditionally operates as an unwritten standard of ethics for the Rajput castes. In further upbraiding and insulting the ungenerous Thakur, Hajari Bhand continues to make use of this normative frame of values:

You are a Rajput. I came to your door to ask for your patronage, but you didn't even offer me water. You are the resident Thakur. A fortunate man worth two, three, or four *lakhs* (hundreds of thousands of rupees), and still you don't invite me for a little food. What sort of Thakur are you? You and your kind are not Thakurs, but the thieves and swindlers of the world. And if the Thakurani had given birth to a real Thakur, he would have looked quite different from you!

More frequently, abuse in a critical bhandai was clothed in wit. Kesari Singh says that court ministers would sometimes try to withhold payment that had been promised by a Raja to a Bhand, but they did this at the risk of being made a laughing stock in front of the court. The following bhandai in Hajari Bhand's repertory is an example of the kind of abuse such a minister would risk:

Your father is a great slave. Your son is nothing but a slave. And your uncle is a slave to paupers. Your brother is a slave to beggars. Your maternal uncle is a slave to men with monkey shows. Your elder brother wears the sky for his clothes. Your brother-in-law is a slave to fools. Your son-in-law is a slave to jogis. This is the kind of family you come from, and you have only increased their baseness. And now I have lost my own honor as a Bhand by requesting money from the likes of you!

In the rough-and-tumble of court life, the Bhand's skills at abusive rhetoric could be turned to sport. Sometimes a Bhand would be threatened with the loss of all he had earned if he could not make the Raja laugh, and Hajari Bhand remembers his brother finally winning such a dare by cleverly and outrageously abusing the Raja himself. Motilal Kemmu, who has worked for many years with the Bhands of Kashmir, tells of a mean-spirited Raja who was blind in one eye from battle and threatened a Bhand with death if he could not make him laugh. After going through his entire comic repertory, the desperate Bhand went up to the King and whispered in his ear: "Why don't you laugh, you blind bastard?" The King roared in appreciation of this mention of a taboo subject and handsomely rewarded the fortunate Bhand (1981, personal communication).

As use of the ethical framework of rajputi in addressing the ungenerous Thakur suggests, the bhandai could extend beyond sport or leverage for payment in its significance. Kesari Singh notes that the acerbic remarks of the Bhand were often warranted, and that a wise Raja would listen carefully for words of warning and wisdom in the privileged man's jibes.

Some very courageous Bhands used to point out to the Rajas where they were mistaken and what their wrong actions were. Clever or wise Rajas would never get angry at them, but would reward their service. Some unwise Rajas, at times they would get angry and turn them out of their kingdom. Such things also happened.

It is startling for those familiar with Renaissance drama to discover such close cousins to Calderon's *graciosos* and Shakespeare's wise fools still alive in this century.

Hajari Bhand now recites bhandais for generous patrons among the merchant castes in the same manner as he did for his royal providers, sometimes even retaining titles appropriate for Rajputs. Thus, the generous payment of cash and a turban by a merchant at Divali was greeted as follows:

Oh Bhandari Raja, you are merciful to the poor and a most lucky King of Kings. Oh great and fortunate Raja, you have brought renown to your family and land. You are like a supreme ruler of the world and your heart is as kind as that of King Hamir. Oh Bhandari

Raja, you are incomparable on this earth and there are no limits to your charity. So many persons stand before you, putting forth their requests, begging for alms and help. Thousands of people stand ready to execute your orders. May the goddess Lakshmi and the god Satyanarayan keep you happy and prosperous. Oh World-Renowned, may you bathe in milk and prosper in children, as a fortunate King of Kings.

Sometimes the concerns of the merchants form an odd mix with the formulaic compliments and good wishes traditionally extended to royal patrons.

You also are a fortunate King of Kings. May you also swim in milk and prosper in progeny. May the goddess Lakshmi keep your coffers and stores perennially filled to the full. May you make a net saving of 35 lakhs rupees in the coming year! Oh Master of the World, Bestower of Food and Sustainer of the Poor, I, your Bhand, have come to the door of your palace!

If the merchant class has inherited the flattering praise offered to generous royalty, however, they have also become vulnerable to the sarcasm and humiliation that can be caused by a Bhand who feels himself slighted. "Raising the bhandai" against a wealthy merchant who has refused payment heaps embarrassment upon the merchant and his entire family. Hajari told a story which exemplifies this power of the Bhands to enforce their means of livelihood:

In our Chittor, _____ (an influential merchant) once stopped our being invited to weddings. Four or five of us made a decision. We all gathered and formed a procession. We made Onkarji Bhand ride a donkey, while my brother disguised himself as a witch. We went to the marketplace. All the members of the merchant community gathered there, and asked us: 'What are you doing?' 'I am _____'s mother, I am a witch!' We were using a shoe as a fan, and Onkarji Bhand was wearing a shoe instead of a bridegroom's crown. Like that, we passed through the market.

In these costumes, they arrived in front of the wealthy merchant's house and began to hurl curses against him, adding the following ill wishes to the recycled curses already cited:

Lord of the Earth, may you never get food or wife, and may your cattle starve for want of fodder! You are killing us, the poor and needy people. May you never enjoy well-being in life! And now this one of us has become a witch in order to take your wife from you and so that you may never enjoy life again. As I have said this, so may it be!

The merchant stayed at home for five days, ashamed by his public abuse. The women begged him to pay off the Bhands, and finally his caste relations gave the Bhands their fee, and assured them that they would always be welcome at Maheshvari weddings.

At times, bhandais can be pointedly satiric, exposing the skeletons in family closets. One Bania who refused to allow payment to Hajari Bhand and his family at a wedding was reputed to have slept with his son's wife and fathered a child. Adapting the vesh that had won him such favor with Maharana Bhupal Singh, Hajari dressed as a pregnant peasant woman and came up to the man in public. He accused him of being the father of the child "she" was carrying, and made not-so-veiled references to the money-lender's extra-commercial exploits. Although this practice is now rare and the Bhands' power has declined with the weakening of the feudal order, Komal Kothari, director of the Rupayan Sansthan Institute, says that in extreme instances Bhands can still make it difficult to marry daughters in families known to have incurred their wrath and scorn for fear of the scurrilous abuse that might be offered by the uninvited guests at such weddings (1981, personal communication).

This satiric strain, directed against the hypocrisy, greed, and overbearing pride of the wealthy and powerful, is also found playing beneath the mimicking of the Bania, the police officer, a doctor who suggests removal of vital organs and sexual abstinence, and a sanctimonious Congress Party politician. Though satire rarely dominates, it surfaces often, as, for example, when the Gaduliya mentions that people call his caste vagrants and beggars because they sleep in wagons, whereas "the real beggars are the bureaucrats who live in their new houses built with the money of the poor."

Hajari Bhand not only portrays and sometimes satirizes holy men, he represents the deities themselves. Thus, within a tradition that may relate back to the origins of mimetic performance in India, he represents Hanuman, Kali, Shiva – and, when he was younger, Lakshmi – in non-comic veshes frequently given on religious holidays. For Hanuman, he uses a papier-mâché Ramlila mask, along with a great deal of red dye, a "tail" improvised from materials about the house, and a picture of Rama and Sita cut from a calendar at his home and glued to his chest. He leaps and shouts "Sri Ram!" as he moves through the Divali market, animating the vision of Hanuman generated by calendars, comic books, and popular religious films. His Shiva glides through the market in a jovial, ecstatic state, blessing goods and people, accepting alms, and dancing joyfully outside of the Shiva lingam and shrine in downtown Chittorgarh. This affinity of the fool with the divine manifests itself around the world. The privilege of the fool to rail and satirize is surely related to these touches of divine grace.

If the mirror that the bahurupiya holds up to nature is a distorting one, often sustaining stereotypes and poking fun at man's pretensions to dignity, the bahurupiya's playful census of Rajasthani types also provides a dynamic method of airing tensions within the culture. Beyond this, in its cumulative effect, the artistry of the bahurupiya challenges the fixed nature of the very categories that it uses for its field of play. Plato, who distrusted mimetic skills, refers in *The Republic* to wandering "pantomimic gentlemen, who are so clever that they can imitate anything" and suggests sending storytellers with such skills promptly away as disruptive influences, "sweet and holy and wonderful beings" though they may be (Jowet 1944: 155). Plato feared that the mimic would further distort life – already imperfectly comprehended – for the sake of a good laugh or a dramatic effect, and that the net result of his fooling with identities would be chaos. The anarchic juggling of identities by the bahurupiya as "pantomimic gentleman" is particularly striking against a social background traditionally dominated by principles of *karma dharma*, which dictate the obligations and duties, as well as social rank, dress, and occupations of caste members.

Feudal societies in general have tried to answer the call of anarchy by sponsoring pockets of disorder within the system itself. The fool chained to the throne of the king served as a reminder of common frailty, but the chain must have also functioned as a means of keeping this human symbol for disorder fixed within the compass of the court. The natural fools and dwarfs that so fascinated the European medieval and Renaissance courts as lessons in humility and images of a disorder that cried out for containment seem to have been less popular (though not entirely missing to judge by the vidusaka's distorted shape) in the courts of India. In Hindu caste society, the bahurupiya's ability to take on many identities is similarly appealing and threatening. It can be no accident that, of all the Bhands, the Hindu Bhands of Rajasthan seem to have taken particular delight in tapping into this tradition to add to their repertoire as jesters. If the rigidities of dress and behavior in caste society facilitate the bahurupiya's work, these same rigidities give added meaning to his ability to function.

The bahurupiya's heretical play with the principles of karma dharma points to a deeper stratum of Hindu philosophy that insists that each human being contains in microcosmic form the powers and potentialities of the macrocosmos. As a joker in the deck, a "wild card" in an otherwise carefully labeled pack, the bahurupiya serves as a reminder that, even in the most rigid societies, identities are not fixed. The wheel of karma takes many turns; a prince in one cycle may find himself a pauper in another as the *lila* – or play – of life continues. Small wonder, then, that the rich and powerful would strive to contain and control this disruptive presence through patronage, and that the Bhand's sycophantic flattery is sought after, while his curses are feared. The Bhand as bahurupiya serves not only as an entertaining reflection and distortion of a Rajasthani "human comedy" but as a reminder and immediate demonstration of the mutability of the human soul and the liveliness of the human spirit.

This is, of course, neither a new nor a peculiarly Asian enterprise. At the end of the middle ages in Europe, Erasmus followed a similar line of thought while meditating on the fool and writing his *Praise of Folly* (Hudson 1941: 37):

> Now what else is the whole life of mortals but a sort of comedy, in which the various actors, disguised by various costumes and masks, walk on and play each one his part, until the manager waves them off the stage? Moreover, this manager frequently bids the same actor go back in a different costume, so that he who has but lately played the king in scarlet now acts the flunky in patched clothes.

We do not know, of course, how much of this analysis would ring true to Hajari Bhand, who in his day-to-day behavior is as polite and modest as he is outrageous in his professional roles. It is appropriate to end this study with his own joking protest about our work with him:

> I wander about, I meet everybody. I get along with everyone. By making people happy, I earn some money. I eat and I drink. I have no problems. Then you people come along and hire me to do all this work and ask me all these questions about this and that. Now I've got problems!

NOTES

1 Funding for this research was provided by the Smithsonian Institution and the Indo-US Subcommission in 1981 and 1982–3 and administered by the American Institute of Indian Studies. In addition to the individuals cited in the text, and many others who must go unrecognized, we are indebted to the people of Bassi, Bhilwara, Chittorgarh, Gangapur, Renwal, Pushkar, Kacheriawas, Jaipur, and Udaipur, where we filmed and conducted research. The bahurupiya's work and our own would be impossible without their good will and sense of humor.

   A 40-minute video tape, *Haraji Bhand of Rajasthan: Jester without Court,* is available through the Asian Theatre Program film rental service, University of Kansas Film Library, Lawrence, Kansas, and for rental or purchase through Documentary Educational Resources, 5 Bridge St., Watertown, Mass.

2 Quotations from Hajari Bhand come from taped interviews and conversations held from November 1982 to March 1983. Translation assistance was provided at various times by Komal Kothari, who first introduced Hajari Bhand to us, Rawat Kesari Singh, O. P. Joshi, Ranchor Singh Ashiya, Dinesh Chandra Bhanawat, Shadashiv Shrotriya, and Kanilal M. Bhandari, whose good faith and assistance were invaluable. Further translation advice was provided by Robert Hueckstedt. Karine Schomer and Joan Erdman offered helpful suggestions for writing and editing.

3 The sections of Hajari Bhand's sangs quoted in this article have been reworked from Dinesh Chandra Bhanawat's literal translation made from out field recordings.

WORKS CITED

Ashiya, Ranchor Singh (1983) Mulakat Hajari Bhand se. *Rangayan* 16. no 10: 13–19.

Bhanawat, Mahendra (1974) Nakal ko Bhand ki. *Rangiyog*: Journal of the Rajasthan Sangeet Natak Akademi.

Bhanawat, Mahendra (1979) Overview of the Folk Theatre of Rajasthan. *Sangeet Natak*: Journal of Sangeet Natak Akademi 53–4: 26–32.

Crooke, W.(1974) *Tribes and Castes of Northwestern India*. 4 vols. Delhi: Cosmo Publications, 1896.

Dash, Dhiren (1979) "Jatra": People's Theatre of Orissa. *Sangeet Natak*. Journal of the Sangeet Natak Akademi 52: 11–26.

Elliot, R. C. (1960) *The Power of Satire: Magic, Ritual, Art*. Princeton, N.J.: Princeton University Press.

Hudson, Hoyt Hopewell, trans. (1941) *The Praise of Folly* by Desiderius Erasmus. Princeton, N.J.: Princeton University Press.

Ibbetson, Denzil Charles (1881) *Punjab Census Report*.

Jarrett, Col. H. S., trans. (1978) *The A'in-i Akbari* of Abu'l Fazl 'Allami. Rev. 2nd edn, 4 vols. Sir Jadanath Sarkar, ed. New Delhi: Oriental Books Reprint Corporation, reprint of 1948 edn, 1st edn of trans., 1894.

Jowet, B. trans. (1944) *Plato: The Republic*. New York: Heritage Press, 3rd edn, 1892.

Mathur, V. B. (1969) *Ethnographic Atlas of Rajasthan with Reference to Scheduled Castes and Scheduled Tribes*. Rajasthan Census Operations.

Raghavan, V. (1981) Sanskrit Drama into Performance. *In Sanskrit Drama into Performance*. Rachel Van M. Baumer and James R. Brandon, eds. Honolulu University of Hawaii, pp. 9–44.

Russell, R. V. and Rai Bahadur Hiralal (1975)*Tribes and Castes of the Central Provinces of India*, 4 vols. Delhi Radjhani Book Centre, 1st edn, 1915.

Sharma, G. N. (1968) *Social Life in Medieval Rajasthan*: 1500–1800 A.D. Agra: Laxmi Narain Agarwal.

Welsford, Enid (1968) *The Fool: His Society and Literary History*. London: Faber & Faber, 1st edn, 1935.

Willeford, William (1969) *The Fool and His Scepter: A Study in Clowns and Jesters and Their Audience*. Evanston, Ill.: Northwestern University Press.

20

CLOWN POLITICS
Report on the International Clown–Theatre Congress

Fred Siegel

Philadelphia, 23–28 June 1991 – The most striking performance at the congress was also one of the most oblique. I had trouble making full narrative sense of *Clomadeus*, performed by the imagistic Soviet troupe, Ilkholm. Nevertheless, Yuri Belov, formerly of the Moscow Circus and currently teaching at the North Carolina School of Arts, assured me that, to the Soviet mind, it made perfect sense. *Clomadeus* was about the dehumanization of oppressed people. In the course of the evening there was a large, threatening hand breaking through a coffin-shaped window and making demands; a game of spin-the-bottle, in which a monster stalked a terrified member of the audience; and a pair of dancing 9-foot giants with balloons for heads. In one scene a man was reluctant to cross over a rope on the floor. Egged on by the others, he finally did, and then, immediately, the others whipped the rope around over his head, like a jump rope, forcing him to cross again. Soon the reluctant crosser was trapped, forced to jump up and down within the frenzied whirl of the rope.

At the panel on censorship in clowning, Belov pointed out a fundamental difference between the political content in the American and Soviet performances. Both can be political, but American performers can explicitly point the finger of blame. In Soviet performance – at least before August 1991 – the political content is veiled, the finger of blame never pointed directly. Belov expressed his fear for the members of Ilkholm: "If the political climate in the Soviet Union slips backward, even a little, they are dead."

Two American performers, Paul Zaloom and Stanley Allan Sherman, also showed political work, though certainly neither is in mortal danger because of it. Zaloom presented *My Civilization*, a three-part full evening show that took on the savings and loan scandal, toxic waste, and Jesse Helms by animating tables full of stuffed animals, appliances, paintbrushes, and other flea-market materials. Helms, for example, was portrayed by a mannequin leg, and a nuclear power plant was represented by three blenders, one of which overflowed. Taking shots at Phillip Morris – a major funder of Zaloom's work and the whole congress – Zaloom showed the company as a giant, coughing cigarette.

Sherman also bit Phillip Morris' hand in his *Aero Show*, which began with an old man forcing himself to smoke a cigarette despite the fact that he could barely breathe. Later in the performance, in an ironic tribute to the Gulf War, Sherman sang patriotic songs while pulling a long string of paper soldiers out of a paper bag, and tossed paper airplanes at the audience while playing "Off We Go, into the Wild Blue Yonder" on kazoo. Sherman finished by shooting off firecrackers and throwing red, white, and blue toilet paper at the audience as we all stood to sing the national anthem.

In an effort to compare clown performances from different cultures, the congress featured two non-western troupes which adapted traditional mask performance styles to the western audience. The *topeng* Balinese clowns featured a western actor wearing academic robes who served as interlocutor. The same actor appeared as an old man who asked the king to help fund the arts, and finally as an American reporter who made jokes about *Roe v. Wade*. In vaudeville fashion, the orchestra punctuated the jokes with the Balinese equivalent of rimshots. Most of the rest of the show was sung in Balinese, with occasional spoken digressions into English. At the end of one particularly long, fiery Balinese monolog, the actor paused, looked up at the audience, and asked, "You understand this?"

In contrast, Magic Buffoonery of Zaire presented *Tundu Mask* featuring the Tundu (buffoon) character of the Pende tribe. The Zaire troupe didn't interpolate much western material. Each member of the audience relied on a program which explained the musical instruments and the idea of each scene. However, the Tundu did exercise his traditional prerogative of imitating the audience. He had a "camera" made from a twelve-pack of beer with a can for a lens, which he used to "photograph" any who tried to record the performance. At the evening's end, the Tundu invited the audience to join the troupe in celebration, as per tribal custom. The audience of clowns, not a shy group, joined in and danced for a good long time.

There was only one African American participant at the congress. Why this underrepresentation? When most Americans think of clowning they think of the European style with its whiteface, auguste, and tramp. While plenty of African American performers are comics, few employ the make-up, costumes, and routines of Euro-American clowning. There are next to no African American clowns to act as role models.

Roughly equal numbers of women and men attended the congress, but women were underrepresented in both the featured performances and the panels. However, they were better represented in the "showcases" – unpaid performances. In her slide lecture on women clowns – which only two males attended – Judy Finelli managed to celebrate a few women clowns, including some of her own colleagues with the Pickle Family Circus. But later, at the panel on women in clowning, a Pickle Family clown, Diane Wasnak, was described as "non-gender specific," and, it was pointed out, people don't always know she's a woman. One way for women to get into the male-dominated clown business is to pass as a man.

Joanna Sherman, the one featured female performer (out of nine), presented a piece entitled *Dancing the Fire*, a series of vignettes tied together by radio announcements and phone machine messages. Some scenes followed a single character through her day – hurriedly getting ready for work, going nuts at work and getting fired, escaping to see a movie (in which she appears as a character), and finally arriving home and finding peace by playing her saxophone. Other vignettes featured a homeless woman looking for shelter, an unsuccessful accordionist on a subway platform, and a political comic in a nightclub. In response to a question about women developing a fourth clown character type, a woman, to add to the three traditional male characters, Sherman said that the way to go was to "not think so much about males and femaleness" but to "concentrate on what you want to say."

Victoria Millard, who appeared in a showcase, dealt with the place of women in the clown hierarchy in a direct, effective way. As Grizelda Le Fou, assistant to the famous clown Monsieur Henri Le Fou, Millard set up the master's props efficiently and lovingly. Then, when the master was late for the performance, she began in his place. Her act went well – she played the concertina and got spectators to participate – but then Monsieur Le Fou appeared as a small, white balloon that Millard manipulated like a puppet. In squeaky balloon language, the master began making recriminations and giving orders until Millard knuckled under, her spirit wilting. Fortunately, as the act progressed, the master accidentally burst, allowing Millard to continue the act herself. By the time she finished the master was resurrected, but Millard had proven that she didn't need him and the two went forward as equal partners.

Millard's baggy, body-concealing clothes and red nose avoided reference to gender, but another of the showcased women performers created characters who were explicitly gendered and sexual. One of Italy's Maria Cassi's creations attempted to seduce Leonardo Brizzi, her pianist, rubbing up against him and placing his hand on her breast. Another of Cassi's characters, wearing a slinky, black costume, mimed a striptease that went haywire, pretending to remove first her clothing, her false eyelashes, and finally her breasts and rear end. Cassi finished her performance in drag, appearing as a male page-turner. Later on at the panel, Cassi said her work is unusual in Italy because her shows are very physical. She sees her work as a way of transcending the stereotypes.

Most of the panels were oriented towards predicting trends in clowning for the twenty-first century. If the congress is any indication, we can expect less make-up, more clowns in theatres instead of circuses, more borrowing among cultures, more adult themes, and a further expansion of the definition of clowning.

And more women. Michael Pedretti, artistic director of Movement Theatre International, which sponsored the conference, suggested a couple of times in his remarks that the next great steps in the field will probably be made by women. Given the number of women at the conference and the quality of their work, this seems like a good possibility. But will Pedretti act on his prediction and hire more women performers for future congresses?

21

PART CIRCUS, PART SIDESHOW, PART BURLESQUE. THOROUGHLY GROTESQUE

Hovey Burgess

She was twice my age, but probably at the zenith of her physical beauty, as she sat motionless in a provocative attitude on the bally stage in front of what was most likely a girly show at a carnival at a county fair in Maine. Her one-piece costume was snug to say the least, and left little to the imagination. Her eyes met mine, and I headed off to locate my parents to ask them to take me to see this show. Then I suddenly had an epiphany – I was much too young for this; surely this would be forbidden to me, and I might even get in trouble for making my desire known. I settled for sneaking back for a final clandestine look at this Aphrodite, whom I never forgot.

There would be other unforgettable sideshow attractions in my life: Percilla the Monkey Girl, The Aztec Child, Prince Randian, Sealo, Joe Allen, Harold Smith, Congo, and sword swallowers Alex Linton and Estelline. I will never forget the mammoth circus sideshow I saw in the off-circus season at Chicago's Riverview amusement park. Nor will I ever forget Hubert's Museum, just off Times Square on 42nd Street, which closed its basement doors in 1965. For many years Ringling Bros. and Barnum & Bailey Circus also exhibited a sideshow, on the road and under canvas, as a separate admission attraction (through the 1956 season), and free, combined with the menagerie, at Madison Square Garden on Eighth Avenue between 49th and 50th Streets (through the 1967 season).

In the spring of 1968 Ringling Bros. and Barnum & Bailey Circus moved to a new Madison Square Garden on the other side of Eighth Avenue between 31st and 33rd Streets, no longer immune from being preempted by sporting events, and having abandoned the sideshow altogether. A similar thing happened in revolutionary Russia, where the lovely and celebrated, but hirsute, Julia Pastrana died in 1860. Under Communism, private circuses, such as Salamonsky, Ciniselli and Truzzi, were nationalized and sideshow attractions were purged – in favor of heroic gymnasts, idealized acrobats, communal animals and presumably political clowns.

In Hitler's Germany, the fate of ten thousand little people was euthanasia. And thus it was that rich heritages were cast aside.

There is peril in the repression of sex, and I think the same can be said of the repression of our fascination with the grotesque – the sideshow. Is such an attraction a monster? Perhaps, but cut off one of its multiple heads and a hundred more grow in its place. The sideshow – exactly thirty years after being banished – returned to Ringling Bros. and Barnum & Bailey Circus as the theme of the main show in the 128th Edition.

Other manifestations include the hairy, anthropomorphic brown bears of the Moscow Circus that were so skilled in circus techniques that the Japanese in Tokyo were convinced that they were seeing men in bear suits. In counter-distinction, the original Pickle Family Circus, denying themselves the use of animals, had a penchant for dressing their performers in gorilla suits. In Chinese acrobatic troupes – where the lack of

Fig. 21.1 Bindlestiff Family Cirkus. (Drawing by Jason Little.)

animals is simply traditional – the inevitable "Lion Dance" is ever popular. Cirque du Soleil, totally lacking in anthropomorphic animals, frequently goes to considerable effort to mask faces grotesquely, pad costumes to create hunchbacks, and choreograph movements to emulate cripples. It is only in the finalé curtain call that the performers are displayed in all their rare physical beauty.

Such outcroppings of the grotesque notwithstanding, a generation has passed since we could see a genuine sideshow at Ringling Bros. and Barnum & Bailey Circus or an odd attraction, alive and living, at Hubert's Museum. We might wonder, therefore, what we would get today if we were to combine the youthful, not-all-that-*sub*-cultural, pseudo-tribal trend of bodily mutilation/enhancement (for example: tattooing and other forms of piercing) with the persistent professional traditions of the American sideshow? This question is not hypothetical, and the answer is The Bindlestiff Family Cirkus.

Enter Keith Nelson, his partner Stephanie Monseu and their entourage. It is hardly unusual that Keith is tattooed, but the large tattoo on his left arm is not at all the usual image. It depicts a tramp clown. Herein lies a clue to the meaning of part of the show's title. In *American Tramp and Underground Slang*, which was published about seventy years ago, "Bindle Stiff" is defined as a tramp or worker carrying his bedding. A stick figure with a hobo's bindle over his shoulder is the ancient Egyptian hieroglyph for "wanderer", according to Sir Alan Gardiner's *Oxford Egyptian Grammar*.

Nowadays Keith's pierced tongue is not so uncommon either, but he is also a block-head, sword swallower, fire eater, female impersonator, clown, diabolist, rope spinner, and plate spinner. Although there have been many Nelsons in the annals of circus history, he is not aware of being closely related to any of them. His clown character is called "Mr. Pennygaff." When in drag, he is known as "Kinkette" in homage to the "Kinko" of Dan Mannix's *Step Right Up* (1951); British title: *Memoirs of a Sword Swallower* (1951).

Fig. 21.2 Philomena Bindlestiff (Stephanie Monseu) and her bed. (Photo by Katie Brennan.)

Fig. 21.3 Kinko the Clown (Keith Nelson) of the Bindlestiff Family Cirkus. (Photo by Maike Schultz.)

Stephanie Monseu is Keith's able partner. They are bonded together by nothing less than having the original Bindlestiff Family Cirkus logo tattooed to their lower backs. Her entire left arm is heavily tattooed. She is also a blockhead, fire eater, male impersonator, whip cracker, aspiring elephant trainer, stilt walker, comedy trapeze artist, and a most unusual plate spinner. Her French last name is actually of Belgian origin, but in the circus she has the title role – identifying herself as "Philomena Bindlestiff."

Scotty the Blue Bunny is the most ubiquitous and supportive of the supporting cast. Well over 6 feet tall, he has a human face with a 5 o'clock shadow. He is a veritable "clothes-horse." He makes himself generally useful, and is equally at home speaking on a microphone between acts or silently holding up clever signs for the audience during acts. One of his acts might be termed pseudo-juggling, and it is quite campy. On occasion he disrobes (ears, tail, and all) to take a tub bath with a gallon jug of red wine.

Una Mimnagh has certainly paid her circus dues and earned her circus credentials. I first encountered Una when she was an electrician with Circus Flora. I later met her when she was an electrician with the Big Apple Circus. Now she is a featured trapeze artist with the Bindlestiff Family Cirkus. She also happens to be the Bindlestiff Family Cirkus lighting designer.

Danny Boy (Daniel Smith) is a very young contortionist, who can make his way through an unstrung tennis racket in much the same way Joe Allen, the Human Cork-screw, once made his way through a wire coat hanger.

The Bindlestiff Family Cirkus usually performs against the background of a banner line, not unlike the one the Florida State University "Flying High" Circus used before it went under canvas, and the one the original Pickle Family Circus used when, having no tent, it side-walled the show outdoors. The Bindlestiff Family Cirkus alternates between making semi-annual tours of the United States, and presenting weekly cabarets in the Manhattan/Brooklyn area – their home base. The tours (New England/East Coast and Mid-west/West) consist primarily of one-night stands. There is no elephant, no big top, and no flying trapeze. Their ambitions and aspirations, however, do not preclude any of the above. Their slogan – "A sight denied past generations *because* not perfected until this year!" Their battle cry – "The Bindlestiff Family Cirkus is a circus with an agenda." Their emblematic mascot – a "Jack-a-lope" (body of a jackrabbit, antlers of an antelope). Their rhetorical question – "Is it Real?" Their paper consists simply of over-printed stock circus window cards (14" x 22").

Just as circuses once found paste more cost-effective than tacks, the Bindlestiff Family Cirkus seems to reach its audience by posting its bill in cyberspace: *www.atomicage.com.bindle*. The recorded announcements on the Bindlestiff Family Cirkus telephone information line (212 726 1935) are frequently updated. As *Spectacle* goes to press, the Bindlestiff Family Cirkus is embarking on a two-month eastern tour in a brand new fifteen-passenger white van.

Bindlestiff Family Cirkus does not seem to have any difficulty attracting guest artists for its weekly cabaret performances. Jennifer Miller – woman with a beard – seems to be the Bindlestiff Family Cirkus's most frequently appearing guest artist. This bearded lady is a talented dancer, actress, comedienne, juggler, escape artist, and light-bulb eater. She has appeared with the Theater for the New City, the Coney Island Sideshow, and Circus Amok, which she also directs. Mary Ellen Mark has photographed her; she is the subject of the documentary *Juggling Gender* seen on public television; and she appears in the recent independent film *Freaks Uncensored! A Human Sideshow* (1998). Jennifer's performance style very much resembles that of the Bindlestiff's.

By contrast, there are frequently repeated guest appearances by world-class acts of pure physical skill and universal appeal. I refer here to Angelo Iodice, from the Bronx, and his "stop-the-show" trick and fancy rope spinning, and Anna Jack, from Russia, and her "bring-down-the-house" hula-hoop manipulations. Other guests, of a more underground nature, include Zero Boy (microphone sound effects) and "Master Lee" (comedian and juggler).

In a political cartoon by William A. Ireland published in the Columbus (Ohio) *Dispatch* on 17 July 1934, the circus was commended for garnering public support without resorting to dirt or sex. The times have changed since then, and the Bindlestiff Family Cirkus, not to mention the first family, has certainly kept pace with the times.

When it comes to sword swallowing, Keith Nelson is a professional. He generally refers to his profession as the art of deep-throating. Fair enough – *Sword Swallower* was the working title for the motion picture, starring Linda Lovelace and released and distributed as *Deep Throat*.

"Deep Throat" was also the metaphorical name used to conceal the identity of the chief informant to the investigating reporters of the *Washington Post* during the Nixon administration Watergate scandal, assuring its place in the lexicon.

"Pardon me, while I clean the [expletive] off … " is the running line that precedes the successive swallowing of a coat hanger, extra-large scissors, a 24-inch sword, and a very special bayonet.

Fakir material may not be everybody's cup of tea, and to gild that cup with erotica may seem to add insult to injury. This might very well be the case were it not for the utter commitment, sincerity, dedication, and vulnerability of the highly imaginative performing artists, who seem to be in touch with the Wisdom of Solomon ("Whatsoever thy hand findeth to do, do it with thy might," *Ecclesiastes* 9:*10*). All this finds expression when Keith Nelson and Stephanie Monseu join forces for their homage to vaudeville plate spinning, a theatrical experience that is both remarkable and rare (and arguably raw). It conjures up the spirits of some of western civilization's greatest painters (Douris of Athens/Thomas Rowlandson of London) at their erotic best – but besets them with an almost unthinkable, and certainly unspeakable, gender bender.

The Bindlestiff Family Cirkus is what it proclaims itself to be – part circus, part sideshow, with a little burlesque.

Part V

CABARET, VAUDEVILLE AND THE FUN PALACE

22

INTRODUCTION TO PART V

Joel Schechter

Joan Littlewood's 1968 proposal for "A Laboratory of Fun" describes a place where "nothing is obligatory, anything goes."[1] Her "Fun Palace" has never been built, but some of the director's vision for this "university of the streets" and "short-term toy" was realized earlier in European cabarets, vaudeville, music halls, and her own Theatre Workshop in the East End of London. In these spaces, visitors and artists were brought together for intimate, relaxed and sometimes disturbing evenings of theatre, song, dance, and highly physical comedy.

Not every cabaret or vaudeville theatre began like Littlewood's Laboratory of Fun, with an experimental, inquisitive attitude toward pleasure. But as John Houchin indicates in his essay, "The Origins of the *Cabaret Artistique*," cabarets like the late nineteenth-century Chat Noir in Montmartre evolved out of Parisian cafés where "painters, poets, composers and novelists met to discuss art, literature, politics and various social conditions, and to present their most recent creations to their fellow artists."[2] These cafés and cabarets were forerunners of modern experimental theatre studios, workshops, and the Laboratory of Fun.

Intellectual and artistic ferment attracted public interest in Paris; as Baron Salis, the creator of the Chat Noir, discovered, segments of the public found provocation and insults entertaining. At the Chat Noir, writes Houchin, Salis

> knew a money-making opportunity when he saw it, and admitted the general public. The programs took on a new dimension. The singers now had the very object of their ridicule [the bourgeoisie] sitting in front of them … . Middle-class morals were attacked and *chansonniers* introduced their audiences to the sullied life of the poor.[3]

If it was not quite "anything goes" at early Parisian cabarets, it was close to that in Germany as well as France. Dadaist cabaret artists in Zurich and Berlin rejected the logic, morality and stupidity that led Europe into World War I, and chose instead to revel in their own consciously chosen poetry of the irrational, and in unsettling, transgressive artistic performances which anticipated contemporary performance art. As a guest says in "Cabaret Dada," "what is too much, is too much."[4]

Cabaret, vaudeville, and the Fun Palace offer their audiences variety entertainments with separated, discontinuous acts. Brooks McNamara observes that in variety entertainment there is usually "no transfer of information from one act to another," and "each act independently determines its own scenic requirements."[5] During intervals, if not during the acts, spectators are encouraged to smoke, drink, dance; as a result of these practices, some cabarets were as popular for what took place offstage as what went on under the spotlight.

The young playwright Bertolt Brecht found himself having fun in a smoke-filled, noisy Munich cabaret where comedians Karl Valentin and Liesl Karlstadt performed. Brecht's concept of epic theatre was inspired by his cabaret experiences, to the extent that he wanted to create his own "epic smoking theatre." Valentin's grotesque comic sketches offered Brecht the finest of pleasures, notes Denis Calandra, pleasures "(presumably intellectual) in an atmosphere of fun in which one can smoke and drink, and thereby remain critically alert."[6] We might question whether smoking and drinking result in alertness; but Brecht's theory called for disruption of the empathic process, and in this regard smoke and drink may be as disruptive as cabaret laughter and applause.

Brecht had an opportunity to see comic versions of class struggle in Valentin's cabaret acts, and it influenced the playwright's later efforts. He recalled that Karl Valentin

> portrayed refractory employees in short skits, members of orchestras, or photographers who hated their bosses and made them appear ludicrous. The bosses were played by his female assistant [Karlstadt], a folk comedienne who tied a belly around her middle and spoke with a deep voice.[7]

This staged conflict between boss and employee offered Brecht a model of class-conscious political comedy before he began reading Marx; first came the fun, then the Marxism.

When Liesl Karlstadt dressed as a man in Valentin's show, as she frequently did, she subverted gender roles. Other cabaret artists performed in drag – notably Wilhelm Bendow, famous for his "Tattooed Lady" monologue – and reflected an era of sexual daring and permissiveness which ended (or at least was officially condemned) under Nazism.

Such "fun" met with political repression and police harassment. When Brecht called for fun in his 1926 essay praising sports events, and anticipated Littlewood's plan for a Laboratory of Fun, it is doubtful he knew how politically objectionable "fun" would become a few years later. In 1926, aesthetics, not politics, motivated his critique of theatres which, despite their

> pretty lighting, their appetite for large sums of money, their imposing exteriors, together with the entire business that goes on inside them, [could not provide] five pennyworth of fun .... And nobody who fails to get fun out of his activities can expect them to be fun for anybody else.[8]

Contact with the audience is a component of the fun for which Brecht called, and in this sense too, Joan Littlewood's Fun Palace is a Brechtian structure. Her plan describes a space for theatre actors and stipulates that "in what has been called the acting area ... there will be no rigid division between performers and audience – a generalization of the technique used in Theatre Workshop for many years."[9] The proposed easing of borders between actor and spectator occurred not only in earlier cabarets, but also music halls and vaudeville houses, where performers would often play directly to the audience, with no imaginary fourth wall between them. Another form of contact between spectators and performers in these entertainments came about through laughter at ethnic and political humor. Anti-bourgeois and anti-Nazi satire in cabarets made audiences part of a subversive community, which explains why Nazi Minister Goebbels officially forbade "comments, including the allegedly well-meaning, on personalities, circumstances, or events of public life ... in theaters, cabarets, variety shows, and any other places of entertainment."[10]

Besides ridiculing those in power, uninhibited Americian vaudevillians used ethnic humor and song to celebrate difference and special identity, and denigrate other immigrants (or even Native Americans) whose poverty and low social standing are much like their own. The Yiddish vaudeville scene in this volume includes some racial stereotyping, as translator Mark Slobin acknowledges. The sketch titled *Among the Indians* is a rare sample of an almost lost popular form; its comic depiction of Jewish peddlers selling dress suits to Native Americans displays immigrant audacity at its boldest (although that hardly excuses its racism). The outrageousness of the situation, in which a naked Indian idol is said to need a smoking jacket, anticipates later Jewish American humor like Mel Brooks' film, *Blazing Saddles*, and his Broadway musical, *The Producers*, which also involves some unreliable peddlers – the title characters selling shares in a play called *Springtime for Hitler*.

That American theatre could move from Yiddish vaudeville's pedlars in 1895 to the multimillion-dollar Mel Brooks Broadway musical about unscrupulous Jewish producers in 2001 testifies to the lasting influence of such popular forms. (If you need proof of a line of influence, there is one comic line praising Yiddish actor Boris Thomashefsky in Brooks' musical, *The Producers*.) Other evolutions of popular theatre can be traced from Joan Littlewood's play, *Oh, What a Lovely War!* back to the pierrot clown show (a popular British entertainment form), and from her staging of Brendan Behan's *The Hostage* back to music hall song and ribaldry.

In recent years, the film and musical theatre versions of Kander and Ebb's *Cabaret* have given millions of viewers the somewhat misleading impression that German cabaret artists were mostly decadent Americans and looked like Liza Minnelli or Joel Grey. Cabaret and vaudeville may now be known best for Hollywood's stellar version of them, in films featuring former vaudeville comedians and popular singers. But some of the most innovative and provocative performances in the twentieth century began less glamorously in small cabarets, nightclubs and vaudeville houses – popular venues which featured appearances by Yvette Guilbert, Frank Wedekind, Bertolt Brecht, Tristan Tzara, Hugo Ball, Rosa Valetti, Trude Hesterberg, Valeska Gert, Lotte Goslar, Erika Mann, Edith Piaf, the Marx Brothers, Burns and Allen, Tony Hancock, Tony Allen, Peter Cook, Dick Gregory, Richard Pryor, Lenny Bruce, Laurie Anderson, Anne Bogart with *No Plays No Poetry*, Eric Bogosian, Marga Gomez, Josh Kornbluth, Charlie Varon, and Sara Felder, to name a few of the artists who turned whatever space they entered into a room of the Fun Palace.

NOTES

1 Joan Littlewood, "A Laboratory of Fun," reprinted in this volume.

2 John Houchin, "The Origins of the *Cabaret Artistique*," reprinted in this volume.

3 Ibid.

4 "Alexis" (pseudonymn of unknown author), "Cabaret Dada," reprinted in this volume.

5 Brooks McNamara, "Scenography of Popular Entertainments," reprinted in this volume.

6 Denis Calandra, Karl Valentin and Bertolt Brecht," reprinted in this volume.

7 Brecht quoted by Calandra, op. cit.

8 Bertolt Brecht, "Emphasis on Sport," in *Brecht on Theatre*, edited by John Willett, New York, Hill and Wang, 1964, p. 7.

9 Joan Littlewood, op. cit.

10 Joseph Goebbels, "Order Prohibiting Masters of Ceremonies and Commentary from the Stage," reprinted in *Cabaret Performance, Volume II*, Baltimore, Johns Hopkins University Press/ PAJ,

23

THE ORIGINS OF THE *CABARET ARTISTIQUE*

John Houchin

The first *cabarets artistiques* were created in France by artists who had witnessed the transition from the Third Empire to the Third Republic. The change in regimes had not been accomplished smoothly. Bismark had lured Napoleon III into war with Prussia in 1870. Defeat followed defeat until, on 4 September 1870, learning that the Prussians had routed the French troops at Sedan, the general populace of Paris stormed the Corps Legislatif. They deposed the emperor and established the Government of National Defense, which eventually evolved into the Third Republic.

During the next decade, the artists who rejected the official Salon painting had as their major forums the cafés of the Latin Quarter, where they held small exhibitions and promulgated their views. Gradually these cafés became homes for organized clubs. Painters, poets, composers and novelists met to discuss art, literature, politics and various social conditions, and to present their most recent creations to their fellow artists. One of the most famous of these clubs was the Hydropathes (Wet Apostles), founded by Emile Goudeau at the Café de la Rive Gauche in October 1878. To this society belonged the noted *chansonnier* Jules Juoy, the illustrator and painter Adolphe Willete, well-known humorist Alphonse Allais and the poets Charles Cros, Albert Samain and Jean Richepin.

In December 1881, the Hydropathes lost its home. During the same month, however, Rudolf Salis, a relatively unsuccessful artist, opened a cabaret in Montmartre in an abandoned post office at 84 Boulevard Rochechouart. At a chance meeting with Godeau, Salis learned that the club had no home. Salis immediately invited the Hydropathes to move into his establishment, and the *cabaret artistique* was born.

Cabaret itself had been in existence for a number of years and did not differ in essence from the *café-chantant*, an eighteenth-century entertainment phenomenon. The *café-chantant* developed when a little wine cellar named Café des Aveugles (Café of the Blind) appropriately hired an orchestra of blind men to play songs during the dinner hour. Eventually the format was expanded to include singers and dancers. This idea was so profitable that more and more cafés began to enhance their menus with entertainers. During the 1860s, the *café-chantant* took on the more respectable title of *café-concert*. This was due mainly to the appearance of the singer Emma Valadon, known simply as Theresa, who eventually became so famous that she was summoned to appear before

Napoleon III. Although the name *café-concert* was more refined, reflecting Theresa's performances, the nature of the programs changed very little. They consisted mainly of second-rate singers wailing sentimental or patriotic songs in smoke-filled cellars, with only a small platform for a stage and an ill-tuned piano providing accompaniment.

Salis, however, completely changed this approach. His cabaret programs were composed entirely of artists who personally presented what they had created; his cabaret was to be a haven for those who wanted to speak out against narrow-minded bourgeois values and traditions. At first, the members of the Chat Noir (Black Cat) – a name Salis chose because of his fascination with the Edgar Allan Poe short story – met only on Friday evenings, and the audience was comprised exclusively of fellow artists. In January 1882, he began to publish a small journal, *Le Chat Noir*, that contained caricatures, sketches and the members' satirical poems and essays. The journal created quite a stir, and the pleasure-seekers who frequented the dance halls of *café-concerts* began to demand admittance to the Chat Noir performances. Although it was agreed that this club would never be handed over to the Philistines, Salis knew a money-making opportunity when he saw it and admitted the general public. The programs took on a new dimension: the singers now had the very objects of their ridicule sitting in front of them. Their vehemence increased. Middle-class morals were attacked and *chansonniers* introduced their audiences to the sullied life of the poor. The *chanson réaliste*, greatly influenced by the writings of Zola, became the primary vehicle for achieving this objective, and such songs as *Un vieux ouvrier* (*An Old Worker*) first gained popularity at the Chat Noir:

Stray dogs have their holes
Swans have shelter by their ponds
Night prowlers have their quarries
And pigs a sort of hotel for murders.

By night at the station the cop
Has something on which to flop
And architects for a heap of saints
Have dug niches in the stones.

Ah well, poor old workman that I am
Since I haven't the means to work
I can't even kip down like Gavroche.

Bah! I don't give a cuss if I haven't a home
For even if I haven't a penny
At least I haven't any rent to pay.
(Raymond Rudorff, Belle Epoch, London 1972)

The greatest attraction of the Chat Noir, however, was Salis himself. His masterful showmanship was indicated by the decor of the Chat Noir. Lighting was provided by old church lamps; the walls, which were remodeled to resemble great ante-chamber doors of the seventeenth century, were hung with antique weapons and the paintings of club members. Salis also had a penchant for spoofs, which he perpetrated on his audiences. On one occasion the audience arrived to find a sign in the window announcing that Salis had died. Several of the artists stood outside to encourage the onlookers to stay and pay their respects. When the doors opened, they entered to find the walls draped with black cloth, candles burning at both ends of a casket, a baptismal font, and a priest delivering a eulogy. As they neared the coffin, they discovered a cello in the coffin and a washbowl in the baptismal font.

Salis' personality was felt far beyond the confines of the Chat Noir, and his antics became legendary throughout Paris. On the day of one of the municipal elections, he called upon the residents of Montmartre to declare themselves independent of Paris and elect him as mayor. With memories of the Commune still fresh in most people's minds, the proposal failed by a wide majority. On another occasion he proclaimed himself King of Montmartre, and paraded through its streets clad in a gold costume while the artists of the Chat Noir followed him, shouting "Long Live the King."

The Chat Noir became so popular that the original post-office quarters grew too small. On 10 May 1884, Salis led an elaborate torchlight procession through the streets of Montmartre to a renovated hotel on Rue Victor Massé. A new era for the Chat Noir began. The hotel, formerly owned by the painter Joseph Stevens, was remodeled to resemble a Flemish hostelry. A gigantic Swiss Guard, halberd in hand, stood at the entrance. On the first floor was an exhibition hall containing such oddities as weapons and Japanese masks, as well as the paintings of Théophile Steinlen, Henri Riviere, Caran d'Ache and Adolphe Willete, all of whom had joined Salis' entourage. On the second story there was a small room where performers sang songs and recited poetry. The third floor, however, became the focal point of the Chat Noir, for the shadow plays were presented there.

The Théâtre d'Ombres, as it came to be known, started quite simply. The painter Henri Sommé had built a small puppet theatre. One night a small tablecloth was hung over the opening, and, while Jouy sang one of his chansons, Riviere moved cut-out figures in front of a light source.

The possibilities of shadow plays became more interesting than puppet shows, and the booth was remodeled to include a complex assortment of color wheels, lights and reflectors. At first, productions were limited to realistic street scenes – such as those depicted in the illustrated Parisian journals of the late 1800s – and were accompanied by a poem or *chanson*. Gradually the artists turned from realistic material to romantic depictions of nature. The following description indicates the range of effects that were achieved:

> We saw the sun sink into the ocean; we saw the desert stretch into eternity! By means of artificial light, the evenings on the great metropolises burst into flame. The moon cast its silvery light onto boat-houses that stood on the bank of a river, down which fishing vessels glided slowly and sullenly.
>
> (Erich Klossowski, *Die Maler von Montmartre,* Berlin, 1908)

Eventually, the Théâtre d'Ombres' productions became extremely complex, costing, in some cases, 20,000 francs and lasting over three hours. *L'Epopée*, by d'Ache, depicted the entire course of the Napoleonic Wars and was responsible for generating a nostalgic, militaristic cult that swept Paris in the late 1880s. An adaptation of Flaubert's *Temptation de St. Antoine* consisted of forty scenes and portrayed such adventures as a gluttonous banquet in Paris, a bacchanalian celebration on the coast of the Aegean, a deep-sea expedition in search of Atlantis, and a trip to Mount Olympus.

Salis died in 1897, the year after he sold the Chat Noir. After he relinquished his interest in the cabaret, it remained in existence for only a few months, for no one with his ability emerged as a leader. Throughout his life, and, to some degree, after his death, Salis was a hotly debated personality. He had accumulated quite a large fortune at the first Chat Noir by selling bock beer at outrageous prices and buying the paintings of men such as Steinlen and Willete. He never paid his performers. Their only remuneration came in the form of public exposure and the free beer he served them. Marguerite Steinlen, wife of the artist who terminated his association with Salis in 1887, referred to him as a selfish wretch who died in a chateau purchased with the fruits of other men's labor. Willy Gaske, a Berlin critic, labeled him "a bock beer merchant upon whom lady luck had smiled." Yet Gabriel Montoya, the famous *chansonnier*, maintained that Salis would come to be regarded as one of the greatest men of the theatre. Apparently Salis himself was of the same opinion, because he had this inscription engraved on his tomb-stone: "God created the world, Napoleon the Legion of Honor, and I, Montmartre."

To say that Salis was responsible for creating the *cabaret artistique* is slightly inaccu-rate, but only slightly. Progressive artists in Paris had lived through the Commune riots and were fully aware of the reactionary nature of the French government. They had also been the victims of stifling traditions in painting and literature that prohibited them from gaining acclaim. The clubs of the Latin Quarter had served as meeting places for these men. These clubs, however, remained outside public scrutiny. Salis' importance was that he provided artists and audiences with access to one another. This union would have undoubtedly occurred, but Salis' love of spectacle, his desire for more exposure and his organizational skills brought about this meeting more quickly and in a more concentrated manner.

The Chat Noir continued its creative output for fifteen years, due, in part, to Salis' leadership, yet – and this point is crucial in terms of later developments within the move-ment – it always remained an artists' club. The adherence to this concept resulted in the two major features of the *cabaret artistique*. First, it continued to be a forum for artistic experimentation. The members were never forced to present material that pandered to the audience's tastes, a work's value was decided by the artist, and represented the performers' desires rather than the patrons' demands. Second, the intimate physical rela-tionship between spectator and artist was retained. No gaudy production techniques were ever allowed to overshadow this all-important element:

> The lasting success ... was essentially based on the intimate connection between the performers and the audience. The artists ... maintained a simple manner of presentation, just as they did at their first Friday evening performances. No make-up, no dinner suits, no polished boots. They performed in the clothes they wore during the day as they walked the narrow streets of Montmartre. They leaned lazily on the corner of the piano. One hand held a burning cigarette, the other they stuck in their pocket. They shot the darts of their witty chansons into the audience, which sat close enough to touch them. No point was ever lost.
>
> (Willy Gaske in *Das Moderne Buvetti,* 15 December 2001)

There were, however, a number of artists who felt that Salis' antics diluted the impact of the Chat Noir's political and social commentary. Godeau, his first partner, opened the Cabaret du Chat Botté (Cabaret of the Booted Cat), and the *chansonnier* Marcel-Legay began the Cabaret de la Franche Lippée (Cabaret of the Big Mouth) in 1885. Both were patterned on the old Chat Noir, but lacked the counterpoint that Salis had provided and closed within a few months. By far the most successful of the first Chat Noir's successors was Le Mirliton (The Reed Pipe), opened by Aristide Bruant. One of the most celebrated *chansonniers* of his era, he started his career in the *café-concert*, where his repertoire consisted mainly of sentimental ballads. In 1885 he became acquainted with Jules Jouy, who introduced him to Salis. He began to sing nightly at the Chat Noir and became one of its major attractions, specializing in the *chanson réaliste*.

When Salis left Boulevard Rochechouart, Bruant borrowed 1,000, francs and started his Le Mirliton in the vacated building. On opening night, 10 January 1885, there were only three spectators, and sparse crowds continued until one night he lost his temper with a fashionable gentleman. Accustomed to all sorts of antics in the Montmartre cabarets, the customer assumed that this outburst was simply part of the show, thought it very amusing, and returned with several friends. Bruant decided to change his approach, reasoning that if the audience desired abuse, he would give it to them. He welcomed his guests with such greetings as, "Oh là là, what a snout you have, oh what a snout you have." Frequently, when a well-known figure visited his cabaret, he brutally attacked his character:

> Well, boys, look who's here – one of our leading burglars, the eminent M'sieur A. coming to spend some of the swag from his last sale of the blue sky. And a new lady with him – another to whom coronets are more kind than hearts! Well, the jails are full of honester people. But there is a just providence that looks after things. One of these days they will be pinning the Legion of Honor on him, and we shall be avenged.
>
> (Quoted in Robert Forrest Wilson, *Paris on Parade,* Indianapolis 1924)

Latecomers were sent into a corner of the room known as the *Institut*, where they huddled together on benches, and any guests who left early were reviled as pigs.

Bruant, however, gave his audiences far more than a pot-pourri of insults. He was the voice of Parisian low life. He was neither sentimental nor political, but concentrated on depicting the plight of the poor and the fate of prostitutes and thieves in an objective manner. His style of delivery was unemotional and his steely voice, according to critic Jules Lemaître, "penetrated one's soul like a knife." On one occasion, the great *diseuse* Yvette Guilbert had decided to add some of Bruant's pieces to her repertoire, and went to Le Mirliton to study his delivery. She was so taken aback by his portrayal of these people that she could hardly believe that humans actually lived and died as they did in his *chansons*. Thereupon he took her to a dive where he had spent many hours studying the wretched of Paris:

> There I saw hell. Old and young people sleeping on top of one another on the floor. The room was lit by one feeble gaslamp and there was an odor, a horrible odor. Everywhere stiff, dirty rags, hats, caps, coats and pants. An old man especially unnerved me. He lay on the floor. His long white hair fell over his shoulders, his arms were spread out as if they were nailed down, his mouth was open, his eyes were rolled back in his head. He was Christ in agony. I emptied my entire purse into his hands. The coolness of the goldpieces awakened him. Oh, that look, the sad astonishment of one eternally lost. In the back we noticed a long table on which children were sleeping.
>
> (Yvette Guilbert *La Chanson de ma Vie,* Paris 1927)

In 1895 Bruant gave up the directorship of Le Mirliton to his most devoted protégé, Marius Herhovchen, who changed its name to Cabaret Aristide Bruant. Herhovchen was so devoted to his master that he dedicated himself to preserving his memory. The cabaret's decor remained unchanged, and he copied Bruant's mannerisms, tone of voice and even his costume. The Cabaret Aristide Bruant remained in existence until 1935.

Berlin critics were in awe of the *cabarets artistiques* and when traveling in Paris always extolled their wonders for their German readers:

> Le Trêteau de Tabarin is the most famous cabaret in Paris in 1900 … . In the evening many coaches wait in front of this little house. The cabaret is only a little room (every seat costs five francs; there are 60 to 80 seats) … . Middle-class people, millionaires, artists … . Such

an enthusiastic crowd. Unspoken friendliness, yet with Parisian restraint. On the walls, are lovely prints. What has happened in the morning is sung about in the evening ... The audacity of these songs is not directed simply at the government. They are directed at heaven itself. Apostles are ridiculed; sinners are absolved ... . Everything is contained in these songs: filth and glory; heaven and hell. In a word humanity, humanity, humanity ... . The poets themselves deliver their poems: without voices, more speaking than singing. Entirely at ease, free of ornamentation. The artist is no servant of the audience ... . Yet above all there is no vulgarity. The songs are bold, vulgar never. They are never blasé. Their basic trait is that they expose humanity. Now they are only popular songs, but some of them will some day become eternal.

(Alfred Kerr, *Die Welt im Drama,* Berlin 1917)

Yet Alfred Kerr, the author of these accolades and one of the most famous critics in Germany, failed to inform his readers that this type of cabaret was virtually an anachronism. After Salis' death the model of the *cabaret artistique* was drastically altered. By 1900 the cabaret had become a competitive, commercial undertaking. Producers and owners, because of the large numbers of people frequenting Montmartre, sought to attract audiences by any means possible. The Cabaret de l'Ane Rouge (Cabaret of the Red Ass) distinguished itself primarily because of a fresco depicting the crucifixion of a large red ass. The singers presented the *café-concert* fare, and the announcer was simply a huckster who encouraged the audience to buy drinks. In the Cabaret du Néant (Cabaret of Death) visitors were served at coffins and lighting was provided by corpse lamps:

A waiter rigged up as an undertaker's man accosts you with a "Good evening, moribund," and serves you with refreshment which by its quality seems designed to hasten your passage to the other world. There are emblems of death all round the walls, with mottos, such as "To be or not to be," or, "Life is a folly which Death corrects." From the café you pass into a vaulted chamber at the back of the premises which is simply furnished with a coffin standing upright. A man takes his place in the coffin, and then fades away into the likeness of a skeleton outlined in light. In a moment he comes to life again, steps out, and with a bow, disappears. This is the Café of Death.

Richard Whiteing, *Paris of Today,* (New York 1900)

More and more cabarets became obsessed with death and its consequences. Cabaret du Ciel (Cabaret of Heaven) featured harp music, a master of ceremonies dressed in the robes of a priest, and a man costumed as an angel who sprinkled the audience with holy water. The programs consisted of a series of *tableaux vivants* depicting the pleasures of heaven. Offering an alternative to celestial bliss, Cabaret l'Enfer (Cabaret of the Infernal Regions) presented a glimpse of hell. The decorations that hung from the ceiling were sculptures of bodies writhing in pain. An acrobat, dressed as Satan, performed a series of contortions, while his wife and her court, accompanied by deafening organ music, were consumed by multi-colored flames.

The artistic merits of these later cabarets is not an issue. More important is the evolution from one type into another. Early cabarets such as the Chat Noir and Le Mirliton were based on the premise that whatever was presented was determined by the performers' standards, not by those of the audience. The successors to the *cabaret artistique* chose their bills of fare according to their commercial potential.

24

A VISIT TO THE CABARET DADA

"Alexis"[1]

Gentlemen, the spectacle begins before you can possibly know it! We walked down a long corridor, each holding a candle with the ladies in front and the men in the rear. The leader, dressed in a white fur coat with a *mitra* on his head, called out several times: "Lift your hands up high and let your belly fall. Grab the kettledrum in your ear and pull the coffin out of your nose – for who knows what good they are?" Then he slammed his earhorn against the wall causing the limestone to break and fall. Yet we felt constantly ill at ease when his voice rang out. Uncertainty rested heavily upon our breasts and upon Councilman Spätzle, a well-known member of the German National Socialist Party. We all began to sink to our knees, although Councilman Spätzle attempted to hold himself erect as long as humanly possible by means of his moral turpitude. We talked for more than two hours through this corridor that stank of coal and garbage ... climbing over rail-road ties, wooden blocks, and rotten mattresses and eventually found ourselves in a room evidently destined for ecclesiastical purposes ... . There stood the first Dada priest whom I have ever seen dressed in violet underpants, holding a cat. On his head, he wore a great wig in which two peacock feathers were stuck. When he spoke, handfuls of teeth fell from his mouth, and in his ears pinwheels rotated to the clash of military music ... . The floor shifted so many times and proved to be so slanted that many of the guests fell down, causing some of the women a good deal of anxiety – lest the sight of their legs turn the liberal men's attention away from the ceremony. Steam came pouring out through a crack in the masonry, and jets of hot water burst forth from the corners. (Ladies and gentlemen – it was simply overwhelming!) The priest lifted a papier-mâché bust and manipulated the eyes, which he controlled by means of a string, to flash back and forth. His voice was like the thunder that ascends from watering cans when the evening sun shines on them. He had a beard in which little mice squeaked "good night," and the express trains were waiting on the abyss of his neck. "I am the priest," he said, "from the beginning until the end. I am the tulip of Valparaiso and the butterchurn from the Bismarck Archipelago." In our party, the voices of those who saw through this swindle grew; they wanted nothing more than to return to their norm of peace and quiet. "We need work and an organized reconstruction of the fatherland," said a gentleman next to me, who later prospered as a very radical politician … . "We want our money, we want our money back," shouted a woman with a throaty delivery. In general, the consensus was that one could have spent a more profitable evening reading a good book, worshipping Goethe, or drinking beer – in short, by promoting German culture. Meanwhile, the priest had sat down on his right side, pulled a rabbit out of his toes, and said,

> I am the young moon which stands on the waterfall. When I laugh, the earth goes out, and the houses, which stand so rigid knowing nothing, reassemble themselves on the Kaiser-Friedrich Platz. Hail! Hail! The heavens burst, the flute splits apart. Still, morning is not all darkness nor even the equinox of the travel bureau.

The man next to me said,

> You may not believe it, but behind Dadaism stands the scantiest intelligence. These men are only crafty frauds, who know very well that the people are enticed by the irrational; and in that cunning manner, they pull the money from the people's pockets. Look there! That guy is laughing so hard that the tears are rolling down his cheeks.

Just then a young woman became indignant. "He isn't laughing," her voice a falsetto, "that is truly enrapture! I've seen the Dadas in Dresden, when chairs were broken over their bodies and pianos shot at their heads. What we call courage is Dada!" The priest in his violet underpants began to roll around the floor. A moving sidewalk brought in the prima donna from the Metropolitan Opera House, who knew how to whistle the ragtime song, "La délice", on one leg. One could hardly look at the leg without becoming flushed with emotion. The sea cows came very close, perhaps when they wanted to eat out of our hands, and the huge green lizard that hung on the ceiling began to spin like a fan. Everyone talked about the hothouse atmosphere and the ventriloquist-voice about which Capasses has so many significant words to say in his famous novel, *Chevilles*. I did not notice it but Councilman Spätzle was growing into a tremendous rage.

> What, [he screamed,] "What? How dare this be offered to me! Me, who was born of respectable parents, who had a good primary education, who took nine years of classes at a liberal arts gymnasium. I have always been in favor of progress. However, what is too much, is too much. [He looked around.] And from a nationalistic point of view [he laughed sarcastically] these Dadas are only opposed to the Entente in order to make revolution. Look at him [the Dadasoph had suddenly appeared], is he a man or an animal?

A heated discussion ensued as to whether the Dadasoph who had just come up out of a trap-door was a man or an animal. The latter was decided upon. No sooner had the Councilman grown silent than a great procession of Dada-like Last Judgments began. It was as if the building would collapse upon our heads. On an immense sofa, they brought in the so-called President of the Universe, Johannes Baader, formerly a tailor who was provided with the necessary accoutrements to distinguish him as a madman and Dionysian dullard. Hot water flowed by the gallons from his ears, and on the seat of his pants he had sewn boxing gloves, on which should have been inscribed the motto of his eternal enterprise: "The Beloved Life of Dadaism." On either side of him stood the Dadasoph Hausmann and Huelsenbeck, who, it is said, is the creator of this nonsense. The Dadasoph rode on an owl, the beast of wisdom, and carried in his hand the symbol of Zarathustra, the serpent and the eagle. "The world as a problem of knowledge," he said, "is Taboo-Dada. From the Eternal One we came to the pigs. Hopsassa!" At these words, a gentleman in our company, who with great difficulty had read Hegel and Schopenhauer, became agitated. The Propaganda-Marshal Grosz appeared with a kettledrum – that symbol of Dada world domination. Close behind him followed the well-known Dada Minister of Commerce and Monteurdada Heartfield. It was an impressive assemblage. An endless procession joined in. The Dadas of all leading countries followed on the backs of cows and horses or on foot. They carried toy trumpets and rattles, and all of them were characterized by the same facial expressions. The troubadour and epicurean of the Paris movement, Herr Tristan Tzara, was there in the uniform of a subway employee. Kurt Schwitters, the world-famous author of *Anna Blume*, was seen at a distance. The din was so great that our eardrums cried like little children. Great soft bones fell from the ceiling. (No one knew what purpose that served.) Then the tailor Baader screamed, "Dada is the victory of cosmic intelligence over the Demi-urgos. Dada is the Cabaret of the world, just as the world is Cabaret Dada. Dada is God, Spirit, Matter, and roast veal at the same time." The man next to me yelled in a rage. "Dada," he said, "is planned nonsense. Dada means the end of the German elementary school and the destruction of the German soul!" I joined in the argument and left the Cabaret with him the very same way from which we had come … .

NOTE

1 This piece appeared in *Der Dada* No. 3 (1920) and the *Dada Almanach* (Berlin 1920) and has been variously ascribed to Richard Huelsenbeck and Johannes Baader. It is not clear to the translators whether the article is an invented description that was possibly read at a Dada soirée in 1919 in the gallery of Dr. Burchard, or whether it is a partial description of an actual performance there. See Motherwell, p. 362 and Mehring (1959) p. 53.

25

KARL VALENTIN AND BERTOLT BRECHT

Denis Calandra

On 14 March 1920, Bertolt Brecht wrote to Doris Hasenfratz (Doris Manheim) that he had just returned to Munich at midday after a fifteen-hour train ride from Berlin and had gone directly to the Cabaret Charivari where the comedian Karl Valentin was playing; Brecht sat "convulsed with laughter until 11 o'clock." Bernhard Reich, a director closely associated with Brecht during the twenties, describes the fascination Brecht had with these performances:

> We often discussed how one could regenerate the stagnant theatre … . The Munich folk comedian Kart Valentin and his ensemble were giving a guest performance at the Kammerspiele. Brecht, the 'enemy of the theatre,' came to every Valentin premiere, and he prevailed upon me to go and see the sketch, *The Musicians Rehearse* (*Die Musikprobe*) … . It was wildly funny. Brecht shrieked with laughter … . (He) enjoyed Valentin enormously, and I suspect he saw particular Valentin scenes so often because he was collecting observations and studying the plays as well as the acting technique of this extraordinary man. Here he may well have discovered that a simple and one-dimensional (*eingleisig*) plot can get across an extremely complicated generalization to an audience, and that a small scene can stand for a big problem. He must have noted a basic difference between Valentin's performance and the commonly practiced form of acting.

Underscoring the important role Valentin played in Brecht's formative years are the direct references to the comic in his writings on the theatre, published and unpublished. In *The Messingkaut Dialogues*, Brecht, speaking of himself in the third person, repeats the story he told to Walter Benjamin in 1938, giving credit to Valentin for the moment when his idea of an epic theatre was born. Valentin inspired Brecht to send on the soldiers in *Edward II* (1924) in whiteface:

> But most of what he learned was from the clown Valentin, who performed in beer halls. He portrayed refractory employees in short skits, members of orchestras, or photographers who hated their bosses and made them appear ludicrous. The bosses were played by his female assistant, a folk comedienne who tied a belly around her middle and spoke with a deep voice. When the playwright was at work on his first play (as director) in which a half-hour battle took

Fig. 25.1 Karl Valentin on accordion. (Photo courtesy of Theatermuseum, Munich.)

place, he asked Valentin what he should do with the soldiers: 'How is it with soldiers in a battle?' Valentin answered without the slightest hesitation: 'They're white: they're scared.'[1]

(Collected Works XVI, p. 599)

There can be no doubt that Brecht had considerable contact with Valentin prior to 1919 and through September 1924, when he left Munich for Berlin.

The Red Raisin (Die Rote Zibebe) was a "midnight show" conceived as "Improvisations in Two Scenes" by Brecht and Valentin and performed only once, on 1 October, 1922, at the Munich Kammerspiele. The first part of the show, entitled *The Host of Abnormalities*, featured Brecht as Benny the Guitarist; Valentin's lifetime partner Liesl Karlstadt as the Lorelei; Joachim Ringelnatz as his recently launched cabaret character, the seaman Kuttel Daddeldu; and actors from the original cast of *Drums in the Night* and others as characters such as "A Plant," "A Virginia Smoker," and "Linda Cow." A "midnight show" like this was usually part of an opening night celebration, with a good deal of the improvisation parodying the "serious" premiere – in this case *Drums in the*

Night. Brecht's name in the show, Klampfenbenke, suggests that he sang some of his ballads, perhaps taking off on the guitar-playing whiskey distiller Glubb in Act IV of *Drums in the Night*, who sings the *Ballad of the Dead Soldier*.

Nothing really concrete is known about this part of the evening, though one can surmise the potential such a performance must have had for Brecht's gestating notions on the theatre. His later ideas on distancing the actor from his role during rehearsals have a possible progenitor in this kind of session where the "serious" play is parodied; and an ideal performance situation is achieved with a mix of popular entertainers, stage actors, and "authors," all of whom are personal acquaintances performing for the fun of it.

Both in his collaboration with and in his "study" of the Munich clown, Brecht saw much of value for his emerging idea of a theatre. Indeed, he seems to attribute to Valentin most of the characteristics for a new theatre that Brecht found lacking in the then current bourgeois *Bildungstheater*, as he describes it in his criticism and notebooks from 1918 to 1926. Valentin offers "the finest of pleasures" (presumably intellectual) in an atmosphere of fun in which one can smoke and drink, and thereby remain critically alert. He "physically portrays" (*leibhaftig vor Augen fuhrt*) his material, in contrast to the literary theatre. And in a new performer-public relationship, he demonstrates for the "simple people" essential relationships where they would normally be overlooked: here between "composure, stupidity, and the enjoyment of life." In sum: Valentin's is a theatre for learning and for the highest of pleasures, with its basis in gesture and its implicit message a need for perpetual change.

Fig. 25.2 Karl Valentin's fairground band, featuring Liesl Karlstadt and Bertolt Brecht. (Photo courtesy of Theatermuseum, Munich.)

Valentin Ludwig Fey (Karl Valentin) was born in a Munich suburb on 4 June 1882 to a reasonably well-off bourgeois family – his father was a partner in and later owner of a furniture-transport company. From 1896 to 1899 he apprenticed as a carpenter, learning the skills he later used in constructing his own sets and handmaking all of his own props. In 1902, he spent three months at a "variety school" in Munich taking instruction from a comic named Hermann Strebel and shortly afterward acquired his first engagement at the variety theatre, Zeughaus, in Nüremberg. His father's death in October 1902 forced him to return to Munich and put off his career for three years. During this period of absence from the stage, however, he built a twenty-instrument "one-man band," and, in 1906, under the pseudonym Charles Fey, took it on a tour of *Singspielhallen*, variety theatres, and guest houses throughout Germany. In engagements ranging in length from one night to four months, the musical clown formed a part of programs that included farces of all types, art songs, acrobatic acts, freak shows, solo comedian acts, and the like. Valentin's love for these shows lasted a lifetime, and he was eventually to assemble what is one of the best collections of material relevant to Munich *Kleinkunst* theatre in existence. This includes many hundreds of different scripts, programs, thousands of photos of freaks, local eccentrics and performers of every description. He meticulously compiled the photos and began a thorough cataloging of relevant data, including descriptions of performance areas, notes on the "artists'" specialties, their reception by the public, and curious personal anecdotes about them.

(The Theatermuseum in Munich has part of Valentin's collection, as do the Valentin Museum in Munich and the Theatermuseum in Cologne.) Many of the scenes Valentin later wrote are stamped markedly with this Singspielhalle atmosphere.

In one particular scene (*Tingel Tangel*, the one Reich claims Brecht took him to) Valentin captured the essential montage character of variety theatre – by having all the acts mistakenly come out onto the stage at once. The orchestra plays away stage right, a cycling artist rolls on stage left, in the center an art song interpretress and a Gypsy dancer compete for position. He carries the idea to its extreme by having the stage technicians, directors and audience appear as well: a worker called in to repair the curtain stands on a ladder in the background, a standing audience member raises her fist in anger down left, while the prompter's solitary hand is raised from his trap in the middle of the stage to try to put a stop to the whole thing.

Though this tableau contains more of the variety elements than any other single Valentin production, many of his others mix variety elements with other types of comedy scenes. There is an abundance of dwarves and giants – often on stilts – very often a mix of folk songs, whether related to whatever else is going on or not, and bits of slapstick comedy.

When Valentin's luck and money ran out in Berlin in 1907, he returned to Munich and tried unsuccessfully to revive his musical act. Then, at the prompting of a friend, he took to writing couplets and comic monologues that he performed to zither accompaniment with a *Komikergesellschaft* (semi-professional performance group) at the Badewirt. It was also at this point that he first capitalized on his odd, gangly appearance by wearing pants that were too short and extremely tight, an evening jacket with cutaway sleeves and oversize shoes to accentuate his large feet. In 1908, Valentin accepted an engagement at the Frankfurter Hof *Singspielhalle* in Munich, where he remained until 1913. There he met his lifetime partner, Liesl Karlstadt (Elizabeth Wellano) and began the type of work that the young Brecht so enthusiastically received.

Valentin's best work is unthinkable without Liesl Karlstadt. She complemented his figure perfectly, a dumpy Mutt to his spindly Jeff, and offered a cool contrast to his unpredictable temperament. When Valentin met her at the Frankfurter Hof, she was the soubrette in the "farce-sing-act ensemble," *Dachauer Bauernkapelle*. The list of her duties in the ensemble gives some clue to her fantastic range in the Valentin scenes:

> The performers were used in many different ways. Fraulein Wellano had to sing in the chorus, sing couplets, dance, yodel, and play in one-acters. One also had to be up to the mark in serious plays, whose deadly earnest could be recognized in their titles: *Condemned!* or *The Spy* or *From Love to Murder*.
>
> (Rudolph Bach, *Die Frau Als Schauspielerin*, Tubingen 1937)

From the time of his first performance with Liesl Karlstadt in 1913 until 1924, when Brecht left Munich for good, Valentin's reputation as a comedian was on the ascendancy. He did go on tour occasionally to Berlin, Vienna and Zurich, but his hypochondria and morbid fear of traveling faster than 10 miles an hour ultimately prevented him from being appreciated quite as widely as he might have been. His successes during the period, however, were hailed by people such as Thomas and Victor Mann and Hermann Hesse. In Munich itself his role was interesting, for unlike his major rivals, who attracted fairly monolithic audiences made up of table-thumping, arm-locking, beer-guzzling "*Weisswurst* patriots," Valentin appealed to a mix of the common beer-hall frequenters, the bourgeoisie, students and intellectuals. By the late 1920s, Valentin had become "chic" among intellectuals, though he refused to have much to do with them personally.

In choosing some of Valentin's skits to describe, it would probably be most useful to concentrate on the ones Brecht undoubtedly saw – those which were first performed before 1925. Among these are *The Christmas Tree Stand (Christbaumbrettl)* and *The Great Fire (Grossfeuer)*. *The Christmas Tree Stand* is a 20-minute skit about "a group of poor, little people who want to celebrate Christmas six months late." The plot, such as it is, concerns the father's difficulty in getting a stand the right size for the miniature Christmas tree he has brought home. Onstage are screaming children, one of whom is played by a dwarf; a contrasting giant as a chimney sweep, who in the closing moments of the sketch sits in the elaborate Christmas cake; a pair of twelve-foot boards as a stand for the two-and-a-half-foot Christmas tree, dogs, toys, etc. A zany string of jokes, puns and sight gags leads to the improbable conclusion: it's all a mistake – the *pater familias* had, since 24 December the year before, forgotten to turn the leaves of the calendar.

The photographs of *The Christmas Tree Stand* give an impression of "naively" over-stated stage arrangements. The set and properties are typical of the *Kleinkunst* stage: a crudely suggested lower-class flat, a spring landscape painted on the window shade, a 4-foot ladder for the 7-foot chimney sweep to climb to the top of the 5-foot stove pipe when cleaning it. In one photograph the bit of action depicted is "father smashing the chandelier lamp with his absurd twelve-foot-long Christmas tree stand boards." (Although there is no proof that the arrangement wasn't "faked" – indeed, in the printed version of the script this set of characters does not appear onstage together – the nature of Valentin's theatre work is such that infinite variation within scenes occurred from one performance to the next, and his penchant for strong contrasts and overstated arrange-ments makes it reasonable to accept the photograph as representative.) The seven people onstage are split into two groups of three, with the one person in the middle, naturally, the center of focus. Two of the children on the left (one played by a dwarf) point at the ceiling lamp being broken; the wife and the giant chimney sweep on the right express their surprise. The father is perplexed. The use of outlandish shapes and sizes for charac-ters, the simple symmetry and attention-focusing technique, the blatant assault on "the natural disorder of things" as well as on stage illusion – Valentin is seen in one photo wearing three wads of cotton on his head and shoulders to represent snow – all of this must have made a strong impression on Brecht in the mid-twenties. Looking closely at Brecht's arrangements as a director in the 1931 *Mann ist Mann* (written between 1924 and 1926), one cannot help but recognize Valentin's stage pictures.

The profusion of grotesque elements – the mother blots her baby with a huge ink blotter, then plays it a lullaby on a trombone – and the nearly silent-filmic racing along of the "story" are two other points worth considering about *The Christmas Tree Stand*. The skit begins at dusk, as the wife (Karlstadt) delivers a 20-line monologue about her son who left for Oberammergau and her husband whom she sent for a Christmas tree; then the sun comes up, abruptly and on cue:

> *Mother:*   It's already so late. The sun must be ready to come up. One-two-three. Aha, there
> we have it now! *(She telephones her husband, Valentin)* … Be careful when you cross
> the street so you don't get run down by a pram. *(A knock is heard.)* Yes, come in! OK,
> adieu Sebastion, come straight home. – I'm waiting for you – Bye bye, Sebastion! *(a
> knock at the door)* Yes, come in! *(She hangs up. In the same instant the father comes in,
> with his Christmas tree.)* … It's him! I was just on the phone with you, and now you're
> already here!
>
> *Father:*   Yup, I hung up quick as a flash, and ran here quick as a flash.

All bother about consistency of any sort – character, story – is subordinated to the one joke, a man struggling with a two-and-a-half foot tree and twelve-foot boards as a tree stand: "the inertia of matter and the insufficiency of all things, ourselves included."

Brecht is quoted as saying: "(*The Christmas Tree Stand*) is, from a literary standpoint, a dramatic product of a high order, like all of Valentin's plays. It derives its inner structure as well as its production potential from the very basics of dramatic art. Since

Fig. 25.3 Valentin's cabaret act, *The Christmas Tree Stand*. (Photo courtesy of Theatermuseum, Munich.)

Valentin, like Nestroy before him, embodies his main characters himself, these plays, which capture the people of the age in a comic mirror, acquire a special character." (Hannes Konig. *Was War Wahr? – Was Wahr War!*, Munich, 1969)

A list of favorite actors, directors and productions that Brecht left on some notepaper from the mid-twenties includes Valentin among the actors and his *The Great Fire* among the productions. (Other actors listed are Helene Weigel, Oskar Homolka, Rudolf Foster and Erwin Faber; the other productions include Engel's *Cariolan*, Brecht's *Edward II* and Arnolt Bronnen's *Pastor* – a play by the Expressionist playwright Hanns Henny Jahnn.)

In its published form, *The Great Fire* concerns a newly rich farmer's wife (widow?) in inflationary Bavaria whose house nearly burns down. A stroke of lightning causes a fire on the *Huberbauerin's* roof. A neighbor comes across stage to tell her about it, and the string of diversions and interruptions that constitutes the "action" of the piece gets underway.

> *(A clap of thunder. The house begins to burn.)*
> *Huberbauerin (L. Karlstadt):*   Come in, come in, who is it? Didn't someone knock? I thought somebody just rapped at the door. I'm curious what the dollar's quoted at today. It's either up or down – or then again up again.
> *(She reads in the newspaper.)*
> *Neighbor:*   *(Appears and goes up to the window.)*
> Howdy do, Huberbauerin.
> *Huberbauerin:*   Oh, it's Ferdinand. What do you want with me, Ferdinand?
> *Neighbor:*   Huberbauerin, I have a secret to tell you.
> *Huberbauerin:*   What, a secret? But if you tell me, it won't be a secret anymore. *(She comes out of the house and puts her ear up to the neighbor.)*
> *Neighbor:*   I have to warn you. This is terribly important for you.
> *Huberbauerin:*   Omigod, don't scare me. Have butter prices gone down after all?
> *Neighbor:*   No, it's not that dangerous. Give me your word you won't tell anyone.
> *Huberbauerin:*   Shake on it. I'll be as dumb as a deaf mute.
> *Neighbor:*   OK then. Your house is on fire.
> *Huberbauerin:*   Jesusmaryandjoseph, how can that be? I would never have thought it. It's so sad. And the little house cost so much.
> *Neighbor:*   I saw it from my window, then came straight here to tell you.
> *Huberbauerin:*   I thank you for the message. And for this trifling matter you made a special trip the ten meters over here. I could cry with joy.

The fire commander enters next, and language remains important as Valentin laces the small talk with dialect jokes, puns and endless digressions on absurd subjects. Although the fire rages in the background, the Huberbauerin forgets her reason for sending for the fire commander, responding to his query "How's it going?" with: "Aggravation, money worries, the mice have munched up a couple of sacks of thousands [inflationary notes], so I put in some gold pieces. The mice don't know about it, and they'll break their teeth." Ultimately, she remembers the fire and shifts to incongruously formal language: "Jesusmaryandjoseph! Now it occurs to me what I wanted to say to you. There's a fire at my place! Would you mind checking into what can be done when you get a chance?" Valentin investigates the type of fire, then helps the Huberbauerin retrieve the more flammable objects from her house – toothpicks, matches, etc. – and goes off to find the rest of the fire brigade.

Part three is another digression, with the Burgermeister of the neighboring town of Untergiging, in which Valentin sells an unwanted fire engine at a bargain price. The fable-like conclusion of the exchange finds the greedy Burgermeister burdened with several tons of fire equipment trapped in a building whose only exit is too narrow by several feet to remove it all. "What's sold is sold!" is Valentin's final remark. During the description of the conflagration in which the engine originally got trapped inside the burning building and later sealed into the rebuilt structure, a characteristic anti-illusionist bit appears:

Commandant: There we were in front of the great fire with the busted fire engine. "Sonuvagoddamseacook," he yells, "the devil take the whole goddam engine." He had hardly uttered the last word when all around a cry could be heard: "The roof's caving in!" and in the next moment, Kaboom! *(A thunderous drum beat is heard from the orchestra.)* The Catastrophe had occurred.

Burgermeister: You told that so true to life that I really did hear a noise just now.

An interlude then occurs in this series of digressions, again in a typical Valentin mixture of styles, as the night watchman comes in – speaking in verse:

I see by the colors higher and higher,
Yon is the Huberbauerin's house on fire.

The fire has been raging since the beginning of the play when the city photographer arrives and requests that the flames be steadied for his camera:

Photographer: Couldn't you stop the fire for a minute?

Wiggerl (L. Karlstadt): Sure, all I have to do is turn off the ventilator. *(He runs backstage, and the sound of the switch clicking is heard. The flames, made of red and yellow bands of cloth that dart about in the rush of air from the ventilator, halt with a sudden jerk.)*

Photographer: Yeah, that's good. OK, hold still now.

The Commandant (Valentin): Naa, I don't feel like it anymore. *(He goes downstage to the ramp, turns around, goes back to Wiggerl and whispers something in his ear.)*

Wiggerl: Oh, that's why!

Photographer: Well, why doesn't he want to?

Wiggerl: He doesn't like to be watched while he's being photographed. He's embarrassed because all the folks in the stalls are looking at him.

Photographer: What people?

Wiggerl: The theatre audience.

Photographer: That's simple, we'll just let the curtain down.

The Commandant: Yeah, then I'll agree.

(The curtain descends rapidly.)

A surviving photo of *The Great Fire* in production gives an idea of the last few minutes of the skit. The stage is crowded with the usual assortment of Valentin grotesques such as the fire brigade: "tall, thin, and short, squat, volunteers stand next to one another." The brand-new, steam-driven fire engine itself is a curious contraption: a multi-colored machine, the main body covered by a cloth in the Bavarian colors – blue and white diamonds – a pipe extending up and tilted at the top toward the backdrop, where smoke is painted as if it were coming out of the thing, the flat surface of the chassis set with beer mugs for the volunteers' refreshment. Valentin as the commandant, with full walrus moustache, strikes a Delsarte-like pose for "pride" or "command," one leg rigid and slightly behind the other, shoulders stiffly back, head cocked to the right, hands clasped behind the back. The "free-standing ladder," taking its name literally, isn't to be leaned up against anything, and therefore faces the wrong way while the "apprentice volunteer fire boy" (also played by Karlstadt) directs a stream of water towards the brigade itself instead of towards the fire. To freeze the cast in this summary tableau Valentin uses the formal device of the photographer, who requests all to remain fixed in place. The effect is totally artificial: "The epic theatre uses the simplest possible groupings, such as express the event's over-all sense. No more 'casual,' 'life-like,' 'unforced' groupings; the stage no longer reflects the 'natural' disorder of things." (Bertolt Brecht, Notes on *Die Mutter*, cited in John Willett, *Brecht on Theatre*, p. 58)

The Midnight Serenade (*Das Mitternachtsständchen*) also concentrates on the theatre as theatre. Valentin, the chief actor and director of the piece, demands proper lighting from his technician, calling for "bright" light when he sings about the sun, "dark" light when he sings about night, "morning red" (*Morgenrot*) when he sings about dawn. And he asks for fitting "emotion" from an audience volunteer when he gives her the cue to "feel." The technician naturally gets confused, then loses control – rainbow colors for "moonlight," and on "pale visage" a red spot; the volunteer laughs when she should cry. The limits of language – dark, light, etc. – and the fundamental contingency of the theatre are demonstrated. Valentin leaves the stage in a huff, refusing to allow them to further "mess up a beautiful dramatic scene."

Another skit based on the performance as performance (*The Alpine Terzett*) ends with the audience and the proprietor forcibly removing the performers from the podium. Valentin rushes back onto the stage after being given the hook and shouts at the audience the truth of the matter in a contradictory tone of reproach: "Just remember this, you don't need us, we need you!" The pathos of the ejected performers, their basic incompetence, the deep bitterness felt as he scolds the audience – all is accentuated by the interplay between the "what" of his words (his dependency on the audience) and the "how" of them (shouted as if they were dependent on him). This element, a form of *Verfremdung*, abounds in Valentin's works.

Valentin's description of an experience of his at the Frankfurter Hof in Munich offers another example of his testing, not necessarily consciously, the nature of performance. A new modernized stage was to be installed in the *Singspielhalle* while Valentin was working there, but, to avoid having to cancel any performances, the management decided to do the demolition immediately after an evening's performance and have the construction done during the night. It occurred to Valentin to do the wrecking in front of the audience: "real" wrecking incorporated into the acted script. The last number on the current program was a rustic scene in which an uxorious farmer comes home late and is scolded angrily by his wife. They fight, and the man loses his temper, smashing his fist down on the table. Valentin secured the management's permission and took the actor playing the farmer into his confidence. Instead of merely smashing his fist onto the table, he was to grab an axe and demolish the scenery – doors, walls, etc. Then he was to cry offstage to Valentin, who would enter with an axe of his own and join the wrecking. Apart from the two of them, no one, including the other actors, knew of the plan. The farmer and Valentin destroyed the set, then turned to the stage itself, tearing up the floorboards. Valentin reports that some of the audience left the hall horrified before they were finished, while others just shook their heads and muttered: "Of course, they were just play-acting!" Some Brecht scholars seem to think this may have been the source for Brecht's idea to dismantle the set of *Drums in the Night* (1922) before the audience. Whether or not this is true, it is certain that Valentin's habit of testing the various elements of performance accounts for Brecht's fondness of him. Valentin loved the "confusion" between playing and not playing on the stage. His favorite of all his own performances was one in which a simple Bavarian woman in the audience took the bungled efforts of one of Valentin's clowns – presumably one of the frustrated musicians – dead seriously and demanded her money back because the blunderer up onstage was incompetent.

Valentin's acting as such is surely the most difficult aspect of his work to describe. First, there is the usual paucity of sources: several films over which he did not have complete control; for the spoken word and singing, a number of reissued phonograph records; and a few sketchy first-hand accounts. Then there is the complex matter of Valentin's relationship to his material. He had an obsessive love of the very material he parodied. As a performer he appeared, with few exceptions, in only his own works, composing largely through improvisation. As a known eccentric (called a *spinnende Teifi* – crazy devil – by his fellow Münchners), he took his work on the stage, as Brecht put it, in "dead seriousness." He brought a decisive reputation to each of his performances; the audience apparently anticipated quite a bit and knew Valentin's various phobias.

In the *New Technique of Acting*, Brecht claims in his directing to have "copied" the "arrangements of the folk comedian Karl Valentin." In 1955, speaking to Giorgio Strehler, director of the Piccolo Teatro de Milano, he used Valentin as a key example of how the actors should sing in *The Threepenny Opera*.

> *The Singing:*
> Brecht offers Karl Valentin as a model, one who 'always represented a low species of art.' He only performed his own material, and he sang in a thin voice, malevolently and sullenly. He always impersonated someone who was just playing for the money, with a minimum of energy, so that he barely filled his obligation. But on top of that he would suddenly have tiny amusements, not really for the public, but for himself; for instance, when he would sing a song and at the same time parody the content of the song and in any case criticize it.
>
> (*Bertolt Brecht Archive*, 1379/13)

Perfectly illustrating what Brecht means here are Valentin's recordings of his songs. Each piece begins with a flat introduction by Valentin: "Allow me to present to you the ballad of 'Loewe's Watch' with zither accompaniment .... I am now going to sing you a song, accompanied by singing." The gist of each piece is to present a man singing a song, rather than to present the song itself. Indeed, in most of the pieces the song proper never gets sung.

The first digression in "Loewe's Watch" is characteristic of the procedure in all the songs. Valentin strokes the zither strings, reflects for a split second, cues on the last word of his introduction (*Begleitung*: accompaniment), and investigates – "criticizes" – the use of the term in itself. The semantic questions raised by the phrase "accompanying oneself" are formidable. Valentin proceeds.

> Thank God I can accompany myself. The other day I accompanied myself home, which looked pretty silly, me there all alone next to myself ... 'Loewe's Watch' ... (*He strokes the strings again.*) ... but the main thing is that one can accompany oneself, for which I have my father to thank for bringing me up so strictly musical. I was only allowed to eat with a tuning fork, and he always trammelled me to a score.

Several more false starts, occasionally allowing a line or two of the song to emerge, lead to the next criticism of the lines:

'Loewe's Watch' (*music*) … I must tell you in advance that Loewe wasn't a watchmaker, but a composer. 'Loewe's Watch' (*music*). Well you see, now that we're on the subject of watches, my great grandfather [Urgrossvater, pun on Uhr–watch], who by the way is still alive … .

Ultimately, Valentin begins sullenly to sing, but he compulsively takes the first line and sets about deciphering it.

'Loewe's Watch': (*singing*) I carry wherever I go, always a watch with me … See, this ballad isn't really fit for zither accompaniment because it says I carry wherever I go [gehen: go, walk] always a watch with me. But I'm not walking now, I'm sitting, and secondly I don't even have a watch; I pawned it. Very honorable members of the audience – because I can't walk while playing the zither, and my watch is in hock anyway, it is unfortunately impossible to offer you a presentation of 'Loewe's Watch.'

"In a Cool Place" follows a similar pattern. This time the digressions begin with Valentin not being able to remember the opening of the song. When he finally does so, after numerous teasing half-starts, the performance is again interrupted while he reflects on the mood of the song. He remains, or gives the impression of remaining, naive in relation to it. He sings the first line, muses, and declares, "it's a very sad song," quite as if he had never heard it before or as though the words produced by his voice-box were totally alien to him. When he has finished the song, his criticism of it focuses on the lines taken literally. The comment, "I find it awful silly!" ends the performance.

The clearest illustration of Valentin's "tiny amusements, not really for the public, but for himself," is found in the piece "Karl Valentin Sings, and Laughs Himself as Well." The framework is similar to that of the other songs: a man singing, having difficulty at it, making inquiries into his material. This "Laughing Song," though, has the very nature of performance as its object of inquiry. Written into the song is a laugh at the end of every stanza, but the performer finds he can no longer bring himself to laugh when he should. He explains that the fake laugh used to be easy; he demonstrates several different types of laughs one can use at the end of the stanzas, then comments on how difficult it is to laugh on cue. Then comes the crux: Valentin laughs at one point genuinely, having apparently responded naively to the lines he had just sung and actually found them funny. Instantaneously, he follows with the fake laugh. That is to say, one has the feeling that the first laugh is real and the second fake. The question raised is the amount of pretense and amount of "honest" reaction involved in the particular moment in the performance. The question naturally remains open, though the questioning itself is necessitated by the situation which Valentin has set up. This balance between being the actor-as-pretender and the actor-as-a-person – a person who is actually open and responsive to his material, capable of being *befremdet* by it, and conveying this duality to an audience – is one quality that made the complex acting of Valentin attractive to Brecht and that makes it useful as a background to Brechtian acting. There is nothing really unusual about an actor conveying this duality in his performance; what is noteworthy about Valentin is the fact that, in his acting in most of his pieces, it was a central element of investigation.

Occasionally in Valentin's films there are moments of apparent improvisation, as in *The Record Shop* (*Im Schallplattenladen*) when he invents parts of a telephone conversation, including the name of the person called, to the surprise and obvious pleasure of his partner. Valentin exhibits that quality of "having a good time" at his work here, something which also concerned Brecht very much in his earliest as well as his subsequent writings on the theatre.

Other comic routines in the films, repeated and altered continually since their inception, point to a different kind of improvisation – in movement. Scenes like those in *Tingel Tangel*, first worked up as early as 1916 and not filmed until 1936, are characteristic. In one, Valentin is having difficulty with the conductor of the orchestra (Liesl Karlstadt). He challenges the authority of the conductor, an action concentrated in the image of Valentin adjusting the conductor's slipping bow tie. At first he is a violinist, sullen, usually off in his timing, but ready to blame the other members of the orchestra for having started "too late." As the piece is being played, Valentin darts out with his bow, adjusting the bow tie; he is slapped away. Without missing a violin stroke he intermittently thrusts with his bow, lightning quick; the music and the harassment become feverish until the conductor takes up the challenge with his baton, and the two of them assume fencing positions, first Valentin, then the conductor. One might say the scene is about the authority-subordinate relationship between the conductor and members of the orchestra and that the physical *gestus* for the scene is the final picture of the fencing duel. Like the tableaux in *The Christmas Tree Stand* and *The Great Fire*, the movement of the shorter pieces has a quality of using simple means to express larger relationships.

Following the period of his association with Brecht, Valentin continued to work in the same manner he had established in the early days, revising and expanding his repertoire until, at his death, it totaled more than four hundred theatre pieces, comical poems, songs and scenes. Several additional visits to Berlin, reluctantly undertaken, in 1929 and 1930 enhanced his popularity, especially among intellectuals, though in his native Bavaria he was never to be as popular as some of his rivals – notably Weiss Ferdl. He was offered parts, at different times, by both Max Ophuls and Max Reinhardt, both of whom he turned down (with the exception of a bit part in Ophuls' *Bartered Bride*), but he did eventually play roles in several feature films by lesser-known directors in the thirties. Besides his performance work proper, Valentin built and attempted to operate a "Panoptikum," complete with a chamber of horrors in the Madame Tussaud style. He lost his own and his partner's total investment in 1934 when the idea failed to catch on with the Munich public. A second attempt at a "Panoptikum"-cum-theatre called the *Ritterspelunke* was a bit more successful, lasting from 1939 to 1941.

Throughout the Nazi era, Valentin tried to remain aloof from politics. An anecdote has it that he once insulted Hitler publicly, and some anti-Nazi skits indeed were written during the 1941–6 period when Valentin was no longer performing. But when asked after the war if he was a party member, he frankly answered, "No! But that's only because no one asked me to join. If they had, I'd have been too scared to refuse." Between 1947 and his death in February 1948 Valentin appeared in public only intermittently.

Since 1948, Valentin's work has revived in popularity, leading to the establishment of the Valentin Museum in Munich, the reissuing of the radio broadcasts and phonograph recordings as long-playing albums, and the intermittent screenings of the films in the cinema and on television. Besides the regular folk theatre performances of his scripts, established theatres in Munich, Frankfurt, and Salzburg have recently done revivals in the form of longer pieces (*Raubritter von München*) and "Valentin evenings" comprised of the more popular shorter skits. The quality in Valentin's work that fascinated Brecht in the twenties and which left a strong enough impression on him as late as 1954 appears not to have totally disappeared with the folk comedian's death.

NOTE

1 There are several versions of this story, all about the same in substance, though some confusion exists about which play was in rehearsal when the exchange took place. Brecht as the Dramaturg in the *Messingkauf* says "It was my first play," which has led some people to assume he meant *Drums in the Night*. Since *Edward II* was Brecht's first play as a director and the anecdote in all versions centers on a director's question, it is more likely than *Drums*, which does not have an actual battle scene between soldiers. Valentin was certain to have been present for some of the rehearsals of *Edward II* in 1924, since he had been hired by the Kammerspiele specifically to help cover the costs of what were then considered elaborate production methods – rehearsal for longer than three weeks – insisted upon by Brecht.

26

FROM VILNA TO VAUDEVILLE
Minikes and *Among the Indians* (1895)

Mark Slobin

Recently the Yiddish theatre has been the object of considerable study, translation and revival; yet the world of Yiddish vaudeville remains virtually untouched. This is odd, considering that what we would now call vaudeville skits and playlets were among the very first products of the Yiddish stage (1870s), while similar material is still being presented to Yiddish-speaking audiences today. It is almost a truism to state that the rise of the Jewish-American comedian in the 1950s and 1960s was rooted in the low humor of the "Borscht Belt", but few have shown any interest in tracing the genealogy further back. One of the reasons for this neglect has been the scorn with which Jewish theatre critics, historians and activists view all ethnic entertainment not directed towards creating an "art" theatre. An even more important impediment is the almost total lack of surviving printed or manuscript versions of early Yiddish vaudeville.

Seemingly the sole exception to this rule is a single fragile copy of an 1895 playlet preserved in the Judaica Division of the New York Public Library. The item is called *Tsvishn Indianer* (*Among the Indians*), and it is included in the program for an evening's entertainment at the Windsor Theatre on 17 April as an afterpiece for a standard Yiddish melodrama. Its author is Khanan Yakov Minikes (1867–1932), whose pen name was *Ish Vilna* ("Man of Vilna"), who wrote the playlet for the benefit held that evening on his own behalf. Also included in the printed program in his "Peddler's Haggadah," an immigrant take-off on Passover ritual texts, and a number of advertisements for East Side businesses. The commercial slant is no accident: Minikes served as advertising manager for the theatre, having already functioned as ticket-taker, accountant and publicist. Later in life he was active in a great many charitable causes, allowing him to be eulogized by the writer Sholem Asch as "the sexton" of the Jewish community. Minikes made only one other contribution to theatre history besides the surviving vaudeville number: a pioneer anthology of Yiddish popular songs, *Di bine* (*The Stage*), published in 1897. There he advertised a major drama he planned to publish, but that project seems not to have come to fruition.

Among the Indians is an illuminating vignette of the "low road" of Yiddish entertainment, as opposed to the "high road" of legitimate Yiddish drama. The brash language, racial stereotyping, and crass commercialism of the piece jump off the page today with considerable force: this is not what we have been taught about the Yiddish stage. Yet

Minikes' playlet is not an anomaly, but rather a pathbreaker in a well-defined line of Jewish-American entertainment that leads to the films of Mel Brooks and others.

The cultural resonance of *Among the Indians*, however, runs even deeper. The moral of the story may be commercial, but Harry's final advice – that only fools believe in luck while the smart believe in themselves – is a didactic message worthy of the grand Yiddish tradition. The low road and the high road were never more than a couple of blocks apart on the Lower East Side. To a great extent, Harry can be viewed as Ragged Dick with an accent; after all, Horatio Alger set most of his stories in the neighborhood of the Windsor Theatre's Bowery address.

Finally, a word on translation. The playlet uses intricate interaction of stylistic levels of speech as one of its main devices. Willie and Harry both speak East Side (i.e. Americanized) Yiddish, but Harry's is on a slightly higher level. Kalomfulo's broken utterances are based on Yiddish, while Dixon's fracture English. Miss Meisel is supposed to be speaking German. She is basically a caricature of the uptown New York German Jew, but not the "farmer's daughter" of the script. However, her German is not "high-class," though better than Willie's mangled attempts at *Hochdeutsch*. In short, it was necessary to compromise to create an English version of the playlet.

AMONG THE INDIANS

or, The Country Peddler

H. L Minikes, *"Ish Vilna"*

performed April 17, 1895, Windsor Theatre, New York

Dedicated to the Premier Yiddish Comedian,
Rudolph Marks

DRAMATIS PERSONAE

Harry, first New York peddler
Willie, second New York peddler
Miss Meisel, a farmer's daughter
Kalomfulo, an Indian chief
Dixon, a black field hand
Indians, field hands, farmers, folk, etc.

place: a small place in Kansas
time: the present

SCENES

1. An Indian holiday
2. Clothing! Clothing! Clothing!
3. He thinks God is an Indian
4. Willie the peddler must be lynched!
5. The rescuing angel
6. A lecture about good luck and bad luck
7. Roles are changed
8. The secret of success

(Scene: a forested area. In the background right and in the foreground open space. Before the curtain rises we hear savage cries from behind the stage, then singing. The curtain rises. Some Indians carry an idol. Other Indians, men and women, enter from all sides. Chorus.)

Chorus of Indians: "Our God is great and strong … " etc.

(They dance around the idol in a wild Indian dance and dance off the stage. The god remains onstage. Pause. We hear from offstage: "You shlimazl! Where are you off to?" Willie enters right, with a large pack. He sets it down and sings.)

Willie's Entrance Song. "Once mankind was foolish … " etc.

Willie: Yes, everyone's coming up in the world with nice clothes; even the biggest ass, the coarsest oaf becomes a gentleman when he puts his wool suit on his crude coachman's body, a regular silk purse from a sow's ear; but things aren't so great for me with my clothing. Here I've been traveling around two whole years, I've already covered half of America with my pack but it doesn't work even if you break your back. Even the wild Indians have become connoisseurs of our goods, so if you make a little cash already you have to pray you won't get lynched when they look closer later and see you've taken them for a ride. *(He sighs.)* Yea, yes. It's no good, my business is six feet underground, and I can't tell whether I'm a *shlimazl* or my customers are worthless. Other peddlers do a good business, and I'm not even fit for the savages. I can't see a ray of hope and I don't know what the secret of their success is. *(He sees the idol.)* Ah, here's a big shot of the barbarians; probably a general or the king's right-hand man! But naked as the day he was born. OK, let's see, maybe I'll manage to sell him a little suit. *(He goes up to the idol.)* Good morning! He keeps quiet? Maybe he's deep in thought; this cannibal, he's probably thinking whether he should have a Jewish peddler for dinner. *(He goes closer.)* How do you do, Mister Hoptsi! *(aside)* The devil with these Indian names! *(aloud)* Nice weather today, Your Honor! Do you need some clothes? A full-dress suit, the latest Paris fashions? Perhaps a smoking jacket, just in from London! Or maybe just a business suit? Or school clothes for your boys, may they be strong and healthy? He keeps quiet? Well, let him look at my stuff, he'll get the urge, the devil take him *(He takes out clothes and puts them on the idol.)* It fits you like it was poured on, Mister. Do you want a jacket? What's your size? You don't know? It doesn't matter. I'll find you something. *(He takes out a measuring tape and measures the idol.)* 46 inches! *(aside)* He has a belly like a Polish pig! *(He takes a jacket out of his pack.)* You see, Mister? Genuine Manchester yard-goods and double-breasted! *(He puts it on the idol, takes a few stops back and looks at it contentedly.)* You look like a real live Cabinet Minister! A royal face, you should only look that way for your children, and since I'm your pal and buddy it won't be expensive! I mean reasonable, $25, no more! Do you want it? Can I wrap up the suit? I tell you, you'll thank me! It's very cheap! I'm selling it cheap because I like you, really I do! You've stolen my heart away! *(Savage cries offstage: he is terror-stricken.)* Oy, a whole herd of wild beasts is heading this way!

(Kalomfulo dashes in quickly from the forest; behind him several Indian men and women. He grabs Willie by the throat.)

Kalomfulo: Hold, you white devil, how dare you offend our holy god?
Willie: *(jumps back)* This is really a god?

Kalomfulo: *(gritting his teeth)* What? You don't know that?

Willie: Yes, yes, of course I know. *(aside)* He's even a worse shlimazl than me.

Kalomfulo: And still you dared to offend him! *(to his companions)* Hang him on that tree, quickly! *(Two Indians approach Willie and want to grab him.)*

Willie: *(jumps back)* Your Highness! Restrain your wrath! Hear me out! *(aside)* Oy, will I trick him?

Kalomfulo: *(calmly)* Speak.

Willie: *(points to the two Indians)* Tell these two good angels to step back. When they look at me with their tender eyes I get butterflies in my stomach.

Kalomfulo: *(to the Indians):* Go! *(The Indians step back.)* Well?

Willie: Last night your god came to me in a dream and ordered a suit. He told me that it's too cold for him to go around naked.

Everyone: Oh! Oh!

Kalomfulo: Well? And did you bring him a suit?

Willie: Ah! Foist quality! Double-breasted and silk lining! Rockefeller always buys this kind from me and Mike Kane ordered three whole suits of the same, deliverable as soon as he gets out of Sing-Sing.

Kalomfulo: *(getting angry)* $25? Rrrrrrl

Willie: *(aside)* Oy, am I an ox! Why didn't I tell him $30!

Kalomfulo: Make sure you're not tricking me with this suit.

Willie: What can you be thinking of, Your Highness? All I need is to trick such a strong and mighty god, and have such a sin on Judgment Day!

Kalomfulo: Fine! But first I'll check and see if the quality is really good. *(He goes up to the idol, feels the fabric, and shouts thunderously.)* Oh! White devil! For this you want $25! Do you think our god doesn't understand business? This suit isn't worth more than $5!

Willie: *(stammers):* Your Highness! The suit is all wool!

Kalomfulo: You can tell that to your grandmother, you thief! I know my dry goods! *(He looks at Willie more closely.)* Holy Hoptsi! What do I see? But you're the same peddler from New York who sold me a rotten suit last year! Rrrrr! Rrrrr!

An Indian: Me too! Rrrrr!

Another: Me too! Rrrrr!

Everyone: Rrrrr! Rrrrr!

Willie: *(aside)* It's bad! They recognized me!

Kalomfulo: Lynch him, and quick! Rrrrr!

Willie: Have mercy! I'm still young – I don't have a boy to say prayers for me!

Kalomfulo: Don't wait! Hang him! Rrrrr! *(Two Indians grab Willie and drag him. Offstage is heard "business is business," etc.)* Wait! Now what's happening? Seems like a familiar voice!

(Harry enters right with a large pack, puts it down and sings.)

Harry's Entrance Song.

Kalomfulo: Ah! Harry! Our dear Harry!

Everyone: *(happily)* You, Harry! Harry! *(They all surround him.)*

Harry: Good morning! Good morning! *(to Kalomfulo).* How's your brown majesty, Lord Kalomfulo? How's your Red Ox? What's up?

Kalomfulo: My Red Ox is a good boy, he sends you regards. But right now we've got a job to do.

Harry: A job? Can I help?

Kalomfulo: Oh, why not? We can give an old friend the honor of holding the rope.

Harry: Can I make some money at it!

Kalomfulo: In the next world for sure!

Harry: A bad business! With the next world I can't pay the clothing manufacturer for my orders from this world, but what sort of job is this anyway?

Kalomfulo: We have to hang this swindler! *(points to Willie)*

Harry: *(looks at Willie, shudders; aside)* What do I see? Willie! My hometown pal? I have to save him. *(aloud)* Hang him? What did he actually do?

Kalomfulo: He offended our god! Rrrr!

Harry: *(angrily): That rascal offended your god? Rrrr!*

Kalomfulo: *(points to the idol)* He dared put that heap of rags on our god!

Harry: Rrr! A terrible crime! *(to Willie)* How dare you offend this dear god?

Willie: I have an order from God, I told them already.

Harry: *(to Kalomfulo)* Kalomfulo! My landsman is innocent; he had the honor of receiving an order from your god.

Kalomfulo: Well, that's as it may be, but why did he give him such a bad suit?

Harry: Don't you see? He gave him a weekday suit, and for Sundays and holidays he'll give him a better suit, right, landsman?

Willie: Of course! *(quietly, to Harry)* Harry, you can be my speechwriter any time!

Kalomfulo: Why didn't you say so earlier? Go, you're pardoned.

Willie: *(bows)* I thank you for my unworthy soul, Lord Kalomfulo, but won't you buy the suit for your god?

Kalomfulo: *(getting angry)* From you? Rrrr! You don't dare come to our country with your rotten rags! We only buy from Mister Harry! *(to Harry)* Harry! Have you bought some new gems with you?

Harry: Milk and honey, Your Highness!

Kalomfulo: Good! Come to our camp, we need a few dozen suits just now. Goodbye, Harry! *(to the Indians)* Take our guest and march off to our camp!

Harry: *(to the Indians, who pick up the idol)* Careful, brothers, he may get a cramp. God forbid!

Willie: And don't shake him up, he needs some sleep, poor thing! *(Kalomfulo and the Indians exit.)*

Harry: How're you doing pal? I haven't seen you in two years! Looks like you were in hot water here.

Willie: I could have gotten to the next world suddenly! I don't know what to do. I'm an eternal *shlimazl*, nobody wants my clothes, and if somebody buys something, they pay me with knocks!

Harry: You're not a *shlimazl*, just a bad businessman.

Willie: A bad businessman? Go on, explain it to me.

Harry: Later. Here comes Miss Meisel, the farmer's daughter, with her field hands. She'll certainly want to buy something.

Willie: Harry! Let me earn something. I haven't seen a penny's worth of earnings for two weeks. You're the favorite in this country and will certainly sell out your stock.

Harry: With pleasure, if she'll buy something from you.

(Miss Meisel, Dixon and several Negroes come out of the farmhouse; Miss Meisel is an old maid, wears elegant clothes and is heavily made up, acts flirtatious.)

Willie: *(to Harry)* An old coquette! That's just the customer for me. I know how to deal with this type as well as you. You'll see, I'll scatter a sackful of compliments and she'll buy from me.

Harry: May God guide you on the right path, but I'm very doubtful. Just speak high-class English with her.

Willie: If I only could! Is it easy to speak high-class? Well, I'll try. *(He goes up to Miss Meisel and bows politely.)* Good morning, my pretty miss!

Miss Meisel: *(smiling)* Good morning, Sir! And how do you know I'm a miss?

Willie: Well, there's no doubt about it. Youth radiates from your face and your charm is like milk and meat, I mean honey!

Miss Meisel: *(smiles coquettishly)* O! O! Such graceful compliments! You're a regular poet, Sir!

Harry: That's no compliment, my pretty miss; my friend really means it. He says what's in his heart straight off.

Willie: Yes, Miss, I'm really a bit of a poet, and my poetic mouse is always inspired by true beauty.

Harry: He must have choked on that one, poor thing.

Miss Meisel: *(enchanted)* Ah! Ah! Such progress! Such evolution! Even peddlers are classic poets these days!

Willie: Yes, my lady, the classier the better! But it's unthinkable for such a relic as you to be out in the country.

Harry: *(aside)* Relic! Now his language is getting too high-falutin!

Willie: Well-read? From top to toe.

Harry: He used to read his prayer book every Saturday back in Shnipeshok.

Miss Meisel: And have you also read the classics?

Willie: I didn't go to classes, but I've read the whole pack! Shelley's "Night before Passover," Shakespeare's "Jalopy," Byron's "1001 Nights," Milton's "Saturday Night" and more and more.

Harry: And he can roll out matzo dough too; he's an expert at that.

Miss Meisel: Unfortunately I've not read these works. Are you also a bit musical?

Willie: *(insulted)* Me a muscleman? Oh, Miss, what do you think of me? I'm a patron of the arts from Shnipeshok.

Harry: And he got out of the Russian draft with an exemption for a mole on his left knee.

Miss Meisel: Harry! You don't understand me! I'm inquiring as to whether he sings or plays an instrument.

Willie: Well, then say so! As for playing, I don't play much, but a bit on the harmonica. As to singing, I'm tops. I can give you a sample of my voice and you'll just lick your fingers! *(He sings a Jewish liturgical number; Dixon listens a while and begins to sing; the other Negroes sing and gesture.)*

Harry: It goes right through my limbs!

Miss Meisel: *(angrily, to the Negroes)* Go to hell, black devil!

Dixon: I wouldn't go, Miss Meisel! I want a new suit for Christmas! Hee, hee, hee! *(He laughs uproariously.)*

Miss Meisel: All right, all right! *(to Willie)* This black devil insists on a new suit for Christmas; could you be so kind as to show me a few of your items?

Willie: *(very quickly)* With the greatest of respect, my pretty miss! You ask if I have articles? From whom else could you find such bargains as from me? I tell you honestly, you're an expert! All pretty girls are expert!

Harry: *(aside)* Expert in radishes and corsets.

Miss Meisel: Do show me a few suits.

Willie: Right away! This minute! *(He takes out a suit and gives it to her.)* See? French-tricot!

Harry: *(aside)* Brownsville rags, Boston patches!

Miss Meisel: *(gives the suit to Dixon)* Here, how do you like it?

Dixon: *(takes the suit, feels it, makes a sour face)* Rags! No good! Hee hee! *(He laughs idiotically.)*

Willie: *(aside)* A plague on his black bones! Some expert! *(aloud)* What does he know about merchandise, Miss? I got it from one of the greatest firms in New York! Ha! How old are you, pretty miss?

Harry: *(aside)* Probably knew George Washington.

Miss Meisel: 23 years old, but what does this suit cost?

Willie: Only $23. But you're fooling me! You're not more than 18.

Miss Meisel: *(flattered)* Really! That pleases me. But $23 is too much.

Harry: A thief's bargain!

Willie: Ah, Miss, it cost even more, but I'm doing this just for you.

Miss Meisel: Why just for me?

Willie: I must speak frankly. When I look at your beautiful eyes, my heart won't allow me to quote a high price.

Miss Meisel: *(coquettishly)* Do you really find my eyes beautiful?

Willie: What do you mean, beautiful! They burn in my heart like two Sabbath candles and I'm on fire! I'm consumed! Love has kindled within me. Oh, goddess! I can't overcharge you! You don't know what my heart feels for you! Give me $20 and take the suit! *(He goes down on one knee.)*

Miss Meisel: *(getting angry)* Back, you shameless man! Are you just trying to swindle me? Your suit isn't even worth $3 and you think you'll take me in with your compliments! Come, Dixon. *(She leaves quickly; Dixon and the other Negroes follow her.)*

Harry: *(cracks up)* Ha, ha, ha! Oh, my sides are splitting! Ha, ha, ha!

Willie: *(gets up, sadly)* You're laughing? And I feel like crying. Now I see I have no luck. You saw yourself how I tried my best. I bluffed, I scattered compliments, I declared my love for the old hag, and the suit's worth $23, isn't it?

Harry: I already told you that you're no *shlimazl*, just not a bit of a business man.

Willie: Do you understand business better than me?

Harry: Of course.

Willie: And how are you doing?

Harry: Brilliantly! I make $100 profit every week.

Willie: *(amazed)* $100 a week? That can't be!

Harry: *(takes out a bank book)* Here's $5000 for the last 2 years. Look, and be convinced!

Willie: *(looks in the bank book)* You've earned $5000 in the last 2 years? Do you really peddle your goods here, or in heaven? Either you're a sorcerer or your customers are angels.

Harry: I'll peddle there in a hundred years. Now I peddle on earth, in the same territory where you wander about with your pack.

Willie: In the same territory, where no one wants to buy a suit? You're just talking.

(Miss Meisel comes out of the farmhouse.)

Harry: Quiet! Here comes the old bitch again! You stay and watch how I'll sell her a suit.

Miss Meisel: *(to Willie)* Kindly show me that suit again.

Willie: *(quietly to Harry)* See? She wants to buy! *(aloud)* At once, my pretty miss! I knew you'd have regrets. My clothing is the best in the world, cross my heart! *(He takes out a suit and shows it to Miss Meisel.)*

Miss Meisel: *(looks at it carefully)* And your last price?

Willie: *(aside, happy)* Oh, she's taking it, she's taking it! *(aloud)* $22, Miss, a dollar less than before.

Miss Meisel: Is that really your last word?

Willie: I'm losing a dollar on it, Miss, but I can't help it, times are hard.

Miss Meisel: $5, not a penny more.

Willie: What are you saying, Miss? God be with you! *(quietly to Harry)* It cost me $8 at sale price, I swear as I'm a Jew.

Miss Meisel: Well? Do you wish to sell it at that price?

Willie: I can't, as God is my witness.

Miss Meisel: *(to Harry)* And you, Sir? Have you brought some wares?

Harry: I have a few things left. *(He takes out a suit and shows it to her.)*

Miss Meisel: *(examines it with an expression of satisfaction)* What does this suit cost?

Harry: *(calmly)* $28.

Willie: *(quietly, to Harry)* What, have you gone mad?

Miss Meisel: Not cheaper?

Harry: I have just one price. $28!

Miss Meisel: Good, I'll take it. *(gives him money, exits)*

Harry: *(laughs)* Ha, ha! Well, Willie, now what do you say?

Willie: Only that you know some magic, and I'm beginning to be afraid of you. Tell me, where did you learn black magic?

Harry: Magic? May such a fate never befall me.

Willie: What then? How can you take $28 for a suit that costs $10 at most?

Harry: There's a secret in this.

Willie: A secret? Tell me!

Harry: With great pleasure – but wait – here comes Lord Kalomfulo and his courtiers!

(Kalomfulo and followers enter.)

Willie: *(terrified)* Harry, my hair's standing up on my head.

Harry: What's the matter now?

Willie: What can it be but that this savage wants to roast me in honor of his holiday?

Harry: May he never have a better meal than peddler steak!

Kalomfulo: Harry! I came to get …

Willie: You hear? He needs to get … I'm lost! *(He trembles.)*

Kalomfulo: *(angry)* Don't interrupt me! Crocodile and devil! Rrrr!

Harry: *(mock-angry)* Don't interrupt! Rabbi and cantor. Rrrr!

Kalomfulo: *(to Harry)* Today is the great festival in honor of our holy god Hoptsi. *(Harry sneezes: Hoptsi!)* So for dinner I want my warriors –

Willie: *(trembles)* Oy vey! He wants to have me for dinner! My poor body will get a burial in an Indian's belly!

Kalomfulo: *(furious)* Scoundrel and lizard! Don't interrupt! Rrrr!

Harry: *(mock-angry)* Ahasherus and Vashti! Quiet! Rrrr!

Kalomfulo: So I want my warriors to have new suits for dinner.

Willie: *(aside)* Oof! A load off my mind!

Harry: How many suits do you need, your Kalomfulic Majesty?

Kalomfulo: As many as you have.

Harry: I have very few; buy some from my buddy, he still has a big stock.

Willie: That's a fact! And I'll sell at my best wholesale price.

Kalomfulo: *(angry)* Keep your clothes for your wild kinfolk back East! Us westerners want good stock and we know what good is!

Willie: *(sighs aside)* When there's no luck, you can't make a broom shoot!

Kalomfulo: So, Harry, let's see your suits.

Harry: *(hands over his whole pack)* Here, brown majesty.

Kalomfulo: How many suits in your pack?

Harry: 25.

Kalomfulo: And the price?

Harry: $30 a suit.

Kalomfulo: Good, here's money. *(He gives him money.)*

Willie: *(aside)* Now that's what I call luck! He gets it coming and going. He'll be a second Jay Gould!

Kalomfulo: Next time bring more clothes. Goodbye! *(He and his followers exit.)*

Willie: No Harry! I can't stand it any more! Either you know black magic or I'm not Willie!

Harry: *(laughs)* Ha ha! I'm just a plain guy and you're you.

Willie: Where do you get this dark power?

Harry: You see I'm skinny and frail, like all the sons of Israel, just skin and bones.

Willie: But with a fat bank book. You get $30 for a suit that costs no more than $10.

Harry: That's the secret, the secret of success.

Willie: Well, I already said that! I'm a *shlimazl*, and you're the fair-haired boy.

Harry: No, you can be a fair-haired boy too, just like me, but you're not a businessman like me.

Willie: And how does one become a businessman like you?

Harry: Just listen, my dear genius, that's my secret.

Willie: And you won't tell me? You're afraid I'll be a competitor? Harry, brother, old pal! Have pity on me! Already three years I wander around America and can't make a living. Tell me your secret, I'll be eternally grateful!

Harry: OK! Close your eyes and I'll tell you. 1-2-3 and open them again.

Willie: *(scared)* Oy vey! Are you really a sorcerer? No, No, I'm scared!

Harry: *(laughs)* Ha ha! You really are a *shlimazl*. I tell you, close your eyes.

Willie: It won't hurt?

Harry: *(mock-angry)* Scoundrel and crocodile! Rrrr! I order you to close your eyes! Rrrr!

Willie: What can I do? I want to know the secret of success. *(He closes his eyes.)*

Harry: *(takes a book out of his breast pocket and holds it up high)* 1–2–3!

Willie: *(opens his eyes, is amazed)* What's this? A book?

Harry: This is the catalog of Louis Minsky of 55, 57 and 59 Canal Street in New York. Get a catalog like this, do you hear? Rrrr!

Willie: Looks like you're making fun of me.

Harry: God forbid! The secret of success lies in this catalog. Whoever buys dry goods from Louis Minsky must have good business, since the prices are low and the stock brilliant. I've been doing business with this firm for three years and to date my customers are satisfied, as you've seen for yourself.

Willie: Is it really so? What did the suits cost you that you just sold?

Harry: $11 and $12 per suit. Good stuff and cheap.

Willie: Oh, what an ox, what a horse, what an ass I am! I paid a lot more for my rags.

Harry: Do you see? There are no tricks, you just have to be a good businessman, you have to know where to buy. Only fools believe in success; the smart ones believe in themselves. Start buying from L. Minsky, the largest, most up-to-date and cheapest wholesale dry goods store and manufacturer of clothing, at 55, 57 and 59 Canal Street, New York. Then you'll see that in a couple of years you too can be a little Jay Gould.

Willie: Oh, I'll listen to you. I won't be a little Jay Gould, a little Astor is good enough for me.

Harry: God willing! From your mouth into God's ears!

Concluding Duet to text of Harry's Entrance Song.

27

A LABORATORY OF FUN

Joan Littlewood

Those who at present work in factories, mines and offices will quite soon be able to live as only a few people now can: choosing their own congenial work, doing as little of it as they like, and filling their leisure with whatever delights them. Those people who like fiddling with machinery and pressing buttons can service and press buttons in the robot-manned factories.

In London we are going to create a university of the streets – not a "gracious" park but a foretaste of the pleasures of 1984. It will be a laboratory of pleasure, providing room for many kinds of action.

For example, the "fun arcade" will be full of the games and tests that psychologists and electronics engineers now devise for the service of industry or war – knowledge will be piped through jukeboxes. In the music area we shall have, by day, instruments available, free instruction, recordings for anyone, classical, folk, jazz, and pop disc libraries; by night, jam sessions, jazz festivals, poetry and dance – every sort of popular dancing, formal or spontaneous.

There will be a "science playground" where visitors can attend lecture-demonstrations supported by teaching films, closed-circuit television and working models; by night, the area will become an agora or *kaffeeklatsch* where the Socrates, the Abelards, the Mermaid poets, the wandering scholars of the future, the mystics, the sceptics and the sophists can dispute till dawn. An acting area will afford the therapy of theatre for everyone: men and women from factories, shops, and offices, bored with their daily routine, will be able to re-enact incidents from their own experience in burlesque and mime and gossip, so that they no longer accept passively whatever happens to them but wake to a critical awareness of reality, act out their subconscious fears and taboos, and perhaps are stimulated to social research.

A plastic area will be a place for uninhibited dabbling in wood, metal, paint, clay, stone, or textiles, for the rediscovery of the childhood experience of touching and handling, for constructing anything (useless or useful, to taste) from a giant crane to a bird cage.

But the essence of the place will be its informality: nothing is obligatory, anything goes. There will be no permanent structures. Nothing is to last for more than ten years, some things not even ten days: no concrete stadia, stained and cracking; no legacy of noble contemporary architecture, quickly dating; no municipal geranium-beds or fixed teak benches.

With informality goes flexibility. The "areas" that have been listed are not segregated enclosures. The whole plan is open, but on many levels. So the greatest pleasure of traditional parks is preserved – the pleasure of strolling casually, looking in at one or another of these areas or (if this is preferred) settling down for several hours of work-play.

Besides the activities already briefly outlined, there will be plenty to engage imagination and enlarge experience. At various points, sheltered or open, there will be screens on which closed-circuit television will show, without editing or art, whatever is going on at a number of places in and out of London, and in the complex itself: it will be possible to see coal-mines, woodmen and dockers actually at work; Monkey Hill, the aquarium or the insect house at the Zoo; the comings-and-goings outside a local authority rest-center, a Salvation Army hostel, the casualty ward of a hospital, or a West End club; newspanels will bring world and local news.

The curiosity that many people feel about their neighbors' lives can be satisfied instructively, and with greater immediacy than in any documentary film … and an occasion of major popular interest – a Cup Final, happenings of international interest, or a royal funeral – would be presented on screens of maximum size. The visitor can enjoy a sense of identity with the world about him.

Many who start by wandering half-attentively, or even sceptically, through the complex will be drawn into these and other elementary exercises in social observation. In what has been called the acting area, for instance, there will be no rigid division between performers and audience – a generalization of the technique used in Theatre Workshop for many years.

As I have described it, it may seem very busy, yet the general atmosphere will be one of relaxation and – equally important and now technically possible – there will be zones of quiet for those who don't feel like listening to music or taking part actively in all that is going on. Here they can watch, lounge about and find enjoyment in wasting time.

The activities designed for the site should be experimental, the place itself expendable and changeable. The organization of space and the objects occupying it should, on the one hand, challenge the participants' mental and physical dexterity and, on the other, allow for a flow of space and time, in which passive and active pleasure is provoked. A maximum range of physical organizational and operational arrangements was prepared on the basis of a design analysis of the preliminary structural, component and servicing design. (Throughout, the shortcomings of using, by name, activities already in existence was realized.) Therefore the next stage consisted of breaking down a wide range of desirable activities into their constituent demands. The resulting activity affinity information was then rehabilitated by a developed structural, component, and servicing kit. The final store of such possibilities was handed over to the cyberneticians with specific requests for threshold conditioning, visiting patterns etc., to be investigated at an early stage. Once satisfactory feedback was achieved then previous hunches on, say, the desirable periods of transformation from one total configuration to another could be tested.

The ephemeral nature of the architecture is a major element in the design, making possible the use of materials and techniques normally excluded from the building industry. Charged static-vapor zones, optical barriers, warm-air curtains and fog-dispersal plants are some of the methods employed, together with vertical and horizontal light-weight blinds.

Within the complex, the public moves about, above the largely unobstructed ground-level deck, on ramps, moving walkways, catwalks and radial escalators. All such equipment is capable of rearrangement – allowing multi-directional movement and random pedestrian grouping, yet capable of programming. The complex itself, having no doorways, enables one to choose one's own route and degree of involvement with the activities. Although the framework will remain a constant size, the total volume in use may vary, thus presenting a changing scene even to the frequent user. While individual enclosures such as theatre areas, workshops, or restaurants have their own particular controlled environment, the total volume is capable of resisting or modifying adverse climatic conditions.

The nature of the enclosures and the degree of control required for these activities are so varied – including as they do large-volume activities such as rallies, concerts, conferences, theatre and screenings – that each is built up of separate units ("walls," "floors," "ceilings") as required. Inflatable enclosures are also used. The smaller enclosures are more likely to be self-contained: these are built-up standard-unit "boxes" of reinforced plastic and aluminum, set on and serviced from open "decks." The construction and arrangement of such enclosures, together with the movement and positioning of fittings and equipment, are achieved by a permanent traveling gantry crane spanning the whole structure.

The movement of staff, piped services and escape routes are provided for within the open-frame, protected-steel stanchions of the superstructure and cross-connected at service basement level, where service access and parking are located, together with the necessary plant.

The whole complex provides valuable site-testing conditions for a wide range of materials, equipment and constructional techniques.

CHRONOLOGY

1961–3: Project designed and programmed.
1962–4: Feasibility studies undertaken, considering various large metropolitan sites.
1964: Fun Palace included in Civic Trust's Lea Valley Development Plan (East London).
1966: Fun Palace Foundation registered as Charitable Trust.
1966: Withdrawal of Fun Palace from Lea Valley site due to strongly contested variation in the extent of particular site.

There is at present no scheduled construction date, since there is no site. As the Fun Palace was designed as a short-term toy (10–15 years), its decreasing validity is being kept under constant review by the Trustees, who meet twice a year.

TRUSTEES

Yehudi Menuhin
R. Buckminster Fuller
Joan Littlewood
Lord Ritchie Calder
The Earl of Harewood

Part VI

POLITICAL THEATRE AS POPULAR ENTERTAINMENT

28

INTRODUCTION TO PART VI

Joel Schechter

"From the first it has been the theatre's business to entertain people," Brecht wrote, and his own plays demonstrated that political theatre can entertain and advance social concerns at the same time.[1] Poverty, hunger, injustice and war are not inherently sources of entertainment, although television news broadcasts daily endeavor to make crises diverting; mass media reports remove events from their political and social context, and focus on sensationalistic and madcap developments, as popular melodrama and farce have done to a greater degree in the past. By contrast, political plays, free of corporate media's constraints, can more fully explore situations of political and social unrest. Their artistic independence allows them to question and protest social injustices, and create innovative forms of political entertainment which would find no sponsor on television.

In the past century, popular theatre artists have employed circus arts, puppetry, vaudeville, melodrama, and jatra among other forms, to promote public interest in social change. In their satiric play, *Throw the Lady Out*, Dario Fo and Franca Rame represented some of the absurd and irrational behavior of the United States in Vietnam with trapeze and clown acts. One senseless hit-and-run murder involved a scooter running over a chorus of clowns; Fo's stage direction notes that the clowns "fall pirouetting. The scooter, proceeding carelessly, exits."[2] These cruel, senseless, and comic acts abound in the allegory about militarism and the USA (The Old Lady). Teatro Campesino founder Luis Valdez discovered in physical comedy a graphic representation of embattled labor relations; in his words,

> if you think that DiGiorgio [a California ranch owner] is living and standing on the backs of his farm workers, you can show it with humor. You get 'DiGiorgio' to stand on the backs of two farm workers, and there it is and nobody will refute you.[3]

Fo and Rame have drawn on a number of popular theatre forms already discussed, including their native Italy's *commedia dell'arte*, circus clowning, storytelling, and puppetry. Commedia was also a source of inspiration for Luis Valdez, who learned about the tradition as a member of the San Francisco Mime Troupe. He left the Mime Troupe in 1965 to create Teatro Campesino in the farmlands of Delano, California. Chicano field workers struggling to start a union saw their fight humorously portrayed and won in *actos*, short plays staged on the portable, truckbed stage of Valdez's Teatro.

Valdez and some of the other theatre artists introduced here developed their popular political theatre in the 1960s, when protests against war, and strikes for equality and justice erupted around the world. In the United States, the San Francisco Mime Troupe and Teatro Campesino were two of many political theatre companies shaped in the crucible of 1960s' turbulence. The Mime Troupe, which began in 1959, has survived over forty years as a political comedy ensemble and an artistic collective. It has gone through many changes in personnel, and its calls for revolution have been less frequent recently, as the Troupe's plays address specific programs for affordable housing, fair trade, non-genetically engineered food, and public control over global corporations. Mime Troupe collaboration with other theatre groups around the world reflects a new, more inclusive vision of theatre, where artistic and social advances are created through multicultural collaboration at the local level, in the United States and abroad. Here, as Eugene van Erven has noted of Third World theatre companies (some of which collabo- rated with the Mime Troupe), there is an emphasis "on *process* and *networking*" among artists, so that in addition to performances, they create cultural and political coalitions.[4]

Popular theatres like the Mime Troupe, and Fo and Rame's La Comune in Milan, developed tour-circuit audiences which would anticipate the return visits of the company, and assemble without the prompting of an expensive advertising campaign. For a time, Fo and Rame were sponsored by the Italian Communist Party; but their senses of humor and justice led them to find fault with their country's bureaucratic Communism, as well as its capitalism. Consequently, their theatre company, La Comune, became wholly inde- pendent and self-sustaining. "We started all over again," Fo tells his interviewers here, "in movie houses, dance halls, places where no one had ever seen a play before." The public had seen Fo and Rame before, on their popular television show, *Canzonissima*; when they left television and its censorship behind, and created their own touring company, the artists had greater freedom of expression, and the public was delighted to see the well-known television performers in person.

During Franca Rame and Dario Fo's tours of Italy, they addressed specific local issues, and re-enacted ongoing political trials and scandals. The experience let Fo know, as he says here, that there is "a public that attends only a type of performance capable of involving it because it is directly related to political actions."

Huge crowds, as many as 20,000 spectators, assembled in India to watch Utpal Dutt's jatra ensemble perform melodramatic speeches and songs. Dutt re-utilized the popular Indian form of jatra for new political purposes, as he explains in the 1967 interview printed here. Before his company created plays about Lenin, the fall of Berlin, Vietnam, Mao Tse-tung, and "current issues indicting the ruling classes" in the 1960s, jatra might have told a less contemporary tale about Lord Krishna, other divinities and royalty.[5] The late Calcutta director, a well-known actor himself, changed the drama's content, but recognized that jatra actors were popular theatre artists long before he approached them; they are, in Dutt's words, "people's artist[s], taking theatre to the masses in remote areas … on tour six months a year, they stay with peasants."[6]

The political entertainments created by Dutt, the Mime Troupe, Fo and Rame draw on popular traditions. They also were influenced by Brecht and Marx. A need for new theory which goes beyond Marx is comically suggested by Tony Kushner in his play, *Slavs*, when the world's oldest Bolshevik, Aleksii Antedilluvianovich Prelapsarianov, declares: "Yes, we must must change, only show me the Theory, and I will be at the barricades, show me the book of the next Beautiful Theory, and I promise you these blind eyes will see again, just to read it … ."[7] But before we entered the era of post-Marxist theory, Marx had tremendous influence on twentieth-century theatre artists. His thesis on Feuerbach arguing that philosophy should not just discuss the world, but change it, resonates throughout Brecht's epic theatre. The politically conscious acting of Brecht's Berliner Ensemble, his plays, and his love of cabaret comedy and songs, inspired several generations of theatre artists to fuse epic and popular theatre forms.

Earlier, following the Russian Revolution, another model for popular political theatre developed through the Moscow collaborations of playwright Vladimir Mayakovsky and director Vsevelod Meyerhold in the 1920s. These artists encountered obstacles in state censorship and bureaucracy, and their work disappeared under Stalin's reign. As a result, Mayakovsky's experiments in popular forms, discussed here by Frantisek Deák, are not well known. The political circus acts, cartoon poster art, and the satiric plays which Meyerhold directed had a lasting impact on Yuri Lubimov and his Taganka Theatre in Cold War-era Moscow. Since the advent of Russian *glasnost* (openness) in the 1990s, books about Meyerhold's rehearsals have been published in Moscow, and his innovations are even finding favor in American theatre training programs.

Perhaps a back-handed tribute to the attractions of popular theatre can be seen in the persecution that Meyerhold, Brecht, Fo, Rame, Augusto Boal and other theatre artists suffered. As David Mayer observed, the fact

> that the popular drama is appreciated by the largest number of citizens makes it of considerable interest to heads of government, the politically ambitious, those concerned with the orderly progress of government, and those responsible to educate the community in religious, ethical and political values.[8]

The "considerable interest" shown by those in power has been quite unfavorable at times in the former Soviet bloc, Asia, Africa, and Latin America. When government repression and illiteracy made free political discourse and dissent difficult, popular theatre provided a means to organize public responses, and create a temporary community of shared interest. Circus clown acts, puppet shows, musical revues are not entirely free of censorship under repressive governments, but often they have been left alone; their allegorical and indirect critiques of oppression were permitted when public rallies were not. Under such conditions, laughter itself becomes a statement; to laugh with others is to create a new, freely chosen community, and side with those who see folly in illegitimate authority, excessive wealth, or their comic stand-ins. As resistance to adversity, laughter is admittedly a small action, only a beginning, but a pleasant one.

With the collapse of the Soviet empire and the alleged end of the Cold War in the 1990s, state repression subsided in some quarters. The South African apartheid satirized in *Woza Albert* has officially come to an end; the play discussed here by Ron Jenkins survives as a document of oppression overcome, and a metaphor for racial prejudices which still exist. The popular forms to which such theatre turned remain viable, as can be seen in the continued, post-1960s' creativity of artists and ensembles introduced here, and new theatrical activism which was widely reported in 1999 when environmentalists dressed as giant sea turtles marched with steelworkers in Seattle to protest against World Trade Organization policies.

One special, hybrid form of political entertainment, Augusto Boal's election to office in Brazil, transformed politics into what he calls "Legislative Theatre." The "popularity" of Boal's legislative theatre, in which the audience is an electoral constituency, and is asked to make decisions before or instead of legislators, can be seen as an answer to Brecht's wry poem which asked whether the repressive East German government should "dissolve the people/ And elect another."[9] Popular political theatre does just the opposite; it brings people together in a new society where artists, not elected officials, give voice to the public's needs and dreams. Boal developed his theatre practices in Latin America during a period of military repression he discusses in his book, *Theatre of the Oppressed* (1974). His work exemplifies a definition of "Third World popular theatre" offered in one source, which states that such theatre is "used by oppressed Third World people to achieve justice and development for themselves," except that Boal and other artists also have pursued justice and economic and cultural development through popular theatre in Europe, North America, and Australia.[10]

Walter Benjamin once described Brecht's epic theatre in terms which also apply to Boal's legislative theatre, and other popular political theatre; provoking laughter, raising questions, positing solutions, such artistry "compels the spectator to take up a position towards the action, and the actor to take up a position towards his part."[11] Here the old calls by Rousseau, Diderot and Mercier, for a people's festival and a theatre for the people, return in new form, as actors and their audience take part in a shared decision-making process which may go on long after they leave the theatre.

NOTES

1 Bertolt Brecht, "Short Organum for the Theatre" in *Brecht on Theatre*, edited by John Willett. New York: Hill and Wang, 1964, p. 180.

2 Dario Fo's play quoted in "Dario Fo Explains," reprinted in this volume. I have chosen to use another translation of the play's title here.

3 Luis Valdez quoted by Beth Bagby in an interview, "El Teatro Campesino: Interviews with Luis Valdez," reprinted in this volume.

4 Eugene van Erven, *Radical People's Theatre*. Bloomington: Indiana University Press, 1988, p. 189.

5 Utpal Dutt quoted in interview, "Theatre as a Weapon," reprinted in this volume.

6 Ibid.

7 Tony Kushner, *Slavs* in *Thinking about the Longstanding Problems of Virtue and Happiness*. New York: Theatre Communications Group, 1995, p. 108.

8 David Mayer, "Towards a Definition of Popular Theatre," in *Western Popular Theatre*, edited by David Mayer and Kenneth Richards. London: Methuen, 1977, p. 263.

9 Bertolt Brecht, "The Solution" in *Poems 1913–1956* Londo:, Methuen, 1976, p. 440.

10 *The Cambridge Guide to Theatre*, edited by Martin Banham Cambridge: Cambridge University Press, 1992, p. 991. The definition of "Third World popular theatre" offered here is quite informative in other respects.

11 Walter Benjamin, "The Author as Producer," in *Understanding Brecht*, translated by Anna Bostock London: New Left Books, 1973, p. 100.

ACKNOWLEDGMENT

The title of this section is taken from Theodore Shanks's essay, and I want to acknowledge my debt; many of his observations about the San Francisco Mime Troupe apply to other political theatre ensembles as well.

29

THE AGITPROP AND CIRCUS PLAYS OF VLADIMIR MAYAKOVSKY

Frantisek Deák

The best known of Mayakovsky's plays are *Vladimir Mayakovsky, A Tragedy* (1913), *Mystery-Bouffe* (the second version, 1921), *The Bedbug* (1928–9), and *The Bathhouse* (1930). These works appeared in 1968 in a book entitled *The Complete Plays of Vladimir Mayakovsky*.[1] However, between 1920 and 1930 Mayakovsky wrote several other dramatic texts. Among these are *And What If? ... May First Daydreams in a Bourgeois Armchair, A Small Play About Priests Who Do Not Understand What Is Meant by the Holiday, How Some People Spend Time Celebrating Holidays* (all three of these playlets were written in 1920 for May Day), *The Championship of the Universal Class Struggle* (written in 1920 for the circus), *Yesterday's Exploit* (playlet, 1921), *Radio October* (1926), and *Moscow Is Burning* (written in 1930 for the circus).

There are also texts that are not literary playscripts but that were intended for the theatre or that were used in the theatre. For example, *L'Idéal et la couverture* is a dramatic libretto, but only the French version is known to us. Also several of Mayakovsky's poems have been staged. Among these are *The Soviet Alphabet*, which was produced in 1919 for the circus; *To all Tituses and Vlasses of RSFSR*, which was published in 1920 with Mayakovsky's instructions for staging; and *Twenty-Five*, produced in 1927. There are also two unfinished plays: *Benz No. 22* (1922?) and *The Play With Murder* (1925–9?).

These plays and texts have gone virtually unknown or ignored. This is mainly because they were written for a particular occasion, such as the anniversary of the Revolution or a political campaign and had a limited but exact and timely purpose. Another factor may be that these works tend to be dramatic scenarios incorporating Communist ideological content, rather than texts with an independent literary value.

THE CELEBRATION OF THE REVOLUTION

The reaction of the artistic community in Russia to the Revolution of 1917 ranged from opposition, ignorance, neutrality and sympathy to complete acceptance and identification. From the very beginning there was no question about Mayakovsky's position. "To accept or not to accept? There was no such question for me (and other Moscow Futurists). It was my revolution," he stated.

In the period immediately following the Revolution, new traditions were established, such as the naming of new holidays that replaced those on the Russian religious calendar. For the first anniversary of the Revolution, Mayakovsky wrote the initial version of *Mystery-Bouffe*, which is historically the first Socialist play. On the ninth anniversary, in the fall of 1926, Mayakovsky, in collaboration with Ossip Brik, wrote *Radio October* for Blue Blouse, a theatrical organization. The play was later rewritten for May Day by the editor of *The Blue Blouse*, a journal published by the organization, and appeared in issue No. 5–6, 1927, under the title of *Radio May*. It was subsequently produced by many troupes of the organization.

In February 1927, the Commission for the Organization of the Celebration of the Tenth Anniversary of the Revolution (directors of the academic theatres in Leningrad) asked Mayakovsky to write a play for the occasion. The Commission wanted a text that would serve as a base for a "synthetic theatre" in which different types of performances could be used. Mayakovsky read the first seven parts of his poem "Good" (first entitled "October") for the Commission. A variant was made from this poem for the production. The director, N. Smolich, used pantomime and film projection in addition to mass spectacle, "living newspaper," and mass declamation. Short scenes followed each other quickly, as in a montage. The performance was called *Twenty-Five*; it was staged in the Leningrad Little Opera Theatre on 7, 8 and 16 November 1927.

THE AGITATION FOR THE REVOLUTION

In the years of War Communism (1917–21), propaganda was crucial for the survival of the Revolution. In an era of limited means of communication – the radio was not used publicly until after 1920 – and a high percentage of illiteracy, the message came mainly through "spoken newspapers," posters, theatre and film. In the first years of the Revolution, propaganda was aimed almost entirely at workers, peasants and soldiers of the Red Army. Many new ways to disseminate propaganda were used. Agit-trains painted with slogans, for example, traveled around the country; agit-ships sailed the rivers. In the theatre, many new ways to stage propaganda were invented. Among these were the "living newspapers" (staging news, diagrams, statistics), mass declamation, theatrical trials, mass spectacles (re-enacting recent historical events), and literary montages, combining documents, poetry, slogans and other texts.

In October 1919, Mayakovsky joined ROSTA (the Russian Telegraph Agency), further identifying himself with the Revolution. Temporarily abandoning his lyric poetry and other artistic interests in favor of the immediate, practical needs of the day, he wrote and drew the propaganda posters known as Window ROSTA. Originally, the posters were put into the windows of empty Moscow shops. Later, with their growing popularity, they were exhibited in railroad stations, clubs and other public places around the country. The function of Window ROSTA was to instruct and inform the masses in a simple but attractive way on different matters – political, economic, military, etc.

In 1928, Mayakovsky wrote:

> Window ROSTA was a fantastic thing … . It meant telegraphed news immediately translated into posters and decrees into slogans … . It was a new form that spontaneously originated in life itself … . It meant men of the Red Army looking at posters before a battle and going to fight not with a prayer but a slogan on their lips.

The political poster influenced both theatre and film. The Window ROSTA posters usually consisted of more than one image (very often a series of four). Each image demonstrated a slogan in a progression. This structure of cartoons is often found in Agit-Prop theatre in which each scene is an image demonstrating a slogan (the play or performance doesn't evolve from one scene to another but one image is replaced by another – a progression of images). The influence of the poster is also found in certain agit-films (film posters). In the beginning, a slogan, such as "All Power to the People!", was projected. This was followed by static images demonstrating and elaborating on the idea of the slogan. Then, another slogan would be projected, followed by an image or images.

The poster also became a part of the scenography. In the "animated poster," a huge poster would be placed onstage. In appropriate places, holes would be cut out for the heads, arms and legs of the actors, who put themselves into the poster. Once positioned, they recited the text. While working for ROSTA, Mayakovsky proposed another simple use of posters on the stage. An actor would travel around the country with a series of posters painted on canvas. Each series would consist of numerous posters that, in progression, would demonstrate some important subject. Performing wherever he could – primarily in workers' and army clubs – the actor would portray different characters from the poster, recite the verses, or simply demonstrate and comment on individual posters.

In 1920, during his work at ROSTA, Mayakovsky wrote three playlets for May Day. These pieces represent the AgitProp genre at its best. In their way, they are the theatrical equivalent of the Window ROSTA, with the same simplicity and explicitness. Only the medium is different.

May Day of 1920 was declared a *subbotnik* (a day of voluntary work for the state on a Saturday or day off); in 1920, Easter fell on the first day of May. Thus, the playlets reflect the peculiar combination of a religious holiday and a *subbotnik*.

The stories are very simple. In *And What If? … May First Daydreams in a Bourgeois Armchair*, a slightly drunk bourgeois, Ivan Ivanovich, has a dream that old times have returned. He wakes up and finds that he has been dreaming and is faced with unpleasant reality. He is then confronted by a character personifying May Day, who asks the bourgeois to join the workers on the *subbotnik*. In *A Small Play About Priests Who Do Not Understand What Is Meant by the Holiday*, Father Svinuil complains to the workers on May Day because they do not ask him to perform the Easter ceremony, which is his means of income. The workers give him a shovel and take him on the *subbotnik*. In *How Some People Spend Time Celebrating Holidays*, days such as Easter, Christmas, and New Year's all end in an immoral way: New Year's Eve, for example, ends in drunkenness. These old holidays are compared to the new May Day or workers' holiday.

These playlets have the same simple, functional character as the Window ROSTA. They are also similar in their use of the forms of popular art – the Russian folk farce is used in the playlets – and in their use of language, which is a mixture of popular folk idioms and political slogans. These playlets were probably intended to be performed together. Their thematic similarity – the use of the same personified character named "Theatre of Satire" – indicates this, along with the fact that they were all written for the same occasion and the same theatre (the Theatre of Satire).

Despite the fact that these playlets literally publicized the *subbotnik* initiated by the government, they were banned by Comrade Kitaevsky, a member of the Worker–Peasant Inspection. Anatoli Lunacharsky, in a letter to the Worker–Peasant Inspection, protested against the ban and expressed the following opinion:

Mayakovsky wrote three rather amusing playlets for the Theatre of Satire. They are not pearls of art but quite well-done caricatures in a good tempo … . I do not understand why these deeply Soviet playlets cannot be done by the Theatre of Satire.

Comrade Kitaevsky's reasons related to personal taste rather than political content. *And What If? …* was staged later in 1920 in the studio of the Theatre of Satire. *A Small Play About Priests …* was given a production in 1921 at the Theatre of Revolutionary Satire. *How Some People Spend Time …* was produced during one of the anti-religious campaigns in 1922 (?) at an army-school club.

The political poster and agit-play also influenced all three of Mayakovsky's major post-Revolutionary plays. In the second version of *Mystery-Bouffe*, which Mayakovsky began to write in October, 1920, we find the themes, characters and slogans from Window ROSTA that were used in the period from October to December 1920. The new fifth act that Mayakovsky added particularly resembles his own posters. In *The Bedbug*, scene 12, for example, is an agit-scene against alcoholism. Mayakovsky, who assisted Meyerhold in staging it, taught the actors the oratorical and slogan-like manner of recitation.

In the production of *The Bathhouse*, slogans ridiculing the Moscow Art Theatre, critics, and bureaucrats were a part of the environment. They were on the stage as well as in the auditorium. All of Act III, in fact, is an attack on the official and middle-class theatre. As such, it is an independent agit-play within a play. The relationships between political posters and agit-playlets in *Mystery-Bouffe* (second version), *The Bedbug*, and *The Bathhouse* are numerous. The few examples mentioned here indicate the influence that the political poster had on the theatre in Russia at that time.

MAYAKOVSKY AND THE CIRCUS

Mayakovsky, like many other avant-garde artists, admired the circus. As a Futurist poet, he saw many possibilities in the circus. He wanted, for example, to read his poems while riding on an elephant in the arena of a circus. But his interest in circus went beyond that. For Mayakovsky, circus was a part of the popular art tradition whose many forms (songs, painting, theatre) he considered his legitimate sources of inspiration.

Mayakovsky's friendship with the circus clown Vitaly Lazarenko gave him first-hand knowledge of the circus. Their friendship began in 1914. At this time, Lazarenko (1890–1939) was already a well-known performer, who had had a successful career as an auguste clown and as an acrobat. In his artistic and political orientation, Lazarenko was very much like Mayakovsky. Before the Revolution, Lazarenko was associated with Futurism: in 1914, he acted in a Futurist film entitled *I Want to be a Futurist*. After the Revolution, he became more political. *In My Life With Mayakovsky*, V. Kamensky describes the first meeting between Mayakovsky and Lazarenko in the circus:

Lazarenko wore the costume of an equestrienne with a huge red hat, rhinestones in his ears, and an enormous black radish on his chest. 'Why the black radish?' asked Volodia (Mayakovsky). Lazarenko explains: 'I'm incarnating an equestrienne who is madly in love with Mayakovsky. You are usually wearing radishes in your buttonhole, and she is trying to please you and seduce you by also wearing a radish. Hopelessly in love, she recites your poetry riding in the arena of the circus and, constantly falling off the horse, she presses the radish to her heart and exclaims: 'Oh! Mayakovsky, Mayakovsky, why did you make me lose my head?' We watched the act. Mayakovsky sent kisses to the equestrienne and Lazarenko yelled frenetically: 'Mayakovsky, genius, take me, with my horse and bridle. I'm all yours. Take me!'

In 1919, after the Revolution, Mayakovsky and Lazarenko met in Moscow in the Poets' Café, where Mayakovsky often read his poetry. At this time, the art of both men tended more toward the political. Lazarenko changed his clown mask from that of a philosophizing vagabond to that of a more politically oriented clown, publicist and propagandist. Independently from Mayakovsky, he staged short political sketches in the circus arena that had been inspired by political posters.

Mayakovsky often went to see Lazarenko in the circus. After the performance they discussed Lazarenko's act and, according to Lazarenko, Mayakovsky gave him themes for his political sketches. Their first concrete collaboration was Lazarenko's staging of Mayakovsky's poem "Soviet Alphabet." The poem is an example of Mayakovsky's use of a popular form for the purpose of propaganda. Soldiers were familiar with a vulgar alphabet-poem. For each letter in the alphabet, there was a verse or two with coarse content. Mayakovsky used the form of the alphabet but replaced the obscene references with timely satirical verses. He printed and distributed the poems personally to soldiers. Lazarenko's staging of Mayakovsky's "Soviet Alphabet" was very simple. He carried huge painted letters into the arena and, showing them to the public, recited or sang verses. Probably some pantomime was also involved.

Lazarenko and Mayakovsky's closest collaboration came in the creation of *The Championship of the Universal Class Struggle* (1920). The form of a circus wrestling match was probably Lazarenko's idea. He certainly collaborated on the subject matter, as the play was written specifically for him.

Lazarenko also acted in the second version of *Mystery-Bouffe*, which was directed by Meyerhold in 1921. He played the role of one of the devils. In Act III, Meyerhold, with Lazarenko functioning as an adviser, used circus tricks and acrobatics. Lazarenko also helped Meyerhold to stage some circus numbers in *The Bedbug*.

Mayakovsky wrote his last play, *Moscow Is Burning* (1930), for the twenty-fifth anniversary of the Revolution of 1905. This was his most elaborate circus spectacle. He described its genre as "pantomime" and later "heroic melomime." A proper classification could have been "montage," because it was a collection of independent scenes, chronologically following events from 1905 to 1930. Different "media" such as poetry, film, pantomime and circus (acrobats and trained animals) were used.

NOTE

1 *The Complete Plays of Vladimir Mayakovsky* was published by Washington Square Press, Inc., translations by Guy Daniels.

30

EL TEATRO CAMPESINO
An interview with Luis Valdez

Beth Bagby

El Teatro Campesino (The Farm Workers' Theatre), founded and directed by 26-year-old Luis Miguel Valdez, deals with the same problems of the San Joaquin Valley that John Steinbeck depicted so graphically thirty years ago. The emphasis, however, is communication to the oppressed, not about them.

The Teatro, (as it is usually called) is a bilingual union theatre established in Delano, California, during the first months of a continuing agricultural strike. On 8 September 1965, the largely Filipino AFL–CIO affiliate AWOC (Agricultural Workers' Organizing Committee) called a strike against the area's grape ranches. On 16 September members of the largely Mexican-American NFWA (National Farm Workers' Association) founded by Cesar Chavez, voted unanimously to join the strike. Later, when the NFWA had also affiliated with AFL–CIO, the two unions merged and became UFWOC, the United Farm Workers' Organizing Committee.

The Teatro's early *actos*, acts of about fifteen minutes developed out of improvisation, dealt primarily with the significance of the *Huelga* (strike), the NFWA, and why farm workers should join. As the problems of the strike have become more complicated, as its targets have changed, and with the union merger and reorganization, the role of the Teatro and the content of its *actos* have become more involved. In the last few months it has instituted a Monday night film series, drama classes for different age-groups, recorder classes, workshops in graphic arts and puppet making, and classes in English.

The Teatro is always understaffed, and never has more than one actress. Consequently, only a few *actos* include female characters. Another factor affecting Teatro material is the necessity of communicating in two languages. Some union members speak little or no English, so actors wear signs – usually in Spanish – designating a character's name or role. Felipe Cantu, 45 years old and a part-time member of the Teatro, is its best comic actor, but does not speak English. However, he reacts so totally with his voice, face, and body that most of the audience never observe that he does not have any lines. Songs are usually Spanish and introduced with English explanations, although Augustin "Augie" Lira, the first Teatro member, recently composed some in English. Dialogue fluctuates between English and Spanish, but with little loss of meaning –

Spanish and English slang are commonly known anyway, and wherever either language is not understood, there is little visual doubt as to the significance of an event.

Valdez' has been as part of a large migrant farm labor family of Mexican-American descent, a college graduate in drama and a playwright. His unpublished three-act play *The Shrunken Head of Pancho Villa* deals with a Mexican-American farm labor family's disorientation in lower middle-class urban life. Working with the Teatro has given him a chance to take some of these problems and propose solutions: first, economic equalization, so that, unshackled by poverty and materialistic dreams, the Mexican-American can then establish an identity which integrates those historic and ethnic elements in which he should have pride. The Teatro has been limited to an audience of either farm workers or urban strike sympathizers, but its unwritten *actos* have established dramatic images which will last the lives of its audiences.

This interview was held in what has been the Teatro's headquarters since last summer, La Azteca, a former tortilleria, on 30 August 1966. The date is important as the day of the first recognized elections for farm labor union representation. The results were a test of the effectiveness of the union organizers, and in the case of the Teatro, of its communication with its audience. UFWOC did win representation for field workers, where they had organized hardest. The Teamsters won representation for non-field workers (truck drivers and grape packers), who constitute a small percentage of ranch employees.

Valdez: I have been interested in drama since the first grade. I started school at Stratford, a small town about 35 miles from here, where we'd been picking cotton and living in one of the bigger camps. We got stuck there when our old pickup was put up on blocks because it was broken down. It started to rain, and the rain kept on for weeks. Then fall came along and school. I started school in October, I think. The only problem was I didn't know a word of English.

The first English word I remember learning was "crawl," and I'll tell you how it came about. The teacher was in charge of the school play that year, and she had this pet – a Mexican kid – who spoke English. She brought him in one day in a monkey suit, with a monkey mask and – well, it was a little suit with a tail – and I was really aghast. This was too much. Then I somehow learned that there was going to be a play, that this was try-outs and this kid was going to be one of the monkeys in the play. It was about the jungle, Christmas in the jungle or something. She told him, "Crawl," like a monkey I guess, but I remember "crawl." He started bouncing around, and I wanted to be a monkey. I thought, "If she tells me to crawl, I'll crawl."

I don't remember if I did, but I got the part. I was one of the monkeys, and we started working on the set with the teacher. I was really fascinated by the fake trees we put up and the stage and the curtain; and the papier-mâché masks – they turned me on. But the thing is that my family moved just before Christmas, so I missed being in the play, and I never forgot that. Shortly after, I started organizing my own plays at school. And then at home in the garage I set up puppet shows.

Bagby: What were the subjects?

Valdez: Fairy tales. I used to dig fairy tales.

Bagby: Did you relate them to the Mexican-American farm worker?

Valdez: No. They were very far out things – the Grimm brothers. They were adaptations, but hardly anything connected with what was going on at home. That continued all through grammar school, and in high school I got in the Speech and Drama Depart-

Fig. 30.1 Luis Valdez (right) in *Two Faces of the Boss*, performed by El Teatro Campesino, 1970. (Photo by Theodore Shank.)

ment and was in several plays. I was a very serious student, and I wanted to make it and eventually got a scholarship.

Bagby: To San Jose State?

Valdez: Yes. I was in math and science at that time, and the whole speech and drama thing was a hobby; the bread-and-butter stuff was mathematics and science. I changed majors my sophomore year; I went into English, and from there started taking all kinds of courses in drama – literature first, reading all kinds of plays. Then I started writing. Toward the end of my sophomore year, I wrote a one-act play called *The Theft*. It won a school prize and a contest that the San Jose Theatre Guild ran. The award was production of the play, and later it was produced at San Jose State.

Then there was a two-year lull, while I worked on *The Shrunken Head of Pancho Villa*. I had a professor working with me from the beginning; I kept working on it and working on it, and he kept asking me to finish. I finally finished a producible version and we got it together and I directed it. After it was produced for the Northwest Drama

Conference at San Jose State, there were still very grave faults with the play that I wanted to iron out. I didn't want to stay at San Jose anymore. It was in that spring, too, that I discovered the San Francisco Mime Troupe.

Bagby: When they were in San Jose?

Valdez: Yes. They were doing *Tartuffe* in *commedia dell'arte* style, and I'd never seen anything like it. I was really amazed by the possibilities of that type of theatre and wanted to know how it worked, so I jumped into it.

Bagby: Had you at that time started to think of theatre's potential among farm workers?

Valdez: No. Before my play was produced at San Jose State, I hadn't decided whether or not I would go ahead or cut out and start hitting the labor camps. I felt I needed some roots again and wanted to get to the Valley and people here, many of them my relatives. Then when I got involved in production of the play, I didn't take off as an itinerant farm worker/writer.

After the play was produced, that idea rolled up again and became very plausible, because it was spring and there would be a lot of work. But it didn't seem right just to leave things as they were. I'd made some headway and was writing plays. It was about that time that the idea of theatre and farm labor came together in my mind, and I thought, yeah, it's a possibility – a theatre group for the Valley.

But I didn't have the resources; so when I discovered the Mime Troupe, I figured if any theatre could turn on farm workers, it would be that type of theatre – outside, that lively, that bawdy. That same spring I had heard about the National Farm Workers' Association. Copies of *El Malcriado* [bi-weekly, bilingual newspaper of the Farm Worker Press] started to seep through.

Bagby: Through what channels, your relatives?

Valdez: My grandmother lives in Earlimart and came to visit my family in San Jose. She brought a copy of *El Malcriado* with Zapata's picture on it, and that really amazed me. Zapata! That's potent stuff. I maintained an active interest in that; but I was still reworking the play. Then the strike broke – 8 September 1965. A couple of weeks passed, and we heard there was going to be a march; that seemed like a good enough reason to come down – to participate in the march.

Bagby: Which march was that?

Valdez: The twenty-sixth of September. I came down with some friends – there were six of us. We were here in Delano that full day and left at night. We'd marched – with all of those people shouting "*Huelga*"; there must have been 1,200 people.

Bagby: These were mostly strikers?

Valdez: Filipinos and Mexicans, yes. This was the *fantastic* thing about it. I couldn't get it out of my head for weeks after that. These were Mexicans and Filipinos, not students or citified radicals; these were poor farm workers. I went back to San Francisco – I thought a lot about a farm workers' theatre then. I knew I had to do something.

Bagby: Were you still with the Mime Troupe?

Valdez: Right. Part of the reason I had to go back and stay in San Francisco was because their performances of *Candelaio* ran into October, and I was committed to that. After the march, I talked to Dolores Huerta [one of UFWOC's five officers] about whether or not they could visualize, see any necessity for a farm workers' theatre, and she said, "Oh, yes, it's very possible. Come on down." That immediate reaction was kind of funny, so I didn't believe her. Then I talked to Cesar Chavez, and apparently Dolores had already talked to him. He said, "Come on down," so I came on down. We had a preliminary meeting in the office, and then we set up another.

Bagby: Who was present?

Valdez: Farm workers, some of the student volunteers. There was a crowd of about thirty-five that night – right there in the little office. They all seemed to like the idea, but what next? How do we go about forming a theatre group? One woman wondered if her sons and their rock and roll band could participate. I couldn't communicate the concept of theatre, because most of them had never been to a play as such. The only way to really show them what I meant was to illustrate it. Frank Cieciorka, the San Francisco artist, had made some signs for me before I came down – *Esquirol* (strike-breaker or scab), *Patroncito* (grower), *Huelgista* (striker), *Contratista* (contractor).

Bagby: So you had already begun to envision *actos*?

Valdez: Yes. Well, I figured that I'd have to hang signs on them. The second meeting started out very slow. We got about twelve people. About four or five were, again, student volunteers, and I was a little disappointed because I wanted farm workers. And with another five – some were very serious. It seemed dismal.

I talked for about ten minutes, and then realized that talking wasn't going to accomplish anything. The thing to do was do it, so I called three of them over, and on two hung *Huelgista* signs. Then I gave one an *Esquirol* sign, and told him to stand up there and act like an *Esquirol* – a scab. He didn't want to at first, because it was a dirty word at that time, but he did it in good spirits. Then the two *huelgistas* started shouting at him, and everybody started cracking up. All of a sudden, people started coming into the pink house from I don't know where; they filled up the whole kitchen. We started changing signs around and people started volunteering, "Let me play so and so," "Look, this is what I did," and imitating all kinds of things. We ran for about two hours just doing that. By the time we had finished, there were people packing the place. They were in the doorways, the living room, and they were outside at the windows peeking in. Dolores showed up later. She stood there watching, and I think it got the message across – that you can do a lot by acting out things.

That was the beginning. The effects we achieved that night were fantastic, because people were acting out *real things*. Then I got together an original group of about five, and we started working on skits – this was all done after picketing hours, by the way. Sometimes we wouldn't get started until eight or nine, but we went on every night for about three weeks. We gave our first presentation in Filipino Hall.

Bagby: Did you do any skits at that first formal production that you do now?

Valdez: None that I can remember. The first formal one that we worked out was *The Conscience of a Scab*, and then *Three Grapes* and *Papelaccion*. *The Conscience of a Scab* involves two actors: the grape worker who "scabs" and the *huelgista*. When the scab hears the striker quote Jack London's *Definition of a Strikebreaker* ("After God had finished the rattlesnake, the toad and the vampire, he had some awful substance left with which he made a Strikebreaker ... "), he joins the strike and goes off shouting "*Huelga!*"

The "three grapes" are the green, ripe, and rotten grapes, who come onto the stage walking in a squat. Each grape wants to be picked by the worker, who has not left the field for the strike. Every time the worker begins to inspect a grape bunch before cutting, a *huelgista* comes on with a *Huelga* sign and chases the scab away. When the grower orders him to cut the grapes, even the green one has begun to smell, so it is as worthless as the rotten and the ripe, which is now too ripe to pick. When the worker discovers that even the green grape smells, he leaves the field to join the strike. If a grower cannot harvest enough crop, he must concede to strike demands.

Papellacion translates as paper play or role play. A grower comes out wearing the sign "Smiling Jack" and proceeds to tell his laborer how much he loves his Mexican workers. The grower's sign changes to "Liar," "Gringo," "Jackass," and finally *Huelga*, as the worker sees through his boss's platitudes.

After about the first month, the boycott against Schenley Industries started and my two best actors were sent away as boycott organizers. There was a lot of work to be done, and sometimes we were too tired after picketing to rehearse; so there was a lull for a month. That was due, in part, to the fact that most of my actors were taken away, and we were involved in picketing and boycotting and chasing trucks. Then we got an offer from Stanford University to perform.

Bagby: Who made the offer?

Valdez: One of the ministers. Canterbury house. We accepted without knowing how we were going to make it – no actors, no nothing. We performed in a student lounge, and there were about fifty people present. It was interesting from the viewpoint that what we had been doing for farm workers in Delano could work outside too, in a university setting. By that time, we had started using a mask, the pig-like mask.

Bagby: Did you have any songs?

Valdez: We had about three *Huelga* songs, and others. The show at Stanford was crude, but they seemed to like it; and that established a pattern we started following: going out to the cities to raise money and spread news about the strike, and then performing in Delano at weekly meetings.

Then in March, we started planning a march to Sacramento. It was decided that the Teatro would be one of the big attractions at each night's rally, so we pushed it as such and organized the rallies to include songs and speeches, reading *The Plan of Delano*, and the use of the Virgin of Guadalupe as symbol and Pilgrimage, Penance, and Revolution as themes, with the Teatro at the end as a drawing card. We performed across the Valley in about twenty-five farm worker towns.

We gained a resilience as a result of those twenty-five performances on the march that made us real veterans; so we had our material down pretty well pat for the performance at *The Committee*.

Shortly after, we had a reorganization, and we felt a growing need to get closer to the farm worker. We had been very effective in the march, but then ran into some snags – a couple of performances, for instance, in Yuba City that really made us wonder. We began to think, how can we influence, get to the farm worker a little bit closer, how can we reach him? Part of the problem was that we had been too busy touring, going from L.A. to San Francisco, across the Valley and to different farm worker towns; we had gotten away from the situation in Delano.

Bagby: Did you ask for this touring to let up, or by that time did the elections at DiGiorgio Corporation's two ranches?

Valdez: It just kind of fell into place again. The elections came on us, and everybody was called into service to help out organizing. The Teatro was drafted to go out in the camps, organize, satirize the competing Teamsters.

Bagby: Had you ever been to a camp as a theatre group before the arbitrators set up the organizers' schedule?

Valdez: Before the first election, 24 June, Cesar called us to Borrego Springs, and we performed in a park. The purpose was for Cesar to explain why the workers should not vote, why they should boycott the election. The Teatro had only pointed references to the elections; we were intended more for entertainment and color. After that, we performed at DiGiorgio's ranch in Arvin. The performance wasn't actually inside the property; it was right on the property line. There is a small fence about knee-high, and so we pulled the truck right up to it. We had the union banners and flags, the Teatro red and black screen and our own *El Teatro Campesino* banner and a mike. We started about 7:30 p.m. It was still light enough so that people could see, and there's this open space between the fence and the camp. There are some trees, and the workers were all underneath the trees, or around the cabins. We were on the truckbed calling them over, but they wouldn't come, so we started singing and then began our first *acto* – Felipe came out. We started to get some stragglers, and as it got darker more and more people came out. By the time we were into the show, all of the people in the camp were out there – a couple of hundred people. They cheered, they laughed, they applauded. It was probably the most successful performance we've had with farm workers since the march, the great difference being that this time there wasn't the whole impact of the march. There was just the Teatro out there by itself.

We've discovered a number of things about farm workers and what they respond to; it verges on slapstick – but it's slapstick with a purpose, it depends who is slapping who. If a DiGiorgio character is beating a farm worker over the head, it may be funny, but it's serious laughter. If the farm worker starts slapping the DiGiorgio character, then it becomes riotous.

I think humor is our major asset and weapon, not only from a satirical point of view, but from the fact that humor can stand up on its own and is a much more healthy child of the theatre than, let's say, tragedy or realism. You can't do that on the flatbed of a truck. If you want to get realistic about the problems, you have to do it in indirect fashion, through dramatic images. But if you think that DiGiorgio is living and standing on the backs of his farm workers, you can show it with humor. You get "DiGiorgio" to stand on the backs of two farm workers, and there it is and nobody will refute you.

We use comedy because it stems from a necessary situation – the necessity of lifting the morale of our strikers, who have been on strike for seventeen months. When they go to a meeting it's long and drawn out; so we do comedy, with the intention of making them laugh – but with a purpose. We try to make social points, not in spite of the comedy, but through it. This leads us into satire and slapstick, and sometimes very close to the underlying tragedy of it all – the fact that human beings have been wasted in farm labor for generations … .

I've noticed one thing about audiences. When they see something they recognize as a reality, they laugh. Here in the Teatro we sometimes work up imitations – of person-alities, animals, of incidents. Impersonations are funny, why? Just because the imper-sonation itself comes so close to the reality. People say, "Yes, that's the way it is," and they laugh. If it's a reality they recognize as their own, they'll laugh and perhaps tears will come to their eyes.

When I speak about comic and dramatic images. I'm speaking about visions of reality. Our comic images are directed at the farm worker; they're supposed to repre-sent the reality that he sees. It's not a naturalistic representation; most of the time it's a symbolic, emblematic presentation of what the farm worker feels. But we can't be stuffy about it, so we use slapstick. Very often the slapstick is the image.

There's a dramatic theory – we used to talk about it in the Mime Troupe. I think we've put a different use to it in the Teatro just out of necessity, but it is that your dramatic situation, the thing you're trying to portray on the stage, must be very close to the reality that is *on* the stage. You take the figure of DiGiorgio standing on the backs of two farm workers. The response of the audience is to the very real situation of one human being standing on two others. That type of fakery is not imitation. It's a theatrical reality that will hold up on the flatbed of a truck. You don't need fancy lights or a curtain. This is what we're working toward – this type of reality.

Farm workers laugh at Summer in *The Fifth Season*. We've used various actors as Summer, and they're not physically funny when they come on; but they're wearing this old shirt with money all over it, and I think with that image we've hit something. This is the way farm workers look at summer. As a kid, I can remember my family going north toward the prune and apricot orchards. My image was of leaves and fruit clustered on the trees, and all of this turning into flows of dollar bills. When you see a ripe orchard or vineyard, the limbs boughing down they're so heavy with fruit, this is money. All you have to do is get up and stretch out your hand. That's money; it's a quarter for every bucket, a penny for every apple or pear. It's a vision of paradise; you're going there – the promised land – you're getting there finally.

Then reality creeps in again, and you end up with less money than you started with. But the dream is always there, the dream that you're going to get rich quick. It isn't just reaching up and holding your hand under the fruit which falls into your palm. More often, it's working like a dog with the snot running down your nose; and you're black with dirt and sweat, and with the blood straining your veins. You're lost in your work; you forget what the hell you're doing. And the contractor's truck is a dirty ugly truck; once in a while it strikes you. But what takes you away from that hard, ugly reality is the dream that you're going to get rich.

Anyway, that is the background behind the image of Summer coming in with his shirt covered with money. I think that is why farm workers laugh. Not because it's funny, but because they recognize that reality. They've been caught.

We don't think in terms of art, but of our political purpose in putting across certain points. We think of our spiritual purpose in terms of turning on crowds. We know when we're not turning on the crowd. From a show business point of view that's bad enough, but when you're trying to excite crowds to go out on strike or to support you, it gains an added significance.

31

DARIO FO EXPLAINS
An interview

Luigi Ballerini and Giuseppe Risso

Translated by Lauren Hallquist and Fiorenza Weinpple

At the Rai Studios in Milan, Dario Fo is just finishing the editing of a series of shows to be aired in the spring of 1978. We are at a delicate moment in the comedy *La signora e da buttare (The Lady Has To Be Thrown Away),* a satire of bourgeois imperialism. At this moment, parts of the dialog are being "reinforced." Dario's finger is pointed at the technician: "Here!" At his command, applause and laughter mingle artfully with the murmur of the audience.

The monitors reflect several sequences of Dario Fo's mocking face. He is a man of fifty – actor, singer, dancer, mime, writer, impresario, choreographer, political activist, and a personality both feared and opposed, like one of the characters in the farces he realizes onstage: opposed by government, politicians, the church, and the petty bourgeois. He is the only actor in Italy who can boast of performances attended by 25,000 spectators; the only one whose visibility, in the history of post-war Italian theatre, can be compared with that of Eduardo DeFilippo and Strehler.

On the monitors, we watch a few scenes from the comedy that takes place under the tent of a nineteenth-century circus.

> *We hear a violent knocking at the window of the caravan … . The window opens and a vulture appears, evidently stuffed, its wings flapping. The clown Bob enters the scene.*

> *Bob:* Here it is again – the vulture (*pointing to the bird that opens its wings in the classic pose of the American Eagle*).

> *Other clowns enter noisily to watch the scene.*

> *Clown Dario:* (*moving toward the caravan*) Away! Away! Filthy animal! Damn beast! Your food isn't ready yet … . The old lady isn't dead yet … And even if she was dead a week and well tenderized – we wouldn't even give you a bite … . Everything to the hyena: Get it?

> *Voice of the old lady from behind the tent.*

> *Old Lady:* So who is it that's well tenderized?

The telephone, hanging from the caravan, rings. The nurse speaks into a hose which also serves as the source of oxygen for the old lady. Dario answers the phone.

Nurse: Hello. Who's the idiot making all this fucking noise?

Dario: The idiot is me. The noise is over.

Nurse: You managed to wake the old lady up.

Dario: It wasn't me, it was the vulture; (*to the vulture*) you filthy creep. But now, I'm gonna make you pay for it, over and out. (*He hangs up the phone and moves rapidly toward the caravan. He goes in. The vulture re-enters from the window through which we can catch a glimpse of a violent fight between Dario and the vulture.*) Come here, sweetie. I've got to talk to you … . Ah! You turn on me!? Ouch! What a beak you've got! I'll pluck all your feathers out! Get this … all the feathers from your ass … and may you catch a nice cold on the above mentioned … and drop dead!

Squealing and croaking from the vulture. Dario comes out of the caravan cooling himself with a feather-fan.

Old Lady: (*barely audible*) Who's crying? Who makes my animals weep?

Nurse: It's nothing, Madam! Don't get excited. Go to sleep. Sleep. La la la la la la …

Lullaby.

Clowns: (*in chorus*) La la la … (*Gathered at center stage, the clowns sway.*)

Preceded by a loud honking, a three-seater scooter with three passengers rushes onstage from the right. It runs over some of the clowns who fall pirouetting. The scooter, proceeding carelessly, exits.

Dario: Murderers, schmucks, bastards!

The old lady peeps out from the canopy of her bed holding a huge rifle, typical of the pioneers.

Old Lady: Injuns! Injuns! Quick – round up the wagons!

Nurse: No, no. It's not the Indians.

Old Lady: No. Well then, I guess I'll sleep. (*She disappears behind the canopy.*)

One reel is finished. Dario Fo comes to meet us

TDR: Your name is known throughout the world as an actor and an author of political satires. ["Now my plays are being performed in an incredible number of German, Swedish, Norwegian, Danish, Belgian and French theatres. My latest plays are being staged above all in West Germany, while those written thirty years ago are being given especially in East Germany, Poland, Bulgaria and the Soviet Union."
It is curious to note that his more extreme political productions have found a forum in many so-called western democracies, while in the countries of Eastern Europe more emphasis is given to his early generically social satires, and perhaps solely to them.] In the U.S. are known, above all, the works that you have written in the last five or ten years. Would you briefly describe the development of your career, so as to give a more complete picture of your work, starting with your first experiences in cabaret?

Fo: That's inexact … I've never done cabaret, but rather a form of theatre tied to popular traditions; if anything, in the framework of *avanspettacolo* [a kind of variety theatre performed between two movie showings. It was very much in vogue in Italy

Fig. 31.1 Dario Fo. (Photo by Corrado Maria Falsini.)

between 1930–40]. All our comics, from Petrolini himself, to Ferravilla and Scarpetta have all contributed to this type of theatre.

When, for example, we did *Il dito nell'occhio* (*The Finger in the Eye*) with the Piccolo Teatro (twenty years ago), the ambience was not that of a cabaret: the space itself, 700 seats, the stage being twelve to thirteen yards wide, the complete set, the number of people acting (there were twelve of us), and finally, the concept of the piece, which yes, was a string of sketches, but had a logical continuity of its own. *Il dito nell'occhio* was based upon a story whose origins go back to the goliard tradition, but mixed with elements from *commedia dell'arte* and modified by my experience with the theatre of Strehler, who, at that time, was truly revolutionary. It had little to do with the French or German tradition in cabaret. That is, it was something better than cabaret, which forces one to adopt a certain unnatural format: a café performance requires a very private and intimate form of speaking. With us, instead, everything was flung out: the action, the amount of physical expression inherent in our way of acting – a pantomime learned not from the tradition of the white mime (Pierrot) but from *commedia dell'arte*. In short, we had with us Lecoq who had worked with Moretti [the famous Arlecchino in *Arlecchino servitore di due padroni*, staged by Strehler in 1947; Lecoq was a pupil of Moretti] whose experience went back to Paduan theatre; De Bosio, [theatre and movie director best known for his staging of Ruzanti], the works of Ruzante, zannis, Harlequins and so forth. We were working along these lines. Moreover, there was a popular element that consisted of the story-teller's visual narration, and this element we used rather explicitly and directly.

The source of my work before *Il dito nell'occhio* is in fact that of the storyteller. I started twenty-five years ago. Then, also, I recaptured the jester's tradition. The story-teller and the jester are two fixed points, the former going back to the seventeenth and eighteenth centuries, while the latter, the jester, is medieval. But the key is the same; they have the same dimension. I had learned it from the storytellers of the north shore of Lake Maggiore, where I was born and where I lived. It is a tradition that has disap-peared, like the balladeers are disappearing in Sicily and the mountebanks or the "poets," as they say in Tuscany (both storytellers and jesters). I learned this lesson early in life from the storytellers who told their stories not in the squares but in taverns or along the lake while people were fishing. There were those who told their stories to children, to the common folk who gathered around them, and one might say they were paid in kind.

Another influence, has been the puppet theatre – hand puppets, not marionettes. Finally, I was acquainted with a popular form of epic theatre staged by traveling players, who performed plots based on fifteenth-century stories such as *Romeo and Juliet* (not the Shakespearean version but the Lombard one), *Othello*, and melodramas with enticing titles such as *Sin Avenges Sin*. The players would stay for a month or so and then move on to another village.

At that time, right after the war, I got involved in the birth of the Piccolo Teatro, which meant an enormous change in the general conception of theatre and of the role of the actor. In my town, I was considered as one who had mastered the teachings of the storytellers. Little by little, I had collected many traditional tales, and others I had invented myself. They all either had Biblical motifs or were based on the cliches of a melodramatic tradition or inspired by sensationalist news items of the day, which I obviously rendered in a satirical way … .

My decision, then, to do theatre was not traumatic; instead, it was a natural devel-opment. I was a student of architecture and I really started for fun: first in my home town, Luino, then in Varese; eventually I also did something in Milan. It was then that I met Franco Parenti (among the first actors of the Piccolo Teatro), with whom I put together shows that were fragmentary and a little amateurish. Finally, still with Parenti and the Nava sisters [Pinuccia, Diana and Lisetta Nava, famous Italian soubrettes of the 1950s], I did a variety show in which my role was really that of a storyteller. It was a show with chorus girls, skits, and it was there that I learned to dance, sing, etc.

TDR: Who wrote the texts?

Fo: In the beginning I wrote my own texts, then in collaboration with Durano [author and actor, active in variety theatre and radio programs. His early success has considerably slackened since the days of his collaboration with Fo and Parenti], with whom I worked for about a year after the experience with the Nava. Soon after, Parenti, Durano, Lecoq and I staged *Il ditto nell'occhio*, which caused a huge stir. The scene was more or less fixed as in the Elizabethan theatre. There were no costumes. There were simply props, a platform, etc., and we wore nothing but black leotards. It ran for a whole summer at the Piccolo Teatro in Milan – a real shock, especially because of the amount of pantomime and the great precision of the improvisations. The performance was always changing, adjusting, modifying itself according to the reactions of the public.

TDR: How were these texts realized – at your desk or through experimentation onstage?

Fo: At the beginning, the text was constructed directly on the stage. Actually, every time I tried to stage a text that I had written, read, and reread, we always arrived at a crisis point during rehearsals, so that we had to elaborate and rewrite. Then we would try it out on an audience, and I would continue to rework it. This holds true for the duration of my experience within a conventional theatrical framework.

   Later, things became even more complicated. Many texts result from downright investigations. Once the investigation is completed, we read the text to our public or, better yet, to those people who directly support our work: laborers, students, workers on strike, members of cultural and political organizations. Texts are discussed; then rewritten; then rehearsed first without, then with, our public; staged a third time only to be questioned all over again. Certain plays, like *Pum Pum qui e la polizia* (*Bam Bam! It's the Police*), *Pinelli* or *Si paga non si paga* (*To Pay or Not To Pay*) have been completely rewritten three or four times. There are three different versions of *Pum Pum qui e la polizia* … the texts are torn apart, composed and recomposed all the time. For example, the original *Grande Pantomima per pupazzi piccoli e medi* (*Great Pantomime for Small and Medium-Sized Puppets*) was transformed, after two years, into something completely different. Even the title was changed.

TDR: The public, then, plays an essential role in your productions …

Fo: Generally speaking, theatre today is still an intellectual product consumed by the public. There is, however, a *public* that attends only that type of performance capable of involving it because it is directly related to political actions. Let's take an example: some of our performances were born and died in the course of two or three days. Let's say that we would give a performance in support of someone being tried in court, as in the case of the Marini trial (young activist of the leftist movement). There, we did an outdoor performance with the townspeople, recounting, in a grotesque and satirical way, the trial itself and, along with it, certain events that had taken place a century earlier in that very same place. We told them about the rebellion of "bandits," who were no other than the peasants from the hinterland of Salerno. We wanted to show that the symptoms of rebellion, oppression, and repression were constant features analogous to those that marked the trial that was now taking place. This performance we gave only twice.

   It happened, also, in Pescara … . There was a trial against fifty rebellion prisoners … and we staged a counter-trial. I could give you countless examples. There is a kind of theatre that we call "Immediate Intervention" and, indeed, in this case, we must act rapidly. Three days after the bombing incidents in Brescia [one of the many Fascist acts of terrorism that have plagued Italian life in the last decade. The bombs exploded during a political rally. Many people died and many more were wounded], we performed in the same square where these events had taken place with 5,000 to 10,000 people overflowing into the adjacent square because it was larger.

TDR: Are these texts of Immediate Intervention based on documentation of facts?

Fo: We begin with an inquiry. For instance, we went to Brescia and we asked for people's versions of the events ... the performance included excerpts from previous work, though they were adapted through improvisation to a new format. The performance for Chile was one that changed from place to place, because of the various ways in which the audience participated. I don't know if you know this, but since many of our performances had been raided by the police, we decided to plant our own policemen led by a commissar – all imposters – who would interrupt the show. Some of our people would be carried off to the police station to be arrested ... we provoked our audiences and there was always a great tension ... people's anger was on the verge of exploding every minute. Some went so far as to pull out knives and assault the commissar.

TDR: At the beginning of your theatrical work what political party did you identify with?

Fo: With the Communist party. We were immediately spotted. We had to contend with Scelba's police [a Christian Democrat Minister of the Interior. His name is linked with one of the darkest moments in the history of the Italian police force], censorship, innumerable difficulties. Our performances were boycotted all the time. It was a real persecution.

TDR: Did the Communist newspaper follow your activities? Did it back you up or keep you under surveillance?

Fo: It backed us up, but the timing was always late. The first ones to act were the students, then the leftist intellectuals, then the laborers; finally, the Communist party ... but then again, they never did very much for us ... the PCI always felt a reverence for the official culture. Our work was accepted, above all, by the rank and file, but there were also some intellectuals who were supportive. Togliatti [the famous secretary of the Communist party, which he had founded with Antonio Gramsci in 1921] for example, liked many of our works. I remember seeing him in the audience once. He was still bandaged after an assassination attempt on his life. Actually, a year had already passed ... and he had a bodyguard. He came to see us at the Piccolo Teatro at the end of the season – toward September ... he was enthusiastic.

There were always debates over the type of theatrical philosophy that we espoused. Many intellectuals, however, didn't make any effort to understand. One who did understand immediately and even wrote an important article on us was Vito Pandolfi. But it's well known that the party never considered Pandolfi orthodox ... in short, a large part of the masses supported us and also the more intellectually sophisticated segment of the bourgeoisie. At the same time certain critics like D'Amico [founder of the Italian Academy of Dramatic Art] could not stomach a theatre with a clearly defined political basis and one so obviously opposed to the elitist type of theatre that they loved and promoted. Then there was the problem of verbal texts versus mime and the art of physical gesture ... not that we went overboard with gesture, but it certainly was the first time that gesture was treated on an equal basis with words. All this, while the prevailing mentality still extolled the written, not the spoken, word.

A new interruption. The scenes on the investigations of President Kennedy's assassination from the comedy *La signora e da buttare* are on the monitors.

Clown Bob: We've got proof!

Clown Arturo: What proof? Tell me what I shot her with.

C. Bob: With this. (*He puts a gun in Arturo's hand.*) You can all testify that we caught him with the weapon in his hand.

C. Arturo: What are you talking about? It's a water gun! (*To demonstrate, he turns to the clown closest to him and squirts some water in his face.*)

C. Dario: (*in the fashion of a town crier*) Exactly. In fact, the old lady drowned.

Clowns: (*in chorus*) That's right.

C. Valerio: Let's not exaggerate. How could she have drowned?

C. Dario: You're right. We've exaggerated just a bit. Actually, how did she die?

C. Valerio: The truth is – the murderer used a technically advanced weapon of the greatest precision: an Italian model '91 with a sight. Here it is. (*He shows them the gun.*)

C. Dario: Where is the sight?

C. Valerio: Here. (*He slides a pair of spectacles along the barrel of the gun.*)

Clowns: (in chorus) Amazing!

C. Valerio: With one bullet …

C. Bob: Just one.

C. Valerio: … he managed to hit the old lady three times plus the chauffeur and a stray dog, not to mention the back-right tire of an ice-cream cart?

All the Clowns: Unbelievable! How did he do it?

C. Valerio: Quiet. Listen to the ballistics expert. How *did* he do it? (*A blackboard is brought onstage. It is covered with lines and diagrams. Dario will use it to give a scientific demonstration of the ballistic puzzle. The clowns follow him as he moves along the complicated trajectory of the bullet, which he physically describes from one end of the stage to the other.*)

C. Dario: It's extremely simple. As we can clearly see on the blackboard, the old lady's murderer was here at point A, that is to say, on platform #1; there he is. An amateur would have aimed directly at point B, where the old lady was. But we are dealing with a specialist. He aims exactly in the opposite direction, at platform #4. The bullet hits the post; bounces back and goes to hit, for the first time, the old lady at point B. It goes through her and strikes the bell of the telephone we see here at a point which we will call Alpha. A new rebound; the bullet lands here with an angle of 116 degrees in the direction of the lamppost, on top of which a stray dog is perched. God knows what it's doing there at the top instead of being at the bottom where he should be, according to the rules. The investigation will clarify this.

C. Bob: Naturally.

C. Dario: The bullet rebounds – not the stray dog, that remains in his place. As we were saying, the bullet rebounds and travels in the direction of the shooter, who, with a baseball bat in hand, sends it once again (*with extreme precision*) back to the old lady. It hits the old lady a second time, goes through her again, and again hits the telephone bell. The impact on the bell, this time, as we can clearly deduce from the markings at point Beta, causes no longer, as before, a rebounding linear trajectory, but a curvilinear one which, moving in the opposite direction, describes a type of parabola known in technical language as Archimede's Protoparabola. A new impact on the ground, a new rebound toward the lamppost on which, in the meantime, has climbed the rescuer of the stray dog: the old lady's chauffeur. The chauffeur, with the bullet in his mouth, bounces toward the shooter who, with a baseball bat, hits him on the back of the head forcing him to spit out the bullet, which then moves along the above-mentioned trajectory and goes through the old lady a third time. The bullet would have run its course ad infinitum had it not been for the fact that the tire of the ice-cream push cart found itself in its path. It was this tire, then, that literally brought to an end the mad race of the bullet. Stop. We'll return after a brief message.

TDR: Let's go back for a second to what you were saying about a theatre with a clearly identifiable political base – that is, if I'm not mistaken, to a theatre understood as a place where not only the conflict between destiny and its modifications is defined, but also where one proposes a physical model of willpower capable of excluding, over-coming, or redeeming the censorship implied by any established truth … .

Fo: This is the basis of all theatre, the fundamental key to everything … . They've always told us that classical theatre is above everything and everyone, that it has nothing to do with class struggle. No, classical theatre is fundamentally a class theatre, planned, written, and developed by one social class to defeat another. You can talk as much as you want about Shakespeare, about the moon and the purity of poetry, etc. Shake-speare's themes reflected class problems. At one moment he sides with power and at another he doesn't, according to the political events of his time. You cannot take Shake-speare out of context with what happened to other poets and writers such as Marlowe, Ford, etc., who were subjected to indirect or even direct repression or death. Men such as these were burned at the stake or met with horrible ends one way or another.

Or else, to point out interpretations that normally are not even mentioned, let's take the theme of *Alcestis*. Let us ask ourselves what is the meaning of a woman's role in a society where she can only sacrifice herself for someone? For her husband, for the male who stands for an entire history, for humanity itself. She can reach the maximum of her glory only by renouncing her own life, thus enabling the male to continue with his.

It isn't an accident that these themes were dealt with. Think of the reactionary dimension of those writers who exploited and reversed popular tradition: Aristophanes, for example. It's more than evident in the way in which they antagonized women. There were feminist movements in those days compared to which today's movement is almost laughable: feminist Communism, women fighting for their own rights. How else would one want to read the official comedies of the satirists, if not as a testimony of the attempt to destroy these extraordinary thrusts coming from the popular movement?

TDR: Don't you think, however, these thrusts should be nourished, not only by *antag-onistic* investigation, but in a truly "tragic" way by a sense of ulteriority and by a courage capable of reconnecting the proponents of those thrusts to the *agonistic* areas of life, that is, those areas where existing and being reflect on one another: the world of enigma, for example – the course of a truth understood as a "wonder" or "awesome-ness" and not as "revelation" or "accommodation" to a deduction?

Fo: I would put it in simpler terms. As far as my, our, experience goes, I would have to say that when I started to have a sense of theatre and my role in it, I realized that there were two fundamental aspects of it that I then found aptly formulated by Brecht, Meyerhold, the theorists of epic drama. What were they? They were what in correct terminology I could today call the "literary" concept of theatre on the one hand and, on the other, the concept of the "situation," which is fundamental.

What do I mean by literary concept? The text first and above all. This notion belongs to a precise social class, that which controls the power.

Opposed to it, there is another theatric lexicon composed of text, pause, rhythm: a lexicon in which, many times, the word is dependent upon an action or a situation. "Situation" means thrusting ahead the conflicts that exist between people; it is *this* conflict that occupies the stage. It even precedes the literary text.

In order to liberate the actor from this pseudo-responsibility of having to represent another, Molière, in the tradition of *commedia dell'arte*, resorted to the construction of a proscenium, an *avant-scène*, forcing the actor to step out of the frame. In this way, he practically destroys the scene, that is to say, the atmosphere, the physical box within which the actor was belittled by the very things that were to support him: voices, sounds, and above all, the physical dimensions of the stage. Without a supportive dimension, Molière said, the actor must himself be the scene, the sound, etc., and Meyerhold added that when an actor needs the tweet-tweet of the birds to create an atmosphere of dawn, this means that he does not have enough power to create it through his gestures, voice, rhythms, tempo. He is dawn, not the spotlights dimming or brightening, producing cold rather than warm light, and so forth. Molière eliminated all scenic effects. This means that the actor must be the exclusive renderer of whatever happens, that he does not have to wear a robe to become a character, but to become a mask.

So, what is this mask? The mask is the dialectical synthesis of conflicts, whereas a character carries with him conflicts without ever achieving their synthesis. He thus tries to be himself, that is, to identify completely with his role and to recount his own *trippe*, as Molière said, the disturbances of his own self. So the actor is an individual entity, while the mask is collective, because it tells of a general concern. In still other words, it is the voice of the story, not the means of acting it out. It is not I who identifies with what I present onstage. Rather, I can criticize, suggest conflicts, contradictions, hypocrisies, and comment under any circumstance. This is the epic fact, the estrangement. The estrangement gives the actor the same possibilities that the puppets give the puppeteer. This is theatre's fundamental ideological condition. And this is drama.

In a basically literary theatre … Chekhov, a fundamental pivot … also, our more recent authors (Pirandello, for instance) did nothing but perpetuate the notion of actor as self-actualizer. Identification. And so, what happens? The spectator is reduced to a voyeur: someone who is there to steal a naturalistic event that is proposed time and again as if it were real life. Even the time sequence is that of a real action … more or less. Agreed, it is shortened, synthesized – but it is presented as if it were real.

The other kind of theatre, instead, destroys completely the notion of historical time because events are not modelled on it; there is only the time of the narration – the synthesis of the telling. The very fact that Chekhov and Pirandello eliminate the prolog is no mere accident. The prolog, in fact, reveals everything, takes away the possibility of unforeseeable events, the suspense.

TDR: Indeed, in classical tragedy, the whole fact is known ahead of time.

Fo: Of course. It is all told in advance. Also, in the theatre of the late eighteenth century, everything is unfolded prior to the action. What counts is the manner of the unfolding, the special machinery reinvented each time on a known theme. How it ends is not important at all; it is a literary degeneration that allows that to capitalize on irrational emotivity and on a sequence of tricks.

TDR: It is a form of cultural terrorism: I know how it ends, you don't. Therefore ... . There is, however, something else that I would like you to clarify. We have this pseudo-theatre, then a theatre that describes approximately, your area of activity: counter-information set off by fact. How do you evaluate that third type of theatre that we would call "formalistic" theatre; one dedicated to the search for a new theatric language and also, really, a new word language in theatre. Artaud comes immediately to mine.

Fo: The new language ... you see, I read Artaud in a different way .... He is important to me because he gave me the courage to reutilize the *grammelot* – the newest language and the oldest of them all, buried in literature because it cannot be rewritten. It must be reinvented every time because it depends so much on the relationship created with the audience. The pace is determined by their laughter, their stillness, the magical mood. I do mean magic, especially when speaking about Artaud, which is not coercion, but the play of the imagination, of the imaginary reconstruction of the world. I think we have worked in the direction of a new language. Take, for example, certain Italian singers' mode of performing: before they begin to sing they know that the song is a pretext to speak, to tell, to invent, etc. These singers are in the *grammelot* tradition, in the storyteller's tradition. Once it was possible to say, "And now a song from Maestro Angelini [conductor. Some of his tunes were extremely popular during the 1940s and 1950s] and his orchestra ... "; today, that's no longer done. Instead, singers talk, chat, narrate; in short, they have rediscovered the prolog. Many times, the songs themselves don't matter much ... as I said, they are a pretext ... .

TDR: Let's go back to your experience with the Piccolo Teatro.

Fo: Yes, there we were able to create a rapport between literary and grassroots theatre ... . My experience with Il Piccolo was very important ... above all because of the mimes I worked with: Covelli and those two very good actresses Galvani and Ridoni, Franca, Tarranti who later married Parenti, and others. [Dario Fo mentions the names of actors who did not become very well known, with the exception, that is, of Franca (Rame), his wife. She is the daughter of a traveling player and is extremely gifted in satirical roles and caricatures. She is also politically involved and heads "Soccorso rosso" (Red Aid), a leftist organization created to assist imprisoned political activists by providing lawyers, etc.]

I remember Strehler used to come and lend us a hand with the lights. He always came to our rehearsals – he would hide among the seats not to disturb us. It was a meaningful working relationship.

TDR: Were you guests of the Piccolo Teatro, or were you part of it?

Fo: Well, half and half. We were guests, but we also belonged there. We were not there as a group who had rented the theatre. Our technicians were the same as those of the Piccolo, the scenes were designed at the Piccolo Teatro school for stage designers, even the costumes were provided by the Piccolo.

Then came the parting of the ways between Parenti and myself. It occurred mainly for ideological reasons. He wanted to stage a socially inclined type of theatre, but not one as directly involved with politics that I had in mind. In fact, eventually he ended up doing Ionesco. I could not possibly bring myself to agree with his choices. So after the two years of our collaboration, I moved to Rome.

Actually the split was also a consequence of the great repression to which we were subjected. Guess who was "Ministro dello Spettacolo" at the time? Andreotti [a Christian Democrat, Italy's present prime minister], and then Scelba as Minister of the Interior, and then the E.T.I. [Ente Teatrale Italiano], a residue of the Fascist regime, which it is, to some extent, even today. Repression took on the usual forms: we were boycotted, forced to move here and there, etc. Times were really bad.

In Rome I worked as a scriptwriter together with Pietrangeli, Zarattini, Age and Scarpelli, and Pinelli, Fellini's scriptwriter. That was also a great experience. I worked also with Lizzani both as scriptwriter and codirector of *Lo svitato* (*The Screwy One*), then with Pietrangeli on other films.

TDR: So you were still associated with a Communist milieu?

Fo: Yes, Pietrangeli had worked with Visconti and Rossellini from the very beginning. After a while, however, Franca and I decided to give up everything and go back to grassroots theatre.

We started again with eight farces. We worked again at the Piccolo for a whole summer when we staged *Ladri, manichini e donne nude* (*Thieves, Store-Dummies and Naked Women*). We even realized some of Franca's scripts. One was called *La comica finale* [scripts from the collection of Franca Rame's father]. Some of these farces are being performed now in Milan … . But they have also been staged all over Europe. Many groups in Sweden, Norway, Denmark and Eastern Europe would choose one of our one-act plays and perform it together with works by Adamov, Beckett, Genet: the big names. This diffusion began right away, practically the year after we had done the pieces. They have also been performed in off-off theatres in the States and in Canada.

Two years later we did *Gli arcangeli non giocano al flipper* (*Archangels Do Not Play Pinball*). It was quite a success, but censorship was still around, and, above all, Scelba was still around. He became even tougher the following year. Our satire of bureaucracy, the common man, power, ministries, and the State hit him where it hurt.

Another play *Aveva due pistole con gli occhi bianchi e neri* (*He Had Two White-and-Black Eyed Guns*) satirized latent Fascism. It was the story of a bandit whose two-sided character was portrayed through the use of doubles, in the tradition of Greek and Roman theatre. Censorship had become just about intolerable, and we almost ended in jail for having refused to submit the text for approval by the authorities, knowing that permission could be obtained only after they mutilated the work beyond recognition.

Subsequently we did *Chi ruba un piede e fortunate in amore* (*He Who Steals a Foot is Lucky in Love*), an allegorical play which, again, hit hard upon bourgeois morality, the art of cheating, etc. It was the year of Tambroni [a Christian Democrat. His short-lived government fell as the result of what was on the verge of becoming a popular insurrection. Right after this experience, the first Center-Left government was formed: it included a number of Socialist ministers and brought about substantial democratic reforms].

TDR: This all ended with the first. Center-Left government … .

Fo: Right, Tambroni fell from power, and we were asked to do *Canzonissima*. [A very popular TV show, Dario Fo's and Franca Rame's participation in it was suddenly revoked before the expiration of their contract. Their performances were considered politically unacceptable. They have only recently returned to work for the state-controlled channels of the Italian TV network.] You know what happened. The trial that lasted for fourteen years ended. The Rai-TV sued us for something like $350,000. I think we ended up paying about $8,000.

After *Canzonissima* we were completely ostracized from the studios. We went back to the theatre with *Christoforo Colombo* and *Isabella, tre caravelle e un cacciaballe* (*Christopher Colombus* and *Isabel, Three Caravels and a Bullshitter*) which dealt with intellectual opportunism. *Settimo: rubba un po' meno* (*Seventh:*

Steal a Little Less), which we did afterwards, was also quite a violent critique. Censorship was finally beginning to slacken.

TDR: It was more or less at this time, however, that you decided to break away completely from official theatrical circuits …

Fo: We broke away from bourgeois theatre. And started again at the *case del popolo* [literally: "houses of the people," Communist social and cultural centers]. There were about forty of us. We ourselves built the stage, the sound and lighting equipment, etc. We staged *L'operaio conosce trecento parole, il padrone mille. Per questo è lui il padrone (The Laborer Knows Three Hundred Words, the Boss One Thousand, That's Why He's the Boss)* and also two one-act plays: *Il funerale del padrone (The Funeral of the Boss)* and *Legami pure che tanto spacco tutto lo stesso (Go Ahead, Tie Me Up, I'm Going To Break Everything Anyway)*. The first was a story based on an investigation of child labor and other illegal forms of employment. The other dealt with the birth of political awareness among workers who had taken over a factory that the owner had closed down.

But even the *case del popolo* were not ideal places for us. The P.C.I. did not find our performances agreeable. Pajetta and Berlinguer intervened. [Pajetta was one of the most outspoken members of the Communist party; Berlinguer is present secretary of the P.C.I. and principal promoter of today's Eurocommunism.] For a while we banged our heads against the party organization, then we realized that there was nothing else to do but to withdraw.

We started all over again, in movie houses, dance halls, places where no one had ever seen a play before. For the most part we performed in small towns. In Torino we stayed only four days and each day staged a new show. Bourgeois newspapers would not review us, although, I must say, there were two notable exceptions: Monticelli and Blandi [theatre critics of *Il Corriere della sera* and *La stampa*, two of the largest Italian daily papers]. The P.C.I. either avoided talking about us or gave us devastating reviews. Then we rented a space, *Il capannone di via Colletta* [a warehouse-type of space situated in Colletta (Milan)] where we resumed *Mistero buffo (Mystery-Bouffe* after Mayakovsky), under the auspices of A.R.C.I. [a cultural association affiliated with the P.C.I.], and put together a work called *Vorrei morire anche adesso se sapessi che non è servito a niente (I Would Want to Die Now if I Knew that It Didn't Mean Anything)*. It was a series of stories from the Resistance narrated by partisans themselves – victorious moments in the history of class struggle and the conflicts those moments created in the very men who lived them. Then we did *Morte accidentale di un anarchico (Accidental Death of an Anarchist)* which had an enormous success.

By then there were two groups of players: one headed by Franceschi with fifteen people and our group of twenty. But we grew even larger and had to form three companies (fifty people). We were more numerous than the company of any major Italian theatre and operated on a budget of a few thousand dollars. We all received the same amount of money: about twelve dollars a day.

We began to tour and could count everywhere on enormous audiences: at the Palazzo dello sport in Milan, for instance, not to speak of outdoor performances. And all the time we were defending ourselves from aggressions and what not. We were registered as a private association and were not obliged to deposit our scripts with anyone. The police could not enter our premises; we managed to block them every time they tried. At Reggio Emilia, however, they arrested many comrades, and since I was officially liable for all three companies, I ended up with forty indictments. So far I have won all the trials that have taken place.

During this period, Franca and I worked in *Tutti uniti tutti insieme, ma scusa, quello non è il padrone?* (*All Together, All United, But Excuse Me, Isn't This Guy The Boss?*). Then we did *Feddajn*, in which Franca played with real Feddajns who spoke only in Arabic. And we took up again *Pum pum qui è la polizia. Mistero buffo* had by then split into three different shows.

Unfortunately, at this point our cell divided into a majority and a minority group which could not agree on such strategic issues as political alliances with this or that organization or segment of the Movement. The gap soon turned into a feud. The majority group, with which I had not sided, seized everything, including records and books (we sell a lot of texts on class struggle, government crime and so forth). They really took everything. We were back to zero once again. To top it all off, I was arrested. Franca was assaulted in a movie house in Quarto Oggiaro, a suburb of Milan. [Franca Rame was sequestered by a band of fascists who attempted to rape her and kill her. Fortuitous circumstances alone prevented a tragic ending.]

To pull us out of this situation, there arrived an invitation to perform at the French Théâtre National. We went and were received enthusiastically. Upon our return, we expropriated the Palazzina Liberty, where we have been performing ever since. Others have followed our example: some young people in need of performing space took over a deconsecrated church, etc. Even without counting the Molotov cocktails thrown at my house, the bomb at the Palazzina, the innumerable court trails that await me, I feel that during this last decade we have lived at least two hundred years.

32

THEATRE AS A WEAPON
An interview with Utpal Dutt

A. J. Gunawardana

TDR: What is revolutionary theatre?

Dutt: Revolutionary theatre is essentially people's theatre, which means that it must be played before the masses. The audience is our first concern; matters of form and content come second. A genuinely revolutionary play put on before an intellectual audience in the city is irrelevant because the intelligentsia simply won't change. Essentially, the revolution is first for workers and peasants. Revolutionary theatre must *preach* revolution; it must not only expose the system but also call for the violent smashing of the state machine.

TDR: Is revolutionary theatre always viable?

Dutt: You can't talk about the general principles of a revolutionary theatre. One must take into account the essential features of a particular epoch and country. In India today we are fighting for a people's democratic revolution, and revolutionary theatre preaches violent methods of overthrowing the present set-up. But after the revolution (which will inevitably come), the theatre must change its content and approach and relate itself to the new conditions.

TDR: How does your play *Vietnam* follow this concept of revolutionary theatre?

Dutt: Our "program" is to bring the stories of the gallant revolutionary struggles of another people to our own people so that they too will be inspired to fight. We also want to teach practical lessons about how a guerrilla unit must be organized and how such a unit fights, in this case in Vietnam. We thought this would be very useful. In 1966, when the play was first done, there were no guerrilla units in India.

TDR: You have been critical of your earlier play, *Angar* (*Coal*).

Dutt: It wasn't a revolutionary play; it was a play of exposure. We exposed cruelty and exploitation in the coal mines by showing that many coal miners are killed when the owners flood the mines to save coal which is on fire. But it did not call for the armed overthrow of the system. *Angar* can at best be called a progressive play, and I consider the term "progressive" damaging, derogatory, almost abusive. Progressives never talk revolution; they will only *sympathize* with the revolutionary from a distance. They will say: "Naturally guerrillas will arise; these boys will throw bombs, because they haven't got jobs and are frustrated. Jobs cannot be distributed or increased because of the nature of our semicolonial economy." But, apart from that, even if it were possible to give our youths jobs – in other words, to bribe them – it does not mean that they would abandon the revolutionary path.

TDR: By progressives you mean middle-class intellectuals?

Dutt: Exactly. For example, there is a Bengali play which portrays the "sufferings" of a group of young revolutionaries who accidentally blow up a passenger train when their real target was a troop train. The author is really trying to criticize our boys and point to the dangers of such extremism, adventurism, Trotskyism (they have all kinds of terms). Actually, the attempt is to dissuade our youth from taking to the road of revolutionary struggle. Our kind or revolutionary theatre cannot take place in isolation. It must be linked with a wider political struggle. The situation in India is very grave. The cultural front is unable to ally itself with political parties advocating and actually preparing for uprisings. At present, the cultural front goes on fighting – without the backing of the parties.

TDR: How effective can theatre be under such circumstances?

Dutt: In 1966, there was a terrible famine all over Bengal, Bihar, and Assam, and the Communist leaders were in jail. The cultural front, though deprived of party leadership, called for the revolutionary overthrow of the government, using the famine as the main theme of their songs and plays. By March 1967 there was a great uprising, throughout Bengal especially, forcing the government to release the Communist prisoners.

In 1967, the peasants of Naxalbari in northern Bengal suddenly burst into armed revolt and guerrilla warfare of the most advanced kind, panicking the ruling classes. Plays and songs came forth almost spontaneously. *Rakter Rang (The Color of Blood)* by Anal Gupta and my play *Teer (Arrow)* tried to recount the daring and heroism of the peasant-guerrilla and expose the brutalities of the soldiers and policemen sent in droves to the area. But there was a hue and cry among "Marxists" and "Communists" that the leaders of the Naxalbari uprising were adventurists and therefore all references to it were taboo. We disagreed. We held that the heroism of armed peasants was important material for revolutionary theatre.

Theatre should not merely agitate for higher wages or reduction of the land tax. A play may take off from any issue involving partial demands but must arrive finally at a call for armed overthrow of reactionary state power. It's not enough to have a rifle in one's hand – one must know how to fire it and must hate the enemy enough to fire it.

But even if this is left-adventurism, there is more heroism in it than in a thousand resolutions and speeches. A pistol held firmly in the hand and a finger on the trigger – such an image can rouse the people to take up arms. You cannot write a play about a legislator who "protests" and "appeals." Even if the time is not ripe for an insurrection, the revolutionary theatre must look forward to the time when, inevitably, it will be.

We want to create plays, songs, ballets, to recapture for the people the important episodes of their past when they took up arms against landlords and the British army. We try to tell them non-violence and passivity are recent interpolations, alien to their nation and history. Several plays by various groups have carried this idea to the workers and peasants in the hope that the strength of previous generations will reassure them that violence in a just war is their birthright.

We must avoid the errors of our predecessor, the Indian People's Theatre Association. In their plays, whenever the proletarian hero walked onstage, conflict and drama disappeared – an over-simplified, anemic, spiritless Symbol of Revolution gesticulated and spoke dull sermons. Whenever the oppressor came on – the landlord, the moneylender, the police officer – the play sprang back to life, because the playwright seemed to have shaken off his nervousness and created an interesting human being.

To portray the proletarian hero as a giant without weakness or conflict is to tell the audience that it's impossible to be a revolutionary. The worker or the peasant in the audience, watching, concludes: "I can never be like him, because I have many weaknesses." Our hero must be as complex as any other human being. He may have many wrong attitudes about life. He may be unhappy at home. He may be a bad lover, or a tyrannous father, or an ungrateful son. In one thing alone he must be simple, direct, and uncompromising: his class attitude.

To make these heroes come to life, we must constantly show them in relation to their class, and, as the hero fights his battles – with the enemy, and with himself, to make himself a better fighter and a better man – we insist that his fellow workers be shown, in a mass or individually, so that the people, and not any individual warrior, are held up as the real maker of history. An audience of workers and peasants, faced with a proletarian hero with many foibles but relying on his class for strength, understands him at once and realizes that, to be a revolutionary, one need not become perfect first.

We have tried to learn Lenin's lesson, which quotes Pisarev and demands that dreams of the future be dreamt, that present reality is not the entire reality, that man's dream of equality and justice which shall surely come to pass is also part of today's reality. Gorki's revolutionary romanticism and his theory of amplification help us to portray life not only as it is but as it should be. And since we realize that the revolution must necessarily be violent and must be led by the armed working class, we have often colored our plays with situations in which action is interrupted and armed workers on the stage address the audience directly and chart the course of revolution, tell the audience in concrete terms of partisan, guerrilla, and people's war, the steps which will lead to liberation.

TDR: In taking theatre to the people you have used traditional forms like the Jatra.

Dutt: I haven't changed the Jatra, but a start has been made. The Jatra actor is remarkable, truly a people's artist, taking theatre to the masses in remote areas. The content of the plays used to be bad; sometimes they led to anti-Moslem riots. But we felt the form had potential. The economic structure of the Jatra is peculiar. The proprietor who sits on the floor of a dingy little room in Calcutta has complete control over the company. The actors, except the "stars," are almost like prisoners while the troupe is travelling, sometimes several hundred miles a day. They play two or three times a day and each performance lasts three and a half hours. This continues all through the winter season.

To change the existing plays and go on to new, revolutionary plays, I needed to have these actors on my side. My first meeting with Jatra actors was a revelation. They may not have possessed "democratic consciousness," but they proved to me what Mao Tse-tung said about living close to the people. These actors truly live close to the people: on tour six months of the year, they stay with peasants. They were able to take up our message far more quickly than the city's petty-bourgeois actors. *Rifle* was my first Jatra play. I was afraid to say certain things in it because I thought that the government might ban the play or arrest the cast. I was wary of asking the actors to deliver certain speeches. But the actors insisted on retaining them because, they said, the play was incomplete without them.

We have done Jatra plays on many subjects, including Lenin, the fall of Berlin, Vietnam, the indigo revolt of 1856–60, Mao Tse-tung, the Indian guerrillas of 1944, the Punjab revolt of 1919, and several on current issues indicting the ruling classes.

Jatra is theatre in the round, and it's very loud. Everything is influenced by sightlines, visibility, and audibility. Jatras are frequently performed in villages without electricity. The carbide gas lamps which are used don't give much light, but the actors have to make themselves visible to a large audience, so the make-up is very heavy and the costumes are very colourful. The gestures and the stage business are stylized. Originally, I think (there's a controversy as to whether the songs or the dialogue came first), it was all sung. But we can understand why, during the late nineteenth and early twentieth centuries, the Jatra had to rely mostly on songs. It is much easier to project song than speech. And continuous acting would be very strenuous in a play lasting from early afternoon until midnight. So the actors would act a little, and then various kinds of singers would come on. There was a character called Vivek ("Conscience") who would enter at particularly dramatic moments and sing a song about what was to be learned from the incident. There was another conventional device – the *juri* – a group of singers sitting on the edge of the area throughout the performance. In the middle of a scene they would suddenly stand up and start singing in chorus. In the scene in which the bad king tried to kill Lord Krishna, they would sing directly to the king, telling him what a bad person he was – "What you have done will earn you a place in hell … ." The action would resume after they finished their song and sat down. That's how the form used to be, but it's becoming more and more corrupt, influenced by the cinema and theatre of Calcutta. (Professional Jatra companies now employ women – one change I do support.) Today the main audience comes from the working class and not the peasants – tea garden workers, railway workers in Assam, coal and steel workers in Bengal. They pay well and the Jatra is now oriented towards them. They won't sit and listen to a Jatra for twelve hours – they have a work shift the next day – so the plays must be shortened. Naturally the songs are the first to go out, and now, instead of thirty, there are never more than five or six, usually only three. Also, the Vivek is no longer used. We are trying to reintroduce these elements but the paying audience is already conditioned. For example, in the original production of my play *Rifle*, I tried to bring Vivek back; I gave him about six songs. After the first two songs, when he came up to sing the third, the audience shouted him down: "Let's get on with the play." I don't blame them, but it's very sad. There are other corruptions. The actors are following what they think is a naturalistic style. They face a big problem: how to perform in a large arena and yet be realistic. The old Jatra actors – at least some of them – achieved a remarkable impression of realism, of absolute control, and yet they shouted at the top of their voices, but skilfully, so that it never seemed they were shouting.

The popularity of the cinema and the commercial theatre in Calcutta for a time pressured our Jatra groups to hire actors from the commercial theatre itself, at fabulous salaries – sometimes 10,000 rupees ($1,300) a month. Luckily, most of them couldn't perform Jatra. It's one thing to be very nice, pretty, and likable before the camera, and quite another thing to appear before an audience of coal miners at 3 a.m., trying to hold their attention.

TDR: How is a traditional Jatra actor trained?

Dutt: Most of the great Jatra actors of the previous generation began training when they were nine or ten, in little boys' and girls' roles – boys played girls' parts too. At fifteen or sixteen they would play the leading lady. At around twenty-one they would be promoted to the men's parts – the prince, villain, king, etc. They had a thorough grounding in the Jatra acting technique before they were permitted the full use of their powers. They never used microphones. Now, I don't mind the use of microphones; every year audiences are becoming larger and larger – a good play may draw 20,000 at one performance. The old actors watch the younger ones perform and say: "Allow us to perform and we'll show you how to do it without microphones." The other day, the amplification system failed when an older actor was performing before a very large audience. But he went on and was quite audible.

TDR: You have done some streetcorner plays. Why did you take up the form?

Dutt: To take our theatre to the masses, apart from our permanent theatre in Calcutta, we have ensured maximum mobility by doing away with sets and lights, and cutting down the number of actors in the cast. We have learned from the Living Newspaper, guerrilla theatre, and other forms abroad, and created Pathanatika (streetcorner plays), in which a group of actors go to a streetcorner or a village market and begin playing; the dialogue is in part extemporaneous, using local subjects. These plays have become very popular in recent years; the audience gathers automatically.

TDR: You admire Brecht. How has he influenced you?

Dutt: I think there is a western conspiracy – conscious or otherwise – to conceal Brecht's real contribution to revolutionary theatre. For example, his development of Gorki's theory of amplification, which became Brecht's "alienation": Brecht was trying to draw attention to the content of drama, to tell us that modern theatre must make people think and not move them by emotion. But the whole world, especially the west, seized Brecht's methods, not the meaning behind the methods. Reading some western critics, one would think that alienation was some kind of an actor's manual. That's not what Brecht said. He said that the actor must face his role squarely, not get lost in it. Most people have carefully avoided the reasons behind this. The actor must capture life not only as it is but as it should be. If he gets lost in a part he is merely presenting an attitude that belongs not to him, and not to the playwright, but to the character. But he must also directly present to the people his own attitude and the writer's attitude – which in my case is Marxist. However, the Brechtian style would interfere with our people's responses because they are used to another kind of theatre, and all forms must arise from the people's understanding.

I think Gorki has influenced me more. As I understand it, epic structure advances the action to a certain point then halts, cuts it entirely and proceeds with another episode, or with the same episode in another light. This directly contradicts our people's expectations. They're accustomed to the dramatic atmosphere getting thicker and thicker, until it becomes almost unbearable. A Marxist believes that form is entirely a tactical question: how to get your ideas across most effectively.

TDR: Do you believe in the idea of a distinctively Indian theatre?

Dutt: Some people have been talking about an Indian theatre in a manner that we do not like, a theatre Indian in its very conception, approach, and form. We think this is rather silly because the modern theatre itself is imported stuff; the first man to do a modern play in Bengali was a Russian called Lebedoff. Theatre as we now practice it is imported from Europe. There is such a thing as an Indian form springing from the people's taste, the sort of thing that people themselves have fashioned through the centuries. But in India we can never talk about an Indian theatre, for there are as many theatre forms in India as there are peoples or languages. The traditional theatre in Kerala and the traditional theatre in Bengal are as far apart as the Bengali traditional theatre and the Burmese traditional theatre.

TDR: There is no quintessential Indian theatre?

Dutt: It doesn't exist. We don't understand each other's languages. The most powerful and effective theatre outside Bengal is in Kerala. But unfortunately we don't understand a single word of it. Plays do depend on the spoken word, despite "total theatre." There are numerous languages in India. There can be a *Bengali* theatre. There probably will be. For example, commercial theatre in Calcutta was deeply influenced by the traditional Jatra. Especially in the nineteenth century, certain forms – acting, music, etc. – were taken from the Jatra and introduced into this imported form. The interaction between the Jatra and the modern theatre is still a valid process. It is possible that in about a hundred years such a thing as a Bengali theatre will rise.

TDR: Does this concept of an Indian theatre – which you don't hold – have anything to do with a particularly Indian way of looking at arts?

Dutt: Not at all. Those who talk about it don't take theatre to the people. They do an Indian production, in the Indian manner, of the great Indian poet Kalidasa – a play called *Shakuntala*, in which men come onstage playing antelopes. It's a great Indian form! These plays are being done in Delhi for tourists, and for Indian government officials, who sleep right through the performance. Women come to the theatre and knit. They sleep, they snore; there are three performances and the run is over. And these are the people who talk about an Indian form. Until a play is done a thousand times, you don't know how the people accept it.

Sanskrit classical theatre has no meaning today. The people are not interested – they've never heard of Kalidasa. Many thousands of Bengali peasants haven't even heard of Rabindranath Tagore. Perhaps they have some vague notion of a bearded man who lived in Calcutta. I think Comrade Tagore reacted so violently to the vices of the professional theatre that he retired into a shell; he organized his own little theatre with his young men and women and wrote special plays for them; they sang and danced plays only for the intelligentsia. And his plays are so difficult; they may be masterpieces – I don't know – in the year 2001 … . We produced two Tagore plays and our experiences were bitter. When we did Tagore's plays they were unintelligible to the audience. We could have been playing in German.

Tagore's spiritual descendants are still active in theatre and cinema. They sometimes do dance-dramas, which are a horror. They sing and dance emasculated versions of what Tagore probably intended. He hinted at some powerful things in *Red Oleanders* and, when Bohurupee did it, it became meaningful; but Tagore's spiritual descendants take the little bit of masculinity Tagore had and emasculate him still further, making him a eunuch. I think that only after the revolution will the people really claim Tagore.

TDR: What about those who reject bourgeois art altogether, as it happened in Paris in 1968, say?

Dutt: I was in Paris then and saw some of these things, and talked with some comrades. It is presumptuous for me to judge comrades abroad, but there is a very strong tendency toward anarchism among the French youth. Inflamed by a misunderstanding of Che Guevara and faulty reading of Marcuse, they have taken to saying, "Down with the entire bourgeois culture." This question came up in the Soviet Union also, and Stalin asked a *proletkultist*: "Why are you against what you call bourgeois culture?" The man replied: "Marxism teaches us that after the base is changed the entire superstructure is changed." Stalin replied with a simple question: "In what language are you speaking to me?" He said: "Russian." Stalin: "Russian was not born under socialism, so it is wrong to say that you change the entire superstructure; it is entirely wrong and un-Marxist and petty-bourgeois romanticist." It's stupid to say that one is going to destroy the entire bourgeois culture.

(Calcutta, November 1970).

33

RIDICULING RACISM IN SOUTH AFRICA

Ron Jenkins

The clash between the illusion of a "New South Africa" and the racist reality experienced by its citizens gave birth to a powerfully subversive style of comedy that expressed the nation's outrage. The two most influential satires in the country's history premiered in the year that President Botha publicly unveiled the idea of a "New South Africa." Fulfilling an essential public need to come to terms with contradictions that the government was content to ignore, both comedies were received with enthusiasm by black and white audiences.

One of these two satires took its title from a pun on an ultimatum made by Botha in a 1981 speech. The leader shocked his white constituents by declaring that the apartheid system would have to change and challenged them to "Adapt or die." It did not take long for the white satirist Peter Dirk Uys to incorporate the phrase into the title of his newest monologue: *Adapt or Dye*. The other play, entitled *Woza Albert*, ridiculed the supposedly Christian principles on which Botha's party had governed the nation for decades, by speculating on what would happen if Jesus Christ chose the land of apartheid as the site of his Second Coming.

Reverberations from both these plays continue to have an impact on the interracial dialogue in South Africa more than a decade after their premieres. *Woza Albert* went on a successful world tour that launched the international careers of its creators, Percy Mtwa, Mbongeni Ngema, and Barney Simon. The original version of the play ran until 1985 and was revived in 1990 by Peter Brook's Paris-based company, which performed it around the world yet again. Mtwa and Ngema both brought subsequent plays to Broadway and the Lincoln Center in New York City, where they played a role in fueling the international public outrage against apartheid that helped force the white South African government to repeal many of the country's most unjust laws. Mbongeni Ngema used the fame of *Woza Albert* to win backing for his worldwide hit, *Sarafina*. Barney Simon followed his work on *Woza Albert* with other interracial collaborations that challenged the country's censorship laws. As artistic director of Johannesburg's Market Theatre, he defied the apartheid system by creating the only theatre in the country where black and white artists and audiences could mix freely.

Woza Albert is the quintessential South African comedy, a play that laughingly dissects the hypocrisies of racism as it calls for social change. Created by the two black actors in collaboration with the white director Barney Simon, *Woza Albert* captures the complexity of South African culture in a multifaceted collage of oral history, physical comedy, muck-raking, and political protest.

The first scene set a tone of comic defiance that enabled the audience to identify immediately with the actors' dilemma. Mtwa and Ngema are two black performers being arrested by a white policeman for playing their music in the streets. The actors convey the spirit of the outdoor concert without real instruments, using an array of melodic and percussive sounds to give the impression of an orchestra in full swing. Mtwa and Ngema are humming, scatting, and whistling a slapdash version of Hugh Masekela's "Stimela." The song is doubly evocative, reminding people of the apartheid laws that forced Masekela to go into exile to find the freedom to play his music without harassment, and telling the story of black workers taken from their homes to work for slave wages in the gold mines of Johannesburg.

The scene is structured so that the outrage evoked by the song is channeled into derisive laughter directed at the buffoonish white policeman who takes the musicians to prison. Mtwa transforms himself into the policeman by putting on one of the pink round noses that both actors wear around their necks throughout the show. These clown masks are ever-present icons of the white race, emblems of apartheid that encircle the throats of the black actors like a ball and chain. Whenever a scene calls for a white character, one of the pair slips on the clown nose and assumes the awkward gait and hypocritical grin of a racist. In the opening scene the pink-nosed policeman tells the black musicians that they should go "back to the bush with the baboons. That's where you belong."

Fig. 33.1 *Woza Albert* **performed by Percy Mtwa and Mbongeni Ngema. (Photo courtesy of Spingold Theatre, Brandeis University.)**

By ridiculing whites as cartoon caricatures, *Woza Albert* exposes the ludicrous foundations of apartheid. The white soldiers, guards, politicians, and TV announcers who appear throughout the play speak in hollow, comic voices expressing idiotic sentiments. The duplicity inherent in their devotion to apartheid is gradually revealed as the play's premise unfolds. Because white South Africans claim that apartheid is based on Christian values, the play explodes the myth of divinely sanctioned apartheid by envisioning what would happen if Christ himself arrived in South Africa and saw how his teachings were being applied.

Woza Albert's fantastical treatment of the Second Coming is a comic jam session based roughly on the New Testament. The imprisoned and exploited blacks await a savior, but when Christ arrives by jumbo jet in Johannesburg and denounces the injustices of apartheid, he is betrayed, persecuted, and martyred by the white government that had initially used his appearance to justify their policies to the world. Wearing a pink clown nose and a sly smile, the prime minister tells an international barrage of television cameras that Christ "is back and South Africa has got him." He cannot hide his contempt for the world leaders who had imposed sanctions on his country and will now be jealous of the public relations benefits bestowed by Jesus' visit. "Tough luck, friends," gloats the politician. "He chose us."

Having welcomed Christ with the key to Sun City and a hospitality tour of its sex shows and gambling casinos, the government is surprised when he denounces the disparities between the excesses of rich whites and the deprivations of poor blacks. Christ is denounced as a terrorist rabble- rouser and imprisoned on infamous Robben Island, where Mandela and other ANC leaders were still being held at the time of the play's creation. When Christ makes his escape from the prison island by walking on the water, he is spotted by two doltish air force pilots who lament that they have forgotten to bring their cameras and missed a chance to get a souvenir photo of the miracle. Following a nonsensical dialogue worthy of their pink clown noses, the pilots drop an atom bomb that destroys Christ along with half of South Africa.

Christ's betrayal had been predicted by an old black vagabond who had appeared earlier in the play. In a comic monologue spoken while trying to sew a button on his coat, the hobo recounts the famous story of Piet Retief. Retief was a revered leader of the nineteenth-century Afrikaans settlers, and his fate at the hands of the Zulu King Dingane has assumed mythic proportions for blacks and whites in South Africa. Dingane invited Retief and his soldiers to put down their weapons and join him in a feast that ended in their massacre by the Zulus. The tramp laughingly predicts that the same thing will happen to Christ when the prime minister invites him inside to "enjoy the fruits of apartheid."

The vagabond's rendition of the encounter between Dingane and Retief is full of comic details that play off the audience's knowledge of African history. Embellishing his tale with snatches of a Zulu liberation song warning that whites cannot be trusted, he contradicts the standard history book version of the event used by whites to justify their mistrust of blacks. The national Voortrekker Monument in Pretoria celebrates Retief's martyrdom in a stone frieze while vilifying Dingane's warriors with a sculpted black *wildebeest* that symbolizes "the barbarism that yielded to civilization."

Civilization for the whites meant the destruction of black culture, but the tramp's revisionist retelling of the tale suggests that Dingane was protecting his people from Retief's intention to steal their land. We know whose side the hobo is on when he imitates the gleeful smile on Dingane's face as he invites Retief inside for dinner. The expression of mock beatitude parallels the look on the face of ex-Prime Minister Hendrik Voerwoerd in a famous newsreel clip from the 1950s in which he defends apartheid as nothing more than a harmless "policy of good neighborliness."

Woza Albert's wry use of Dingane's legend calls attention to how the story is used frequently by both blacks and whites to appropriate history to their own ends. Mtwa, Ngema, and Simon offer it as yet another comic salvo in a satirical battle that can be traced back to the nineteenth century when black Africans were caricatured on the English-speaking stage as ooga-booga Zulus in grass skirts.

A large part of the black struggle for political power in South Africa is waged in the arena of international public opinion, and popular comedies like *Woza Albert* have played a role in exposing the injustices of the apartheid system to the outside world. In 1982 *Woza Albert* was presented in London to a storm of critical acclaim. The play overturned the tradition of racial caricature that had become an institutionalized part of European culture. Now it was the whites who were depicted as comic savages, brutalizing blacks and nuking Jesus with their silly pink clown noses. *Woza Albert*'s fierce comic indictment of white savagery can be imagined as the Zulus' revenge for having been caricatured as barbaric cannibals in the past. Somber tragedies, like those of the white South African playwright Athol Fugard, have also been influential, but the resilience of the black liberation movement is most eloquently expressed in the cathartic release of laughter.

Comedies have happy endings, and the political comedies of South Africa end on a note of hope for the future rather than despair over the past. Because *Woza Albert* is a comedy that combines religion with politics, its happy ending takes the form of a resurrection. Christ is killed by the white government's atomic bomb, but he comes back after three days and brings back to life the ghosts of South African freedom fighters who were also victims of the government's repressive policies. The finale is an exhilarating musical duet sung by Christ and the grave digger as they call out the names of Steve Biko, Ruth First, and other political martyrs they will bring back to life. Each of the names is preceded by a shout of "*Woza*," which is Zulu for "rise up." Their resurrection of the Nobel Peace Prize-winning black activist Albert Luthuli gives the play its title, *Woza Albert*.

Woza Albert expresses the frustrations and longings of black South Africans with pithy comic grace. Its protagonists are put in jail, but they find freedom. Its heroes are killed, but they come back to life. There is a lot of suffering at the hands of the whites, but there is also a lot of laughter at their expense. The play is imbued with the same irrepressible spirit displayed by the clown commando at the head of the march on Pretoria when he challenged the government's soldiers with a mock machine-gun. Displaying the power of the powerless, the characters created by Mtwa and Ngema use laughter as a weapon to ensure their survival.

Mtwa, Ngema, and Simon shaped their satire from personal experience with the raw suffering of South African blacks. Mtwa received a lesson in the caprice of the legal system when he spent weeks in jail for going to a restaurant without his identity papers. When he and Ngema first began working on the script, they didn't have enough money for food or a bus fare and depended on the largesse of a Soweto gangster who bankrolled their project with a stipend that amounted to little more than pennies a day. Simon, a director with a passionate commitment to socially relevant theatre, encouraged Mtwa and Ngema to gather material for the play by interviewing street vendors, bricklayers, and children of Soweto. This authenticity resulted in rapt audience attention whenever the play was presented in black townships.

Woza Albert was created during a time when censorship laws in South Africa were tightly enforced. Black people had no opportunity to see their suffering portrayed realistically in films, television, or newspapers. The play's gritty comic realism fulfilled their hunger to see the hypocrisy of white authorities publicly unmasked. Nothing like this had ever appeared before on the South African stage. Audiences in black townships like Soweto thronged to performances and responded to its bleak humor with wild enthusiasm. From the opening sequence they were totally engaged in the play's mockery of the white regime that had restricted their movement, limited their economic opportunities, and imprisoned their heroes. In the repressive conditions of 1981 all this injustice had to be endured without question. Laughing at *Woza Albert* was the only permissible form of public insubordination.

34

POLITICAL THEATRE AS POPULAR ENTERTAINMENT
The San Francisco Mime Troupe

Theodore Shank

In the exuberance of revolutionary zeal, it is natural that certain political theatre groups should turn to forms of entertainment associated with fun, with the common man, with people in general regardless of social, economic, or educational status, in contrast with the traditional aristocratic forms that have "artistic" pretensions and tend to be more contemplative than energetic. It is also predictable that such groups should shun ballet, opera, the symphony, and literary theatre, and use instead techniques from *commedia dell'arte*, circus, puppet shows, music hall, vaudeville, parades, magicians, carnival side-shows, buskers, brass bands, comic strips, striptease, melodrama, minstrel shows, and other means of exhilarating celebration.

Since the present seemed to hold no answers, it was inevitable that the search by these groups for political theatre forms would turn to the past, a past which, through education and television, had become more accessible than ever before. Such breaks with the present served another purpose as well – they demonstrated a disassociation with the Establishment and its theatre. Some of the characteristics of bourgeois theatre were realism, psychological characters, an intellectualism that was seen as pretentious, a reliance on words that came to be considered the chief device of hypocrisy, and an estheticism that rejected political statement. Thus, in trying to distinguish themselves from the Establishment, young political theatres attempted to find bases for theatre outside Realism.

Political theatre has done more than adopt past entertainment forms, it has also adopted their spirit of fun. Jean-Jacques Lebel, the Happener and political activist who was making street theatre during the Paris events of May 1968, says that the Revolution should be fun, even the planning of it. It is this sense of living, of vitality, that must imbue all revolutionary political activity, coming as a continual demonstration of the energy of the Movement toward desired goals, in contrast with the boredom of the status quo. It is this vitality, which comes in part from taking on the Establishment, that is the most obvious characteristic of the contemporary political theatre groups. These groups see themselves in contrast with the effete, lifeless, decadent theatre of those in power.

In part, the energy inherent in the works of political theatre groups is related to what Peter Brook calls the "rough theatre." The works incorporate a collection of styles and techniques taken from many times, places, and other groups. These styles and techniques are used in whatever ways seem most effective, and mixed together every which way. Everything is at the disposal of these political groups; they have not eliminated poten- tially expressive materials, characters, or events in the interest of unity, beauty, style, decorum, or other theoretical values. While some experimental work of the 1960s attempted to find the unique essence of theatre through an economy of means that focused on the performer's body and voice to the exclusion of all other materials, the political theatres were expansive and eclectic, assimilating everything that could further a spirit of freedom and demonstrate their political objective.

The energy and roughness of such theatre also comes from the need to remain open to changing political circumstances and the specific needs of the occasion. They must be able to adapt at a moment's notice; polish is not always possible. Further, since the polit- ical efficacy of their work depends on creating a sense of "we" with the audience against "them," the Establishment, it is essential that the performer – the human being – remains visible under the character. If the illusion of character is so opaque as to hide the performer completely, there can be no sense of "we." In practice, then, the character is used by the performer as a means of demonstrating something, just as a puppeteer might operate a puppet while remaining visible. At the very least, the humanity of the actor must come through the cracks of the illusion he creates.

The feeling of community between the performer and spectator is enhanced by keeping the performance open to improvising so that the performer can respond directly to spectators and to situations that arise in the immediate area during the performance. This is in much the same way that a political speaker might respond in taking advantage of a particular moment.

The political theatre groups have attempted to create the ambiance in which popular entertainment forms, such as commedia and circus, took place. In reaction to the expected audience behavior in the traditional theatre, where the spectator is isolated in contempla- tion that approaches reverence, the political groups promote a relaxed natural atmosphere and encourage spectator reaction and interaction. The spectators feel free to share their enjoyment with each other, to talk, eat, smoke, move around, and even leave without embarrassment if they wish. Thus, most groups usually avoid boring their audiences. The opposite of boredom is the feeling of being free and energetically alive, which is conveyed by popular forms of entertainment and the atmosphere that surrounds them. A sense of community results from this atmosphere and from the feeling of being the good minority standing against the evil Establishment. Such easy moral distinctions suggest one of the reasons stereotype commedia-like characters and symbolic characters are so often used.

There is an important difference, aside from political intentions, between the Estab- lishment's use of popular entertainment forms, such as television and movies, and the use by political theatre groups of popular entertainment forms and techniques. Commer- cial television and motion pictures aim for the broadest possible audience. That is how they make a profit. The audience is extremely varied, often including people of different countries and certainly of different political convictions, religions, races, education, and economic status. The spectators are exploited to support the industry and the status quo. Political theatre groups, on the other hand, while designing their works for popular appeal, often make their pieces for specific audiences, to be performed in specific locales, perhaps even on specific occasions. The focus is on the immediacy of the moment, of performers and spectators being together in the same place at the same time, where two-way communication can occur. Frequently communication continues after the performance in a discussion of the pertinent political issues. While the performance may depict the evils of the Establishment, the system, and the status quo, the event surrounding the performance creates a community between the performers and spectators, demonstrating the society that can exist and the means of bringing it about.

The San Francisco Mime Troupe, which gave its first performances in 1959, is one of the oldest of the contemporary political theatres and one of the most varied in its use of popular entertainment forms and techniques. In its fourteen years, it has adapted elements from *commedia dell'arte*, circus (including clowning and juggling), minstrel shows, puppet shows, comic strips, popular band music, carnival sideshows, vaudeville, and movies. In the beginning, in an attempt to find a non-realistic means of expression, they performed wordless pieces while making it clear that their interest was in the mime of Charlie Chaplin and Buster Keaton rather than that of Marcel Marceau. They focused on the use of body movement to convey action, character, and attitude, thus already beginning to use techniques traditionally associated with commedia. Their first commedia, however, was a couple of years later – about the time they began performing outdoors. For several years, the staple of the group was adaptations of scripts by Molière, Goldoni, Machiavelli, Beolco, Bruno, and Lope de Rueda, performed in the manner of *commedia dell'arte* with the traditional stereotype masked characters, exaggerated movement and voice, and sufficient flexibility to incorporate news events of the day and to permit impromptu responses to unplanned events during the performance. These were performed on a portable stage in the parks of San Francisco and the commedia style served well in holding attention and competing with the usual outdoor distractions. Each of these adaptations, while keeping the traditional characters and costuming, was infused with the general political radicalism of the San Francisco "hip" scene in the mid-1960s.

Fig. 34.1 *The Independent Female* staged by the San Francisco Mime Troupe, 1979. (Photo by Theodore Shank.)

"Adaptation" may be a misleading term for the relation of our commedia shows to their origi-
nals. We do not usually set ourselves the task of translating an author's intentions; rather, we
exploit his work to suit our own; using what we can and discarding the rest, writing in new
scenes and characters, to say nothing of new emphasis … Our interest in this sixteenth-
century form is not antiquarian: we use it because it is popular, free, engaging, and adaptable.

(Program Note)

An adaptation of Goldoni's *L'Amant militaire* in 1967 became their first long anti-
Vietnam play. The plot was mostly from Goldoni. The Spanish army is fighting in Italy, a
clear parallel with the US army in Vietnam. Pantalone, the Spanish mayor, connives with
the Spanish general to profit from the war. The general is determined "to pursue peace
with every available weapon." Pantalone would marry his daughter off to the old general,
but she is secretly in love with a young lieutenant. Arlecchino disguises himself as a
woman in order to avoid military service. In the end, the soubrette, dressed like the Pope,
appears above the curtain and stops the war. She then tells the audience: "If you want
something done, my friends – do it yourselves." Joan Holden, who adapted the play,
considered the Mime Troupe production quite militant for 1967. "The heroine debunks
pacifism as an answer. She says that you have to fight war with war. It called for a revolution, but it didn't say who the revolutionaries should be."[1]

The commedia stereotypes of authoritarian well-to-do old man, general, young lovers,
soubrette, and tricky servant had undergone some changes, but in appearance were still
very much traditional commedia because of the half-masks and costumes. Further, the
names were unchanged and the plots, while somewhat adapted, were still more from an
Italian past than an American present. A partial solution was found in 1970 with *The
Independent Female*, or *A Man Has His Pride!* written by Joan Holden as a parody of
nineteenth-century melodrama.

For several years, we had been dissatisfied with commedia because it was foreign, and we
had been talking about what would be an American equivalent. We liked commedia
because the characters were so clear, it had a broad comic style, it was funny, it was highly
stylized, and it was really good for us to work in. We didn't know what could work as well.
We sort of stumbled on it when we did a melodrama, *The Independent Female*. We didn't
know then that we were replacing commedia with melodrama, but that is basically what we
have done. We found American stereotypes that can be used the same way as the commedia
stereotypes – the capitalist, the young naive man, the strong woman.

(Joan Holden, San Francisco, 1 September 1972)

This women's liberation play, set in the nineteenth century, concerns Gloria Pennybank
who is engaged to marry a junior executive, John Heartright. Gloria, however, is
unhappy because, although she likes her job, John insists that, when they are married, she
must quit. He wants "a wife, not a business partner." The villain, in the eyes of all but
Gloria, is Sarah Bullitt, a feminist who eventually succeeds in corrupting Gloria, who
comes to realize that "femininity is a drug to make us slaves." Together they lead a
women's strike for equal pay, free nurseries, and free transportation. To frustrate
Gloria's leadership, John resorts to deception. He holds a gun to his head and threatens to
kill himself if Gloria does not sign an agreement to renounce all of her political activities
and live for him alone. She relents and is about to sign when Sarah pulls a gun on John
and exposes his deceit. Gloria's mother arrives and discovers that the big capitalist, the
President of the Chamber of Commerce, is her long-lost husband. The sight of the

mother causes the President to collapse with a heart attack. John takes advantage of the confusion and shoots Sarah who dies after making a speech. After all, she is the villain. Gloria renounces love forever and vows to work for the cause. When the play has ended the performer of the role of Gloria comes forward and makes a speech for women's power in San Francisco.

Originally, the play followed the melodrama form more closely, but when the play was ready for performance, it was seen by a group of feminists who strongly objected to two things about the piece and suggested some changes. In the original version, Sarah was much more villainous. She was a manipulative woman who cast a spell on innocent Gloria so as to destroy all men. Also there was a typical "happy" ending in which Gloria gave up her fight, returned to John, and everything came up roses. At first the group resisted the changes because inherent in the melodrama form was the requirement of sharp contrasts of good and evil, and of course the happy ending was considered important. However, during the course of discussions the members of the Mime Troupe gained an awareness about the women's struggle that they had not had previously. They came to feel that the conflict between the form and what they wanted to say had to be resolved on the side of their political intent.

Another potential danger in *The Independent Female* was the possibility that some spectators might not distinguish between the parody of the melodrama form and the seriousness of the political statement – that they might take the play as a spoof of the women's liberation movement. In the major piece the following year this problem was averted. Its form was not specifically from the past but borrowed elements from the old melodrama, from commedia, from the adventure movie of foreign intrigue, and even from comic strips such as "Terry and the Pirates." In part, this more diffuse form may have resulted from the fact that the scenario of *The Dragon Lady's Revenge* (1971) was developed collectively by five members through discussion, and then each wrote the scenes assigned to him.

> We were looking for a play to do against the war, against imperialism, but we didn't know what line to take. Somebody heard that *Ramparts* was going to come out with an article that linked the C.I.A. to the drug traffic. So somebody had the idea that that would be a good subject.
>
> (Joan Holden, San Francisco, 1 September 1972)

The Dragon Lady's Revenge is set in the present in the "capital of Cochin, a small country in S. E. Asia." A young American lieutenant, the son of the US Ambassador, sets out to find the man who murdered his friend with an overdose of heroin. He becomes a pawn in the power struggle between those running the drug traffic – the Dragon lady; General Rong Q, who is head of the country; and the C.I.A. In the end, they are exposed by Blossom, a member of the National Liberation Front who works as a B-girl in the den of iniquity run by the Dragon Lady. When Mr. Big, the man behind the drug traffic, is disclosed to be the American Ambassador, his son changes sides and joins Blossom.

The stereotypes are mostly a blend of those from forms previously used by the Mime Troupe. The lieutenant and Blossom are the young lovers from commedia or melodrama. The US Ambassador is a blend of Pantalone and the capitalist boss of *The Independent Female*. General Rong Q resembles the Capitano of commedia and the intriguing villain of foreign espionage movies. An agent of the Ambassador, who makes each appearance in a different disguise, is like one of the commedia zanni. And the Dragon Lady is the evil woman of the Orient.

While masks were not used in *The Independent Female* or *The Dragon Lady's Revenge*, the acting style was broad enough to accommodate a man playing the mother and a woman playing General Rong Q. Both pieces used devices such as overheard conversations, disguises, mock heroic speeches, slapstick comedy, surprise revelations, and endings that provided models for action by the spectators.

While the principal steps in the Mime Troupe's development of a mode for their longer pieces are from commedia to melodrama parody to their own unique eclectic form, they have experimented with other forms as well. *A Minstrel Show*, or *Civil Rights in a Cracker Barrel* (1965) used the form of the black minstrel show made popular in the second half of the nineteenth century by such groups as the Original Christy Minstrels for whom Stephen Foster wrote his best-known songs. The Mime Troupe used some traditional material and invented some of their own in putting together a melange of songs, dances, jokes, skits, and a short film by Robert Nelson, all geared toward exposing racism and liberal poses. In the traditional minstrel show manner, which reflected the amused paternalism of white people toward black people, there was a white interlocutor and several minstrels in exaggerated blackface sitting in chairs on each side of the inter-locutor, who acted as a master of ceremonies. Among the songs were old favorites such as "Old Black Joe," but the skits, quite different from those of the nineteenth century, showed the blackface minstrels cavorting in skits on the racial cliches of black history, society, and physiology.

Each year the repertoire of the Mime Troupe includes a play of an hour or so on a broad political subject, such as the Vietnam war or women's liberation, and short plays of perhaps twenty minutes in reaction to specific political events as they occur. While the long plays have relied on forms drawn largely from commedia or melodrama, the short pieces have been more varied and have incorporated juggling, dancing, puppets, clowns, and crankies – a kind of comic strip that moves on a roll of paper a frame at a time.

Two problem–solution pieces concerning parking meters (1968) and telephones (1970) used both actors and puppets, called Gutter Puppets by the Mime Troupe. Problem: how can one park free? Solution: stick a tab-top from an aluminum can in the parking meter. Problem: how can one phone long distance without charge? Solution: use a corporation's credit card number, according to the method explained by the performers.

The Gutter Clowns replaced the puppets. The short plays made use of performers dressed and made-up somewhat like clowns and used some slapstick movement sugges-tive of circus clowns. *Highway Robbery* (1971) uncovered "the biggest all-time swindle … the used-car-credit-insurance-time-payment trap."

A style reminiscent of vaudeville replaced the clowns for the short pieces. *High Rises* (1972), originally developed in opposition to redevelopment in San Francisco, which was resulting in inexpensive housing being replaced by expensive executive apartments, was subsequently revised as a protest against a planned multimillion-dollar performing arts center that would have the same effect on inexpensive housing. The new version of the piece, called *San Fran Scandals of '73* (1973), concerns Stella and Frank, a former vaudeville song-and-dance team whose number used to include their now lost daughter Baby Tap Toes. The show opens with a dance routine and one-liners, in the manner of George Burns or Jimmy Durante. The couple are being evicted so their home can be razed to make way for a new performing arts center. They pay a call on the man respon-sible, millionaire patron of the arts, Mr. Smellybucks. The couple are mistaken for the world's greatest soprano, Carlotta Snotta, and her manager. Smellybucks has dreamed of one day having Carlotta sing in his new opera house. When the real Carlotta arrives, she

Fig. 34.2 *Frozen Wages* by the San Francisco Mime Troupe, 1972. (Photo by Theodore Shank.)

is induced to hide in a vaudeville trunk to escape the public. Smellybucks, threatened with the disclosure that the toilet paper he manufactures has chafed the opera singer, finally signs a contract agreeing to devote his fortune to the restoration of vaudeville in neighborhood theatres and the rebuilding of inexpensive housing within the city. The vaudeville couple do their song-and-dance number and Smellybucks' secretary, who has schemed with them to trick her boss, begins to dance with them. They discover she is their long lost daughter, Baby Tap Toes.

In recent years, beginning with the group's interest in circus techniques, they have also begun most of their performances of short pieces with juggling, a skill developed by most members of the group. In *Frozen Wages* (1972), a protest against Nixon's price and wage control policies, juggling was integrated into the action of the piece to represent an assembly line. At first, six workers juggle six clubs, leisurely tossing them to one another. Then, a figure resembling the Statue of Liberty suggests to the Boss that while price controls prohibit him from raising prices, he can increase profits by reducing expenses. How? By firing some of his workers. One by one, he fires workers until only two are left to juggle all of the clubs. The Boss is still not satisfied with his profits, so, at the suggestion of the government representative, he steps up production – faster and faster until one of the worker-jugglers flips out and becomes rigid. Eventually, a strike provides a solution for the workers.

The Mime Troupe uses a number of techniques to achieve a spirit of unity among the spectators and between the spectators and the performers. At outdoor performances, the spectators sit on the grass and it is daytime so they can see each other, making interaction more likely than in a darkened auditorium in rigid theatre seats. They watch performers make final preparations, seeing them as human beings, not as characters. There is no attempt to create a mystique that would tend to separate them. The performers are people just like us. Without assuming characters, they warm up by singing and clapping in unison, the Gorilla Band plays, and they parade around the audience and sometimes through them. Often there is a comic juggling competition between several of the performers. The spectators encourage them. Then one or two performers speak directly to the audience, asking them all to get up and move closer to the stage, and telling a couple of jokes involving recent political events. On the day Spiro Agnew resigned as Vice President, part of the speech went something like this:

> Hey, you know that Agnew resigned? (*Spectators respond.*) One down, one to go. He had to resign because of his hemorrhoids … . No, that's not really true, he doesn't have hemorrhoids, it's a medical impossibility. Do you know why? (Spectators say "No.") He's a perfect asshole.

The band music, the jokes, the friendly manner of the performers, and the responses of the spectators all help to create an ambiance of fun and a sense of "we," the performers and spectators, against "they," the Establishment.

NOTE

1 All quotations of Joan Holden are from the author's discussion with her on 1 September 1972, in San Francisco.

35

LEGISLATIVE THEATRE

Augusto Boal

The similarity between Theatre of the Oppressed (in which spectator is transformed into actor) and the Legislative Theatre (in which citizen is transformed into legislator). The proposition advanced by the *vereador's* mandate, the fallacy of Greek direct democracy, and of representative democracy, and the idea of a 'transitive', or 'participatory', 'interactive' democracy.

THE PROPOSITION

Theatre as politics and transitive democracy as theatre

Theatre cannot be imprisoned inside theatrical buildings, just as religion cannot be inprisoned inside churches; the language of theatre and its forms of expression cannot be the private property of actors, just as religious practice cannot be appropriated by priests as theirs alone!

Paulo Freire talks about the transitivity of true teaching: the teacher is not a person who unloads knowledge, like you unload a lorry, and heaps it up in the head of another person – the bank vault where the money-knowledge is kept; the teacher is a person who has a particular area of knowledge, transmits it to the pupil and, at the same time, receives other knowledge in return, since the pupil also has his or her own area of knowledge. The least a teacher has to learn from his pupil is how his pupil learns. Pupils are different from one another; they learn differently. Teaching is transitivity. Democracy. Dialogue. An Argentinian teacher from Cordova relates: "I taught a peasant how to write the word 'plough': and he taught me how to use it."

Conventional theatre is governed by an intransitive relationship, in that everything travels from stage to auditorium, everything is transported, transferred in that direction – emotions, ideas, morality – and nothing goes the other way. The tiniest noise, the smallest exclamation, the least sign of life the spectator displays, is the equivalent of driving the wrong way down a one-way street: danger! Lest the magic of the stage be shattered, silence is required.[1] In Theatre of the Oppressed, by contrast, dialogue is created; transitivity is not merely tolerated, it is actively sought – this theatre asks its audience questions and expects answers. Sincerely.

Legislative Theatre is trying to do the same thing. We do not accept that the elector should be a mere spectator to the actions of the parliamentarian, even when these actions are right; we want the electors to give their opinions, to discuss the issues, to put counter-arguments; we want them to share the responsibility for what their parliamentarian does.

Our mandate's project is to bring theatre back into the centre of political action – the centre of decisions, by making theatre as politics rather than merely making political theatre. In the latter case, the theatre makes comments on politics; in the former, the theatre is, in itself, one of the ways in which political activity can be conducted.

In Greek tragedy the action led to catastrophe for its protagonists and produced catharsis in its spectators, after a phase of euphoric, transgressive violence. At the same time as the 'tragic flaw' (*hamartia*) of the protagonist was extirpated by death (Antigone) or by terrible punishment (Oedipus), the same transgressive desire which had been vicariously stimulated in the spectators was now eliminated. In Legislative Theatre, the aim is to bring the theatre back to the heart of the city, to produce not catharsis, but dynamization. Its objective is not to pacify its audiences, to tranquillize them, to return them to a state of equilibrium and acceptance of society as it is, but, again contrarily, to develop their desire for change. Theatre of the Oppressed seeks not only to develop this desire but to create a space in which it can be stimulated and experienced, and where future actions arising from it can be rehearsed. Legislative Theatre seeks to go further and to transform that desire into law. (We must be aware that law is always someone's desire – it is always the desire of the powerful; let's democratize this desire, let's make our desire become law too!)

NOTE

1 I am not against any kind of theatre: I love them all. I am a playwright myself, and a director, and I would not like to hear any member of the audience shout "Stop!" and come up on stage to take Hamlet's place and shoot Claudius. But the world of theatre is large enough to accommodate all theatrical forms, including Theatre of the Oppressed. In any case, all forms of theatre can interact. I was extremely happy when the Royal Shakespeare Company, in July 1997, invited me to train twenty-six of their actors how to use the introspective techniques of *The Rainbow of Desire* to create characters from Shakespeare's plays. It was a wonderful experience for all of us.

BIBLIOGRAPHY

Artaud, Antonin (1958) *The Theatre and Its Double*, trans. by Mary Caroline Richards. New York: Grove Press.

Bakhtin, Mikhail (1984) *Rabelais and His World*, trans. by Helene Iswolsky. Bloomington: Indiana University Press.

Bell, John, ed. (2001) *Puppets, Masks and Performing Objects*. Cambridge, MA.: MIT Press.

Benjamin, Walter (1996) *Selected Writings*, Vol. II. Cambridge, MA.: Harvard Belnap.

——(1973) *Understanding Brecht*. London: New Left Books.

Bentley, Eric (1967) *The Playwright as Thinker*. New York: Harcourt, Brace and World.

——(1980) *The Theory of the Modern Stage*. New York: Penguin Books.

Blumenthal, Eileen, and Julie Taymor, (1995) *Julie Taymor, Playing with Fire: Theatre, Opera, Film*. New York: Abrams.

Boal, Augusto (1998) *Legislative Theatre*. London: Routledge.

——(1979) *The Theatre of the Oppressed*. New York: Urizen.

Brandon, James (1967) *Theatre in Southeast Asia*. Cambridge, MA: Harvard University Press.

Braun, Edward, ed. (1969) *Meyerhold on Theatre*. New York: Hill and Wang.

Brecht, Stefan (1988) *The Bread and Puppet Theatre,* Vol I and II. London: Methuen/Routledge.

Bristol, Michael (1989) *Carnival and Theatre: Plebeian Culture and the Structure of Authority in Renaissance England*. London: Routledge.

Brook, Peter (1968) *The Empty Space*. New York: Atheneum.

Coult, Tony and Baz Kershaw (1983) *Engineers of the Imagination: The Welfare State Handbook*. London: Methuen.

Craig, Gordon (1962) "The Actor and the Ubermarionette" in *On the Art of the Theatre*. London: Mercury Books, pp. 54–94.

Davis, R. G. (1975) *The San Francisco Mime Troupe: The First Ten Years*. Palo Alto: Ramparts Press.

Disher, M. Willson (1942) *Fairs, Circuses and Music Halls*. London: William Collins.

Ducharte, Pierre Louis (1965) *The Italian Comedy*. New York: Dover.

Edwards, Glyn (2000) *Successful Punch and Judy*. Great Britain: DaSilva Puppet Books.

Emigh, John (1996) *Masked Performance*. Philadelphia: University of Pennsylvania Press.

Findlater, Richard (1978) *Joe Grimaldi: His Life and Theatre*. Cambridge: Cambridge University Press.

Flanagan, Hallie (1940) *Arena*. New York: Duell, Sloan and Pearce.

Fo, Dario (1991) *The Tricks of the Trade*, trans. by Joe Farrell. London: Routledge.

Gilbert, Douglas (1953) *American Vaudeville*. New York: Dover.

Goodlad, J. S. (1972) *A Sociology of Popular Drama*. New Jersey: Rowman and Littlefield.

Goorney, Howard (1981) *The Theatre Workshop Story*. London: Methuen.

Gordon, Mel (1997) *Grand Guignol*. New York: Da Capo.

——(1983) *Lazzi: The Comic Routines of the Commedia dell'Arte*. New York: Performing Arts Journal.

Grimaldi, Joseph (1838) *Memoirs of Joseph Grimaldi*, ed. Boz [Charles Dickens]. London: Routledge.

Hauser, Arnold (1951) *The Social History of Art*, Vol. I., Baltimore: Penguin.

Hollis, Wyndham, ed. (1987) *Mr. Punch's Progress and Other Observations*. Norfolk: Monkeypuzzle.

Irvine, David (1996) *Leather Gods and Wooden Heroes: Java's Classic Wayang*. Singapore: Times Editions PTE Ltd.

Jenkins, Ron (2001) *Dario Fo and Franca Rame: Artful Laughter*. New York: Aperture.

——(1994) *Subversive Laughter: The Liberating Power of Comedy*. New York: Free Press.

Keene, Donald (1973) *Bunraku: The Art of the Japanese Puppet Theatre*. Tokyo: Kodansha International Ltd.

Kelly, Catriona (1990) *Petrushka: The Russian Carnival Puppet Theater*. Cambridge: Cambridge University Press.

Kerr, David (1995) *African Popular Theatre* London: Heinemann.

Kirby, E. T. "The Shamanistic Origins of Popular Entertainments," *The Drama Review*, 18(1): 5–15.

Kott, Jan (1966) *Shakespeare Our Contemporary*. New York: Anchor.

Laurie, Joe, Jr., (1953) *Vaudeville*. New York: Henry Holt.

Lipovsky, Alexander, ed. (1967) *The Soviet Circus*. Moscow: Progress Publishers.

Littlewood, Joan (1994) *Joan's Book: Joan Littlewood's Peculiar History as She Tells It*. London: Methuen.

McCormick, John (1993) *Popular Theatres of Nineteenth-Century France*. Cambridge: Cambridge University Press.

——and Bennie Pratasik (1998) *Popular Puppet Theatre in Europe, 1800–1914*. Cambridge: Cambridge University Press.

McGrath, John (1981) *A Good Night Out: Popular Theatre: Audience, Class and Form*. London: Eyre Methuen.

McKechnie, Samuel (1969) *Popular Entertainments through the Ages*. New York: Blom.

McNamara, Brooks, ed. (1983) *American Popular Entertainments*. New York: Performing Arts Journal.

——(1976) *Step Right Up!* Garden City: Doubleday.

McPharlin, Paul (1969) *The Puppet Theatre in America*. Boston: Plays, Inc.

Mason, Bim (1992) *Street Theatre and Other Outdoor Performance*. London: Routledge.

Mayer, David and Kenneth Richards, eds (1977) *Western Popular Theatre*. London: Methuen.

Mayhew, Henry (1968) *London Labour and the London Poor*, Vol. III. New York: Dover [reprint].

Mitchell, Tony (1984) *Dario Fo, People's Court Jester*. London: Methuen.

Nagler, A.M. (1952) *A Source Book in Theatrical History*. New York: Dover.

Nicoll, Allardyce (1963) *Mimes, Masks and Miracles*. New York: Cooper Square.

——(1963) *The World of Harlequin*. London: Cambridge University Press.

O'Brien, Mark, and Little, Craig (1990) *Reimagining America: The Arts of Social Change*. Philadelphia: New Society Publishers.

Orenstein, Claudia (1998) *Festive Revolutionaries: The Politics of Popular Theatre and the San Francisco Mime Troupe*. Jackson: University of Mississippi Press.

Rémy, Tristan (1945) *Les Clowns*. Paris: Grasset.

Rolfe, Bari, ed. (1982) *Mimes on Miming*. Los Angeles: Panjandrum Books.

Rudlin, John (1994) *Commedia Dell'Arte: An Actor's Handbook*. London: Routledge.

Sandrow, Nahma (1975) *Vagabond Stars: A World History of Yiddish Theatre*. New York: Harper and Row.

Schechner, Richard (1985) *Between Theater and Anthropology*. Philadelphia: University of Pennsylvania Press.

Schechter, Joel (1985) *Durov's Pig: Clowns, Politics and Theatre*. New York: Theatre Communications Group.

——(2001) *The Pickle Clowns: New American Circus Comedy*. Carbondale: Southern Illinois University Press.

Scott-Kemball, Jeune (1970) *Javanese Shadow Puppets*. London: British Museum.

Scuderi, Antonio (1998), *Dario Fo and Popular Performance*. Ottowa: Legas.

Senelick, Laurence (1988) *The Age and Stage of George L. Fox*. University of New England Press.

——(1989) *Cabaret Performance, Europe, 1890–1920*. New York: PAJ Publications.

——(1993) *Cabaret Performance, Europe, 1920–1940*. Baltimore: Johns Hopkins.

Shank, Theodore (1982) *American Alternative Theatre*. New York: Grove Press.

Skipitares, Theodora (2000) "Once Were Warriors: The Struggle to Preserve Tradition in Southern India, in a Changing World" in *Puppetry International*. Atlanta: UNIMA-USA, Spring.

Solomon, Alisa (1997) *Re-Dressing the Canon: Essays on Theater and Gender*. London: Routledge.

Speaight, George (1955) *The History of English Puppet Theatre*. London: Harrap.

——(1970) *Punch and Judy, A History*. Boston: Plays, Inc.

Stead, John Philip (1950) *Mr. Punch*. London: Evans Brothers.

Toole-Stott, Raymond (1958, 1992) *Circus and Allied Arts. A World Bibliography 1500-1982*. Derby and Chippenham: Harper and Sons, five vols.

Towsen, John (1976) *Clowns*. New York: Hawthorn.

——(1974) "Sources in Popular Entertainment," bibliography published in *The Drama Review*, 18(1): 118–22 (March). New York: New York Univerisity.

UCLA Museum of Cultural History (1979) *Asian Puppets, Wall of the World*. Los Angeles: UCLA Museum of Cultural History, University of California.

Van Erven, Eugene (1988) *Radical People's Theatre*. Bloomington: Indiana University Press.

Variot, Jean (1942) *Théâtre de Tradition Populaire*. Marseille: Robert Laffont.

Weimann, Robert (1978) *Shakespeare and the Popular Tradition*. Baltimore: Johns Hopkins.

Welsford, Enid (1935) *The Fool: His Social and Literary History*. London: Faber & Faber.

Wettach, Adrian (1957) *Grock, King of the Clowns*, trans. by Basil Creighton. London: Methuen.

Wiles, David (1987) *Shakespeare's Clown*. Cambridge: Cambridge University Press.

Willett, John, ed. (1964) *Brecht on Theatre*. New York: Hill and Wang.

Williams, Raymond (1976) *Keywords: a vocabulary of culture and society*. New York: Oxford University Press.

Wilmeth, Don (1980) *American and English Popular Entertainment. A Guide to Information Sources*. Detroit: Gale Research.

——(1982) *Variety Entertainment and Outdoor Amusements: A Reference Guide*. Westport: Greenwood Press.

Wilmut, Roger (1985) *Kindly Leave the Stage: The Story of Variety, 1919-1960*. London: Methuen.

Wilson, A.E. (1935) *King Panto: The Story of Pantomime*. New York: E. P. Dutton.

Zhengbao, Wang (1982) *The Art of Chinese Acrobatics*. Beijing: Foreign Language Press.

INDEX

Sophocles 133, 212
Soviet Alphabet 221, 225
Speaight, George 9
Springtime for Hitler 179
Stalin, Joseph 252
Stanford University 231
Stanislavsky, Konstantin 137
Stattel, Robert 72
Steinbeck, John 226
Stiefel, Erhard 99
street parades 19, 38
Strehler, Georgio 80, 198, 234, 237, 243
Styles, John 4
sword-swallowers 131, 170, 172–2

Taganka Theatre 219
Tagore, Rabindranath 252
Talma, François-Joseph 27, 30
Tartuffe 229
Taymor, Julie 9, 10, 37–8, 64–75, 80
Teatr Loh 67
Teatro Campesino 217–18, 226–33
Tempest 70
Terry, Megan 92
Théâtre de l'Aquarium 91
Théâtre des Funambules 27–9
Théâtre National Ambulant 3
Théâtre National Populaire 3, 9, 246
Theatre for a New Audience 73
Theatre for the New City 172
Théâtre d'Ombres 182
Theatre of the Oppressed 219, 266–7
Théâtre du peuple 3
Théâtre des Pygmées 25–6
Theatre of Satire 223–4
Théâtre du Soleil 10, 81, 97–103
Theatre Workshop 8, 177–8, 213
theme parks 73
Thomashefsky, Boris 179
Three Grapes 230
Threepenny Opera 198
Throw the Lady Out 217, 234–5, 240–1
Tingel Tangel 192, 200
Titus Andronicus 64–5, 70–3
To Pay or Not to Pay 238
Tom Shows 16
top bananas 84
topeng 4, 79–81, 107–26, 130, 166; and *topeng pajegan* 107, 110, 123–4; and *topeng panca* 117; and *topeng wali* 124
Transposed Heads 66
transvestites 61–2, 170, 178
Travail Théâtral 98
Trotskyists 103, 248
Tse-tung, Mao 218, 249
Tussaud, Madame 200
Two Faces of the Boss 228

Tzara, Tristan 179, 188

Ubu Roi 35
United Farm Workers Organizing Committee 226–7
Uvarova, Irina 41

Vakhtanghov, Yevgeny 80
Valadon, Emma 180
Valdez, Luis 217–18, 226–33
Valentin, Karl 178, 189–201
Valetti, Rosa 179
Variétés 24
Variot, Jean 8
Varon, Charlie 179
vaudeville 3, 4, 7, 9, 14–15, 24, 26–9, 73, 173, 177–9, 217, 260, 264
Verfremdungseffekt 50, 197, 251
vesh 149, 156–7
Vietnam 247
Vilar, Jean 3, 9
Voyage to Switzerland 16

Washington, George 208
Wasnak, Diane
Watergate scandal 172
wayang kulit 3, 4, 9, 36, 53–8, 60, 62, 66–7, 116, 126
Wedekind, Frank 179
Weigel, Helene 195
Weimann, Robert 7
Weisman, Jael 90–1, 93–4
Welsford, Enid 152
Wesker, Arnold 97
whiteface clowns 138–40, 145–6, 148, 166
Whiteman Meets Bigfoot 93–5
Wild West shows 19
Wilder, Thornton 92
Willeford, William 149
Willett, John 197
Williams, Raymond 11
Wilmeth, Don 9
Windsor Theatre 203
Wise Fool Puppet Intervention 38
Woodruff, Robert 131
World Trade Organization 219
Woza Albert 219, 253–7

yeti 94
Yiddish vaudeville 3, 179, 202–11

Zaloom, Paul 38, 165
Zanni 79, 89, 237, 262
Zapata, Emilio 229
Zaslove, Arnie 134
Zazezizozu 30
Zulus 255–6